COLLECTIVE BARGAINING AND GOVERNMENT POLICIES

Conference held at Washington, D.C.,
10-13 July, 1978:

Papers presented and Report
of General Rapporteur.

ORGANISATION FOR ECONOMIC CO-OPERATION AND DEVELOPMENT

PARIS 1979

The Organisation for Economic Co-operation and Development (OECD) was set up under a Convention signed in Paris on 14th December 1960, which provides that the OECD
shall promote policies designed:
- to achieve the highest sustainable economic growth and employment and a rising
  standard of living in Member countries, while maintaining financial stability, and
  thus to contribute to the development of the world economy;
- to contribute to sound economic expansion in Member as well as non-member
  countries in the process of economic development;
- to contribute to the expansion of world trade on a multilateral, non-discriminatory
  basis in accordance with international obligations.

The Members of OECD are Australia, Austria, Belgium, Canada, Denmark, Finland,
France, the Federal Republic of Germany, Greece, Iceland, Ireland, Italy, Japan, Lux-
embourg, the Netherlands, New Zealand, Norway, Portugal, Spain, Sweden, Switzerland,
Turkey, the United Kingdom and the United States.

TABLE OF CONTENTS

PREFACE

"Trying to generate a sense of common purpose is not the same as trying to get everyone to conform to detailed goals set from the centre. Indeed, the more diverse and complex the society or organisation, the more important it is that (we) recognise the different interests that have to be accommodated if they are to be harnessed into constructive endeavours rather than dissipated in anti-social behaviour.".

Sir Frank Holmes
Chairman, New Zealand Planning Council

In the efforts made by OECD Member governments to achieve sustained non-inflationary growth and to reduce high unemployment, the interaction between the processes of collective bargaining by employers and trade unions, and governmental policies in the fields of general economic, employment and related social policy, has become increasingly important.

The work of OECD's Industrial Relations Working Party has highlighted the many changes which have been taking place in the operation and institutions of collective bargaining in a number of countries in recent years, creating new problems and challenges for governments in the development of such policies. Unions and employers have also had to face new problems in their collective bargaining in reconciling the demands of their constituents with the often conflicting needs of public policy. To review these developments and initiate policy discussion of the critical issues, an OECD Conference was organised on the topic "Collective Bargaining and Government Policies" and was held, at the invitation of the U.S. Government, in Washington D.C., from 10 to 13 July 1978. The main objective of the conference was to explore the character of the two-way interrelationships between the institutions and operation of collective bargaining on the one hand, and general economic, employment and related social policy on the other — in the perspective of the need for sustained non-inflationary economic growth in the medium term. It was probably not possible, nor indeed desirable, to attempt to reach conclusions representing the position of Member governments on the important policy issues faced in the conference. Rather, the conference provided a forum for the exchange of experience between government and other experts, and an evaluation of policy approaches in different OECD countries, thereby providing an opportunity to clarify issues and options.

The conference papers comprised those prepared by rapporteurs and also the written comments of selected discussants. First, reports by trade

5

union and employer experts appraised the nature and extent of the changes in collective bargaining which are at present having an impact on government economic and employment policy-making. Next, the conference turned to the economic environment in which collective bargaining is operating, and is likely to operate in the medium term. Following this, the ways in which collective bargaining and government policies have been interacting were examined, building on country studies made by the Secretariat[1]. The conference then turned to some key problem areas, including the relationship between the subject matter of collective bargaining and government policy, in sessions dealing respectively with wages, with employment and working time, and with the concept of policy "trade-offs" between government, unions and employers. Finally the potential future interrelationship between collective bargaining and public policies was considered.

The edited conference papers, together with the report of the general rapporteur on the discussions, are now presented to a wider audience for information and to encourage discussion of one of the most important public issues of our time. In preparing the papers for publication it has been thought desirable for ease of reading to adopt a different order of presentation from that of the conference.

The contents of the papers in this volume are the responsibility of the respective authors and do not engage the responsibility of the OECD or any of its Member governments.

The conference received reports on collective bargaining and government policies from ten Member governments. These reference sources are being published in a separate volume "Collective Bargaining and Government Policies in Ten OECD Countries".

---

1. Certain of these studies were published; see OECD (1975) and Addison (1979).

I
OPENING ADDRESSES

OPENING ADDRESS

Charles G. Wootton[1]

This Conference has been designed to deal specifically with the issues arising in OECD Member countries from the many-faceted and highly complex interactions of governmental, economic, employment, and social policies on the one hand, and of free collective bargaining defined in a very broad sense, on the other, in the context of the compelling need for sustained, non-inflationary economic growth both now and in the medium term.

I believe that the subject we will be addressing comprises one of the most important policy interfaces in our free societies. As to the immediacy of our subject, I share fully the view of the Rapporteur for our session on *"Trade-offs" between Collectively Bargained Decisions and Public Policies,* Professor Bram Peper, that "the gravity of the situation is greater than is usually assumed". I think that the presence here to-day of so many leaders in the decision-making processes involved underlines the validity of this conclusion.

Although you are all very well informed on the economic environment in which we are seeking to find the right policy solutions to these interrelated problems, I will nevertheless allow myself a few comments on the difficult economic situation in the OECD community.

Firstly, I would like to say that our countries have brought about some improvement in economic conditions as compared with the crisis period immediately following the massive increase in oil prices, and our own excessive stimulation of our economies in the early 1970s. We have moved out of recession into modest real growth and we have brought the rate of inflation down substantially. Very importantly, we have generally succeeded in avoiding protectionist responses to our problems.

But our OECD economy has changed drastically, and we have a very long way to go to adjust to our new environment. Inflation is a persistent curse in nearly all of our countries. We have only begun the process of adapting to a radically different energy situation; my own country, the United States, has an enormous responsibility vis-à-vis the entire world to expedite this process. Protectionist pressures threaten our market economies and our open trading system from all sides. Trade and payment imbalances also persist. And the unemployment rate remains at the highest level in the OECD as a whole since the world-wide depression of the 1930s.

Now our modest growth rate and our present economic policy posture will not, in our community as a whole, deal at all adequately with the

---

1. Deputy Secretary-General, OECD.

unemployment problem. The outlook for the next twelve months, according to the OECD Secretariat's analysis on the basis of current policies, is for a real increase in GNP of three to three-and-a-half per cent in the OECD area. Thus, unemployment could be expected to rise further, unless policy changes, as we require a real growth rate of 4 - 4 1/2 per cent just to keep up with our growing labour force.

It does seem likely that the overall policy stance will shift sufficiently to avoid this outcome of even greater unemployment. At the Ministerial Level Meeting of the OECD Council in June, OECD Ministers agreed on a programme of concerted action, differentiated according to the widely varying situations in our individual Member countries. A number of our countries undertook to expand domestic demand significantly; these were Belgium, Canada, France, Germany, Italy, Japan, Switzerland and the United Kingdom. All other countries are to concentrate on reducing inflation and improving their balance of payments position, and most of them stand to gain some real GNP increase via higher exports to countries in the first group, although there are still a few of our Member countries where reinforced stabilization policies are called for. While our governments have set no specific target this year, our hope in the OECD Secretariat is that, in the aggregate, these policy moves will prevent any further increase in unemployment and may even fractionally reduce the current level.

But even with these policy changes we are still bogged down in a very high unemployment situation, facing the prospect of more years ahead of unsatisfactory employment conditions unless we can find better ways back to full employment. There are many reasons why we have reached this regrettable point in our development. They can be classified as constraints on economic growth and in itemizing them one would surely include: high rates of inflation, low profits, large budget deficits, depressed business confidence, energy problems, increasingly complex governmental regulatory actions, international payments disequilibria and periods of disorderly exchange market conditions.

Of these constraints, all of which are interrelated and interactive, I expect we could conclude that persistent inflation is the main limitation on faster growth and hence on the more rapid reduction of unemployment in our countries. If it were not for stubbornly high inflation rates and continuing inflationary expectations, our governments and our central banks would be able to carry out more expansive demand management policies and all three parties represented here to-day - governments, business and labour - could realise the higher revenues they require.

My own view is that a renewed commitment to thoroughgoing co-operation among government, business and labour, aimed at achieving broader and deeper consensus on government policy and on wage and price policies, would greatly facilitate our effort to break out of the inflation constraint on growth. Having read the papers by our Rapporteurs and our Discussants, I am all the more convinced of the necessity of such a consensus. And I am all the more convinced of the three-sided nature of such a consensus. I was struck in this connection at how strongly this message came through in our papers. That is, that "responsive collective bargaining", in Professor Conrad Blyth's terminology, means that responsiveness by labour at the collective bargaining table is both dependent upon and a precondition for responsive pricing policies by business, and both in turn require responsive government policies, not only in the field of demand management, but also, *inter alia*, in energy, taxation and regulatory policies.

Our papers also point up how difficult a three-sided "social bargain" of this type would be and I am certainly not underestimating the political, social and other limitations that would apply and that would vary greatly from country to country. But I share the concerns of the authors of many of our papers at the gravity of our present predicament and at the political, social and other repercussions that could flow from a failure to meet the challenge of the inflation constraint on growth.

While you are evidently not asked to reach agreed solutions in the course of this conference, I hope that you will succeed in reaching a number of more modest objectives, as a result of which this conference will lead to a greater international understanding of the nature of the interdependence of free collective bargaining, price setting and government policies, and provide an opportunity for a purposeful exchange of experience and views, thus yielding some guidance and new perspectives to all of you on the kinds of policies that have proved successful in these complex interfaces, as well as those that have not been successful, and the reasons for such success or failure.

I wish you every success in your task.

Finally, I want to express the thanks of the Secretary-General of the OECD and the Organization to our hosts. We were delighted when last September Secretary Marshall let us know that not only did the United States welcome the proposal to hold this conference but that it wished to offer facilities for the conference to take place in Washington. Thank you very much indeed for your gracious hospitality. I would also like to thank the Chairman of our Manpower and Social Affairs Committee, Mr. Tadhg O'Carroll, and the Chairman of its Working Party on Industrial Relations, Mr. Frank Burkhardt, who have given us all possible help and encouragement in preparing this conference. Thank you very much.

ADDRESS

Tadhg O'Carroll[1]

The Conference marks the culmination of a major work programme carried out under the direction of the Industrial Relations Working Party of the Manpower and Social Affairs Committee of the OECD. As will be seen from the documents, that work extended to every aspect of wage policies and collective bargaining. The programme, extensive and diverse as it was, has had the full support of the member governments. That support has been forthcoming in various ways, through participation in the Working Party's deliberations, through contributions to the budget, but also through co-operation with the Secretariat in the preparations for this Conference, and notably in assembling and evaluating the material contained in the selected national reports now presented to you.

The OECD is also indebted to the employer, trade union bodies, and independent experts who gave so much of their time in assisting the Secretariat in the preparation of the country studies upon which this Conference has been built.

I should say that in another important area of the work of the Manpower and Social Affairs Committe, that of employment and manpower policies, Member countries have found it beneficial to monitor and study the measures taken by one another. The Committee has, therefore, been encouraged to develop a clearing-house role through which information on national policies and programmes in the field of employment and manpower is made available to all Member countries. We have all benefited through these arrangements; we have been encouraged by one another's successes; we have been stimulated by one another's initiatives and experiments; we have been alerted by one another's failures. And we have done so with an economy of time and effort.

The Committee considered whether some similar procedure could be developed for innovations in industrial relations. However, it soon became clear to us that national systems of collective bargaining are deeply rooted in history and tradition and that they tend to reflect the distinctive features in our different countries; so that, while possibilities for comparative studies exist, there are limits to the extent to which forms developed in one country can be applied in another. Besides, experience shows that collective bargaining systems do not always transplant well.

The particular dimension of the subject to be discussed at this conference, namely, the relationship between the working of collective bargaining

---

1. Secretary, Department of Labour, Ireland, and Chairman of the OECD Manpower and Social Affairs Committee.

13

and the policies of governments, is one that has already exercised the minds of many in the Member countries, but it would appear that, despite varying degrees of success from time to time, no country can claim to have found the solution, that is, a solution that would be sufficiently flexible and responsive to the ever-changing scene. It would indeed be a remarkable coincidence if the point at which rival parties in the system of collective bargaining settle their differences were automatically to reflect also the wider interests of the community, including the interests of those who have not taken part in the bargaining process. This is not to suggest that the signatories of negotiated agreements set out to disregard or ignore, much less damage, the interests of those who are not parties to their settlements. It is to recognize that the mandate of negotiation is a narrower one than that of governments.

In the papers presented to this Conference, it is assumed that a degree of co-ordination between collective bargaining and government policies is necessary for orderly progress; it is recognised that that co-ordination will not occur of its own accord; it is being suggested, therefore, that some measures will have to be devised, by agreement, to secure that the conflicts can be eliminated or at least contained. The obstacles to be overcome in achieving the desired relationship are formidable. To quote one as an illustration, government policies are decided nationally, but a significant and far-reaching development in collective bargaining can occur at the most local of levels, the shop floor, and the parties to the settlement may not feel at all obliged to look out for repercussions beyond the factory gate once they have reached an accommodation between themselves.

All participants in this Conference will be seeking the solution for their own countries. It would appear that many of the differences identified in the papers relate less to ends and objectives than to the means by which agreed objectives are to be pursued. Such things as full employment, stable growth and social security are sought by all. All participants know from experience that there is no blueprint, no common formula, and that each country has the task of devising its own solution and securing support for it through consensus at home.

The exchange of experience and the structured discussions arranged for the Conference will hopefully throw light on the problems which all countries have, and will help participants to arrive at workable and acceptable solutions to meet their own unique and individual needs.

II

REPORT ON THE CONFERENCE
Lloyd Ulman

REPORT ON THE CONFERENCE

Lloyd Ulman[1]

The Conference discussions were exceedingly rich in variety and view-point, as are the papers and the written comments, but this report cannot hope to do more than deal broadly with problems and policies which seem to have been generally regarded as important and to record some of the main areas of consensus and, where opinion diverged, to do rough justice to divergent opinion. It proceeds, *first,* by viewing a set of contemporary problems in a collective bargaining context and, *second,* by referring to three broad macro-economic policy approaches and some of the ways in which they interact with collective bargaining institutions.

A. Current Problems in a Collective Bargaining Context

General consensus was reached on two points.

a) that contemporary governments have an interest in the outcome of negotiations over pay and other elements in labour costs; and

b) that major increases in non-wage as well as bargained wage costs have played a role in generating stagflation - or a deterioration in the trade-off between inflation and unemployment - which seems to have characterized the current decade, when the most rapid inflation was followed by the deepest recession since the Second World War and when high (although recently declining) inflation rates and high rates of unemployment have persisted together.

The second proposition emerged from observations to the effect that in most of the countries (in the period prior to the date of the Conference) prominent increases in costs, which have been associated with high or rising unemployment and/or inflation, have not arisen within the context of collective bargaining between enterprises and trade unions. The most dramatic cost increases were not increases in labour costs, but rather in the cost of foodstuffs, raw materials, and, above all, oil. Other non-labour cost increases have resulted from the adoption of increasingly stringent environmental standards. Increases in labour costs did indeed occur but they were especially great in non-wage labour costs, many of which are determined by legislative or other official authority; these have included increases in payroll taxes to cover rising social security payments and increasing protection of worker health and safety. Finally, some rising wage costs, such as minimum wages, overtime premiums, and equalisation of women's and men's pay have also

---

1. Professor, University of California, Berkeley, Director, Institute of Industrial Relations.

resulted from governmental mandate, while others have resulted from unilateral employer action, at enterprise or plant level, either in unorganized labour markets or as wage drift, i.e., pay increases in excess of increases negotiated at more centralised levels.

Unless such cost increases happen to be associated with corresponding increases in productivity or by increasing demand for the good or the service in question, they tend to result in rising selling prices and/or reduced output and hence in reduced demand for unionised labour. If the union responds by accepting a sufficiently large reduction in negotiated pay – in real terms, i.e., by allowing the cost of living to rise relative to money pay – then total costs and selling price would not rise, and neither output nor the employment of the union's members would fall. But if the union seeks instead to "protect" or to advance the real negotiated wage in such a situation, it would ensure that rising non-bargaining costs would be translated into rising total costs of production and prices. That a union should seek at least to protect its members' real wage rate is understandable, but its ability to do so is less certain, for real wage protection can mean, under the conditions assumed above, deterioration of profits. Increased union militancy, which is called forth by threatened real wage erosion, is then countered by increased disposition of employers to resist union wage claims, which is called forth by threatened erosion of profit margins.

Discussion of two topics considered in the papers and in the conference discussion is relevant in this context: real wage rigidity and the indexation of money wages to consumer price movements. The Schelde Andersen paper (p.194) finds that, between 1972 and 1976, real wages rose relatively to real per capita GNP corrected for changes in terms of trade (defined as the "norm") in all of the 16 OECD Member countries covered except the U.S. (the only one of the 16 in which real wages actually declined), Germany, and Austria. The paper also attempts indirectly to measure the extent to which real wage earners in the various countries might have succeeded in "catching up" with past increases in both income taxes and prices and concludes that they appear to have done so in the Scandinavian countries, Australia, Belgium, and the United Kingdom, but not elsewhere. The discussant of this paper, Michael Wachter, (p.243), expressed doubt that catch-up norms can be a significant cause of real wage rigidity in the face of declining demand, offering the view that "individuals adjust their norms in reaction to labour market realities", as witnessed by the increase in two-wage earner families. On the other hand, conference discussion developed the point that unions, as institutions, are likely to strive for catch-up targets. In fact, unions typically represent individual members rather than their families in wage negotiations, charging the rate for the job; and union dues do not vary with family size.

The increased adoption of "escalator clauses", "thresholds", and similar indexing devices in the 1970s may also be regarded as a manifestation of attempts by unions to protect and indeed restore real wages, because they generate money wage increases in response to past price increases. On the other hand the fact that, at least in the U.S., escalators typically do not compensate for the entire increase in the cost of living is consistent with the view that the cost increases which they generate encounter employer

18

resistance (although it must be added that indexed wage increases usually comprise only part of the bargaining settlement). Indexation of wages – as well as other incomes and of tax brackets as well – has been defended by some economists as a way of preventing inflation from altering the distribution of incomes, but the Dodge paper and its discussion at the conference pointed out that full indexation prevents real wages from falling in response to inflation generated by exchange rate depreciation, which of course could result from increases in the prices of imported raw materials and energy and are the means by which resources are transferred from the importing country to the exporting country. Nevertheless, some union and employer experts present regarded widespread indexation as inevitable and desirable as a device for minimising social conflict over the distribution of national income, the level or rate of increase in which might have been reduced by increased costs of imported resources. The two viewpoints might be reconciled by allowing for something less than full indexation; indeed, the more widespread the *coverage* of indexation, the more feasible it may be to adjust the *degree* of indexation up or down, as indicated by changing economic conditions. But indexation does not receive universal support, even from the union side. It has been opposed by unionists in some countries as weakening their bargaining function by making it more difficult to secure non-indexed wage increases when the latter must comprise only a small increment to increases generated "automatically" under indexation. And some employers oppose it by drawing the opposite conclusion from the same basic hypothesis; they fear that, as a result of indexation, the total negotiated package will be larger than in the absence of indexation, because unions would lack neither the ingenuity to formulate additional demands nor the bargaining power to push them.

If a union in one economic sector were to permit its real wage to fall more than unions in other sectors in response to a reduction in demand, its relative wage would also be reduced. And unions are generally regarded as seeking to protect their relative, as well as their real, wages against reduction – whatever the source of potential reduction might be – and their efforts to do so might result in a leapfrogging process which could add to the rate of inflation of the general level of wages. The Schelde Andersen paper (p.215) claims some empirical support for two propositions in this area. The first is that inter-industry wage structures are affected by the level of the general demand for labour, as depicted by the rate of unemployment: in some countries, like the U.S. and Japan, an increase in demand benefits the low-paid more than the high-paid groups and compresses the wage structure; while in others, like Sweden, increased demand widens wage differentials as it results in more wage drift in the high-paid categories. The second proposition is that the smaller the dispersion of wages in one period, the higher the rate of overall wage or total labour cost inflation the next; this seems to be the case, however, only in Sweden and Denmark. In most of the countries, the greater the dispersion of wages, the higher the subsequent rate of inflation. Either situation is consistent with a relative wage "catch-up", whether, as in the first case, the higher-paid groups are attempting to restore their relative position, or, in the latter case, the catch-up is performed by the lower-paid groups. The discussant rejected the conclusion that the degree of wage dispersion can be an independent cause of wage inflation, since both dispersion and wage inflation depend on the level of unemployment (or aggregate demand) and on the rate of price inflation. Therefore, the leapfrogging phenomenon is a result, rather than a cause, of inflation. In conference discussion, however, it was argued that changes in wage structures have been induced by policies or by *relative* changes in demand or supply, as well as by inflationary conditions, and, to this extent, could add to overall inflationary pressures.

Finally, trade unions are interested in protecting jobs, employment, and incomes of their members as well as real and relative wages. Thus, when employers might not wish to maintain existing levels of employment unless wages are reduced, unions might wish them to maintain employment at existing wage levels. But the more complete the degree of employment protection and the wage protection in the face of decreased demand, the greater the increase in costs. Hence unions and employers have negotiated a considerable variety of income security devices, many of which are discussed in the McBride (p.305) and the Hart and Sloane (p. 247) papers. Some are employed in conjunction with others. At one extreme are a range of work practices which are intended to oblige the employer to hire more employees than he might otherwise wish to at prevailing rates of pay; however, these rarely oblige him to hire a minimum total number of man-hours per year, although plant seizures by workers in order to prevent plant closings may be viewed as a supermake-work rule. At the other extreme are what were termed work-spreading devices during the Great Depression and which involve reductions in hours per employee with no corresponding increase in hourly pay; collective agreements which provide for the reduction of overtime and even straight-time hours before layoffs may occur fall in this category, as may arrangements for flexibility in working hours ("flexi-time") or voluntary part-time work. A counterpart to spreading work consists of layoff in accordance with seniority, which is a form of job-rationing, which is frequently combined with such reductions in pay as are involved by "jumping"; but sometimes with varying degrees of "wage rate protection" provided. Various pension and early retirement schemes can also be regarded as a form of job rationing, with reduced worker income. In addition, negotiated supplemental unemployment benefits imply acceptance of layoffs but with income maintained − in some cases at very high levels. Severance pay, or redundancy payment, on the other hand, leaves the employer free to lay off (subject to whatever additional restrictions may be in the contract) but penalises him economically for doing so. Then, in contrast to work-spreading, there is work-sharing, or reduction in the standard work week − or, through increasing vacations and holidays at full-time pay − in the standard work year. Work-sharing differs from work-spreading in that it calls for full compensation to the worker for extra time off the job, by increasing the standard hourly rate in proportion to the reduction in standard weekly hours or by providing that holiday and vacation pay be at full standard rates.

Since most make-work, share-work, or income maintenance arrangements involve raising either direct or indirect labour costs per unit of output, they offer the employer some incentive to substitute overtime for engaging new workers, as Hart and Sloane (p.248) argue, and to this extent would be inefficient in providing new jobs. This effect could be countered by negotiating maximum limits on overtime or increases in overtime premium pay, but the latter would constitute a separate rise in labour costs. The adverse employment effect of a relative rise in non-wage labour costs would also be countered by a growing preference of individual workers (notably women) for part-time work; to the extent that negotiated reductions in working hours reflect increased preference for non-working time, the negotiators' work wins them the approval of the economics profession (as exemplified in the remarks of Charles Schultze, (p. 56). Moreover, to the extent that increases in non-wage labour costs represent increased investment in employee recruitment or training, substitution of overtime (or other ways of more fully utilizing existing labour force) for new hires would be regarded as consistent with the requirements of economic efficiency — although it implies decreasing responsiveness of employment to increases in demand and output. (However, two cautionary comments were reflected in discussion of this point). First, it remains to be demonstrated that employer outlays on recruitment and training per employee have indeed increased in the past decade, when non-wage labour costs have in fact increased. And second, if, as conventional economic theory holds, employers pay employees, in whom they have "sunk" recruitment or training outlays, premium wages in order to prevent their quitting, they need not "hoard" such labour during recessions, because they need not fear that these relatively high-paid workers will be reluctant to return after layoff).

However, discussion made it clear that negotiated increases in labour costs to provide employment protection or income maintenance would be confined to increases (like the two examples cited in the previous paragraph) which employers would be willing to incur in the interests of efficiency and absence of bargaining pressure. In particular, the discussion reflected the opinion that negotiated reductions in the length of the standard workweek would probably occur although those who shared in this forecast did so with varying degrees of enthusiasm. Thus, the conference discussion reflected appreciation of the fact that unions would seek to protect the interests of their members in both dimensions — employment as well as real wage rates. The Oswald (p.277) paper stressed the defensive role of trade unionism and collective bargaining in the seventies, holding, in effect, that these institutions have been like King Lear — "a man more sinn'd against than sinning". The Roberts (p. 287) discussion, however, did not rule out some original sin as well; and, while this point was not debated, the general discussion did reflect at least tacit consensus on two interrelated points which would most probably have eluded consensus a short decade ago. The first is the proposition that, although negotiated (or legislated) increases in wages and benefits might be responsive to inflationary or deflationary conditions arising from other sources, they can result in further increases in costs and prices. The second point is reflected in the absence of any reference to the "purchasing power theory" which argues that pay increases negotiated under conditions of unemployment and excess industrial capacity tend to increase demand rather than (or more than) costs and prices. Beyond these two points a further general consensus might be informed from the fact that the following statement in the Oswald paper provoked no challenge: "Collective bargaining was called upon to respond to broad economic issues that were beyond its abilities to redress": Two questions in this connection emerge:

i) whether the bargaining responses are consistent with appropriate governmental policies of economic stabilisation and expansion, granted that they had been elicited in the absence of such policies; and

ii) whether or in what ways appropriate governmental policies would require modification or supplementation in the light of the interests of the parties to collective bargaining.

B. Government Policies and Collective Bargaining

The same increases in non-wage costs, and especially in the prices of imported resources, which signalled the need for wage protection to the unions, signalled the need for domestic cost flexibility to governments, most of which were intent on maintaining or restoring equilibrium on external account. Adverse shocks of external origin carry the potential for both inflation and deflation or unemployment. Authorities could in principle choose either to counter the deflationary effects of such import price rises by adopting expansionist policies or to counter their inflationary effects by adopting deflationary policies. Most governments have reacted with policy mixtures compounded of (a) deflation of aggregate demand, (b) policies to maintain employment and incomes threatened by (a), and (c) policies aimed directly to achieve wage and/or price restraint. The proportions can vary in direct proportion to the effectiveness of (a) and (c) in bringing domestic costs "into line" or for accommodating price and employment objectives. All three classes of policy were considered in conference papers and discussion, especially in the light of their interrelationships with collective bargaining.

I. Demand Deflation

The purpose of deflating aggregate demand has been to force down money wage and price inflation so as to adjust real labour costs sufficiently to restore (or attain) desired levels of exports, although, to the extent that such relative cost reduction proved not to be feasible, deflation would also reduce demand for imports by reducing domestic income. One of the preconditions for the effectiveness of deflation has in fact been present. According to the Schelde Andersen (p.187) paper, countries with the lowest rates of increase in money wages have tended to be those with the lowest rates of increase in real wages. Therefore, a policy which is supposed to produce combinations of higher rates of unemployment and lower rates of increase in money wages should also produce lower rates of increase in real wages. And in fact the policy may be said to have worked in the sense (again according to the same paper) that countries which pursued more rigorously restrictive policies in the 1970s – notably, Germany, the Netherlands, and Switzerland – and which consequently experienced relatively great increases in unemployment and labour market slack, also brought down their rates of increases in real wages most rapidly; while in countries which adopted expansionist policies – i.e. Canada, Italy, Norway and Sweden – real wages rose more rapidly than productivity (as measured by per capita real GDP, adjusted for changes in the terms of trade). On the other hand, in other countries – such as Belgium, Denmark, and Japan – real wages rose more rapidly than productivity despite restrictionist policies and weakened labour market conditions.

In general, the consensus of discussion appeared to be that, while demand deflation, if carried far enough, might indeed constrain domestic costs to the degree required to meet desired targets of relative price stability and balance-of-payments equilibrium, deflation was not *per se* an efficient instrument for such purposes. The efficiency of demand deflation might be decomposed into two components :

i) the responsiveness of wages and labour costs to reductions in demand, including decreases in employment; and

ii) the responsiveness of employment to reductions in the rate of wage inflation.

If, under the first criterion, wages are responsive, a fall in demand could be transformed rapidly and almost completely into a (relative) reduction in labour costs, and almost not at all into unemployment. Thus a theory by the Norwegian economist Odd Aukrust has held that wage movements in a small "open" economy should be determined by changes in the prices of products moving in international trade (and by changes in productivity in those industries in the country in question which are exposed to foreign competition). Hence a fall in the rate of increase in export prices, resulting from a decline in foreign demand, would be reflected in a corresponding fall in the rate of increase in wages in the country's export sector and thence in the other sectors of the economy. In fact, the central federations of unions and management in Sweden have tried to make wages respond flexibly to world price movements; and if they had succeeded in doing so on a year-to-year basis the expansionist policies originally followed by the Swedish authorities would indeed have been justified as a response to the world price increases which occurred in the early 1970s; it would have been possible for them to bring down their rates of domestic cost inflation without suffering increased unemployment. Unfortunately, the bargaining parties were not able to produce the requisite degree of fine tuning; and when the rate of inflation in world prices declined in 1975-76, the rate of inflation in Swedish labour costs actually increased, and more deflationary policies had to be resorted to. The Aukrust theory (like the purchasing power theory) never made its way into the conference, although the older Phillips Curve did. However, the Phillips Curve appeared flatter than it used to be. According to the Dodge paper (p.166) the tendency of lagging wages to catch up with the rest is pronounced, and it means that wage movements in general do not respond sensitively to opposite changes in levels of demand and unemployment.

Thus, it is well known that, instead of working directly and primarily on the rates of wage and price inflation, deflation results first in increased unemployment, which in turn is followed only sluggishly by a decline in the rate of inflation. It has been estimated that, in Canada and the U.S., an increase of at least two percentage points in unemployment would have to be held for two to four years in order to reduce average wage increases by one percentage point.

The resistance of wage movements to deflationary demand conditions is enhanced by the operation of collective bargaining. This point emerged from a discussion which followed an argument against governmental intervention in collective bargaining on the grounds that, in the country concerned, it would result in a greater share of wages in the national income than would emerge from free collective bargaining. According to the latter argument, the government should be responsible for maintaining a politically acceptable rate of price stability but should deploy only fiscal and monetary instruments in attempting to discharge that responsibility. That would leave the determination of (both money and real) wages largely to the outcome of collective bargaining, so that, with the government setting its monetary policy according to its price target, the larger the rate of wage increase emerging from collective bargaining, the lower the levels of employment and output. But the discussion generally agreed that the government is held responsible for unemployment as well as inflation; and it was also claimed that collective bargaining might generate greater wage increases than would be compatible with acceptable levels of unemployment. This would be so because under collective bargaining the pace is often set (a) by powerful unions which (almost by definition) may not experience much of an increase in unemployment as the result of wage increases in their own jurisdictions, or (b) by the frequently large groups of workers within unions whose own expectation of being laid off is quite low. If either situation prevails − and it may do so even under highly centralised bargaining − both wage increases and unemployment are likely to be too great from the viewpoint of the general community. This is one aspect of a phenomenon referred to several times in the discussion: that unions are naturally most concerned with the jobs and wages of their own members, whereas governments need to be concerned with both the general level of unemployment and its distribution. The high incidence of unemployment among the youth, where job attachments are frequently short-term or non-existent, was cited as the leading case in point.

The argument was raised that deflating the economy has begun to prove a less and less effective way to reduce labour costs, as a result of some developments discussed solely in the context of collective bargaining in Part A.

    a) Insistence by unions on targeting wage increases on after-tax earnings, which means that raising taxes could yield higher rather than lower rates of inflation, presumably by obliging the authorities to reverse deflationary monetary policies before unit costs have been sufficiently stabilized;

    b) increasing proportions of non-wage (and possibly fixed wage) labour costs over time, partly as the result of the socialising of costs of job protection and of care of the inactive population. Such costs, especially of the public variety, (it is argued), have also contributed to

c) compression of pay differentials, which allegedly make for higher overall rates of wage inflation as the more highly paid wage and salaried groups try to restore former (and what they regard as "equitable") differentials.

These factors have allegedly made for what the Sylvestre discussion (p.181) regarded as an increased "autonomy" of wage movements, or "lack of sensitivity of wage increases to changes in the general level of activity". As we have seen, (a), and, to some extent, (c) have been challenged; but (b) was generally accepted, although strongly defended on policy grounds in various discussions.

It was also asserted, in the Scharpf (p.301) discussion of the Verschueren paper (p.291), that employment has been growing less responsive to reduction in the rate of wage inflation, due to :

a) the approach of "relative saturation" among consumers in high-income, industrial countries;

b) increasing competition from newly industrialized economies where wages are much lower than wages in the older industrialized economies; and

c) the development of labour-saving micro-electronic control technology.

This aggregates into a provocatively pessimistic view which, while its separate components have not been subjected to quantitative assessment, is currently held and advanced. It is not, however, unchallenged. Explicitly or implicitly, it was not subscribed to by discussants and commentators from the U.S. (Schultze and Dunlop comments p. 53 and p. 127). Possibly this reflected the fact that people in the U.S., having experienced a slower rate of economic growth than most Member countries in the postwar period and, perhaps, a lower level of expectations, did not suffer as severe a letdown by the events of the seventies as people who might have grown to expect rapid improvement as the order of the day. (But who had become sated ?. Perhaps the North Americans recall their own automation-cum-satiety scare of the early 1960s, which, on balance, turned out to be a false alarm.) In any event, the pessimism generated by this analysis may be a function of its incompleteness in at least one respect. If rapidly developing countries can increase their exports of manufactures (while they and less developed countries can charge higher prices for exported resources), then they should be able to increase their imports as well. The great postwar economic expansion of Europe occurred against the background of greatly increased international trade. It ought not be too fanciful to expect new mass markets to grow up in some of those more rapidly developing countries — provided that trade policies are sufficiently liberal.

Nevertheless, in the short run and from the perspective of the individual firm or industry which the bargaining parties share, diagnoses are likely to run at least as much in "structural" as in "cyclical" terms. Structural diagnosis leads to pessimism over the efficacy of conventional demand management in coping with unemployment: deflation is not likely to bring down relative costs far enough or soon enough; reflation is likely to spill over into inflation while unemployment is still at high levels. This viewpoint seemed to run like an undercurrent through much of the discussion, and it helped to account for the emphasis which the discussions of income maintenance and employment protection policies placed on the second of these two objectives.

II. Income Maintenance and Employment Protection

While restrictive demand management and real wage protection under collective bargaining have worked at cross purposes, government policies to maintain incomes or protect or create jobs have the same objectives as protective bargaining arrangements. As the Oswald paper (p.277) put it, "...unions attempted to negotiate employment protection and inflation protection and used their political powers to influence governments to create jobs and protect purchasing power". In the U.S., collective bargaining protection has been tailored to supplement legislated protection; historically, as the McBride paper (p. 305) notes, some of the bargaining supplements were intended by the unions involved to furnish an incentive to the employers to support increases in legislated programs and were originally regarded as temporary expedients. In other cases, as in negotiated supplemental unemployment benefits, they were always regarded as permanent arrangements, but they were related to unemployment compensation so that, in certain situations (e.g., exhaustion on entitlement to unemployment compensation) private benefits would move inversely to the amount of governmental assistance. Thus, while the discussion of official measures to counter unemployment has tended to be concerned more with unemployment compensation and job creation in the public sector than with job protection and creation in the private sector, precedent exists for extending the latter from the bargaining arena to the official domain. Indeed, some of the conference discussion (i.e., of the Hart and Sloane paper, (p.247)) favoured substitution of governmental for private efforts. That would reduce fixed labour costs (and the ratio of non-wage to wage costs) to the firm and thus reduce their incentive to substitute overtime for new hires.

The American concentration on unemployment insurance undoubtedly reflects greater exposure to and acceptance of higher levels of unemployment in the postwar period. It also reflects collective bargaining arrangements (which may be copied in non-union firms) which ration reduced employment according to seniority. Seniority arrangements may also have contributed to a predisposition to accept unemployment which has been high by European standards – at least until the mid-1970s – since they make for a more uneven incidence of unemployment. Finally, acceptance of unemployment may also be based on the implicit assumption that the unemployment is for the most part transitional, or cyclical, rather than "permanent", or structural, in nature. Given that belief, relatively high compensation for joblessness may make the latter more supportable. Recently revived criticism of American and other earnings-related benefit systems are not irrelevant to this last point, as related in the Dodge paper. The criticism goes mainly to the effect that unemployment compensation increases inflation mainly by decreasing the cost of either idleness or searching for better jobs, and that people who choose to be unemployed for those reasons do not exert downward pressure on wages in the labour market.

There is some evidence that changes in the unemployment insurance benefits or systems have tended slightly to increase the rate of inflation at any level of unemployment, but no allowance is made for the obvious fact that increased or more widely available unemployment benefits increase the public tolerance of layoffs and generally make it politically feasible for the economy to be run at higher levels of unemployment and lower levels of inflation than would otherwise be the case.

However, discussion at this conference dwelled more on measures to promote job security and work-sharing than off-the-job compensation; and in fact wage or employment subsidies to protect employment have been urged as superior to compensation for "open" unemployment, for the following reasons:

a) They can be linked to on-the-job training programs, thereby helping to prevent the development of what might be termed full employment skill deficits from developing during periods of slack, and consequently the emergence of occupational bottlenecks during ensuing recoveries in demand.

b) They could increase demand while − and by − reducing unit labour costs, in contrast not only to unemployment insurance, but also to negotiated makework and sharework schemes which raise unit labour costs to employers.

c) They could result in greater relative increases in employment in groups where the incidence of unemployment is particularly high (such as school-leavers and ethnic minorities), in contrast to the "trickle-down" effects of general reductions in payroll or income taxes.

d) They could neutralize any effect of job protection schemes, negotiated or public, in "exporting" unemployment to unprotected groups by "strengthening the selective approaches to creating employment and educational opportunities for the groups which are most severely hit under the recession". (Rasmussen discussion p. 318).

But if quantitative research attributes only a limited perverse effect to unemployment insurance in increasing unemployment, it credits subsidies with only limited effectiveness in increasing employment. (However, in the case of Sweden, where subsidies have been extensively resorted to, the ratio of open unemployment to changes in GDP fell dramatically in the mid-1970s.) Conference discussion also treated the subsidy approach warily and paid as much attention to the debit side of the ledger as to the credit side:

a) Subsidised training on the job is productive to the extent that unemployment is transitional rather than structural in nature − to the extent that it can be expected that jobs destroyed by reduced demand will later be revived. Otherwise the danger exists that subsidies will turn out to be like work-sharing and negotiated job protection in that they might tend to lock labour into jobs and patterns that are no longer appropriate (Crispo discussion p. 321).

b) The ability of subsidy programmes to increase demand by reducing unit costs presupposes a high degree of responsiveness (elasticity) of product demand and output to reduced costs and prices. If all countries producing and exporting a particular product subsidise

27

employment to the same degree, none can expect to reduce its price relative to the world price (although total international sales of the product in question would presumably be increased to some extent).

c) On the other hand, if differential subsidisation among countries can gain differential cost and price advantages in international competition, it can reinforce charges of "dumping" and support of protectionist devices in retaliation, as mentioned in the McBride (p. 305) and Robinson (p. 111) papers.

d) Targeting of cost reduction to high unemployment groups is more efficient than general tax reduction only if there are substantial "leakages" out of general tax reductions which delay their effectiveness and if it is not very feasible for employers to substitute subsidised for non-subsidised labour – e.g., to fire young workers as soon as they become ineligible for subsidy.

In general, sentiment appeared to converge on keeping subsidies temporary and targeted as closely as possible, although the advantage of a device which protects employment without raising enterprise costs was appreciated. On the other hand, trade union support of legislated work-sharing through shorter hours was strongly in evidence, although the drawback of a device which protects employment by raising private costs was recognized. Finally, there was at least implicit preference for both of these approaches over protectionism. Protectionism is a political make-work rule in which even sophisticated and liberally oriented bargaining parties seek refuge when they are convinced that their unemployment is so deep-seated that conventional negotiated palliatives and policy prescriptions are of little or no avail.

A partial alternative to unemployment insurance on the one hand, and job subsidies on the other, is public employment. Public employment is a classic device for coping with temporary reductions in employment in the private (and nationalized industry) sector; but it is not a very appropriate instrument for dealing with protracted unemployment. It is inferior to subsidies in coping with unemployment among those laid off from jobs in the private sector; but when linked with appropriate training it may equip those without much, if any, job experience to qualify as replacements in permanent positions in the public sector. In the latter capacity, public employment would – unlike subsidies – avoid the risk of overmanning and potentially reducing productivity in private industry, but in the case of the unemployment among the youth and historically disadvantaged minority groups there is much to be said for "crowding" them into sectors from which members of their groups have been crowded out. Finally, public employment is inappropriate to the extent that, as in the case of subsidies, it cannot be financed indefinitely on a major scale by deficit creation without risking unacceptable balance-of-payments problems or domestic inflationary consequences. In fact, public employment was not much discussed at this conference, possibly because of a feeling that the secular growth of the public sector, which has been regarded as both effect and cause of inflation, now limits recourse to it as an employment-creating device in many countries.

A policy which was strongly (if not unanimously) championed, however, is the requirement that employers notify employees, unions, and appropriate authorities well in advance of intended layoffs, especially in cases where plant closures are contemplated. This can reduce managerial discretion in an important area. In U.S. law the obligation of management to bargain "under any circumstances" on "such larger entrepreneurial questions as to... how capital shall be invested in fixed assets, or what the scope of the enterprise shall be" has not been established,[2] although National Labor Relations Board orders to require the employers to give the union advance notice of the closing of operations and to bargain over the effects on the employees involved have been upheld in superior courts. (However, American unions have negotiated such provisions as severance pay, early pensions, rights to transfer to other company facilities with moving allowance, extended supplemental unemployment benefits, or guarantees against loss of wages; and these in many instances have raised closing-down costs to very high levels). In some cases advance notice may provide the union with an opportunity to attempt to get the decision reversed, by mobilizing political pressure or by taking industrial action in other plants owned by the company in other communities or even in other countries. In the extreme case, it may facilitate seizure of the plant and other assets by employed groups and/or governmental decisions to subsidize the operation with public funds, with or without nationalization. In such cases, policies requiring advance notice might prove conducive to the policies of subsidy or of public employment, which might prove difficult to reverse. But against such eventualities must be set the opportunity which advance notification, combined with union-management consultation, provides to consider "alternative ways to tackle the company's economic problems so that the workers' jobs may be protected and the company may re-establish its competitiveness" (Rasmussen p.316). (Such means have included suspension of recruitment and elimination or reduction of overtime). On the other hand, where no effective alternatives exist, advance notification and consultation may convince the employees concerned of this unfortunate fact, and it should make it possible for public agencies (e.g., labour market boards) to publicize educational, relocational, or other assistance programmes.

III. Wage Restraint and Consensus

In view of the limitations of both private institutions and public policy-making — i.e., of collective bargaining, demand management, and policies of income maintenance and specific job creation — in coping with the problems of high and possibly rising unemployment combined with high and possibly rising rates of inflation, it is inevitable that incomes policy should become the subject of renewed interest. It was remarked that the case for incomes policy is the case against the alternatives; but if that is all that can be said for the policy, it is hardly enough — especially in view of the spotty record. However, a bit more can be said for incomes policy, at least in principle. The Robinson (p.115) paper claims that the positions of the "extreme monetarists" and those of the proponents of incomes policy

---

2. Fibreboard Paper Products Corp. *v.* NLRB, 379 U.S. 203, 215 (1964) at 225, Justice Stewart concurring.

are really not as opposed to one another as the monetarists claim, since both regard the deflation of expectations as an essential component in a counter-inflationary process. In fact, the monetarist case seems to proceed as follows: While the amounts of services and goods which people wish to buy and sell depend on how much they expect wages and prices to rise (or fall), their expectations — conditioned by experience — are governed by the going or announced rate of increase in the supply of money. Thus, if, when the latter remains unchanged, people somehow are persuaded to reduce wage and price increases below their previous rates, they will be left in the lurch; shortages will develop and wages and prices will "explode", making up for lost time and wrecking incomes policies in the process. Thus, the expectations which play such an important role in the inflationary process are, according to this theory, ultimately governed by the rate of increase in the money supply. However, (a) there is nothing to prevent expectations from being altered by other things as well; moreover, (b) monetary policy is not as autonomous as the monetarists would like to believe, but is responsive to international pressures as well as domestic pressures — including prior or anticipated increases in wages and prices. Therefore, if expectations can be made responsive to norms and the like established by incomes policy, there would appear to be no reason why the rate of increase in the money supply cannot be responsively reduced to conform to such lowered expectations, so that neither shortages nor unemployment need develop, as David Soskice has shown in unpublished work. In principle, inflation and relative labour costs could be reduced without the prior painful intervention of unemployment and lost output, or at least with less "real" economic pain. If expectations could be modified by an incomes policy, the task of monetary and fiscal policy-makers would be lightened (which is one reason why central bankers have typically been attracted to incomes policy).

Since, conceptually, the lowering of inflationary expectations may precede the reduction in the rates of increase in money supply and aggregate demand, incomes policy would (if effective) have the effect of inducing unions to bargain less "militantly" — that is, to exploit their market power less fully. Quite frequently, authorities have attempted to persuade unions to bargain more moderately during upswings in business activity, so as to minimize inflation (a) when there is still substantial unemployment and underutilization of capacity or even (b) in the neighbourhood of full employment. Indeed, in order to make such abstention more palatable to the unions, the Blyth paper (p. 65) suggests that union moderation during the upswings be matched by employer moderation during recessions, so that employers would grant more generous settlements than they would otherwise be willing and able to grant. Discussion, however, while appreciative of the ingenuity of the proposal, revealed scepticism of its feasibility — e.g., "a policy which runs diametrically against existing market forces... is just too much to expect". Contra-cyclical policy is not very productive in dealing with "stagflation", when wage and price increases are likely to be inflationary even during slumps, when unemployment is high. Indeed, there is something to be said for a policy which can be said to be "pro-market" in the sense that it induces *union* restraint to minimize inflation during *downswings* in demand — or, as the Liinamaa paper (p.136) puts it, "to reduce the residual pressure on pay and prices remaining from the boom". With recessionary inflation reduced, unions would be under less pressure either to "catch up" with or anticipate inflation in the ensuing upswing — or, to put it in the context of stagflation, the monetary and fiscal authorities would thereby find themselves less inhibited by the fear of wage and price inflation in expanding aggregate demand so as to increase employment and output.

Even a policy which succeeds in deflating the general level of expectations might not producre the desired deceleration in overall wage increases. As we have noted earlier in this report such normal developments as changes in technology, consumer tastes, or minimum wages, which may make for increases in specific (relative) wages may tend to generate increases in the general level of wages as other groups seek to maintain or restore traditional (and hence "equitable") wage differentials; in some cases this has resulted in retention of labour in the occupations or industries where restoration has occurred and perpetuated bottlenecks in industries to which such labour might otherwise have moved. Designers of incomes policies have sometimes sought to reduce the force of wage "comparability" by narrowly restricting the circumstances in which "exceptional" wage increases would be admissible — e.g., in cases of specific labour shortages, or where wage increases could result in compensating increases in productivity. However, while exceptions are intended to make wage structures conform better to the changing requirements of the market place than they would in the absence of any incomes policy, they also tend to make the overall policy less operational — more subject to challenge, more in need of bureaucratic clarification and interpretation. And while exceptions are intended to counter the influence of comparability, they have sometimes included allowances to bring the pay of closely comparable occupations or jobs into equality; partly because market efficiency may well require "equal pay for equal work", but partly because gross departures from customary wage relationships would entail seriously adverse consequences for industrial relations and labour productivity. On the other hand, it might be noted that an incomes policy applied during recessions, when employer bargaining power is relatively great, might minimize the effects of comparability by making it more difficult for "exceptional" wage increases — e.g., in sectors where demand has been increasing relative to supply — to "spill over" into other sectors.

While incomes policy is supposed to work by influencing bargaining behaviour, its effectiveness may depend on the structure of collective bargaining; in general, it has been supposed to vary directly with the degree of centralization of bargaining structures and the structures of trade unions and employer organizations. In addition to the obvious advantages to the government in dealing with fewer and larger centres of authority — including the minimisation of leapfrogging inherent in centralised negotiations — there is the fact that the effectiveness of changing expectations is presumably greater the more centrally located is the target of persuasion. If persuasion includes confronting the parties with the beneficial effects to the economy as a whole of moderation on employment and output, the lesson is better appreciated and, more importantly, more readily acted on by centrally

31

located union and management representatives than by those in smaller units. The latter may view their own welfare as only tenuously affected by and affecting macro-economic developments but as directly impaired (improved) if they alone act virtuously (transgress) while their neighbours transgress (act virtuously). Sweden has been, or used to be cited as furnishing the highest testimonial to the power of centralisation to make bargaining "responsible", since the parties attempted to constrain their bargaining to conform to the requirements of international competitiveness while remaining opposed to governmental intervention and incomes policy in principle.

If highly centralised bargaining is not only conducive but essential to the effectiveness of incomes policy, then what the Verschueren paper (p.293) identifies as a counter-cyclical movement away from centralised bargaining (in recession) does not augur well for the future of incomes policies in the countries of Western Europe. (However, to the extent that decentralisation is caused by the desire of management to avoid the larger total cost increases which they believe have been generated by bargaining at both industry and enterprise levels, a movement away from industry-wide negotiations *per se* could make for reduced cost inflation, compared with a dual system of bargaining — in the absence of incomes policy). In fact, a very high degree of centralisation may be neither a necessary nor a sufficient condition of the effectiveness of incomes policy. As both the Blyth (p.77) and the Dunlop (p.127) papers point out, industry-wide bargaining (in the case of Germany) and company-level bargaining (in the case of the United States), both countries having strong national unions, can furnish the bases of central tripartite arrangements which include the government and some independent agent; indeed, the effective functioning of such central tripartite institutions could conceivably result in the accrual of influence or authority within the central union federations and perhaps within employer organisations as well. On the other hand, if incomes policy is not effective in reducing union bargaining pressure, the result may be to deflect that pressure from the top institutions to the local units and effectively to decentralise the bargaining system in the process. Thus, in the process of inducing restraint in the centralised (industry-wide) negotiation of basic rates of pay, some incomes policies have contributed to "explosions" of locally-determined wage drift. Moreover, as Hart and Sloane (p.252) suggest, incomes policies might have contributed to the increase in non-wage labour costs relative to wages; and included among the non-wage labour costs, as the McKenna (p.103) discussion of the Blyth paper emphasizes, are those work rules which unions have established for job protection, which may reduce the growth of productivity and which are mainly determined at plant and enterprise levels.

Discussion of the problems created for economic policy-making by the attempted protection of real wages and jobs through collective bargaining, and discussion of the modifications of bargaining behaviour and institutions required to minimise those problems and make incomes policies effective were counterpointed throughout the conference by discussion of the propriety of such governmental intervention. There was, as we have noted (page 17), consensus that the government has an interest in the outcome of collective bargaining that derives from its accountability for the performance of the economy as a whole. There was also consensus that, if the government does adopt a policy of wage restraint, it should not be implemented through legal sanctions. Opposition to legal sanctions was in part based on instrumental grounds – i.e., that, in the absence of a general consensus, it is unworkable – although it has been argued that, with general consensus, a "stick in the closet" (that is, legal authority held in reserve) would come in handy should it be necessary to prod any "rogue elephants" back into the herd and thus preserve the consensus. Some of the opposition to legal controls over wages derived from opposition to legal restrictions on collective bargaining for any purpose (or, as the General Secretary of the British National Union of Railwaymen told the Chairman of a Royal Commission, "I would be much happier, with great respect to you, my Lord, if we didn't have anything to do with the law at all"). But some of the opposition to legal controls reflected opposition to even a purely "voluntary" policy. Opinion was divided on whether the government should be allowed to sit in on the game, even if it parks its guns outside the door.

Opposition to even a purely voluntary incomes policy, with the government advocating restraint, did not necessarily reflect opposition to the exercise of restraint *per se*. Incomes policy has been criticised on the grounds that unions inherently exploit their market power to the hilt, just as business firms are presumed to maximise profits, and that expecting them to do less would be flying in the face of nature. However, the papers and comments which discussed the responsiveness of negotiated wages to such "external shocks" as consumer price increases and actual or potential reductions in relative wages implicitly rejected the view of the union as an inveterate maximiser, for if an institution is able to summon the extra bargaining power required to "catch up", it must have been satisfied to exert less than its full potential prior to falling behind. In any event, there was no objection to self-restraint, no disposition to object to bipartisan bargaining which takes account of its own impact on the national economy. But some drew a hard distinction between self-restraint and guided restraint. It should be up to unions and employers alone whether collective bargaining should be purely an adversary relationship (democracy's version of "class warfare", according to the Scharpf discussion) or "social partnership" (which the Dunlop paper found distasteful). Or at least their freedom to select the degree to which their mutual relationship should be adversary in nature should weigh in the scales of the national interest against the desirable level of employment and degree of price stability.

It was naturally appreciated that governmental intervention in the structure and conduct of collective bargaining has, in varying forms, been found in every country and in many cases has come to be accepted or even welcomed by the parties themselves. Thus, in the United States, legal prohibition of "secondary" boycotts (largely absent elsewhere) and work assignment strikes have been defended as in the interests of "neutral" parties, while the National Labour Relations Board's powers to decide disputes over the boundaries of bargaining units is responsive to problems raised by inter-union rivalry and to the right of the individual employee to decide which, if any, union he wishes to designate as his bargaining representative. But it is argued that, even after the government has a hand in drawing the boundaries, the parties are free to go at it inside them. This would not be true if the determination of bargaining structure were to be made an instrument of incomes policy (a possibility considered in the Blyth paper (p. 77), for in that case the object would be to increase the degree of structural centralisation, thereby running counter to a trend discussed by the Verschueren paper (p.292), in order that the government would be better able to affect behaviour.

In seeking to promote industrial peace, governments provide mediation services and sometimes oblige the parties to avail themselves of them. But mediation is intended to serve the interests of both parties — as well as the public interest — by helping them discount the outcome of stoppages, and thereby to reach settlements which are free of strike costs. This is also true when the law steps in to delay or even prohibit strikes from occurring in situations in which governmental officials are empowered by law to determine that stoppages would adversely affect public health or safety or other aspects of the "national interest". In any event, mediation consists typically of reconciliation; in this it is distinct from compulsory arbitration over "interests" which, incidentally, is neither widespread nor outstandingly effective. Hence mediators do not take too kindly to incomes policy when a minimum strike-free settlement happens to exceed the incomes policy norm. In thus frustrating the will of the parties — adversaries or partners, as the case may be — incomes policy runs counter to the requirements of industrial peace, in itself an important policy objective of long standing.

Incomes policies may strain the institutional fabric of collective bargaining and of trade unionism in particular. If leaders of central federations are persuaded to lend their support to the policy; e.g., by participating with government and employer agencies in policy formulation or administration, they may experience withdrawal of support from affiliated national unions (as noted above). If national unions cooperate, they might find themselves cut off from local units in the grass roots. Postwar history is long enough to have been rewritten: outstanding figures in national trade union movements who once were hailed for being "responsible" and "statesmanlike" were later denounced as dupes or even sell-outs. The argument against incomes policy here is that, apart from being counter-productive in weakening the bases of its support, it threatens the viability of institutions which have been traditionally regarded as sufficiently valuable to society to receive specially protected status under law.

Yet no right is absolute; no policy is sacrosanct. The privileged status of unionism has commonly been qualified by the protected rights of individuals not to join or to disaffiliate and by the right of employers not to reach agreement with them (even when under law they are obliged to bargain with them in good faith). The right to strike has been circumscribed by public policy to preserve industrial peace. Since it is also public policy to secure levels of employment as high as possible together with rates of inflation and levels of relative costs as low as possible, why should these economic policy objectives play second fiddle to the objectives of industrial relations policies? Should they not be permitted to enter the trade-off among all related policy targets?

That proposition could hardly be denied. But members of what might be called the industrial relations community nevertheless remain anxious lest the terms of trade-off be regarded as too unfavourable to the institutions of collective bargaining and the individualistic values which it inherited from an age in which the manufacturing economy was less complex and the unit of enterprise smaller and more subject to competitive discipline. Hence the charge in the Dunlop (p.128) paper and the McKenna (p.103) discussion that, out of ignorance or insensitivity, macro-economic policymakers are reluctant to accommodate their own instruments and objectives sufficiently to the essentials of collective bargaining and the perspectives of its practitioners. Essentially, the Dunlop paper views this problem as the latest chapter in a long chronicle of the antagonism between the "intellectual" and his global concerns and those lewd fellows of the baser sort who must be concerned with the unromantic "nuts and bolts" of economic life. ("Never the twain shall meet" is the gloomy conclusion — but economic necessity — and OECD conferences — may yet drive home to the policymaker what to the bargaining parties are the facts of life). The Rasmussen (p.318) paper, in dealing with the argument that job security for unionised groups may intensify unemployment elsewhere, offers no apology for the trade union perspective: "It is difficult to see why missing employment opportunities for one group should be used as an argument to worsen conditions for other wage earners". The McKenna (p.105) discussion of the Blyth paper reaches the same general conclusion about inclusion of collective bargaining activity as a social objective:

"There are many general goals that we want in free societies in addition to price stability, full employment and economic growth... Above all, though, we need to accept, no matter how painful, a final role for freedom that governments too must respect".

And the Blyth paper itself, in attempting to reconcile "free" and "responsive" collective bargaining, "emphasizes that bargainers must be leaders who keep the support of their members (whether employers or employees)".

Since this problem seemed to be viewed as a trade-off rather than a stand-off, the next problem to engage the conference dealt with how far a community is prepared to go in trading between bargaining freedom and the macro-economic goals. The mirror images of the two most prominent of these goals — high level of employment and price stability — have been implicitly bundled together in so-called "discomfort indexes" which simply add the rate of unemployment to the rate of inflation prevailing in each period of time. Similarly, the degree of collective bargaining freedom might be depicted in terms of its opposite, the degree of external restraint imposed on the conduct of collective bargaining. Hence the swap between the goals of price stability and high-employment and the goal of bargaining freedom can be seen as acceptance of more restraint in order to secure less "discomfort". Moreover, it is a fair inference from conference discussion that this process is sooner or later subject to diminishing returns: as the rates of unemployment and inflation are brought down and as bargaining becomes more restricted, there is less willingness to surrender still more of the latter in order to gain further reductions in the former. The process can be pictured in the following diagram in which SS might be regarded as a Supertrade-off

Curve because reducing the degree of "discomfort" may well involve improving the (Phillips) trade-off between unemployment and inflation.

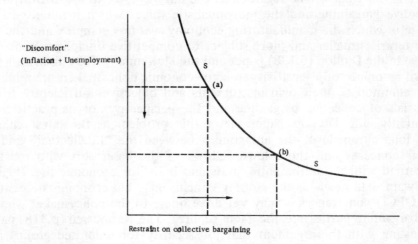

Restraint on collective bargaining

Thus, under incomes policy, it may be necessary to slide down the curve, reducing the rate of discomfort and increasing the degree of restraint — although in reality the process is hardly smooth and continuous, as the graph depicts it.

Now one problem for the community is to determine the point on the Supertrade-off Curve on which it wishes to stand e.g., "(a)", with more "discomfort" but less bargaining restraint, or "(b)" with less "discomfort" but more restraint? Another problem is to determine the level of the curve itself: the more persuasive the policy is to individual workers and their employers, the less it needs to rely on restraint (whether exercised by central bargaining institutions over their respective affiliates or by government over the private parties) to hold the economy down to a given degree of discomfort. In other words, the greater the popular persuasiveness of the policy, the lower the level of our SS curve. Both the level of the curve and the roosting point on it reflect political decisions, and these decisions are influenced by the fact that the bargaining parties, in particular the union side, may demand and may be willing to obtain compensation for the acceptance of restraint. From the viewpoint of the entire community, including the bargaining parties themselves, such compensation might be regarded as a cost, in economic and/or political terms. Thus there may be a cost in securing less "discomfort" (or, in other words, in shifting the Phillips Curve downward). Much of the discussion in the sessions devoted to "The Interaction between Collective Bargaining and Government Policies" and to "Trade-Offs" attempted to identify and evaluate what the private parties, at least the unions, may want from the government in exchange for bargaining restraint and hence as a condition for achieving "consensus". The remaining paragraphs in this report deal with these issues as summarised under the headings of Information, Performance, Compensation to Firms or Wage Earners, and Institutional Protection.

Incomes policies have almost always included wage "norms", "targets", "guiding lights", or "guideposts", although they have sometimes been criticised for being counterproductive. (The maximum could become the minimum target for unions and managers who might otherwise have settled below the target figure). Norms have usually been generated out of economic forecasts; for, although past trends in productivity have sometimes formed the basis for norms, as in the case of the U.S. guideposts during the Kennedy and Johnson administrations, norms cannot readily take account of highly relevant changes in the cost of living, and they cannot preclude inflationary movements in labour costs in years when productivity increases are below trend values. Finally, forecasts and norms have usually been provided by the government, or by some independent agency supported by the government, because it was frequently the sole repository of forecasting capability and also because the government was usually regarded as an impartial neutral in bipartisan labour disputes. (In Sweden, however, both parties have frequently agreed on the economic data and forecasts, the data being generated by the Swedish Employers' Confederation; in this case, however, the two central federations have tried to exercise bipartisan self-restraint in order to obviate the necessity of taking the government into explicit partnership).

With provision of the official information from which the official forecast and the guiding light was generated, it was even hoped that little additional guidance would be necessary. Underlying this optimism were two implicit assumptions; first, that the forecasts were accurate enough to furnish the basis for this kind of policy, and that they were unbiased; and second, that the true selfish interests of both the parties themselves would be served if they acted in the public interest as set forth in the guidelines. Unfortunately, events have revealed that neither assumption can be taken for granted.

In the first place, forecasts have been revealed increasingly to be "chancy", as the Blyth (p. 72) paper puts it, and public confidence in them has correspondingly declined, especially during the turbulent and puzzling seventies. Moreover, official forecasts have sometimes been biased conservatively when presented in conjunction with wage targets. Officials naturally wish to avoid situations which could occur when, as a result of the adoption of a wage norm based on an over-optimistic forecast, wages rise too rapidly relative to prices, and profits are squeezed or export prices get pushed up too rapidly relative to world prices and the external balance deteriorates. But if the forecast proves too conservative, the wage norm turns out to be too low, with the result that prices outpace negotiated wage rates, profit rates increase "abnormally", and earnings drift, abnormally, above negotiated rates as individual employers and rank-and-file wage earners take things into their own hands. (This, as the Blyth paper notes, has been known to occur in Germany).

The private parties have been developing increasing competence of their own in forecasting techniques. Given the large margin of error to which forecasting is prone, even unbiased forecasts may vary considerably. And if official forecasts are sometimes biased conservatively, trade union forecasts may err on the side of optimism. Thus, even if both the private parties and the authorities share the same employment objectives, they may differ over the prospects for meeting those objectives in the coming period, and hence they may differ over the appropriate policies to be followed and over the "room" for wage increases. Thus it may become increasingly important to reconcile governmental and private information and projections; and given the uncertainties involved, a certain amount of information bargaining may be in the cards. A precedent might be found in the history of Dutch incomes policy between 1959 and 1963, when the policy called for wage increases in the different sectors to be in line with increases in productivity within the respective sectors. Since the data on sectoral productivity movements were very poor, a good deal of the bargaining took the form of bargaining over productivity statistics.

Finally, government officials (representing the general public) and the bargaining sector may differ in their choice of macro-economic targets. The second assumption in the second of this subheading paragraph does not necessarily hold. Discussion of real wage and employment protection under collective bargaining (above) raised the possibility that the union side's targets might possibly imply a higher rate of aggregate unemployment (associated with a higher level of real wages) than the official target, or even a higher rating on the discomfort index (e.g., corresponding to point (a) rather than (b) in the diagram on page 36). Conversely, the union side's objectives might translate into unemployment rates lower than the official targets; they frequently do so since the public policy objectives of union movements typically embrace the employment prospects of the entire community. Thus, if the public authorities should choose to present their forecasts as an array of predictions which are conditional on the outcome of pay negotiations, as the Blyth (p. 71) paper mentioned, it must reckon on the possibility that the prediction which it prefers may not be adopted by one or both of the bargaining parties. It must be prepared to bargain over the norm. Even generally accepted information, while it might indeed constitute a necessary condition of an effective incomes policy, would not constitute a necessary condition of effectiveness.

The same point holds when the parties and the government disagree with respect to the distribution of income, a point which is emphasized in the Lachs (p. 95) discussion of the Blyth paper. Short-term forecasts and especially wage and price norms under incomes policy are frequently predicated on the assumption of constant shares, an unchanged distribution of income. (Thus the Schelde Andersen (p.189) paper compares movements in an overall productivity "norm" with movements in real wages to ascertain whether or by how much profit margins and comparative costs might have been reduced in the various countries). Nor may the publication of a simple productivity-based norm effectively guide negotiations even if the union side is content with the existing distribution of income; if labour costs rise no faster than productivity and prices rise nevertheless, labour's distributional share will have shrunk.

Performance

While it was agreed that wage increases can lead to price increases (as well as the other way around) and that high rates of inflation may lead ultimately to higher rates of unemployment, it was by no means taken for granted that moderation in wage increases will ensure moderation in price increases, nor that the latter will ensure rates of unemployment. The super-trade-off curve on page 36 is drawn on the basis of two assumtions: *(a)* that restraints on the conduct or structure of collective bargaining can restrain increases in wages (and other labour costs) and *(b)* that wage restraint under collective bargaining produces lower rates of inflation and/or unemployment. With regard to *(b)*, discussion indicated that even effective wage restraint is not a sufficient condition for attaining the desired degree of price change. Thus it was argued that if the bargaining parties are expected to live up to their side of the contract with government and deliver restraint in wage negotiations, the government must also perform under the contract by delivering the required degree of moderation in price increase. That is why trade unions invariably try to insist that price restraint accompany wage restraint; it is also why price restraint policies are sometimes accompanied by subsidy programmes. More recently, trade union movements have been replying to governmental requests for wage restraint with demands for assurance that governments deliver lower rates of unemployment; hence they frequently support employment subsidies and other job creation programmes. Whether demands for performance centre on price behaviour or employment behaviour, they signify that public authorities can no longer regard incomes policy as costless or riskless to themselves. They cannot accompany policies of wage and price restraint either with lax demand management, which imparts a "pull" to prices, or with demand management as restrictive as would be required to restrain inflation in the absence of an incomes policy. As the union side sees it, demand management must be restrained together with collective bargaining; if the latter is required to be "responsive", the former must be as well.

Compensation

While the effectiveness of incomes policy depends on its ability to moderate expectations by means other than monetary restriction (see above), those other means may themselves be costly if they involve compensation to firms or wage earners. Compensation to firms may take the form of encouragement to resist above-norm wage claims of unions more strongly than they would otherwise have been inclined to do — perhaps by constraining the institution of mediation (p. 34) or by providing a penalty, in the form of a special tax increase, for acceding to such demands. Conversely, when the community is unwilling to incur the social costs of additional labour unrest, subsidies may be provided to compensate firms for absorbing increases in labour costs without raising prices commensurately. But of course the community must pay in the end, for subsidies must be financed; moveover, they are almost inescapably wasteful to some extent.

Discussion of incomes policy in the context of a "social contract" implies that, under a variety of circumstances, unionised wage earners may require compensation for restraint in the exercise of their collective market power. Compensation may take many forms. *Indexation* may be considered a form of compensation for risk-taking, as suggested above; as such it involves a transfer of risk from the wage earner to the community, for, if price inflation occurs, indexation would result in increased labour costs to the enterprise. *Tax reduction*, especially reduction of income taxes, is the most widely discussed form of compensation, since it is the most obvious one and potentially the least costly one to the community. Substituting a tax reduction for a rise in wage rates can mean expanding demand without a rise in negotiated labour costs; if sales and payroll taxes are reduced, costs may be actually decreased. Thus, this form of compensation can be almost pure gain – as long as there is significant unemployment. Under conditions of high-level employment, tax reductions may have to be balanced by off-setting tax increases elsewhere; hence the substitution of income tax reductions for cost-raising increases in employer payroll taxes in Sweden, referred to in the Blyth paper (p. 70). Thus tax reductions which are co-ordinated with incomes policies may involve a substitution of increases in non-wage labour costs for increases in wage costs; or even, when sales taxes are increased to balance reductions in income taxes, substitution of increases in non-labour costs for increases in wage costs.

Incomes policies and wider "social contract" deals have frequently provided special compensation for low-income groups. "Exceptions" which allow above-norm increases to low-paid groups have been a common feature of such arrangements. Arrangements which in effect trade off bargaining restraint for increased social welfare benefits, which are either of the flat-rate variety or provide services "in kind", accomplish the same results. How effective can such differential compensation be as an incentive to wage earners higher up on the income ladder to accept wage restraint? More equal distribution of labour incomes might evoke an altruistic response by the more well-to-do members of unions with strong socialist traditions of egalitarianism. On the other hand, differential compensation might backfire in demands for the elimination of "inequities" and the restoration of traditional differentials and in damaging wage drift at the local level. Hence the Blyth paper (p. 73) warns that "it is difficult to pursue for very long a policy of raising the pay of the lower paid worker at a faster rate than the better paid worker and at the same time achieving a deceleration of inflation". However, the "policy" should be read as the *total* policy: a low-pay exemption or allowance might simply offset other parts of a deal which favours medium- and high-paid workers, such as income tax reductions which would tend to increase real after-tax wage differentials.

Worker "participation" – which can range from various forms of "job enrichment" at the workplace, through worker representation on the board of directors, to profit-sharing and co-ownership – was also mentioned in the Treu discussion, in connection with "socially responsible" collective bargaining. It can be regarded (at least in part) as a form of non-pecuniary compensation; in this respect it bears some resemblance to the altruistic appeal of policies which favour the low paid, except that participation supposedly satisfies more selfish, if not more materialistic, yearnings. To the extent that participation encourages wage earners to acquire, or at least appreciate, a management perspective, it could induce greater productivity as well as wage restraint. In the former respect it would achieve the results of efficient incentive systems, including so-called "productivity bargaining" under (British) incomes policies. However, whereas productivity bargaining, etc., depend for their effectiveness on the allowance of "exceptional wage increases" in exchange for the reduction of restrictive labour practices, participation may not. Nevertheless, participation schemes can have adverse, as well as beneficial, effects on productivity and growth when they oblige management to consult and negotiate before instituting changes resulting in altered work conditions, including reductions in the work force.

Institutional Protection

Compensation in its various forms may be too ineffective or too costly to produce the politically desired or economically required degree of moderation in wage movements; when such moderation implies a reduction in the level of real wages, or even in its rates of increase, the costs of compensation which the community is prepared to incur may be quite limited. And when compensation of firms or wage earners cannot do the job by itself, it will require supplementation by restraint over bargaining activity to effect a desired reduction in the community "discomfort index". But since the various forms of compensation are alternatives to collective bargaining, they might weaken the bargaining institutions through which restraint must be exercised. As the Robinson paper (p.118) observes, "Improvements obtained by government intervention... are less easily seen as the result of trade union action, so that the perceived benefits of trade union membership are accordingly less. "This may be less true in countries where unions have traditionally devoted more of their energy and resources to political activity and legislation, relative to collective bargaining, but collective bargaining has been developing relatively rapidly in those countries, so that members might well be coming to expect more from their unions in this sphere of activity than used to be the case.

Incomes policy, accompanied by compensatory devices, could thus either weaken membership interest in collective bargaining or, alternatively, it could induce greater militancy and wage drift at the grass roots. In either case, the central bargaining institutions would be strained and weakened (p. 34), and so policies of wage restraint and compensation might be accompanied by measures intended to strengthen the authority of national unions or union federations. An example of such institutional protection is furnished by American experience during the second World War: when a combination of wage controls and no-strike pledges by the national unions left the latter exposed to wildcat strikes and inter-union rivalry, they sought and obtained a considerable extension of "union security" arrangements, including "maintenance of membership" arrangements and dues check-off (Ulman, 1976). The repeal of the Industrial Relations Act in 1974, which has been regarded as part of the "social contract" between the union movement and the Labour Government in the United Kingdom is an example of at least institutional compensation, if not protection. (Although that legislation was intended in part to strengthen the authority of the national unions, the latter had strongly opposed it as restrictive and counterproductive). In addition, potential elements of institutional protection appear in various versions of worker participation. The strengthening of works councils, representation on company boards, and schemes of capital-sharing all contribute to the decentralising tendencies in collective bargaining discussed in the Verschueren (p.292) paper. Therefore, provisions which tend to protect the distinctive status of the trade unions in plant and enterprise nominations and elections and which provide for industry-wide or economy-wide funds on which national unions are represented tend to act as counterweights to the decentralising effect of "participation".

The Political Trade-off

Thus, conference discussions have agreed *(a)* that economic policies, especially when they include wage and price restraint, have tended to induce what the Peper paper refers to as the "politicisation of industrial relations (p.146)", and *(b)* that incomes policies have afforded the trade unions, and in some instances employers, both additional incentive and heightened opportunity to divert their energies into political channels. The Lachs discussion argues that "a responsible bargaining policy... would probably necessitate a very large measure of union involvement in economic policy (p. 95)." And one of the participants expressed the opinion that, if collective bargaining is regarded as too important to be left to the parties directly involved, then social and economic policies must be regarded as too important to be left to governments. So, having discussed the propriety of governmental intervention in collective bargaining, the conference ultimately dealt with the propriety of trade unions' backing their political intervention with their economic power and, according to Peper (p.144), obliging the government to arrive at consensus via "accommodation". Both this paper and the Treu comment regard the existence of this process as a measure of the weakness of representative government *vis-à-vis* powerful interest groups in the community; indeed the Treu discussion asserts that "the practice of, and need for, trade-offs as a necessary means of acquiring consensus, demonstrate the inadequacy of parliamentary democracy... p.156)." Another delegate even argued that the influence of the trade union movement could be powerful enough to obliterate, for all practical purposes, the distinction between the public and the private institutions. ("In the night all cows are black").

However, the discussion also made the point that representative governments have never functioned in the absence of pressure groups, even when they conform to what Peper (p.144) terms "the political model", in which they retain a good deal of independence. It might be added that countries like the Netherlands and Sweden have been able to incorporate powerful interests explicitly and, in some respects, formally, into legislative and administrative processes without calling into question their outstanding reputations as democratically governed communities. Yet, even in those countries, the issue has been subject to serious political debate and is regarded as a problem to be contained. In fact, there are forces at work which make for containment; compensation and institutional protection tend to be self-limiting phenomena. Since restrictions on the autonomy of collective bargaining and restrictions on the "sovereignty" of parliament both become greater as "compensation" increases, the private interest may become progressively less willing to press for, and the public interest less willing to grant, more compensation (and, in the latter case, more protection). Further reduction in unemployment and/or inflation then depends increasingly on the effectiveness of persuasion without compensation — in acquainting the parties to collective bargaining with the implications of external developments for their own behaviour and in the implications of their own behaviour for the welfare of the entire community.

III

GOVERNMENT POLICY TOWARDS THE PROBLEM

The papers in this section approach collective bargaining from the point of view of implementing anti-inflationary and full employment policies of government. The three papers by Marshall, Schultze and Blyth broadly take the view that price stability and full employment remain unachieved objectives in almost all Member countries. While neither the unions nor the collective bargaining process are seen as to blame for the failure to achieve these objectives, a greater degree of co-ordination of the results of collective bargaining with government aims, within a framework of adequate demand management and control of the money supply, is seen as essential in most countries if price stability and full employment are to be achieved. The challenge to governments and collective bargainers is to find the ways to get this co-ordination and at the same time preserve the essential features of free collective bargaining. Marshall argues that we do not face a simple trade-off between unemployment and inflation; "inflationary pressures are created by both *low* and *high* levels of unemployment", and that collective bargaining can "transmit and accelerate inflationary pressures". In the light of experience of various policies, and with a recognition of the difficulties involved, he suggests that solutions to the problems of co-ordination lie in some form of tripartitism. Schultze provides a review of the broad economic background of OECD countries, emphasising the constraints on faster growth and lower unemployment imposed by fears of accelerating inflation, especially in the United States. The paper draws attention to the nature of the present unemployment problem, especially its structural aspects, arguing that an enforced reduction of labour supply is no proper solution and pointing to the ways in which collective bargaining directly affects these issues. Blyth's paper uses the recent experience of Member countries, reviewing the varying ways in which collective bargaining and government policies are interrelated in Member countries. Following the earlier OECD report on *Socially Responsible Wage Policies and Inflation: A Review of Four Countries' Experience*[1], he develops the concept of " responsive collective bargaining" involving counter-cyclical pay and price policies[2], tax and welfare policy and the provision of information. Blyth stresses the constraints of administering such a policy imposed by uncertainty, powerful market forces and the problems of equity and rigid pay differentials. Four key institutional factors which may be candidates for reform are discussed: centralisation of structure and level of bargaining, wage rounds and leap-frogging, the role of government as employer, and co-ordination between government policy and the results of collective bargaining. Lachs and McKenna criticise Blyth from different viewpoints. Lachs takes the view that collective bargaining is about real wages and he criticises most incomes

---

1. OECD (1975)

2. See also the comments of Liinamaa in this volume, pp. 133.

policies – and Blyth – for inadequate attention to price policy. McKenna questions the assumption underlying Blyth's paper that government can and should increase its involvement in collective bargaining, arguing in particular that government is by its nature a coalition of differing interests and an unsatisfactory "third man".

COLLECTIVE BARGAINING AND GOVERNMENT POLICIES

Ray Marshall[1]

It is an honour for me to be the keynote speaker at this important OECD Conference. On behalf of President Carter and the rest of the Administration, I would like to welcome you to the United States.

The United States strongly supported this conference because we believe that all Member countries will benefit from sharing experiences and ideas about collective bargaining and government policies. Recent economic developments have made it very clear that all of our countries will have serious difficulties reconciling stable prices with low levels of unemployment. In varying degrees, we all have suffered from the international dislocations resulting from such problems as rapidly rising energy and food prices. The world faces the challenging situation where some countries have excess savings, others have inadequate sources of productive capital and still others have excess industrial capacity. This situation cries out for institutional innovations to recycle savings to areas of need in a way that will utilize productive capacity to meet pressing human needs. This is one of many examples that could be given to illustrate a problem we all face — dynamic economic forces are no longer compatible with relatively static institutions.

In the United States we are making steady progress in reducing unemployment. When President Carter was elected, unemployment was 8 percent; today it is 5.7 percent. Over five million jobs have been created in the American economy in the last 18 months. While many problems remain, it is now very clear that selective labour market policies can be used to complement macro-economic policies to produce full employment. The major uncertainty in the United States is whether or not we can control inflation as well as reduce unemployment. I do not believe, however, that we face a simplistic trade-off between unemployment and inflation. The relationship is very complex and not one-directional. Inflationary pressures are created by both *low* and *high* levels of unemployment. I believe we have paid too little attention to the upward pressures on wages and prices created by high levels of unemployment and partial utilization of productive capacity.

A major problem for the United States and other OECD countries is the reconciliation of collective bargaining with the coordination that is required to achieve full employment and stable prices. I do not believe collective bargaining has been a major source of inflationary pressures in recent years, but collective bargaining, along with other economic institutions and processes, can transmit and accelerate inflationary pressures.

---

1. United States Secretary of Labor.

This reconciliation of government policies and collective bargaining clearly is one of the most pressing and difficult problems facing democratic market-oriented economies. It would not be difficult at all to demonstrate that the health and even the survival, of democratic societies will depend heavily on whether and how they deal with inflation and unemployment problems.

Our support for this conference is based on the assumption that OECD member countries can learn much from each other. While our economic, political, and institutional differences require different policies, there is enough unity between our countries to make it possible for us to derive some basic principles that cut across international boundaries. Diversity is created by different union, economic, and collective bargaining structures, different degrees of dependence on international trade, and different governmental structures. However, OECD countries are unified by commitments to relatively low levels of unemployment, being relatively industrialized, having democratic governments, and relying heavily on collective bargaining and free market forces. We also are united by the fact that we *all* are searching for ways to minimize inflationary pressures at low levels of unemployment.

Experience with collective bargaining and inflation policies supports the following tentative conclusions.

1. No inflation or "incomes" policy can succeed if it ignores collective bargaining.
2. Traditional efforts to control wages and prices have rarely succeeded, although temporary freezes can momentarily break inflationary expectations. A major problem for traditional wage and price policies is the difficulty involved in devising a formula for wage and price determination that will simultaneously *a)* provide sufficient flexibility for collective bargaining and *b)* not produce dislocations in either product or labour markets. It is difficult enough to conceive of such a formula but even more difficult to apply it.
3. It does not follow from the failures of past efforts at wage and price controls or the inadequacies of present inflation policy that we can adopt *laissez faire* attitudes or that all of these efforts have been complete failures. Government policies are rarely complete successes or failures. The question before us is not whether to have a policy to coordinate wage and price determination with economic policy – the question is what kind of policy we should adopt.
4. While each country will have to adopt policies to fit the realities of its situation, the experiences we have had to date and the ideas to be discussed at this conference provide useful insights into the factors that will influence the success of policies to coordinate collective bargaining and economic policy. We know, for example, that the structure of bargaining will be very important.
5. The failure of past systems to reconcile wage and price determination with reasonable price stability at low levels of unemployment does not mean that we can adopt *laissez faire* policies. Indeed, it is essential that all of our governments develop policies to combat inflation – which means must attempt to reconcile wage and price determination with anti-inflation policy. We will rarely, if ever, develop perfect reconcili-

ations of collective bargaining and wage and price stability. We must, however, effect the best reconciliation possible at any given time.

A centralised bargaining system provides some advantages in coordinating policies to moderate wage and price pressures, but centralized bargaining can exacerbate the coordination problem if government officials and industry or union representatives are unable to find acceptable bases upon which to establish agree-upon policies. Decentralized bargaining can lead to price and wage instability through leapfrogging and whipsawing, but the pressures of a large competitive non-union sector can moderate wage increases and stimulate productivity and efficiency in the unionised sector.

We also know that governments can either work with collective bargaining systems in order to attempt to control wages and prices or they can work against those systems. The dangers in attempting to work against the collective bargaining system include not knowing how to influence the outcome of bargaining without damaging collective bargaining as an institution; and the counter-productiveness of activities of government intervenors if they do not thoroughly understand industrial relations systems and lack adequate power and effective tactics to influence the outcome of bargaining. If, for example, public officials intervene in bargaining they might create contests with union leaders that cause those leaders, for intra-union political reasons, to press for higher wage settlements than they otherwise would have. Efforts to reduce wage demands also risk strikes and other forms of strike.

An examination of experiences with collective bargaining and inflation suggests an exploration of the following considerations :

1. Mechanisms must be established for the government to exchange information and enter into tripartite agreements on principles governing wage and price determination. These mechanisms might include the exchange of technical information about economic assumptions and forecasts. These tripartite mechanisms should exist at the national level and in key sectors. The discussions should be based on an understanding of the actions the government is prepared to take in response to different outcomes of the collective bargaining process. Of course, the success of these discussions will depend on the parties' ability to carry out their policies. On the government side, a parliamentary system might have some advantages in entering into "social compacts". In the United States it is difficult for any branch of government to enter into a binding agreement with unions and employers in exchange for desired behaviour on wages and prices. For example, my actions require Congressional concurrence, making it difficult for executive branch officials to negotiate an agreement.

2. Mechanisms also should be established for the joint or tripartite exploration of problems outside the collective bargaining process. These mechanisms can deal with long-range problems and develop programmes to improve productivity and efficiency. These mechanisms can work *with* collective bargaining systems rather than *against* them. A number of such mechanisms have been established in the United States and others are in process of being formed.

3. The key to an effective inflation policy is to work with the most inflation-prone sectors of the economy to try to moderate these inflationary pressures within that sector. Such an approach does not exacerbate the collective bargaining process. Rather, it helps establish a climate in which productive and ultimately non-inflationary negotiations can take place.

I wish it were possible to enunciate an anti-inflation policy that could apply to all OECD countries at all times. Obviously, the problem is much too ingrained in our economies to be resolved overnight. Equally obvious is the principle that all countries must develop policies that take into consideration the unique strengths and weaknesses of their economies.

I am delighted to have been able to speak to this conference today. I would like to express my appreciation to the OECD for making such an important conference possible.

THE OVERALL FRAMEWORK
IN WHICH COLLECTIVE BARGAINING TAKES PLACE

Charles L. Schultze[1]

Growth, Inflation and Employment

I would like to try to provide an overall economic framework for the conference discussions: to try at least to deal with those particular economic problems that face our nations and the policies that are, or are likely to be, in place to deal with them, particularly those which have a particularly important impact on collective bargaining.

For virtually all of our countries, the period between 1972 and 1975 saw the worst inflation of the post-war period immediately followed by the worst recession. In the past three years we have made some important progress in recovering from those difficulties. Inflation rates in the major OECD countries, which ranged at the peak from 6 per cent to 25 per cent annual rates, have been brought down to a range of 3 per cent to 13 per cent. In the OECD countries as a whole, real output grew by 9 per cent between 1975 and 1977. Some countries in the OECD whose balance of payments situations were extremely perilous in 1975 and 1976 have made significant improvements. The surplus of the OPEC countries with the rest of the world has been reduced from over 60 billon dollars in 1974 to a projected 20/25 billion dollars in 1978. On balance – and with some lapses – we have not in the main erected new trade barriers among ourselves in response to the economic difficulties of the past 5 years.

But despite this progress we still face some serious economic problems. First, in the OECD as a whole economic growth has slowed substantially since 1976. Outside of the United States, growth in the past year-and-a-half generally moved parallel, or slightly below parallel, to economic potential, the rate being insufficient to pull down the high rates of unemployment and the high rates of excess capacity among our countries. In the OECD countries as a whole there are still more than 15 million people unemployed and the total is not moving down. Only in the United States has the unemployment rate continued to fall significantly. In Europe the economic growth in 1977 was a shade under 2 per cent and it is likely to be only modestly higher than that in 1978.

While inflation rates have come down they are still quite high in most countries. Those countries in which inflation is the lowest are growing very slowly in relation to their economic potential. In the United States, which has made progress on the unemployment rate, inflation has not fallen since late 1975 and in recent months the rate of inflation has increased; also it is quite clear that in virtually all of our countries fear of re-igniting inflation has inhibited policies to promote faster growth and lower unemploy-

---

1. Chairman of the Council of Economic Advisers to the President, United States of America.

ment. And in virtually all of our countries the rate of unemployment thought to be consistent with full employment has apparently increased. Investment in virtually all of our economies has lagged in the economic recovery. It has put more burdens on governmental budget deficits as the means of economic stimulation. It has threatened the longer-term growth of productivity and living standards.

With respect to the balance of payments, as I indicated earlier, while the rest of the world's deficit with OPEC has grown significantly less among OECD countries there are increasing imbalances. Within the OECD countries a small number of nations have a very strong surplus position which will probably amount in the aggregate to something between 25 and 30 billion dollars in 1978, whereas among the remainder of the OECD countries there will probably be a deficit of 40 to 45 billion dollars in 1978, roughly half in the United States and Canada and half among other OECD countries. These deficits add uncertainties and turbulence in the foreign exchange markets and add to the difficulties of economic recovery.

The Prospects: Employment and Inflation

What can we say about prospects for dealing with these problems? We have made some progress; we have more to make. What are the prospects for making that progress? What policies are required; in particular, what policies which may have important implications for the collective bargaining institutions and arrangements in our different countries? First, it should be possible to increase economic growth within the OECD by moderate amounts over the next several years without reigniting inflationary pressures. That is not true in the United States. In 1977 — from the end of 1976 until the end of 1977 — our economy grew by almost 5 per cent. In the last 18 months the employment rate has fallen by over 2 percentage points. Over the 18 months to come our economy will grow at a slower rate, a fact which is both desirable and necessary, given the progress we have already made against unemployment and the problem of restraining inflation. In a few other OECD countries faster growth will not be possible since those countries are still facing major internal adjustment problems. But for most of our countries, and especially those with strong balance of payments positions and those who have made substantial reductions in inflation, stepping up growth is clearly possible in the period ahead. That stepped-up growth is more likely to be realistic if it is done on a concerted basis since the balance of payments limitations and constraints which might otherwise face some of our countries would thereby be lifted. Moreover, continued slow growth in most of our countries would not accomplish very much to reduce inflation further in any event.

The continued high levels of inflation stem not from overheated economies with strained resources and excessive demands. Instead, they are heavily a matter of momentum and inertia in which yesterday's inflation drives today's inflation so that each group, trying to protect its income against past inflation, presses its claims hard and thereby helps to keep inflation going. Even though there can be faster growth in the OECD area without

54

setting off new inflationary pressures, and even though persistence of excess-ively slow growth would not contribute much to a further reduction of inflation, inflation remains a problem that cannot be ignored. To the extent that it persists at high levels, even if not accelerating it will inhibit economic growth. We have learned the painful lesson of how hard it is to eradicate inflation once it accelerates and because of that lesson governments have been very reluctant to take risks or take expansionary chances.

Inflation and Collective Bargaining

In dealing with this question many OECD governments have according-ly turned to one form or the other of voluntary policies affecting private wage and price decisions. They have tried various measures through tech-niques other than direct controls to influence directly the outcome of individual collective bargaining and pricing decisions. The institutions of collective bargaining vary widely among our countries in terms of the degree of centralisation of bargaining. They are also strikingly different with respect to the timing of bargaining — in some countries concentrated in a few months and at the other extreme, like the United States, spread out over a number of years. There are also wide differences among our countries in terms of the general reliance placed on fixed wage increases as compared with indexing to consumer prices and therefore no single approach within governmental policies towards effecting prices and wages is, or has been, suitable for all. The success or failure of these policies has varied widely from country to country and from time to time.

I am not enough of an expert to know the extent to which the particu-lar collective bargaining institutions in a particular country heavily influence the chance of success of such policies or whether that success hinges on more general political and cultural attitudes. Developing a relationship between the outcomes of a free collective bargaining process on the one hand and general national policies with respect to inflation and growth on the other is a matter that inherently brings tension and even logical contradictions. How, for example, do we reconcile the necessary flexibility and adjustment in relative wages that a dynamic economy needs with specific objectives in terms of overall wage and benefit changes? While I am fully aware of the major issues involved, I suspect that the problem of the relationship of collective bargaining institutions to national policy objectives with respect to growth and particularly inflation is one that is going to be with us a long time and needs careful and systematic attention, both by technical experts and by practitioners.

Barriers to Faster Growth

Next, with respect to our economic policies I believe we must be careful that in seeking to alleviate the problems which have accompanied high unemployment and low growth we do not institute measures which reduce the prospects for future growth in employment and living standards. In the face of high unemployment and large excess capacity in some important in-dustries, many of our governements have adopted particular policies to deal with specific industries, sectors and regions. To the extent that such national policies are adopted, we must be careful not to set up barriers to the necessary economic adjustments which must take place in healthy economies. Economic prosperity in the long run depends both upon a suitable rate of overall economic growth and on adaptation to changes in technology, tastes and trade patterns. One of the costs of slow growth is the fostering of particular kinds of subsidies and protective devices which throw up road blocks to dynamic adjustments. How to choose the appropriate mixture of measures which on the one hand alleviate the costs of unemployment and bridge temporary difficulties, without at the same time increasing the rigidities and inefficiencies in our economies, that is a path that is both economically and politically very difficult to walk. And again I believe there is a strong interaction between the institutions of collective bargaining and government policies dealing with economic adjustments in particular industries, sectors and regions, and there will continue to be a major challenge both to governments and to the parties to collective bargaining agreements to design and carry out adjustment policies which ease the burden of unemployment and insecurity without introducing rigidities into our economy.

Reducing the Supply of Labour

There may be a temptation in some of our countries to deal with the problem of unemployment and slow growth by following the old maxim, "if you can't beat them join them"; that is, to deal with the problem of unemployment not by measures to improve the growth of output but by measures to slow or reduce the growth of labour input, shorter work weeks, earlier retirement ages, and the like. A shorter work week or earlier retirement or longer vacations can be a perfectly appropriate way for a nation and its workers to realise their increases in living standards. It is a perfectly appropriate choice to opt for more leisure and less consumer goods, and indeed over the past three-quarters of a century there has been in all our countries a major shift to a shorter work week as one aspect of the increase in productivity and living standards.

But such measures, however desirable as a free choice between leisure and work, are no solution to the problem of unemployment. We do not have high unemployment because our countries cannot find a use for the potential output of the unemployed in additional consumer goods, or in private or public investment. Rather we have slow growth because we are reluctant to speed up the rate of growth of output by monetary and fiscal measures fearing that the faster growth will put pressure on labour markets, drive up wages and prices and stimulate inflation. A national policy of reducing hours of work or similar measures is obviously not an answer to this problem. To the extent that it is the fear of inflation that inhibits growth-inducing measures, policies which reduce labour input will not help the unemployment problem. Such policies do not address the problem that we face, and leave us no better off than we now are in dealing with the twin phenomena of high unemployment and inflation. While individual collective bargaining arrangements which seek to increase workers' leisure are therefore perfectly appropriate, national policies which encourage these trends as the answer to the unemployment problem, seem to me to miss the point.

Structural Unemployment

The problem of structural unemployment now looms larger in most countries than in any time in the recent past. Its seriousness as distinct from overall cyclical unemployment varies from country to country but it is a problem for most of us. Policies to deal with structural unemployment have a direct impact upon both economic growth and inflation. Structural employment policies do not generally negate the need for a satisfactory rate of economic growth as the condition for reducing unemployment. Rather such policies make it possible for growth to occur and for unemployment to be absorbed without giving rise to the inflationary pressures which might occur in the absence of such policies. As economic growth becomes sufficient to reduce the cyclical component of unemployment to low levels, further increases in the demand for labour generally will tend to create shortages of skills and increase the upward pressure on wages and prices. But to the extent that the growing demand for labour can be satisfied through the hiring of the structurally unemployed, for example from among youth and minorities, economic growth can be sustained and the overall unemployment rate lowered without a build-up of inflationary pressures in the labour market.

We generally tend to think about structural employment policies in the context of governmental programmes of various kinds, and that is in one sense correct, but collective bargaining arrangements can also have, I think, an important effect on the degree to which structural unemployment can be reduced. Again I do not pretend to be an expert on these matters but it seems to me that herein lies another important area in which national economic policies and collective bargaining are related. Through collective bargaining we affect wage structure, private training and apprenticeship arrangements, seniority systems, agreements with respect to hiring and firing and a number of other elements of industrial relations which clearly have an important effect on structural employment and structural unemployment in our countries.

The Way Ahead

Our countries face an important set of challenges in the years immediately ahead. Most, though not all of us, need to increase our rate of growth to make inroads on unemployment, idle capacity and lagging investment. At the present time that can be done for the area as a whole without increasing inflationary pressures if undertaken on a concerted basis, carefully and selectively. Dealing with inflation will nevertheless remain a prerequisite for long-term sustained growth and substantial further reduction in unemployment. In the process of promoting growth while dealing with inflation and promoting structural adjustments in our economies there are going to

57

be important connections between collective agreements and national economic policies, I have chosen to cite in particular the area of government policies directly affecting private wage and price decisions, and the field of industrial, regional and other adjustment measures in the area of structural employment policies. These are very important connections and there is a very important contribution that collective bargaining can make in dealing with our common problems.

THE INTERACTION BETWEEN COLLECTIVE BARGAINING
AND GOVERNMENT POLICIES IN SELECTED MEMBER COUNTRIES

Conrad A. Blyth[1]

Introduction[2]

Full employment and stable prices have been two of the most important objectives of the governments of OECD countries ever since the Second World War, and the economic history of the last thirty years could well be written around the attempts of governments to attain these two objectives while at the same time constrained by the need to balance their countries' foreign accounts. While other important economic and social objectives like growth and the raising of average living standards, and greater social and economic equality, have been pursued, most governments have acted in the belief that a failure to achieve economic stability, i.e. failure to deal with the problems of unemployment, inflation and external deficits, would make other economic and social objectives more difficult — perhaps impossible — to achieve.

The experience of three decades has shown that the sustained achievement of stable economic growth is difficult and presents a continuous challenge to governments. Stable economies can be thrown off balance by events like wars, strikes or large rises in the prices of primary commodities, while the interdependence of economies through trade, migration and capital flows means that no country, however large, can be insulated against events in the wider international sphere. In recent years it has even appeared that the challenge to governments has increased, the problems if anything getting bigger.

Orthodox policy to attain stable economic growth received its modern shape during and shortly after the Second World War. The instruments of policy were the five traditional tools of government - monetary measures, public finance (expenditure and tax) measures, exchange rate alteration, direct controls and the fifth category, which will be described here as persuasion. What was new was not so much remodelling of the tools — although there was some of that — as the deliberate effort to use these tools to achieve stability. The real novelty lay in the conscious attempt of governments to manage their economies to avoid unemployment and inflation, and at the same time to attain higher standards of living.

---

1. Professor, Department of Economics, University of Auckland, New Zealand and Consultant to the Social Affairs, Manpower and Education Directorate of OECD.

2. This paper attempts to draw out the implications of a series of OECD studies of the relationship between collective bargaining and government policy in eleven countries: Australia, Canada, Finland, Germany, Ireland, Japan, Netherlands, Norway, Sweden, the United Kingdom and the United States. Earlier OECD studies (e.g. of Austria) as well as the experience of other countries (e.g. Denmark, France and New Zealand) have been drawn on. The published OECD studies are listed in the Bibliography.

Over the years the particular mixture of tools used has varied, and different countries have shown preferences for particular tools to be used in particular ways, reflecting perhaps the fact that the use of all tools involves costs, and some costs are felt more strongly in some countries than in others. Thus countries like Germany and Switzerland have continuously relied heavily on monetary measures. France and Austria have used price controls more or less continuously as an important instrument, the United Kingdom relied considerably for many years on tax and public expenditure changes, but in recent years has used a mixture of monetary and fiscal measures. After two decades in which orthodox exchange rate policy was designed to hold rates fixed, the 1970s have seen new policies of greater flexibility and relatively free exchange markets. The use of direct controls over production, domestic expenditure, imports and capital movements, because of the costs involved, has been reduced over the years, but most governments have resorted to direct controls over incomes and prices from time to time, usually briefly in emergency situations. Some governments have tried over lengthy periods statutory control programmes over incomes and prices: the United Kingdom 1966-1970, and again 1972-74, the United States 1971-74, the Netherlands for many years until 1967, and Canada 1975-78.

Persuasion covers a broad category of measures including, for example, statements suggesting or urging citizens or interest groups to follow certain courses of action (such as exercising restraint in spending or in raising prices and incomes); formal or informal meetings of government representatives with trade union and employer leaders to discuss pay and prices, and one another's points of view; and published guidelines for the activities of particular economic sectors, such as suggested maxima for bank lending or price increases. The rationale behind measures of persuasion is that the government's policy to achieve stability rests on certain assumptions about the decisions to be taken in certain parts of the economy, and by telling the decision-takers what these assumptions are the government hopes to influence the decisions in the direction of its assumptions. It can thus be seen that successful persuasion presupposes some degree of social consensus about economic and social objectives. While it is likely to be most effective in wartime or other emergency situations, there are many examples of its use in less extreme situations. Examples of the use of persuasion as a measure to moderate pay and price rises are the United States' voluntary guidelines 1962-66, the United Kingdom's *Social Contract* from 1974 to date, and the occasional interventions of governments into centralised collective bargaining as in Norway in 1977, in Finland frequently in recent years, in Ireland in 1970 and in subsequent years, and in the Netherlands since 1976. Austria provides an example of continuous involvement of government in centralised pay settlements and pricing decisions. In Germany under the *Concerted Action* policy since the 1960s representatives of the Federal Government and other official agencies regularly meet the representatives of trade unions and employers to exchange views and information about the state of the economy and its future prospects. Obviously interventions can take a variety of forms depending on the circumstances: in some cases the extent of government influence is so slight that even persuasion is too strong a word; in other cases governments have used threats or actual sanctions to achieve their objectives and the measure of persuasion merges into a form of direct control.

Reference has already been made above to examples of government's interventions in centralised negotiations in recent years. This is not however a new interest of governments : the concern with the influential social and economic role of collective bargaining goes back to the early days of active policies to promote full employment and price stability. It is because of the important part that collective bargaining plays in the overall determination of labour costs − and the part that increases in labour costs play in the inflationary process − that governments have become much more concerned in recent years with the settlements that emerge in collective bargaining. Most governments are now in a position where just as they must have a co-ordinated set of policies about household spending, enterprise investment, housing and energy, so they must have a policy towards collective bargaining which is properly co-ordinated with the rest of their social and economic policies. A policy towards collective bargaining has become for most governments an essential part of their overall full employment and anti-inflation programmes. The three following sections of this analysis successively examine the nature of the case for a policy towards collective bargaining, the way in which such a policy works, and the changes in collective bargaining and government relationship to it required to make such a policy effective as an instrument contributing to stable economic growth.

A Positive Policy Towards Collective Bargaining

The simplest way to state the case for a government policy towards collective bargaining is to say that an activity like collective bargaining has such an enormous influence − directly or indirectly − on all parts of the economy that a responsible government intent on securing full employment and price stability must ensure that the outcome of collective bargaining is in accord with its other economic and social objectives. This very general statement contains two central themes, firstly, the influence of collective bargaining on the economy (and the influence of the economy on bargaining), and secondly, the accordance between bargaining outcomes and national objectives. These will be examined below.

Collective bargaining between employers and their employees (represented usually by the officers of the trade union) settles the pay and other working conditions of the employees through the negotiation, administration, interpretation and enforcement of agreements or joint understandings. In almost all OECD countries collective bargaining is the normal method of settling pay. Thus in countries like Sweden where a very high proportion of the labour force is unionised it can be said that pay is generally settled by collective bargaining. However even in countries with lower levels of unionisation, such as Germany and the United States, the influence of collectively bargained settlements extends beyond the unionised part of the labour market, both through the legal or customary extension of such settlements to other groups of workers, and through the workings of the competitive parts of the labour market. Although it is not possible to measure precisely the influence of collective bargaining, it is likely that in most OECD countries the pay of a majority of — in some cases nearly all — employees is settled directly or indirectly by collective bargaining. Thus governments which seek to influence pay settlement must influence the decisions taken by the parties to collective bargains.

Governments who wish to influence pay settlements do so because they see such actions as part of their wider policy of attaining stable growth, and in particular of price stability. The action may be indirect, using monetary and fiscal measures, or direct, using controls or persuasion. Indirectly, governments may influence the forces of supply and demand in both the markets for labour and the markets for goods and other services. For instance, governments may through monetary and fiscal measures so reduce the aggregate purchase of goods and services that enterprises reduce output and reduce their labour force. This reduced output and reduced demand for labour will affect the attitudes and expectations of the parties to collective bargains. Most people would expect that, if output and demand fall enough, pay settlement will be lower than would otherwise be the case[3]. Direct action to influence pay settlements can take a variety of forms ranging from wage freezes (as in the United States in 1971, and in the Netherlands in 1974), statutory control programmes and statutory enforcement of settlements (as for example in Denmark in 1977, when, following the failure of unions and employers to agree on a new settlement, Parliament enacted the official mediator's draft proposal into law), to attempts to influence national collective bargaining, examples of which have already been referred to above.

Governments through experience have found that their efforts to achieve stability can be frustrated if pay settlements do not accord with their overall objectives. This is not an exceptional experience of a few countries on occasion; it has been the general experience of all countries at least since 1974, with the single exception of Switzerland. The level of pay settlements has been such that most governments have been thwarted in their attempts to achieve either full employment or price stability. In the first place, the level of pay settlements in many countries, however justified on grounds of cost-of-living increases, has through its effect on costs inevitably meant that prices have kept on rising rapidly. In the second place, attempts to slow down pay increases by the indirect methods of deflation have inescapably led to high levels of unemployment[4]. While depressed conditions in the labour and output markets have in most cases slowed down the rise in pay, governments have been fearful that recovery measures leading to too rapid rises in output and employment would reaccelerate the rise in pay and lead to renewed accelerating inflation. As a result, in recent years the objectives of no party to the process have been achieved: employees have in most countries seen price inflation reduce the value of their pay rise, and have

---

3. This does not necessarily imply that the rate of increase of pay will decline — it may in fact accelerate: the comparison is with what would have happened if output and demand had not fallen.

4. Deficient demand as a primary cause of present high levels of unemployment is stressed; there are other causes of high unemployment.

also experienced high levels of unemployment; employers have experienced low profits and stagnant markets; while very few governments have achieved their goals of full employment, price stability, growth and external balance.

There is an emerging realisation that collective bargaining is too important a factor in modern, highly interdependent economic systems for governments to neglect it in framing their policies. To neglect it is like attempting to drive a car with no brakes: if one is driving uphill there is no problem, but if the car starts on a downhill path... In the past governments have attempted to intervene directly in collective bargaining in exceptional situations, as when they feared that expansionary policies to reduce unemployment would raise already high rates of inflation (as in the United States in 1971 and in Britain in 1972), or as a response to large accelerations in the rate of inflation (which has been the case in many countries in the years since 1973). In some cases the fear of a worsening competitive position, as in Canada in 1975, has been the factor leading to the imposition of controls.

Experience of direct intervention through freezes and statutory policies has been unsatisfactory. Freezes, by their very nature, are crisis measures and must be quickly relaxed in market economies if distortions and black markets are not to emerge. Statutory policies, such as those of the United States and the United Kingdom, appear to be fairweather systems, introduced in periods of recovery from recession, and showing strains when the recovery turns into boom and excess demand pressures emerge in the markets. The United States phased out its statutory policy of controls in the boom years of 1973 and early 1974, while the British controls were dismantled in 1974 after a serious industrial confrontation and a change of government. This recent American and British experience has convinced some governments and their citizens that statutory controls which interfere with or stop the normal processes of collective bargaining, especially when they try to stem the tide of excess demand, are useless and even dangerous in their legacy of distortions, suppressed inflation and real or imagined injustices.

Instead the trend of current thought and development is towards a policy for methods of settling pay — and as explained this means primarily a policy for collective bargaining — which is very different from freezes and statutory controls. It is towards a government stance which attempts to co-ordinate the objectives of collective bargainers with the government's objectives of stability, growth and social equality, in a continuous way such that each party — trade unions, employers and government — is responsive to the objectives of each other. This trend of both thinking and experience appears to be towards a patient policy of continuous co-ordination designed to produce the optimal degree of responsive behaviour that satisfies the social, political and economic aspirations of the people.

The governments, differing in the social, political and economic aspirations of their people, will almost certainly differ in their methods of achieving continuous co-ordination and in the degree of responsive behaviour they expect to achieve. The ultimate objective of the policy towards collective bargaining of all governments however must be the same: *it is to get results from collective bargaining which do not upset the government's other aims.* Policies to achieve this objective can embrace a variety of institutions and methods of persuasion. The next section of this paper considers how, taking into account a variety of institutions and methods, and the events of the 1970s, responsive collective bargaining might work in the new social and economic environment of the 1980s.

How Responsive Collective Bargaining Works

There are four areas where important decisions will determine the success of responsive bargaining: pay, price, taxes and welfare policy, and information. These will be discussed in turn, taking into account two serious constraints on the process: the strength of market forces and the difficulty of economic prediction.

Counter-cyclical pay policy

Responsive collective bargaining would adopt a pay policy that can best be described as counter-cyclical, which is the opposite of how the bargaining process works at present. At present, as an economy recovers and boom conditions develop, excess demand emerges in markets including parts of the labour market. The profits of enterprises usually start to recover. In this situation unions' bargaining position strengthens at the same time as employers are willing to increase pay to keep good workers and attract others. In other words, market forces are pulling in the direction that unions are pushing, and employers in general have little or no incentive to show resistance. Furthermore, the prospect of a share of higher profits encourages a more aggressive union attitude. In contrast, in a recession, when excess supply and slack emerges in markets, employers are in general under no pressure to keep labour – in fact some will be laying off workers and reducing new recruitment. In these conditions employers are in a strong position to resist pay increases and unions are in a correspondingly weak bargaining position. Market forces are pulling employers in the direction they want to go.

It would hardly be worthwhile to have drawn attention here to these obvious and familiar situations, were it not for their significance in propagating inflation when inflation is already at a high level. If in the boom period pay increases are, for whatever reasons, substantially in excess of productivity growth, prices will inevitably rise (in general by the excess of labour cost increase over productivity growth). Consequently, in the ensuing recession, it has been the workers' experience that they find themselves ground between two millstones: one, the reduced demand for labour and weakened union bargaining strength and two, rising prices as employers attempt to maintain their profit margins in the face of the rising labour costs. This very generally describes the position that workers in most OECD countries have been faced with in the years since 1974, although the rise in prices during the period of recession has been aggravated by other factors like the rise in oil prices,while the experience of countries with a high propensity to import has been that rises in import prices has been a further aggravating factor. The reason for drawing attention to the link between inflation of labour costs in the boom period and continued price inflation in the recession is firstly because labour costs are the major cost in GNP, and secondly because unlike the prices of oil and imports, labour costs are potentially within the control of the parties to collective bargains.

The natural response of workers to price rises during recession is to bargain for pay rises which at least compensate them for the rises in the cost of living. If they are successful — and the experience of many OECD countries is that employees in general have been successful in recent years — the consequence is that the inflationary spiral is perpetuated. The continued pressure on prices is likely to be aggravated by the declines in productivity that arise in industry during periods of recession. In this way economies become trapped in continuously high rates of inflation, due not to excessive greed on the part of either workers or employers, but to a system of settling pay which, however successful it has been in the past in non-inflationary situations, has shown itself to be inadequate in inflationary situations — unresponsive to the problems and dangers of rapid inflation. And the consequences are not only in perpetuated inflation. It has been suggested in some countries — the Netherlands and Germany, for example — that in the recession period the combination of low output and continued rising labour costs has put such pressure on profits that not only has employment been directly affected by the recession but employers' unwillingness or inability to undertake investments has retarded or delayed economic recovery.

A counter-cyclical pay policy, instead of allowing collective bargains to be pulled all the way by market forces, would take a middle way in both boom and recession. In the boom, unions would refrain from exerting their full immediate strength; in the recession employers would moderate theirs. The intention would be to keep labour costs in the boom at a level which would avoid rapid price rises in the recession, and to ensure that in the recession the real purchasing power of pay did not fall or possibly rose by some acceptable standard. Such a policy might involve transferring some of the gains in real income, which unions hope to win in a prosperous boom, to the recession when by supporting consumer buying power they would have the effect of limiting the depth and length of the recession: the policy is not only counter-cyclical in the market forces sense, but is counter-cyclical in its effect on boom and slump — the top of the boom is scraped off to fill in the hole of the recession[5].

The foundation of such a policy is the link between pay settlements and real income growth. Agreements would contain a normal annual increment linked to the long-term productivity growth of the economy. Protection against rises in the cost of living would take the form of an increment at intervals to compensate for rises in the cost of living during the previous period. At this point two major complications arise. Firstly, if it is generally agreed that the rate of inflation is at a dangerously high level and must be reduced, the compensation for previous cost of living rises must normally be less than full. Secondly, if despite a country's productivity growth, its real

---

5. The analogy is with Keynes, deferred pay scheme. See *How to Pay for the War,* in Collected Writings of John Maynard Keynes, Vol. IX (Macmillan).

income is growing less than proportionately because of a decline in its terms of trade (e.g. import prices rising faster than export prices), the combined productivity and cost of living increments must be reduced by this loss due to the fall in the terms of trade. Correspondingly, if the terms of trade improved, pay packets would contain a terms of trade bonus[6].

A pay policy of this sort on the part of unions and employers is not at all an idealistic dream. Austrian unions and employers have in recent years discussed and attempted to implement some aspects of such a policy. The policy of the Netherlands' unions shows such a conception of pay policy in their claims for a guaranteed growth of real income protected by automatic cost-of-living adjustments (indexation or escalator provisions), although a period of recession is not the best time to get such a proposal accepted at the bargaining table. Countries where collective bargains are normally for periods greater than a year, such as the United States or Canada, would appear to be in a better position to introduce deliberate counter-cyclical policies into collective agreements not only because the span of such agreements (say, three years) covers a large part of a cycle of boom and recession, but also because in recent years the introduction of automatic cost-of-living adjustments in agreements has become common. But it hardly needs to be pointed out that unless the pay rises agreed on for the boom are less than they otherwise would have been, an agreement with full or near full cost-of-living adjustment may be yet another powerful propagator of inflation.

In the proposed counter-cyclical policy neither party to a collective bargain is being asked to give up any of its bargaining power. The parties are being asked to take a longer view in their own long-term interests. Both are concerned with the long-term growth of real incomes: unions because it provides the workers with their rising standard of living, employers because it provides them with the growth of output and sales. Both are asked to consider an elementary trade-off between occasional large rises in income in booms on the one hand, and on the other, steady growth in real income every year. The extent to which indexation should be automatic or periodically negotiable, full or partial, will depend upon the underlying assumptions of counter-cyclical policy – the real income growth, the effect of changes in terms of trade and exchange rate, the severity of inflation – and will obviously vary from country to country, and from period to period.

Price policy

Pricing decisions are not independent of the counter-cyclical pay policy discussed above, nor indeed of collective bargaining in general. Profit levels and pay claims flow from pricing decisions, and price increases flow from pay rises. Responsive collective bargaining requires that employers reduce prices (or minimise their increase) as much as possible following productivity increases, and that to make this possible collective bargains should minimise the pay increases won from productivity increases. Both wage and price

---

6. Both of the Schelde Anderson (Section 1) and Dodge (p.170) papers in this volume deal with the terms of trade problem.

policies, if they are to be responsive to the aims of government and the interests of other groups in society, must aim to spread the benefits of productivity growth as far as possible to all counsumers by means of price reductions, insofar as this is feasible. Usually, in competitive industries, such an aim will work with market forces. But enterprises in less competitive situations will not be under such pressures and in a realistic situation a considerable effort by government would be required if both employers and employees were to make this possible. Because of the extent to which many governments are responsible for the price decisions of enterprises in their countries (either because of ownership or of different forms of statutory control), these governments have a special responsibility to ensure that price decisions are co-ordinated in the fullest way possible with the wider economic objectives. An aim of steady levels of money pay with a declining price level may be somewhat unrealistic, but it is a good guideline for bargainers and government to accept.

Real income is the underlying concern of all pay settlements, and the argument of this paper is that responsive bargainers must consider money pay and prices in all their relationships. An essential complement to this is that employers should avoid large, disruptive price rises at critical points in the economic cycle. To the extent to which the long-run interests of an enterprise allow it, the pricing policy of an enterprise should be adapted in a counter-cyclical way. Large price increases in a boom will obviously create unmanageable strains in a union's counter-cyclical pay policy.

Taxes and welfare policy

It has been suggested above that the underlying concern of collective bargainers should be growth in real incomes over a period of several years. Real income is a concept that not only relates money pay to prices, but also takes into account tax payments and the benefits households receive under welfare (social security or insurance) schemes[7]. Fiscal decisions as such are not taken by collective bargainers, but their decisions are and can be considerably influenced by fiscal and welfare policies. Responsive collective bargainers would reach agreements explicity with levels of taxes and welfare payments in mind. What is suggested here is that governments should, through their tax and welfare policies, make it possible for collective bargainers to arrive at pay settlements that fit in with governments' objectives. In other words there is for unions a trade-off between gross pay increases and net tax and benefit changes, such that if a government offers a reduction in tax payments or a rise in benefits (or a combination of the two), unions settle for a smaller pay rise than would otherwise be the case. Similarly, employers can be persuaded to accept larger pay increases than would otherwise be the case if a government offers a reduction in the taxes or social security contributions they pay.

---

7. Real income may of course be defined in many different ways and could include the real value of all public consumption expenditures. Here, for practical and illustrative reasons it is limited primarily to the real value of household net cash receipts. But non-cash benefits are considered later in the discussion.

This very important instrument of government policy towards collective bargaining has increased in scope and use greatly in recent years, both as a method of dealing with difficult industrial situations, and as a deliberate anti-inflation device. In 1974 the new *British* Government dismantled the previous government's statutory control policy and came to an arrangement (the *Social Contract*) with the Trades Union Congress who agreed to encourage negotiators to moderate their wage claims, while the government promised to repeal legislation disliked by unions, continue statutory price controls and subsidies, improve the position of low paid workers and take measures to increase employment and foster growth. By early 1976 it appeared that the policy was having some effect and for 1976-77 (what was called Phase II of the Social Contract) the government offered tax reductions conditional on acceptance of a further voluntary agreement to limit pay increases, which was in fact entered into. Next year, however, the government's new offer of another income tax reduction in return for another voluntary agreement was declined[8].

The British experience concerns largely the dealings of government and unions. Other countries give examples of governments employing tax and welfare policy initially at any rate to resolve difficult bargaining situations between unions and employers. Since 1962 there has existed in *Norway* a formal means of bringing together government and representatives of the central bodies of trade unions and employers, together with farmers and fishermen, to discuss the economic forecast and its analysis before the bargaining commenced. Norway in 1973 was starting to experience the effects of the international inflation, and the government, as part of an anti-inflationary package deal, took an active part in a combined settlement with employers and unions. 1974 witnessed an unusual episode of decentralised, industry level bargaining, the government playing only a minor part by providing economic information. By the end of 1975, with inflation still high and Norway suffering from the effects of the international recession, the government was able to bring unions, employers and the other interest groups together to agree on a modest pay settlement in the framework of a comprehensive stabilization policy which was worked out over several months during the end of 1975 and early 1976. The government made it clear that tax concessions would only be granted if pay increases were moderate. The important part of the pay settlement was that pay rises could not be expected to fully compensate for price rises: workers, along with others, would have to accept slow growth in real income. An attempt was made, through industry-wide discussion, to adapt the overall agreement to local conditions and the whole agreement was approved by referenda amongst the members of the participating groups. This agreement allowed pay negotiations to be reopened on the basis of price rises and general economic developments. While the 1977 negotiation promised to be difficult, it was resolved after the Krone was devalued in April. Government policy was

---

8. After two years of voluntary restraint during a period of high inflation, living standards had been eroded to a point where many unions were becoming dissatisfied. The TUC opted for a return to free collective bargaining although it continued to support the policy of a twelve-month interval between pay settlements (or the consequential pay rises).

to achieve by tax reductions an increase in real disposable income of 2 1/2 per cent p.a., even though money wages and prices were rising at about the same rate. Norway has thus embarked on what appears to be the first stages of a British-type Social Contract, although there are some important differences from the British model, including a centralised bargaining system which appears to have the support of most unions and a partnership which extends to farmers and fishermen.

Over the last decade, the policy of the *Finnish* Government has been to secure voluntary agreements within the framework of its stabilization policy. The experience has been a checkered one, partly because of political crises (which affect union behaviour as well as government policy), partly because of labour market pressures such as the dissatisfaction of workers who are not benefiting from wage drift. The 1971 agreement broke down and political difficulties prevented the signing of an agreement in 1973. Since 1974 the agreements have been much wider than those signed earlier, and embrace a number of government measures including personal tax reduction, welfare payments and price controls. The most recent agreement signed in early 1977 (for two years) was the product of hard bargaining. Several unions had opted out of the previous agreement and negotiated better terms, and a strong move towards decentralised bargaining was only warded off by a government package deal offer including the compensation of those workers who had not benefited from drift. The government agreed to adjust income tax scales to compensate for inflation, not to raise particular indirect taxes for a year, and to temporarily reduce employees' employee pension contributions. This Finnish experience reflects to some extent the British difficulties of organising a voluntary policy when the policy itself becomes part of politics, when the policy allows normal differentials to be distorted and where a lack of central authority makes leadership difficult to exercise. As in Norway, fluctuations in international trade make goals set in terms of real income growth exceptionally difficult to achieve.

In *Ireland* in 1970 after a period of rapid inflation and public discussion of the benefits of a voluntary incomes policy, the Employer-Labour Conference was established to provide the organisation for an attempt to establish such a policy. After initial trade union opposition to the policy proposed by the government — which led to a brief incomes freeze (not actually applied) at the end of 1970 — a national pay agreement (NPA) was worked out at the Conference after much give and take on all sides including the government's abandoning of some of its original proposals. An important feature of the agreement was a cost-of-living escalator clause. New NPAs were negotiated in 1972 and 1974, the latter being difficult to achieve in the face of accelerating inflation. On this occasion the government smoothed the trade union path by committing itself to tax reliefs and improved welfare benefits. By 1974 Ireland was experiencing the effects of the international recession together with continued accelerating inflation. The government was successful in getting the partners to agree on virtually no rise in real incomes in 1975, although during the year it negotiated arrangements to alter the linkage of wages and consumer prices in return for reductions in indirect taxes and measures to reduce unemployment. In 1976, after a draft NPA had been rejected by trade unions because it severely limited the possibility of public sector pay rises, an interim settlement protecting real incomes was worked out, with agreement on a tripartite conference on general economic issues to precede the negotiations at the next Employer-Labour Conference. After an inconclusive tripartite conference the government early in 1977 set out its proposals – modest increase in pay which would not fully match the expected rise in consumer prices, with tax reductions and policies to promote employment – which eventually became the basis of the 1977 NPA.

Norway, Finland and Ireland provide interesting examples of evolving systems of centralised collective bargaining, with governments as a third partner deliberately using fiscal and welfare policy as a tool to bring about satisfactory national agreements. This open role of government contrasts with the absence of formal intervention by government in *Swedish* centralised bargaining. Although the Swedish Government does not deliberately play the part of a third partner, it has however been willing in recent years to offer tax and other fiscal concessions to trade unions in return for moderate pay settlements. This began in 1973 before the negotiations over pay in 1974 commenced and was repeated at the beginning of 1975 for the negotiations which covered 1975 and 1976. On this latter occasion a two-year agreement for blue-collar workers was only made after the three main political parties had come to an agreement on additional income tax reductions for 1976. For 1977 the government again reduced income tax rates but without making the reductions conditional on moderation in wage increases. However, possibly because the effect of the tax cuts was estimated to be equivalent to wage rises of over 10 per cent, and possibly because the government raised the social security contribution of employers, the 1977 pay settlements were modest.[9]

Collective bargaining experience of the *Netherlands* in recent years has been different from that of the countries mentioned, but it is interesting to note the ways in which the Dutch Government has viewed collective bargaining within the wider framework of economic policy. The long-lived statutory incomes policy came to an end in the late 1960s, and the subsequent attempt to operate a voluntary policy with residual veto powers in the hands of the government was not particularly successful. However, the voluntary bargain that emerged in 1972 was remarkable in that the government as a third partner agreed to a list of political demands regarding taxes, social services and employment. In 1973 tripartite negotiations started for a new agreement with a fresh list of political demands from the trade unions. Before the issues could be resolved (which looked doubtful: negotiations reached a stalemate) the oil crisis caused the government at the beginning of 1974 to take special temporary powers (for six months) to control prices, incomes and conditions of employment. These powers the government used, together with tax reductions, to prevent a slow-down in the growth of real wages and consumer demand, and to avoid industrial unrest. Again, in the autumn of 1976, when national negotiations broke

9. The raising of taxes paid by employers, as a way of strengthening employers' resistance to high pay claims, had been earlier suggested in Sweden and elsewhere. As a policy it is somewhat different from levying a special tax on employers who grant "excessive" pay rises.

down on the issue of indexation, and the ensuing industry negotiations were accompanied by strikes, serious by Dutch standards, the government assisted the eventual mixed national and industry level settlement by a promise to reduce slightly employers' social security payments.

All of these examples, even including the British experience and the Dutch which has wider political and industrial relations aspects, show the willingness of some governments to use tax and welfare measures to achieve acceptable pay settlements, and the willingness of unions in particular to think in real income terms. No government would regard its steps in this direction as ideal; several of the countries concerned in fact would be judged to have poor records in achieving price stability and full employment. Some critics have argued that the poor records are the *results* of government intervention in the processes of collective bargaining. The view taken in this paper is that even if such critics were correct, the failures or inadequacies of previous government interventions is no reason to cease searching for improvements in the co-ordination of the results of collective bargaining and government policy, within a framework of adequate demand management and control of the money supply.

Information

If the government is to have an effective policy towards bargaining it is essential that the information on which the government is basing its policies be available to trade unions and employers. The reason for this is that the government is attempting to create an environment in which collective bargaining decisions are co-ordinated with its own plans and actions. Those parties responsible for pay settlements, if their decisions are to be responsive to government and other groups' interests, must know what will be the effect of their decisions upon the actions of government and other groups. To know this they need to understand the governments' policy alternatives and what the government will do in various circumstances. Obviously, some of the information provided by government must be confidential – matters concerning the financing of an external deficit, for instance. But the most important part will consist of the government's economic forecasts, which are usually conditional predictions – conditional on particular policies and particular decisions such as those arising in pay settlements.

A good example of an information-providing process comes from *Norway*. Since 1962 there has been an organisation providing a forum for the bargaining parties and the government to discuss wage and prices developments. Originally this meeting gave the government an opportunity to explain its policies before and during the actual bargaining. Since 1965 the organisation has been supported by an expert technical committee which provides formal forecasts and analysis of alternative policies – including their effects on other sectors of economy such as farming and fishing. The inspiration behind this development came from the government's own statistical organisation, although the French planning system also served as a source of ideas. But quite apart from assisting in the technical aspects of forecasting, the Norwegian Government has continued to respond to requests for information. For instance, in March 1976 when pay negotiations were at a difficult stage in a very inflationary situation, the central union and employer bodies asked for and got from the government up-dated forecasts and statements on contemplated economic measures. This sort of collaboration has become even closer in recent years as the Norwegian economy has experienced considerable difficulties from inflation and changes in foreign trade.

All of the governments mentioned above who play the role of a third element in the bargaining process provide information of the Norwegian sort in different ways. Although the German Government is not a third element in the sense of being a party to bargaining, it also has evolved an interesting relationship with the parties. In *Germany* the authorities started in the mid-1960s to set out criteria for relating pay increases to the aims of stability and growth and since 1967 representatives of employers, trade unions and government and other official bodies (including the Bundesbank and the Council of Economic Advisors) have met several times a year to discuss the government's economic forecasts and analyses. The intention of such *concerted action* has been to provide an opportunity for the co-ordination of private decisions and official policy, and on occasion the government has quite explicitly given its view of the consequences of alternative actions. For instance, at the meeting before the 1975 pay round the government presented three alternative scenarios showing that the higher the money wage rise the lower would be the increase in real GNP[10].

Economic prediction is a chancy business, and economic forecasts, even when the conditions are fully set out, must be understood as providing a range of outcomes with different probabilities. What decision-takers should do in uncertain situations is perhaps the whole art of management and solutions will not be propounded in this paper. But it is perhaps useful to point out that one of the rational ways of dealing with uncertainty is to be flexible, to keep options open, and to be prepared to review decisions. In the informed bargaining situation being considered here, this means that the parties must be fully aware of the uncertainties and the possible need for revision. Germany again provides interesting examples of the problems of tying settlements explicitly to forecasts. In 1969 and again in 1973 pay agreements were made on the premises of official forecasts which proved to have underestimated the strength of economic expansion, with the result that rank and file pressure forced the later reopening of the agreements.

Equity and Differentials

This section has set out four legs of responsive collective bargaining: a counter-cyclical pay policy, a complementary price policy, a tax and welfare policy, and a policy for information. It has not attempted to play down the difficulties surrounding these policies. The uncertainties of prediction have just been referred to, and the role of market forces and the need for lengthy time horizons avoiding distortions has been stressed above. It also needs to

---

10. In subsequent years this supposed negative correlation between wage inflation and real growth has been criticised on technical economic grounds by German trade union economists. For a review of the issues see *Germany, Economic Survey (1977)*.

be pointed out that one of the main features which can endanger or disrupt responsive bargaining appears to be an overly-ambitious set of goals and in particular the need to reconcile in a pay policy pressures for equality, the lowering of rates of inflation and pressure of market forces. Whether government has been a party or not, most centralised bargaining experiences in recent years show that it is difficult to pursue for very long a policy of raising the pay of the lower paid worker at a faster rate than the better paid worker and at the same time achieving a deceleration of inflation.

The experience of the United Kingdom and Sweden shows that eventually a combination of market pressures and worker dissatisfaction bring about attempts to reverse the narrowing of differentials[11]. This inevitably leads to an acceleration of wage inflation especially if there is a renewed movement for equality. This leapfrog between lower paid and higher paid has its counterpart in leapfrog situations that can develop between workers in different industries and in particular between the public and private sectors. All leapfrog situations are inflationary and responsive collective bargaining would attempts to countain them: the subject is considered again in the final section. Here the stress is on the need to avoid, not egalitarian aims — each country will have its own ideals in that respect — by overly-ambitious means of bringing them about. No collective bargaining system can sustain the pressure of having to solve *all* of society's problems! Tax and public expenditure policies are acceptable means of solution also.

New Instruments for a new Policy?

This paper has argued that responsive collective bargaining has a vitally important part to play in stabilizing our economies and enabling governments to attain their wider and deeper social goals in the years ahead. What procedures and structures in collective bargaining, and what actions of government, are likely to encourage and develop moves towards the more responsive collective bargaining policies discussed in the previous section? What modifications of present procedures, structures and actions would assist responsive bargaining? What is attempted in this section is to provide a framework for answering, and to review the major issues behind any proposals for change or reform. The method is based on a comparison of collective bargaining procedures and structures in different countries with the aim of isolating those procedures and structures which appear to be of most assistance to responsive bargaining.

There is however one important preliminary issue which must be raised. In the minds of most of its supporters, collective bargaining must be *free* if it is to function properly, and in fact freedom to negotiate is by many regarded as an ultimate political objective in itself. The position of this paper is that nothing that is being discussed or suggested need be in any way, necessarily,

---

11. Egalitarian policy in Sweden is known under the title of "solidaristic wage policy". In the United Kingdom egalitarian elements entered into the Social Contract. Such a policy is by no means peculiar to these two countries, although both show clearly the pressures to reverse the narrowing of differentials. See Robinson (1974) and *Sweden (1978), Economic Survey.*

in conflict with free collective bargaining , providing always that we enjoy this freedom — like all our other freedoms — with due regard to the responsibilities it brings. What this paper attempts to do is to explore and delineate in today's conditions, under the title of responsive bargaining, the nature of these responsibilities.

Some would interpret this approach to free and responsive bargaining as the sort of action that parties to bargains take when they act intelligently in their own long-term interests: those who take this view do not see the problem as one of reform of processes or procedures but as a matter of a change of attitude, away from actions based on short-term, temporary advantages, towards long-term policies of permanent improvement. Such a view, stressing the primacy of the intelligently thought-out interests of groups which must live together, does have some implications for processes and structures. It emphasizes that bargainers must be leaders who keep the support of their members (whether employers or employees) and who can use technical expertise in no way inferior to that at the command of government. There must also be procedures whereby government's views are received and discussed by the bargainers and whereby negotiations with government can take place over what combination of gross money pay rise, taxes and welfare receipts are acceptable in the light of expected economic conditions including the expected rise in prices. And government itself must also act as a responsible employer towards its own employees engaged in responsive bargaining.

This way of considering collective bargaining is not an alternative to other ways. It is the foundation of any reasonable approach to the problems. In democratic societies any government policy must be predicated on people following intelligently their best interests. All of this must be taken for granted: it is not the purpose of this paper to recommend the obvious, i.e., that trade union and employer leaders should be intelligent and hire the services of experts, that members should vote and support the leaders, and that governments arrange to meet unions and employers either publicly or privately, formally or informally. There are however, some processes and procedures in collective bargaining that will possibly make these foundations more effective in supporting responsive policies, and these will be discussed.

Procedures and organisation of collective bargaining in settling pay and conditions vary greatly from country to country. Studies show that important features like degree of internal democracy and relations of members to leaders in both trade unions and employers' organisations, extent of federal or central organisation, level or levels at which bargaining usually takes place, degree to which collective agreements are enforced, size distribution of unions, extent of indexation, degree of wage drift, role of trade union and employer bodies in a country's political structure, education and professionalism of leaders, together with the framework of law within which individuals and organisations operate, show large differences between countries as well as over time. As has already been pointed out, the importance of collective bargaining itself differs from country to country: there are varying proportions of the national wage and salary bill that are fixed outside the collective bargaining system, by minimum wage laws and tribunals and by employers in non-unionised industries and occupations, and these systems

74

are affected by collective bargaining in varying degrees. Furthermore, the effectiveness of collective bargaining in making pay different from what it would otherwise be may also vary from country to country, as well as over time. Generalisation, beyond this stress on variety, about the collective bargaining experience of OECD countries is possible but hazardous. Four related subjects are selected for consideration here: centralisation of structure and level of bargaining (treated as one subject), wage rounds and leapfrogging, governments as employers and steps to co-ordinate collective bargaining with government policy.

Centralisation of Structure and Level of Bargaining

By centralisation of structure is meant the extent to which trade union and employer organisations are federated or joined into strong central bodies at the national level with substantial executive (negotiating) powers capable for instance of negotiating with one another and dealing with government on behalf of their members. Level of bargaining means the level at which bargaining over pay usually takes place: e.g., national, industry, region, enterprise (or firm), workplace (or a combination of some of these). There is a rough correspondence between highly centralised structures and the prevalence of national bargaining shown by comparing on the one hand Sweden and Norway, where the organisations on both sides are highly centralised and bargaining takes place at the national level (amongst others), with, on the other hand, Canada and the United States, showing probably the highest levels of decentralisation amongst OECD countries with a high proportion of bargains made at the enterprise or workplace levels[12].

It has been argued that the relationship is not by chance, but that it is the level of bargaining that determines the degree of centralisation, and the main influence upon the level of bargaining is the structure of management and employer organisations[13]. If in fact the level of bargaining and hence the degree of centralisation are dependent on the level at which enterprises and employers wish to negotiate, it might be thought that the increased government involvement in pay settlements (e.g. tripartite discussions, mediation, statutory controls, representative bodies) in several countries over the last decade might have led to an increased degree of centralisation on the part of unions and employers. There has been such a tendency but it has been weak and it could be argued that government intervention has served to weaken it by reducing the authority of central bodies, lowering the degree of effective centralisation.

In the light of this it is instructive to consider the experience of the Netherlands, where there have in recent years been lengthy periods of government intervention along with periods of free collective bargaining. The trade union and employer movements have traditionally been divided on

---

12. This correspondence is shown in a schematic way in the Appendix to this paper.
13. See Clegg (1976). Clegg supports his thesis that the main influence upon the structure of trade unionism is the level of bargaining, with examples from several OECD countries, but his explanation of variations in level of bargaining itself, while plausible, is presented as an unsubstantiated assertion.

grounds of religion and there is a growing independent group of white-collar unions. In 1976 the Catholic and Socialist Federations united in a new federation covering nearly two-thirds of Dutch unionists, particularly strong amongst urban blue-collar workers. Since then the difference between this new federation, the Protestant Federation (strong amongst white-collar workers and in rural areas) and the independent unions have if anything widened — although the various groups were able to join in opposing employers in the 1977 wage round. Most workers are covered by collective agreements at the industry level, with large enterprises having supplementary agreements, and there is a growing tendency towards plant agreements with stronger plant organisation on the part of the unions. In 1972 there was the first and only national level agreement under collective bargaining, but in 1974, 1975 and again in 1976 attempts to reach national agreements broke down. Generalisation is dangerous but the Netherlands may be a case of limited centralisation with a lowering of the level of effective bargaining taking place. In this respect the parallel with the evolution of plant level bargaining in Britain over the last 40 years is interesting. Furthermore, it should be noticed that it is not only in the Netherlands that white-collar workers find it difficult to follow the policies of predominantly blue-collar unions — Sweden presents another, clear example of such a division.

Another warning, along with that against assuming that there is a natural tendency to centralise, or that events have conspired to foster centralisation, may be issued. Bargaining which takes place formally at the higher levels may require much negotiation at the lower levels to sustain it[14]. There is conclusive evidence in those countries where bargaining is undertaken by centralised bodies at national and industry (or regional) levels — as in Finland, Germany, the Netherlands, Norway, and Sweden — of a high degree of wage drift caused by both authorised and unauthorised pay settlements at the enterprise and plant levels, suggesting that centralised, high level bargaining needs a "safety valve" at the lower levels to prevent frustrations and distortions. Centralised, national negotiations are frequently the tip of an iceberg which contains predominantly local, if sometimes informal and unwritten, decisions. Furthermore, there are examples, although it is difficult to say how typical they are, of rank and file workers not accepting agreements that have been made by their leaders under some forms of government pressure, or that have been arrived at through politically influenced settlements[15].

The reason for this emphasis on centralised structures is obvious. If a government is to discuss its views on the state of the economy and on acceptable pay settlements with unions and employers, and must have a responsive audience whose technical experts can clarify issues with the governments' experts, there is a natural presumption that it is only possible to do this effectively with the leaders of both the national trade union movement and the national employers organisation, leaders who have adequate authority, and can expect appropriate support and consent, from their members

---

14. Of course any system, however centralised, must leave much of the administration of agreements to managers, trade union officials and workmen on the factory floor level.

15. Recent examples are the 1978 East Coast coal mining dispute in the United States and the German dockers' dispute in 1978.

back at the grass roots level. And whether the discussions take place publically or privately, formally or informally, this presumption becomes very strong when the government wishes to negotiate on the matter of pay, taxes and welfare payments. On the surface, it would appear that a government can most effectively pursue its policy of encouraging responsive bargaining if it can deal with the leaders of unions and employers who represent highly centralised structures.

Examples of governments pursuing such a policy, dealing with centralised structures, have been referred to above. Norway is a recent example of the leaders of highly centralised organisations forming a type of partnership with government. In Austria the highly-organised and long-standing system of voluntary partnership between unions and employers, in which government has a voice, has produced a highly centralised, national system of pay settlements and price control. There is no clear pattern, however. Swedish trade union and employer organisations are highly centralised but the government's influence is much less obvious and informal than in Norway or Austria. In Germany, where at the level of providing information the government institutions are active in the Concerted Action organisation, the degree of effective centralisation appears to be lower than in Sweden (partly because of the German federal structure). In Finland, where effective centralisation is not high, the government has frequently played an important part in assisting the negotiation of national agreements on difficult occasions. The action of the Danish Parliament in giving settlements proposed by a national mediator but not accepted by the parties, the force of law has already been referred to. In Ireland, in a situation of low effective centralisation, the establishment of a national body — the Employer-Labour Conference — provided the organisation for national bargaining, and the Netherlands Government has used an older institution, the Foundation of Labour, in a similar way.

While it is clear that the absence of highly centralised institutions does not preclude a dialogue between government and the bargaining parties, the most outstanding examples of policies of overt government influence do occur in countries with such institutions. Other governments wishing to pursue such policies in less centralised surroundings, appear to have been forced to create or support the establishment of new organisations as in Germany and Ireland. Experience then does support the presumption that a high degree of effective centralisation, implying effective union and employer leadership, is significant if a government is to encourage responsive bargaining, although this tentative conclusion should not be taken as a judgement about the success of centralised, high-level bargaining in achieving national economic and social objectives.[16]

Wage rounds and Leapfrogging

Nearly 20 years ago an OECD report by a group of independent experts (Fellner, 1961) was convinced that collective bargaining was an important

---

16. The withdrawal of the British TUC in 1977 from explicit support of pay policy might be attributed to pressure on the leadership from its members, who were dissatisfied with the fall in living standards (see above, under subheading Taxes and Welfare Policy) as well as with the distortions and apparent inequalities emerging from many years of control and restraint.

cause of inflation and discussed what it called the "wage-wage spiral". Drawing attention to the uniformity in negotiable increases in each country on each occasion, and the maintenance of existing differentials — which seems at variance with that would happen in a competitive market — the report commented upon the frequency with which negotiations and arbitrators "fell back on the wage increases set elsewhere as the easiest way of reaching agreement. This was most apparent at times and in countries where demand was excessive and in countries where collective bargaining is centralised at the industry level". The report then went on to make the point that stability of the pattern of differentials has not been the objective of negotiations. "Indeed, it is the continued attempt to upset it which is one of the main reasons why the process of wage negotiation has produced inflationary results". The expert group's views on leapfrogging are worth quoting in full :

> With wages as a whole rising faster than productivity and with prices rising, any labour group which hangs back in the wages spiral will suffer a relative, or even absolute, decline in real wages. Hence, it is immaterial whether the object of any particular section of labour at any time is to catch up with, or get ahead of, the general movement of wages. This process of "leapfrogging" takes its most obvious form when wages are negotiated separately for individual industries. But it operates also inside individual industries and individual establishments, between classes of labour and especially between skilled and unskilled labour and between time-rate and piece-rate workers. The "leapfrogging" process operates particularly between workers whose wages are highly standardised for each grade of labour, as laid down specifically in collective agreements, and those whose wages are subject to more latitude of negotiation with individual managements. This is frequently the underlying reason for the competition often observed between workers in the public and private sectors of industry. Its forms are manifold, but we believe that the "wage-wage spiral" has been one of the major causes of excessive wage increases. (Fellner, 1961, pp. 53-54).

While a more recent expert group reporting on inflation and instability observed that in recent years wage bargaining has not seemed to be a main cause of inflation, it drew attention to three specific aspects of collective bargaining relevant to inflation: the tendency for a wage increase obtained in a particular sector of industry to spread regardless of the state of demand and inter-industry or intra-industry productivity differences; the tendency to maintain or re-establish traditional wage differentials by skill or trade; and the disadvantage suffered by any group which hangs back in the wage spiral when wages are rising faster than productivity (McCracken, 1977). It thus followed the earlier report in regarding leapfrogging as an important factor in maintaining or propagating inflation, whatever its initial cause.

It is important to draw a clear distinction between the "going rate of increase" and the process of leapfrogging. The Japanese Spring Offensive system, and the German system of regional and industry negotiations, both produce as the bargaining round progresses an emerging notion of what is likely to be the average or typical increase for the current year. United

States bargaining patterns, while over the country as a whole showing little evidence of a going rate of increase — because of the variety of circumstances existing in a large country including the lengthy periods the agreements refer to — do reveal the existence of going rates of increase in negotiations with firms within the same industry, while the name "pattern bargaining" implies a concept of going rates of increases (or comparable non-wage benefits). The point is that none of these systems of bargaining is inevitably associated with leapfrogging.

Criticism is levelled at systems which propagate inflation by a circular sequence of pay increases such that there can be no end to the process. For instance, in the simplest case (which probably never exists in the real world) if union A gets a 10 per cent pay rise, union B bases a successful claim for a comparable increase on the grounds that its differential over A has been altered. The process could stop there, but if union A now argues that its differential position has been altered and successfully claims another 10 per cent rise, the process could continue. This is the simple leapfrog which over a period of time produces stable differentials with continuous inflations. In practice it would be affected by the price increases flowing on from the rising labour costs.

A wage round spread over a long period of time, in which individual unions negotiate in sequence, industry by industry (or enterprise by enterprise), appears to be conducive to this leapfrogging, whereas a wage round concentrated into a relatively short period of time with a lengthy interval between wage rounds, would appear to suppress the leapfrog. The United Kingdom is an example of the former; Japan is a clear and classic example of the latter. It is noteworthy that one of the features of the British Government's Social Contract with the TUC was the support by the latter of the policy of a 12-month interval between pay settlements (or the consequential pay rises), and that the TUC continued to support this policy even after it formally withdrew from other aspects of pay policy in July 1977[17].

Although differentials are a continuous problem in those countries which practise national bargaining, the leapfrog aspect of differentials does not appear to be a major problem in such countries: the leapfrog problem is more a problem in countries with decentralised structures and lower level bargaining, and no firm tradition of a concentrated wage round as in Japan. For such countries, practices which would be likely to minimise the effects of leapfrogging include fixed intervals between pay settlements — either by the British approach or the North American institution of agreements covering fixed intervals — and the reduction of the period within which all pay settlements are made in order to avoid too great a difference between the circumstances surroundings settlements made at the beginning of a round and settlements at an end.

Governments as Employers

The bodies through which governments discharge their functions as employers vary from country to country and the roles of unions in fixing

---

17. On ending a wage freeze in August 1977, the New Zealand Government reached agreement with unions and employers on a similar 12-month rule.

pay of public employees also vary. In Sweden, for example, the degree of centralisation in public sector bargaining, while less than in the private sector, is high. On the employer side there are four bodies dealing with government offices, state-owned firms, municipalities and county councils which bargain with three national federations embracing nearly 50 unions. In Britain on the other hand each part of the public sector has its own machinery. In the civil service collective bargaining is carried on through joint union-employer bodies (Whitley Councils), assisted by regular surveys of private sector pay made by a Civil Service Pay Research Unit[18]. There is no central body for the nationalised industries, each industry having its own bargaining system, usually a descendent of what existed before nationalisation.

Even if the government is separated from bargaining by the sort of bodies that exist in Britain and Sweden, it cannot avoid being directly concerned with the results, if only in its role as ultimate paymaster (either of civil service wages and salaries, or of subsidies to nationalised industries). The government's budgetary situation is immediately and directly affected by any pay settlement in the public sector, just as it is indirectly affected by pay settlement in the private sector. Governments are the largest employers in all OECD countries and it is essential that neither should their anti-inflationary policies make them bad employers nor should soft or extravagant actions as good employers ruin anti-inflationary policies. For a government, being a good employer is a complicated concept, involving trade-offs of highly sensitive, political kinds. A government which operates a public service like fire-fighting or electricity may have a responsibility to maintain the service and may lose electoral support if it fails to do so. Strikes may be a serious threat to its political position. The weakness of governments in the face of strikes suggests that governments may regard the political damage from strikes to be much worse than the political damage from inflation. In recent years governments which have debated the issue have had the fate of the British Conservative Government in February 1974 as a warning. The high weight governments give to industrial peace has been a major constraint in fighting inflation through intervention in pay settlements.

Being a good employer also means paying wages that in terms of the labour market as a whole are suitable for the particular grades and occupations. "Fair and competitive" wages perhaps describes the objective. Some governments in the past have forgotten this objective. The authors of *The Problem of Rising Prices* were led to say in memorable words, "[The government] so often fixed the wages of some group of its employees... as if this settled the matter for eternity. Then time passes and a day of shocked surprise comes when it is found that schoolteachers, or civil servants, or bus drivers have been woefully neglected. The result is a wage adjustment of a size that should never happen in the interests of stabilisation policy, which is bad in itself and bad as an example (pp. 59-60)". Unfortunately since that was written governments have not shown they have learned the lesson, and many of the confrontations that arise between governments and their employees are the result of narrowed differentials and changed relationships with other occupations and sectors in the economy. The Swedish confron-

18. The Unit has not operated in this way in the recent period of the Social Contract.

tation in 1971 and the German in 1974, while each had its own peculiar features, are typical of most countries' experiences. To some extent, of course, this reflects changes in trade union structure; the growth of white-collar and professional unions is not just a feature of the public sector. On the other hand not all public sector unions are white-collar — some countries with nationalised industries have a large proportion of blue-collar workers in the public sector.

Just as there is evidence that governments have used restraint over public sector pay (where it has been under their control) as an anti-inflationary weapon — with explosive results — so there is evidence in some countries that public sector rates of pay have pushed up private sector rates, leading to a type of leapfrog of the sort described above. A co-ordinated policy on the part of government to both public and private sector pay settlements is essential. If as, for example, in Ireland different groups in the public sector have different bargaining arrangements, with different principles being applied by different arbitrators and independent chairmen, a steady leap-frog inside the public sector is produced which may eventually affect the private sector. This problem, and the government's desire to deal with it, has created great difficulties in the negotiation of successive National Pay Agreements in Ireland. The government has tried, not always successfully, to exclude the public service from provisions in the NPAs which permit special pay increases to deal with anomalies and productivity deals. The draft 1976 agreement, eventually rejected by the unions, contained a provision that an inability to pay clause would apply to the public service: the government could withhold the standard increases written into the agreement if they were judged to have serious budgetary effects. A similar provision was retained in the 1978 agreement.

The Irish example has been referred to because it illustrates a solution (which would not necessarily be followed elsewhere) to a problem which arises when a government has little direct control over the pay of its employees. It suggests that systems of arbitration which have grown up haphazardly over the years, involving several unco-ordinated centres of decision-taking, in an inflationary situation are not satisfactory ways of settling pay. The Irish way of dealing with the problem leaves unchanged the basic institutional arrangements — which some may wish to preserve for other reasons. But the example also suggests that there is a case for replacing a system of unco-ordinated decisions by a single source of decision-taking or arbitration — possibly by a single judicial arbitrator[19].

It is noticeable that in several countries there is a high degree of resort to arbitration in the public sector — higher than in the private sector. In view of the general nature of this phenomenon, the most likely explanation is the budgetary constraints imposed by Finance Ministers who are not themselves negotiators. Because the government negotiators' hands are tied, arbitration is inevitable. In countries where the rate of voluntary settlement in the public sector is low it has been suggested that arbitration

---

19. In Ireland disputes over inability to pay are examined by the Labour Court (or appropriate public service Arbitration Board) which issues recommendations following a report from an independent assessor.

is a face-saving device. In a sense this explanation may be true of other countries as well: governments are unwilling to take pay decisions themselves because of the political consequences, therefore they allow the odium to fall on the arbitrator[20]. If, in forcing resort to arbitration, governments were sure that the resulting decisions on pay would fit into their overall policy, there might be sense in the action. But that certainty can never exist, certainly not when arbitrations are unco-ordinated.

It will be clear from what has been said that the public sector problem, viewed as one of co-ordination both between parts of that sector, and between that sector as a whole and the private sector, is in essentials yet another version of the total pay settlement problem. It has been argued above that no pay settlment can escape the interest of a government committed to growth and stability. The real significance of public sector pay settlements is not the narrow financial budgetary effect (although that is not unimportant as a practical issue); the real significance is that the settlements must fall in with the government's overall objectives and strategies for achieving those objectives. The more ambitious is a government, the more closely it must ensure that public sector settlements are co-ordinated. It is significant that in three of those countries — Britain, Ireland and France — where governments have attempted directly over several years to influence the results of collective bargaining the public sector has been a centre of difficulty. In others, like Sweden, where national bargains have been achieved, although the role of government has not been so overt, the public sector has presented comparable difficulties. For governments, there is no royal road to the successful acting out in a harmonious way the triplet of roles of employer, manager of national economic policy and guardian of the peace.

To Improve Co-ordination

This paper has so far identified three aspects of collective bargaining where certain procedures or structures are conducive to a responsive policy. They are :

a) centralised union-employer structure, and experience in national bargaining;

b) a concentrated wage round; and

c) consistency in the pay policy of the public sector.

Each of these procedures or structures is designed, by some type of co-ordination procedure, to offset what might be termed the decentralised myriad of decisions that form the basis of bargaining[21]. There is a sense in

---

20. In New Zealand in 1977 the government set up a new tribunal to determine cost of living adjustments to the general level of wages, which had been controlled by the government since 1973. The Government's views, along with those of trade unions and employers, were presented to the tribunal. When the tribunal awarded an increase somewhat larger than the government had recommended, it was publicly criticised by the Prime Minister.

21. It is tempting to refer to the myriad of decisions as the *natural* basis of bargaining, and while in one sense this is true, it does not always describe accurately the actual history of bargaining. The sense in which it is true is that all bargains have to be made to work by the workers, foremen and managers at the local level.

which the concept of *collective* bargaining is a deliberate device to co-ordinate what might otherwise be several separate bargains between individual workers and their employer (so as to protect weaker workers and improve bargaining strength). Thus from the point of view of any particular group of workers there will be some optimum degree (or degrees) of "collectiveness" or *co-ordination*. This co-ordination is subject to constraints, two of which facing workers are the attitudes of management and employers, and the law regarding unions and bargaining. Subject to these, it is expected that the degree of centralisation of structure will influence the co-ordination that is achieved, and that the optimum degree of co-ordination arising from collective bargaining will be associated with a particular degree of centralisation that workers will try to attain in their union structure. This optimum degree of co-ordination we call here the *workers' optimum* and is simply what they think is best for their collective interests.

In this paper we have considered another degree of optimal co-ordination – that co-ordination of bargaining decisions which best enables a government to follow an effective policy for responsive bargaining. Let us distinguish this from the workers' optimum by calling it simply the *government's optimum*. We have already suggested three basic factors determining the government's optimum: degree of centralisation, concentration of wage rounds and consistency in public policy. We also have suggested that if centralisation is pushed too far the leader-member authority relation weakens and because of such phenomena as wage drift and non-ratification of agreements co-ordination declines. Concentration of wage rounds and consistency in public sector pay policy may also have offsetting costs if pushed too far. The government's optimum is then the result of a delicate balancing of the positive and negative effects of the three factors identified (and further analysis may well bring to light more).

The practical problem, in the terms defined above, is that the degree of co-ordination of pay settlements that satisfies unions (and possibly the degree that satisfies employers) produces a level of centralised structure which in general does not make it possible for governments to attain the degree of co-ordination in pay settlements (and between pay settlements and government economic policies) which they desire. Unions (and employers) in general are pleased with the actual degree of centralisation because it gives them what they want; governments in general are dissatisfied with the degree of centralisation because it produces a degree of co-ordination which is inadequate to deal with the problems government have to face.

The objective of reform is to make a government's presence felt in collective bargaining, even if it does not sit at each table or on each shop floor. To achieve this the government must change the degree of centralisation. The approach suggested here for study is that of bringing the degree of centralisation of bargaining structure closer to that needed by government – by altering the benefits received and costs incurred by workers and employers from the existing degree of co-ordination.

In general altering the degree of centralisation of bargaining structure means raising the degree of centralisation. We have stressed above that increasing, or high, degrees of centralisation carry costs which may actually lower the extent of effective co-ordination of pay settlements. Already some countries such as Norway may have gone beyond the levels of centralised, national bargaining which create desirable co-ordination. A few countries such as Switzerland and Austria may in their own different ways be at levels of centralisation that suit both workers and government. But many countries like the United Kindgom have a level of centralisation that, while it produces co-ordination acceptable to workers, does not necessarily produce a result that governments can be satisfied with.

The centralisation that produces the government's optimum, and the extent to which that optimum differs from the workers' optimum, vary from country to country. There can be no prescription to suit all — let alone Austria and Switzerland which may feel they need no change. The objectives are to lower the net benefit to workers and employers of low levels of centralisation, and to increase the net benefits of higher levels. To get a change in net benefit, this can be done by altering costs or benefits or both. The means available to governments are:

i) encouraging one partner to centralise his structure and co-ordinate his bargaining activities so as to influence the other partner: most observers believe that in the past this influence has flowed from employers to unions rather than the other way;

ii) improving the co-ordination of public sector bargaining and ensuring that the settlements the government agrees to are consistent with overall economic policy: if we are realistic this will mean educating the electorate to accept more strikes and disturbances;

iii) altering the law so as to change the degree of protection given to unions and employers for actions undertaken by decentralised organisations: as experience shows that it is difficult to force people to work or put workers in jail, attention could be directed to reducing financial protection of unions as well as legal and financial protection of management and employers (although experience also suggests that in fact it is extremely difficult to make such actions effective);

iv) establishing new centralising, co-ordinating institutions: the possibility of such innovation is considered below in a little more detail.

There have been within the framework of free collective bargaining several recent instances of the establishment of new centralising institutions to assist in the co-ordination of pay settlements and overall economic policy. There is in fact a spectrum of institutions ranging from primarily investigative and reporting bodies to bodies which set guidelines, on to organisations which endeavour to achieve positive co-ordination of pay settlements and price increases by a variety of methods short of statutory controls. In the United Kingdom, the Council for Prices, Productivity and Incomes, established in 1957, was an early example of a body whose function was to "review and report". This was succeeded in 1962 by the National Incomes Commission with a more closely defined purpose but no powers; it reported on pay claims submitted to it by both parties, by the government in public sector cases, or retrospectively in private sector settlements. In 1965 the Commission itself was succeeded by the National Board for Prices and

Incomes, to which the government could refer cases it wished to have reviewed, and whose activities became in 1966 incorporated in the government's statutory incomes and prices policy[22]. Other countries have had a similar experience of an institutional evolution from reporting to statutory control and as was mentioned at the beginning of this paper, the unsatisfactory experiences with statutory controls have caused the renewed interest in co-ordinating institutions operating in a free bargaining framework.

There are basically three sorts of such institutions depending on whether bargaining takes place in a centralised, national setting, or whether it is decentralised at plant and enterprise levels. In the first sort, the co-ordinating institution can be a body on which sit government, union and employer representatives as in Austria, the Netherlands and Norway. Or the co-ordinating institution can be an arbitrator or a mediator who assists in obtaining national agreements, as in Finland or Denmark. These institutions presuppose an already high degree of centralisation and a tradition of national level bargaining. (In Ireland we see one of the few examples where the government entered into a new tripartite organisation because of the existing high degree of centralisation).

The second sort of institution, found in countries of decentralised, plant level bargaining, is the investigatory and reporting agency, as in the United Kingdom 1962-66 with the Commission and the Board, whose influence is primarily exerted by publicity (and possibly delay) and by informal pressures on the partners in critical negotiations or on firms planning to raise prices. A recent example of this sort of institution is the United States' Council on Wage and Price Stability, set up in August 1974 after statutory controls had expired. Its extensive duties include consulting with the parties, making specific recommendations and holding public hearings. It has powers to obtain information.

The third sort of institution is the national arbitration commission or court found in Australia and New Zealand[23]. Although this institution is indigenous to these countries, having evolved within a specific framework of collective bargaining institutions, it contains two features relevant to the present discussion: the centralised nature of the arbitration system permits a co-ordinated policy; and the views of government can be brought to the attention of the court or commission through the normal judicial processes of advocacy and evidence[24]. Although the systems of these countries have

---

22. Abolished in 1970, the Board emerged in 1973 in a new guise as a Pay Board and a Price Commission, independent bodies to administer the new statutory controls. The Pay Board was abolished in 1974, but the Commission continued to operate, and under a new Act of 1977 is empowered to investigate price rises, recommend freezes and apply sanctions against firms.

23. Some authorities would not regard the Australian and New Zealand systems as exemplifying what in other countries is called free collective bargaining. Under Australian compulsory arbitration most arrangements about minimum pay and other conditions of employment are embodied in legally enforceable "awards" of federal or state arbitration tribunals. But in most cases the parties have first negotiated all or most of the provisions before submitting them to a tribunal for approval (and for adjudication on the unsettled issues). In New Zealand the Arbitration Court in effect ceased to function after 1971; after some years of experimentation, with the resumption of a less controlled form of collective bargaining, a reconstituted Court was established in 1977.

24. Government representatives normally only appear before the commission or court for national wage adjustment hearings, not normal wage negotiations.

their critics in respect of both guiding principles and the failure to achieve those principles, what makes them interesting here are the opportunities they might offer to achieve a degree of co-ordination in pay settlements and between pay settlements and government policy, while at the same time maintaining the essential features of collective bargaining. A single court or commission could avoid the haphazard aspects of other systems or arbitration, and in particular can avoid leapfrogging and distortion of differentials; it can produce and apply consistent principles and reach co-ordinated results. Access to the court by the government is essential: the government's representatives, either by advocating the government's policies or through expert witnesses presenting statistical and other evidence, are able to ensure that the government's views are discussed and understood without the government imposing its will on pay settlements.

There appears to be one further essential requirement for such a system to produce a completely co-ordinated pattern of settlements: all settlements, whether disputed or not, must be reviewable by the court. Disputed settlements must automatically go to the court for arbitration. There is a case for taking non-disputed settlements to court for review and possible alteration, but this case depends on the degree of co-ordination desired and which can be made effective. The success of such a system does depend very much on the attitude of the parties in bargaining to the rule of law and to the preservation of industrial peace and the willingness of society in general to allow government to intervene as a third party − representing the public interest − in the judicial process. However, while the Australian and New Zealand experiences may provide other countries with ideas, it is unlikely that the systems themselves could be transplanted.

Conclusions

With the great international economic and social changes of recent years, the results of conducting collective bargaining in traditional ways have increasingly appeared inconsistent with broad economic and social goals. Advanced industrial market economies appear to be faced with two clear alternatives. On the one hand, a continuation of existing ways of settling pay and other working conditions is likely to condemn many of these economies to economic stagnation, high unemployment, continued inflation and the threat of controls; in fact, these problems may worsen. On the other hand, there is the possibility of regaining prosperity and stability by closer co-operation between governments, unions and employers. The analysis made in this paper clearly suggests that, looking to the future, closer co-operation between governments, unions and employers will be necessary to ensure that government policies and the outcome of collective bargaining serve the best interests of the community at large. The form and extent of such greater co-operation will naturally vary from country to country but if our societies are to enjoy the full prosperity, stability, and social justice and advance open to them, the parties to collective bargaining must be responsive to the wider national interest.

It is readily apparent from the experience of many countries that the results of traditional free collective bargaining have too often caused governments to adopt generally restrictive economic measures or to intervene directly -- and sometimes clumsily and hastily — in collective bargaining. Where government intervention has been judged necessary it has commonly been against a background of economic crisis; hardly the most propitious environment for developing what this paper has termed responsive collective bargaining. Even when tried institutions already exist they have rarely been adequate to meet the challenge posed by unexpected fluctuations in the terms of trade or unprecedented high rates of inflation.

Collective bargaining inescapably means that pay and other conditions of work which affect labour costs and efficiency are settled by a myriad of decisions. Even in more or less highly centralised systems, where unions and employers bargain at the national or regional levels, provision — sometimes extensive provision — is made for bargaining right down to the workplace level. In fact, a realistic look at any system of collective bargaining will surely show the sustained, vital role of workplace bargaining, administration and grievance resolution. This is the strength of collective bargaining as a system — the feature which gives it the flexibility that makes it such an efficient economic and social instrument. But from another point of view the role of workplace bargaining makes it a serious threat to national co-ordination. It is important to recognise that at least three conflicting principles are involved and that compromise is necessary. One principle concerns the allocative economic efficiency of workplace collective bargaining; another concerns the macro-economic need for co-ordination between pay settlements and government policies; and the third is the payment of a just wage. A good compromise will explicitly acknowledge the costs of failing to achieve not only both full allocative efficiency and full macro-economic co-ordination, but equity as well.

The concept of co-ordination that has emerged in this paper, from the study of the experience of Member countries, is that of collective bargaining which is responsive to the needs not only of workers and employers, but of government also; government representing the wider public needs, including those of groups not represented at the bargaining table, like the unemployed and pensioners. As has sometimes been said, there has to be a "national interest" presence, a "third man", whether present physically or not, at the bargaining table where the most important bargaining takes place. Several Member countries have already explicitly accepted this point of view; in some it is effectively but tacitly held; in most of the others the view is widely canvassed even though it may not be official policy.

The lessons about responsive bargaining with a government presence that can be drawn from past experience seem to be clear. Firstly, governments must continuously work to achieve co-ordination. Discrete, stop-go interventionist policies are disruptive and likely to incur more costs than benefits; rapid changes in policy leave behind them anomalies that produce later reactions and resistance. The government presence must be continuously felt and understood by the bargaining parties: the form of the presence is relatively unimportant compared with its continuity. But it is important to remember that government has no more monopoly of wisdom than unions or employers; what is needed is open-minded and statesmanlike discussion of policies towards common goals and ways of reaching them.

Secondly, without a considerable degree of consensus and general acceptance of what constitute national needs, the problems of reaction to attempts to check political and market forces may render the government's position ineffective or even disruptive. The problems show themselves clearly in the reaction to narrowing pay differentials. Narrowing can be brought about in several ways, such as attempts to suppress inflation by controls, or by deliberately egalitarian national bargaining. Experience in many countries shows that a reaction is almost inevitable; sometimes market pressures working to restore differentials, at other times work-group pressures exerted through threats and strikes being the driving force. Where wage rates are held firm the pressure will be shown through wage drift. Experience also shows that the problems of dealing with these political and market forces are well enough understood in most countries. The authors of the 1961 OECD report (Fellner et al. 1961, p. 58). warned "... that it is not a wages policy to try to keep the lid on wages, by whatever means, as a substitute for adequate monetary and fiscal measures when the situation is one of excess demand. It is precisely this which has often frustrated efforts by governments to obtain a reasonable rate of wage increase". Equally, the political and economic forces behind the "wage explosions" produced by trying to achieve price stability through restrictive demand management policies are now better understood even if the containing of these forces still presents great problems. Understanding appears to be not enough: a degree of co-ordination is required which avoids the reactions from strong uncontained market and political forces.

Thirdly, governments, whose ambitions in their long-term goals need no comment, must learn moderation in their short-term aims. This means that if a large number of aims need to be pursued for political reasons, it must be understood that the extent to which all of these aims will be achieved is likely to be small. False hopes are always dangerous, and much dissatisfaction with government intervention in pay settlements is undoubtedly due to the inability of employers or unions and their members to see any short-term effect on rates of inflation. But moderation also means avoiding measures which produce disruptive economic and political reactions: the combination of egalitarian with anti-inflationary measures, while attractive politically in the short run, appears costly in the long run. Governments should not expect collective bargaining to bear all of the weight of their objectives; there are other instruments of policy available for achieving them.

Fourthly, many governments need to increase the educational element in their policies of persuasion. While dire alternatives and offers of trade-offs will always play a part in persuasion, information is also important. However, much economic information is nowadays somewhat sophisticated, and threats and offers of trade-offs produce little or the wrong effect upon those who find it difficult to assess what is really involved. Education, in the sense of using the same yardsticks and understanding the issues involved in pay settlements — seeing beyond the selfish basis of a single settlement to the wider community of interests affected — requires a sustained effort, and possibly in some countries new independent institutions. Educational efforts by special interest groups, however good, are usually regarded as simply the statement of the groups concerned. Governments' efforts in this field may be damaged by political criticism. Independent sources of education and understanding have an important part to play.

Fifthly, governments must themselves be responsive bargaining partners in their role as employers in the very important public sector. History shows that co-ordination has frequently broken down in public sector pay settlements and it has been stressed above that many governments as employers have an unsatisfactory industrial relations record. Part of the reason undoubtedly stems from the fact that it is difficult for governments to dissociate their role as employer from their roles as guardian of the national economy and, in some cases, as industrial peacemaker. To ensure responsive bargaining and effective co-ordination will require just as important changes in attitudes and behaviour on the part of governments as for unions and private sector employers.

Finally, the precise ways in which the parties to collective bargaining will respond to wider national needs will inevitably be determined by each country's goals and traditions. Broad, if somewhat ambitious, lines of long-term policy for pay and prices have been set out above, together with the related issues of tax, social security and welfare policies. The conditions of agreement on feasible long-term rates of growth of real income, and what should be the response to change in terms of trade and to inflation imported from abroad, is a matter which will vary from country to country, and will undoubtedly be influenced by the circumstances surrounding each country. It is clear, however, that the greater the number of countries that adopt responsive bargaining the easier all will find the achievement of their objectives.

Experience shows a great variety of institutional means to bring about co-ordination. It is possible to identify four basic types of formal co-ordinating institutions:

a) deliberative and consultative tripartite organisations, representative of government (or its agencies), employers and unions, as in Austria, Germany, Ireland and Norway;

b) mediative or arbitral bodies, as in Australia, Denmark, Finland and New Zealand;

c) independent investigative and reporting bodies, such as the present United States Council of Wage and Price Stability;

d) agencies of statutory control, such as the Canadian Anti-Inflation Board and the British Pay Board.

To this list needs to be added the type of relationship that exists between government and the bargaining parties in France, Japan and Sweden — informal and largely non-institutional, but which nevertheless provides a basis for co-ordination and understanding.

It has been suggested above that centralised bargaining systems with traditions of bargaining at the national level are more conducive to effective co-ordination, than are more fragmented systems. (This does not necessarily mean that centralised systems have produced better records of growth and stability). The more decentralised systems, with their numerous points of decision-taking, present the greatest problem of co-ordination. Government intervention in the past has not noticeably increased the degree of centralisation, and the evidence of a natural tendency towards centralisation in the highly localised systems of Canada, the United Kingdom and the United States, for instance, is mixed. From countries like Australia, Ireland, and New Zealand come experiences with national co-ordinating institutions which work in largely decentralised systems and this study has drawn attention to those aspects of the Australian and New Zealand system of judicial arbitration that might have lessons for co-ordination elsewhere.

In trying to develop a vital system like collective bargaining into forms that suit future needs, workers, employers, and governments are dealing with one of the major problems of modern industrial society. In all countries systems of settling pay and other working conditions have developed over long periods of time, and collective bargaining, like all social systems, has developed rules and procedures based on custom, law and a knowledge of what "works". There is a natural resistance by social and economic relationships to interference and change of certain kinds and in certain degrees. No society has ever found it easy to reform an essentially conservative institution. The basic issue is how far people can be encouraged or persuaded to alter their behaviour.

Attitudes to collective bargaining undoubtedly reflect not only vested interests but also political beliefs. Those who find the free, peaceful, localised solution of social problems a source of value in itself will wish to encourage the further development of collective bargaining within the framework of certain, workable laws with a minimum of government intervention. Others — and recent experience suggests they are a large and growing group — will attach importance to the establishment (or re-establishment) of a stable total economic environment within which free individuals and free social relationships may develop. Such an environment requires compromise and the giving up of some freedoms in return for others; it requires some reduction in the use made of freedom of collective bargaining in return for more effective reaching of social goals in general. At this point those who take this view divide. On the one hand are those who believe it is imperative that government should exercise control by statutory means over the institutions that settle pay. On the other hand are those who see government entering into what might be called a partnership with unions and employers to settle pay. Such a limited sharing of power in a responsible way by the three partners may be the most beneficial, and least costly, way of achieving stable economic growth.

The conclusions of this paper have been set out in the previous paragraphs. The lessons can be summarised very simply. It is desirable, in order to achieve full employment and stable prices in all Member countries, to co-ordinate in each country the results of collective bargaining and government policies. To achieve this the parties to collective bargaining must recognise the interest of all groups and citizens in the outcome of their negotiations by accepting the presence of the public interest — seen or unseen — at the bargaining table. In some countries the unseen presence is effective. Most countries, however, face the challenge of designing new institutions or procedures to obtain an acceptable and effective presence. Without such changes in the present system of collective bargaining and government policy the path to prosperity and stability will remain difficult to find.

Appendix

Level of Bargaining

This note is intended to show briefly the strength of the relationship between degree of centralisation and level of bargaining. Each country is graded subjectively according to the degree of effective centralisation in its trade union and employer federated organisations. The extent of union and employer membership of federations, number of federations and extent of power wielded in central bodies are considered in placing countries into three basic grades: high, medium, and low. The usual or typical level of bargaining is likewise graded, less subjectively, into national, industry or region, and enterprise or workplace. Where bargaining is mixed an intermediate point on the scale is chosen. Diagram 1 shows the results. While the subjective nature of the grading means that different graders would probably produce different results, it is not thought that the rough relationship depicted would be substantially altered. The countries upon which Clegg based his study (op. cit.) were Australia, France, Germany, Sweden, the United Kingdom and the United States.

It is interesting to observe that there is a somewhat similar relationship between the degree of unionisation (measured by proportion of total employees belonging to unions) and level of bargaining. Diagram 2, based on union membership data from a variety of sources, shows the relationship. Clegg has suggested that some aspects of collective bargaining, including the attitudes of employers, explain the degree of unionisation, and the correlations shown in the diagrams do not disprove his argument.

Diagram 1. RELATION OF CENTRALISATION OF STRUCTURE TO LEVEL OF BARGAINING

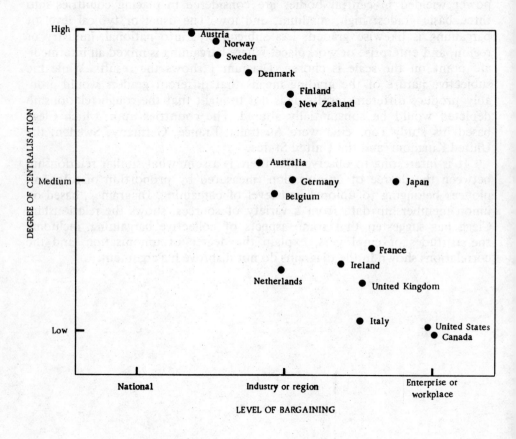

DEGREE OF CENTRALISATION

High — Austria
Norway
Sweden

Denmark

Finland
New Zealand

Australia

Medium — Germany · Japan
Belgium

France

Ireland

Netherlands

United Kingdom

Italy

Low — United States
Canada

National   Industry or region   Enterprise or workplace

LEVEL OF BARGAINING

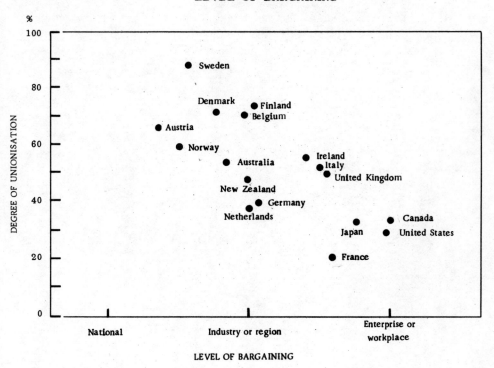

Diagram 2. RELATION OF UNIONISATION TO
LEVEL OF BARGAINING

COMMENT ON BLYTH'S PAPER

Thomas Lachs[1]

As Blyth points out unions today are concerned with much more than just wages. Problems such as employment, social security, distribution of wealth, workers' participation in management and others are very much in the forefront of their thinking. These are problems that can only be solved with the help of governments. If governments want to achieve a partnership with unions in the pay field they should be willing to extend this concept of partnership to other fields that interest unions as well.

In the given medium-term economic situation of OECD Member countries the aim of achieving a much higher level of employment than at present is paramount in trade union thinking. Any government wishing to gain the confidence of trade union leadership will therefore have to convince the unions that it is sincere in its efforts to achieve this goal. If union leadership can demonstrate to their rank and file that their co-operation with government in the incomes field is contributing towards making the government more active in combating unemployment the willingness of the rank and file to accept this policy will be greatly increased.

Blyth has devoted almost no attention to questions of income distribution. In almost all Member countries it is a declared aim of trade unions to alter the existing income distribution (which they consider unfair and unjust) in favour of the working class. The attempts to achieve this aim by means of large wage increases for workers lead to compensatory price increases and thus to spiralling inflation. Trade unions will presumably not be willing to give up their demands for a redistribution of income. They can, however, perhaps be persuaded to forego their attempts to reach this goal by wage increases if they see an alternative possibility by way of secondary income distribution through public expenditure. Technically this is certainly possible. The question is whether governments are willing to embark on such a course of income redistribution, to what extent they are willing to do this and how they can convince the unions of the sincerity of their intentions and the success of the measures taken. The latter will depend to a large part on if and how they are willing to involve trade unions in the formulation and carrying out of the necessary policies.

This would mean that a responsible bargaining policy, as Blyth sees it, would only be acceptable to trade unions if they are convinced that they can achieve their stated aim of redistribution of incomes by other means. And this in turn would probably necessitate a very large measure of union involvement in government economic policy.

It also seems logical that a more responsive bargaining attitude of trade unions will also depend on the scope this leaves for increases of real wages.

1. Dr Thomas Lachs, Director, Konsumgenossenschaft, Wien (Vienna).

In stagnating economies this margin will be too small. Governments that want trade unions to co-operate with them in their collective bargaining policies will therefore on their part have to adopt economic policies that leave sufficient leeway for regular increases in real wages.

Counter-cyclical Pay Policy

From the point of view of general economic policy a counter-cyclical pay policy would certainly be ideal. But Blyth himself acknowledges that such a policy, which runs diametrically against existing market forces, is just too much to expect. Even his aim of a somewhat less pro-cyclical pay policy is going to be hard enough to achieve.

The first big problem is when to begin, or in other words : who takes the first step ? Should employers begin by giving more pay increases than they would have to during a recession or should unions begin by taking less than they could get in a boom ? Who would or could guarantee that the other side would then take the equivalent second step ? One side or the other in taking the first step — however small it may be — is going to have to place enormous trust and confidence in its partner. Which in all probability means that you have to have quite a history of responsive bargaining before you can even try to launch such a counter-cyclical pay policy.

Furthermore one could point out some of the dangers of wage indexation in general and particularly in the context of such a policy. Blyth seems to take indexation for granted even though a large number of Member countries have never adopted or have given up this system. Indexation may be unavoidable in situations of existing rapid inflation. But it certainly has its disadvantages.

After the initial success of having won an index clause it leaves unions with very little achievements to show their members in ensuing periods — notably if economic conditions make small real wage increases a necessity. Though such clauses may protect workers from the effects of inflation they make it almost impossible to reduce inflation rates.

Price Policy

While Blyth has devoted considerable energy to devising better methods of wage determination he has given price policy much less thought. This is unfortunate because — as he himself points out — the basic issue of collective bargaining is real wages. Real wages depend on price increases. With all our economies experiencing a continuous decrease in price competition and an increase in business-administrated pricing it seems to be imperative that any success in improving the responsibility of wage policies be accompanied by similar measures to make price policy more responsible. To rely on market forces to achieve this end appears to be hopeless after the experience of almost all Member countries in the seventies.

Of course some Member governments — even though they may be quite willing to introduce wage restraints — on ideological grounds reject all genuine interference in the freedom of suppliers to set prices. It seems ironical that some of these same governments are quite willing to interfere in free price determination in the interest of higher prices for producers. That — after all — is quite obviously the main purpose of the farm products price policy of the Common Market.

Blyth's references to the Fellner et al. study of 1961, need to be seen against the background that the unions criticised this study severely because in their eyes it favoured restricting wages without complementary restriction of prices.

Any successful policy for more responsible wage bargaining will have to include provisions for a more responsible price policy. Such a policy will be easier for trade unions to understand and accept if they themselves are given an opportunity to take part in any mechanism designed to control price determination.

Tax and Welfare Measures

It is certainly correct that governments can, do and should, use tax and welfare to make it possible for collective bargainers to arrive at pay settlements that fit in with governments' objectives. But reducing taxes and welfare contributions does not seem to be enough. Governments have much more to offer as incentives to collective bargainers and they should not hesitate to make use of these opportunities.

Blyth has drawn attention to the fact that both Ireland and the Netherlands offered policies for reducing unemployment as an incentive to trade union negotiators. In other countries an improvement in labour legislation has served the same purpose. It would seem that not only the contributions towards welfare services but also the extent of these services could be an argument at the bargaining table. Maybe even laws regarding holidays, vacations, the work week or similar matters could have an influence on wage demands.

Information

Here again Blyth, it seems, does not go far enough. To be informed is fine and necessary. But at least from a trade union point of view consultation with both partners as to the formulation of policies would be even better.

It is a fact that in capitalist societies (and all OECD Member countries can thus be described) governments have always developed their economic policy in close co-ordination with business interests. This is presumably a necessity and not even socialist governments have been able to act differently. Thus government and business are always partners — be they more or less happy with this arrangement. If governments want trade unions to be more responsive to their policies in formulating wage demands they are going to have to admit the trade unions into this partnership.

This will certainly not be easy and in most cases it may even strain the already difficult relationship between government and business as partners. In some cases trade unions may even shy away from any such proposition. After all they will soon realise that more influence on the formulation and carrying out of government economic policies will invariably lead to a certain measure of public responsibility for these policies − and that this may be a more severe restraint on their wage policies than any law would be. However the recent developments in the Italian trade union movement have convinced many that such a course will eventually be accepted and even demanded by almost all trade union movements.

Also in the context of information it may be worthwhile to note that in his conclusions Professor Blyth emphasises the need for more and better education for trade union officials involved in a more responsive bargaining system. This is true both for those officials taking part in more or less centralised negotiations and for those who have the responsibility for explaining the decisions taken to the rank and file on the shop floor. Therefore it may be interesting for governments and employers to study the results of laws existing in some Member countries giving union officials at the workplace level the right to take part in a certain limited number of union education courses without loss of pay from their employers. It may be found that paying a union official to take part in such education programmes − if they are properly conducted − could be one of the best investments an employer can make.

Leapfrogging

The effects of leapfrogging on wages tend to be exaggerated and certainly do not exist at all in many Member countries. Blyth's proposals for those cases where this is a problem seem reasonable. On the other hand it would probably have been interesting to look a bit further into the transposition of wages from protected to competitive sectors of the economy as described by Aukrust in Norway. At least for small countries this seems to be a vital factor in wage determination.

Centralisation

The arguments for a high degree of centralisation of structure and level of bargaining are most convincing. From the point of view of governments this is almost imperative if they want to gain a certain measure of influence on collective bargaining. Such centralisation, however, calls for strong organisations on all sides. Employers and governments have in some cases considered it to be in their best interest to keep unions weak and divided. Employers have fought unionisation and some governments have designed laws specifically to weaken trade unions. It may very well be that they now must conclude that all these efforts have only made life more difficult for themselves.

As an aside, it may be worth considering that a tripartite partnership also calls for a strong government. A government that cannot assure the success of its proposals in its parliament will certainly be a relatively weak partner in a tripartite negotiation — as will a central employers' or trade union organisation that has little influence on its membership.

The concept of an optimum degree of centralisation and co-ordination of wage bargaining from the government point of view is logical. Chart 2 of Blyth's appendix proves that there is — quite logically — a strong positive correlation between the degree of unionisation and the centralisation of bargaining. Therefore it would be in the interest of governments that want a stronger centralisation of bargaining to improve the legal framework for unionisation efforts. This might be of particular interest in the United States. Furthermore it might be worthwhile looking into the legal framework for centralised collective bargaining. Some Member countries have laws that under certain conditions make collective agreements binding for individual employers and employees even if they are not members of the negotiating organisations. Other countries might want to evaluate the effects achieved with such arrangements.

Finally, most trade unionists would have very strong reservations about any system of compulsory centralised arbitration. Where negotiations are already highly centralised this boils down to third party determination of wages and would be the end of free collective bargaining. Even in the setting of highly decentralised bargaining such arbitration would be unacceptable for most trade unions.

All in all, a closer co-operation between governments, employers and unions in all fields of economic policy would indeed seem to be a vital prerequisite for solving the problems at present facing almost all Member countries.

COMMENT ON BLYTH'S PAPER

Sidney F. McKenna[1]

Many practitioners have worked hard to make mature collective bargaining a responsible process and they are constantly exploring alternatives, structural and procedural, which might help remedy its shortcomings. Many of these same practitioners have questioned, however, if collective bargaining is not sometimes stretched beyond its limits, both as to the scope of the subject matter which it is expected to encompass and as to its ability to meet the expectations of those who see it as a mechanism for mitigating the adverse effects of external economic developments. This questioning is particularly acute when economic conditions have deteriorated, such as in periods of high inflation or rapid disemployment.

Nevertheless, despite its limitations, collective bargaining remains an important institutionalised device for resolving sometimes conflicting interests in free societies. In trying to improve the working of collective bargaining, we must not lose sight of this central contribution. In considering, therefore, how to improve collective bargaining, especially by enlarging the role of government as advocated in the Blyth paper, one must not be afraid of addressing oneself to the issue of freedom, even though the debate loses some allure because it has been raised so often.

There are two elements of basic significance that should be addressed in reviewing the Blyth discussion of further centralising collective bargaining in order to facilitate greater government influence on its outcomes. These are : the nature and macro-economic performance of free government, and the ability of free collective bargaining to serve as an effective counter-cyclical tool of national policy.

The Nature and Performance of Government

Underlying the thesis of the need for an enlarged role for government in the collective bargaining process is Blyth's assumption, largely unexplored, of the benign, unitary nature of government policy, short-term and long-term, and an unexpressed view of government as a single, predictable source of decision-making. This view fails to recognise sufficiently that the political motivation of elected government, which is the necessary essence of its existence, frequently constitutes an important impediment to the development and implementation of economically sound and balanced programmes.

There is the indigenous instability of democratic organisations reflected in various mercurial combinations of relationships: the power split between central and local entities; the balances and imbalances that pervade legislative,

---

1. Vice-President, Labor Relations, Ford Motor Company, Dearborn, Michigan.

executive and judicial structures; official and unofficial political party mechanisms and splinter groups; the changing values and goals of electorates; periodic elections and their implications for policy; competing aspirations of existing and emerging leaders and power groups, confrontation and challenges by minority interests even in the face of majority decisions; and seemingly ineradicable and growing bureaucratic units. Government is not a distinct entity clearly separate from the many interests that comprise it. If government is invited to the bargaining table, as proposed, it is not likely to come as a pure "third man". More likely, it is apt to come as a labour government, or a management government, or a consumer government, or, in a possible caricature, as all three. Also, it is apt to come with only one hat, as the executive, or as one part of the executive. It is an unworkable assumption to view representative government as a simple, consistent, rational prescriptive third party.

With respect to the macro-economic functions of government, relatively few informed groups or individuals would seriously dispute that governments have a large measure of responsibility in today's economies for establishing the general macro-economic climate in which key economic decisions are made, including free collective bargaining decisions. The principal tools available to government include monetary, fiscal, trade and welfare policies, regulatory mechanisms affecting the factors of production and the distribution of income, forms of national planning and in some cases outright ownership or management of some major productive units.

Although macro-economic tools are relatively well known, experience indicates that their interrelationships are less so and the consequences of application are frequently unpredictable.

The record of macro-economic policy determination is clear in one regard : many of the national problems of inflation, unemployment and insufficient growth are themselves the product of policies, or lack of policies or of conflicting actions, of various government groups. The reality of conflicting, contradictory, partial and reversed courses of government action cannot simply be brushed aside. It provides an infertile setting for superimposing upon it government intrusion into the collective bargaining process as a new major tool for national economic decision-making.

Price instability, unemployment, and economic stagnation or overheated growth existed prior to collective bargaining and occur in economies where there is no well-established system of collective bargaining. With respect to inflation, changes in prices and wages are largely manifestations of basic causes which lie in increased demand or reduced supply, or combinations thereof, and in government management of fiscal and monetary policies. We cannot ignore, either, the key factor of national productivity and its rate of improvement. I believe, for example, that relative productivity growth would explain Germany's and Japan's lower inflation more satisfactorily than would the degree of centralised bargaining or the degree of bargaining involvement by government.

Even if there were a universal and demonstrably cogent link between macro-economic statistical aggregates and the degree of centralization of bargaining it would be presumptive to conclude that government intervention would in fact produce the desired results. One effect, of course, would be certain : more government control of the economy and further erosion of private decision-making.

Interestingly, this exploration of how collective bargaining and government policy might be better coordinated implies notably greater government intervention in the economy, and more specifically in collective bargaining, but also an expansion of the topics considered by bargainers and a potential intrusion by the bargainers into public policy determinations.

Tax, welfare and related public policies have uses and purposes beyond the control of economic activity. Determining such uses and purposes is a proper exercise of representative government. The proper forum for all groups and citizens to participate in fashioning these national policies is the political arena. Free societies are not ready to subject themselves in these matters to the additional power of economic disruption inherent in the collective bargaining process.

This risk of economic breakdown is worth a more extended comment. By risk of economic breakdown is meant the possibility that highly centralised bargaining could result in strains and intolerable disruption in the event that the bargaining leaders cannot settle without strikes or lockouts. Centralised bargaining, or even bargaining for a large sector, increases the impact of failure in the bargaining on the public generally. The larger the ambit of bargaining the greater is the risk of destructiveness if a breakdown occurs, and, if collective bargaining is truly free, one cannot rule out the risk of breakdowns. Although public tolerance for the economic disruptions caused by breakdowns in collective bargaining is essential if free bargaining is to work, clearly there are limits in democratic countries (both politically and economically) to what amount of destructiveness the electorate will accept. Severe ultimate breakdowns which cause widespread economic dislocations lead eventually to the threshhold of mandated terms and complete government control.

Collective Bargaining as a Counter-cyclical Tool

The second basic element mentioned above is the ability of collective bargaining, assuming its desirability and virtues for other reasons, to serve as an effective tool of counter-cyclical national policy. It cannot. Some reasons why are as follows. Firstly, the ultimate control in unions is the test of rank and file acceptance of the bargain. Union leaders in their deliberations fashioning the terms of the bargain cannot guarantee such acceptance. This manifests itself not only in ratification rejections but sometimes also in lengthy strikes before the leadership will take terms of agreement to the membership, and frequently in the case of highly centralised bargains, in wage drift and in enterprise and plant deviations from national settlements.

Secondly, national control of the economic terms of settlement would not affect the so-called "non-economic" or work rules aspects of bargains. These revolve around work place amenities, schedules, subcontracting, and a myriad of practices that affect productivity, output and quality. Such elements are often an expensive part of a settlement and typically cannot be controlled from a single source without risking a breakdown in enterprise and plant-level relationships.

Thirdly, centralized bargaining and settlements lead to a reduced measure of freedom for individual firms. Results are apt to be a squeezing out of some firms, more industry concentration, strikes on issues not germane to a particular company and less innovation in industrial relations.

Fourthly, the final imperative for all groups is a large degree of self-preservation. In free societies there is a vast diversity of interests, and in the end each group faces the stern, harsh and immediate realities of the marketplace. The economic interests of individuals and groups do not disappear in the face of broader social goals, and in the end group needs will reassert themselves, destroying major bargains or requiring acceptance of countless deviations and exceptions.

Finally, collective bargaining is not the proper instrument for determining prices, as suggested. To do so would usurp the management function, eventually embracing all associated decisions such as investment, cost expenditures, production and market expansion or contraction. The final result could only be a complete change in production and allocation mechanisms.

The present writer cannot agree with the directions suggested in Blyth's paper. This is not to say that everything is well in the world of collective bargaining and that there is no need to continuously explore new approaches and seek modifications of existing systems. The search for constructive change must continue. No single approach is likely to provide all the answers needed in a complex, dynamic, ever-changing system of national and international relationships.

What can government do to influence the pattern of settlements determined by collective bargaining? Two principal interrelated courses of action, short of a direct or indirect takeover of bargaining, can be seen.

First, government can lead the way by adopting sound policies in the areas where it has principal responsibility and by integrating its actions into a consistent whole. It should be even-handed in the development and administration of the policy framework within which collective bargaining is conducted.

Second, as Blyth indicates, government can engage all parties, including the electorate, in an open, constructive, consistent dialogue on basic economic issues and develop the public consensus necessary to provide an appropriate framework for private decision-making. All elements of the society must be sensitized to the social and economic responsibilities they must exercise when making decisions that affect the destinies of their fellows and of the nation. Part of this dialogue must include a frank discussion of group and individual expectations and value systems and an honest admission that there must be priorities.

Although these comments have been in general terms, they seem to have broad applicability to all free societies. The intrusion of government into the collective bargaining arena on a regular basis as opposed to in emergencies, contributes to ultimate state control or to social anarchy as powerful groups grow restive when their essential interests are not met. Greater centralisation of collective bargaining power and expansion of the factors to be considered in bargaining, in the direction suggested in Blyth's paper, could be as detrimental to government and the social fabric as it could be destructive of the free collective bargaining process.

There are many general goals that we want in free societies in addition to price stability, full employment and economic growth. We also want peace, justice, freedom of speech and activity and a host of socio-economic and cultural values. Above all though, we need to accept, no matter how painful, a final role for freedom that governments too must respect.

IV

SOCIAL AND ECONOMIC ISSUES

The papers in this section explore some of the broad, practical issues involved in closer government involvement in collective bargaining. The papers are noteworthy in that they illustrate how different national experiences result in different solutions, and different ways of thinking about, common problems. In the light of the experience of the United States, where there is little communication between macro-policy makers and the parties to collective bargaining, Dunlop holds out little hope of voluntary partnership in fixing wages, although he identifies a number of areas for reform where government influence could be beneficial. Liinamaa's paper draws on Finnish experience, which shows the problems of co-operation "in a small national economy sensitive to external disturbances". To achieve this co-operation Liinamaa stresses two factors: agreement on the underlying economic analysis and centralised negotiations. Robinson points out that pay is determined by both economic and non-economic factors, and that in the light of likely developments in employment and inflation, and the responses of unions and employers, governments will be compelled to intervene. Robinson foresees increased tripartitism, with governments offering trade-offs against restraint. He recognises the difficulties faced by unions "who will be in danger of getting too far ahead of the views and expectations of their own members", raising basic questions of democracy and leadership — referred to in several papers in this volume, and dealt with in particular by Treu.

For Peper, trade-offs are not a new phenomenon, being a form of the "politicisation" of economic processes which prevails in varying degrees in OECD countries generally. In industrial relations, Peper argues the phenomenon is irreversible: "it will become more difficult for the political systems to shirk the responsibility... for the outcome of more or less unobstructed negotiations by the social partners". Furthermore, in view of a likely future with slow or zero growth, income distribution policy will become a major factor in the irreversible process. In commenting on Peper's paper, Treu supports the view that income distribution policy is of vital importance, but also makes the point that trade-offs usually require substantial resources and hence zero growth does not appear feasible. Treu argues that decentralised participation is necessary to counter-balance "the centralisation which generally goes along with trade-offs and with closer relations between the State and interests groups", and cites West Germany as a successful example of this development[1].

---

1. The papers of Verschueren and Scharpf can be usefully read alongside those of Peper and Treu.

THE DEVELOPMENT OF COLLECTIVE BARGAINING IN RELATION TO NATIONAL ECONOMIC, EMPLOYMENT AND RELATED POLICIES

Derek Robinson[1]

In this paper collective bargaining will be used in a wider sense than is usual so that various forms of consultation, bipartite or tripartite discussion of analyses of trends and developments in the economy and proposals for dealing with economic, social and industrial problems are included. It is recognised that these might not fit in the usual definition of collective bargaining, but if the intention is to discuss the possible developments in bargaining and the determination of terms and conditions of employment and these other activities are thought to be relevant or to influence collective bargaining and the outcome of bargaining, it is appropriate that they be included in this discussion.

Three aspects of the development of collective bargaining might usefully be distinguished although there are likely to be interconnections between them. Firstly, there are developments in the processes of bargaining; secondly, in the agenda or content of bargaining; and thirdly, in the results of bargaining.

The most important premise assumed in this paper is that pay is determined by both economic and non-economic factors. Thus, while the economic forces which operate in both product and labour markets are relevant and influence pay determination, so too are such things as attitudes, expectations, perceptions of fairness and equity, and other factors which arise from a range of social and political beliefs and objectives of individuals and trade unions. Further, it is believed that the particular institutional arrangements which exist in different countries can influence the development of collective bargaining and, perhaps more importantly for present purposes, the outcome or results of collective bargaining.

It is accepted that governments will seek to influence the outcome of collective bargaining, either directly or indirectly.

If this is not accepted then the whole emphasis of the discussion changes. Thus, while it could be assumed that governments will not seek to influence the outcome of collective bargaining, but leave this to the social partners, it then becomes necessary to assume that governments will, in the pursuit of the various, and frequently conflicting, economic, social, political and industrial objectives which they are now required to accept, merely respond to the outcome of bargaining and adjust their own policies and actions to seek to obtain their objectives. While to a greater or lesser degree there is some element of this in all OECD Member countries, there are also present attempts by governments to exert some influence on the results of bargaining.

---

1. Fellow of Magdalen College, Oxford, England.

Certain other assumptions underlie this paper. Firstly, society requires governments to accept a much wider range of responsibilities than was the case, say, fifty years ago, and governments have, to varying degrees, accepted these increased, broader responsibilities. Further, in all countries trade unions are established and there is an acceptance that collective bargaining is in itself desirable as a preferred way, in a democratic society, of determining the terms and conditions of employment. In many countries there are legislative provisions to encourage the extension of trade union recognition and the establishment or strengthening of collective bargaining, and in some cases, its extension to cover aspects of the employment relationship which might not previously have been the subject of bargaining or consultation.

The Medium-Term Issues

Although conditions in individual countries vary and can be expected to vary, certain features apply to some extent or other in all of them. Currently they are experiencing higher levels of unemployment than they have been accustomed to in the past twenty years or so. At the same time they have experienced higher rates of inflation and slower rates of growth. The initiating factor has been the dramatic change in the terms of trade and particularly the increase in the price of oil. The failure adequately to re-cycle oil revenues has led to a substantial depressive effect on international trade. It is assumed that these depressive forces will continue to operate, at least for the next three to five years. After that, the future is extremely hazy, and it may well be that actions and developments over the next few years will themselves determine the later position. Emphasis here will therefore be placed on the more immediate future.

The general problem is seen as that of attempting to stimulate growth and reduce unemployment levels. The particular aspects to be considered centre round the question of what role collective bargaining might have in helping to achieve these objectives, either in a positive way, or, in the negative sense, that collective bargaining might lead to a worsening of the situation. The latter aspect might be crudely summarised by the argument that collective bargaining in which trade unions are influenced by the expectations and attitudes of their members, might seek to obtain increases in real wages which are higher than the economy can somehow "afford", with the result that inflationary pressures will be intensified, leading to a decrease in employment both through a loss of cost-competitiveness in some countries and by reductions in investment in those countries, either because enterprises are unable to undertake the required level of investment activity or are unwilling to do so in the countries concerned but prefer to invest elsewhere.

This admittedly crude and over-simple formulation of the issue is not merely a restatement of the old question of whether trade unions do or do not cause inflation. It starts from a recognition of the effect on living standards of the substantial shifts in the terms of trade at a time when in all OECD Member countries there were widespread expectations of constantly rising living standards.

112

Moreover, this paper asserts that in the past few years there have been general changes in attitudes regarding the role of individual employees, and their trade unions, in the decision-taking processes surrounding the employment relationship. This has led to a desire by employees to play a greater role in decision-taking and to their rejection of traditional views of managerial prerogatives. The response to this general tendency differs between countries. In some it may be that the noticeable features are a lengthening of the agenda of collective bargaining as more issues are considered to be appropriate to joint regulation. In others it may take the form of employee participation on the boards of companies. It is assumed that this trend will continue. Indeed it is possible that if unemployment worsens, either because employment levels fall or the potential labour force increases for demographic reasons or as a result of higher participation rates, efforts to strengthen job security for those employed could well lead to greater demands for more involvement in decision-taking.

Employment

Changes in participation rates could mean that both employment and registered or measured unemployment rise in an individual country. Structural changes appear to be such that we are witnessing either the emergence of a new problem, or more likely, the much increased development of something that has been present for some time on a smaller scale; an imbalance or mis-match between the demands of employers for certain skills and the qualifications and abilities of the unemployed to meet those demands. Increases in unemployment and employers' vacancies can take place simultaneously. It may be that without measures to correct the imbalance, and more particularly the greater imbalance that might result should economic growth occur, it may not be possible to obtain much faster economic growth. There is a strong possibility that bottlenecks in skilled labour supply could prevent much higher economic growth in a number of countries and attempts to obtain faster economic growth without attendant active manpower policies might well generate higher inflation. Mere reliance on stimulating the general level of demand is unlikely to be successful and could worsen the inflationary problem.

Proposals are being made in a number of countries for reductions in the working week, or other variants which are intended to reduce the number of effective labour hours expected of individual workers so that a given level of output would require a larger number of people to produce it. (Reduction or abolition of overtime, longer holidays, sabbatical leave, lower retirement ages and job sharing can all be seen as having the same economic implication for the labour market and labour supply).

From the viewpoint of reducing unemployment the crucial question is whether these measures would actually lead to more people being offered employment. Two main arguments are advanced against them. Firstly, as most of the measures would involve no reductions in the pay and living standards of those whose hours of employment (weekly or per annum) would be reduced, and there would be additional labour costs involved in employing the additional workers, costs would rise. The effects on employment in any one country would be influenced by measures taken, or not taken, in other countries. Moreover, if the real living standards of those currently unemployed who would be provided with employment as a result of these measures rise, then unless there was some increase in output, the living standards of some other sectors of society would fall. Attempts to maintain their living standards by the groups affected could either lead to greater inflationary pressures, or strong political pressures if the burden was passed to groups receiving transfer payments. Demographic factors in some countries are such that politicians might well be averse to taking such steps. Indeed, these factors and the resulting shifts in political power could well lead to developments which would generate reverse trends, e.g. the extension of the retirement age, thereby making it more difficult for the unemployed to obtain employment.

Secondly, it is argued that because of the imbalance between the skills required by employers and those possessed by the unemployed it would not be possible to make any significant reduction in the numbers unemployed. Considerable training and re-training measures would be needed as a precondition of this approach to reducing unemployment.

It is also argued that the present provisions of collective bargaining and/ or legislation, whereby labour is much more a fixed cost, e.g. employment guarantees, redundancy provisions, possibilities of discrimination on sex or race grounds, create a situation in which employers are reluctant to hire additional employees, this being one of the causes of the present high levels of unemployment.

At the same time it should be recognised that many trade unions will nevertheless continue to press for these or similar measures. In some cases they may dispute the economic analysis. In other cases they may well argue that while some of these developments might occur, it is open to government to minimise or negate their effects. Thus, any redistributional problems that occur can be dealt with by taxation of the higher-income groups, thereby enabling those taken into employment to have higher living standards without other large groups of employees suffering. The burden would be passed to those with the "ability" to bear it. This difference of opinion, while amenable to some consideration of the facts of income distribution, will be much influenced by value judgements regarding the possibilities as well as the desirability of further redistribution.

It can also be argued that reductions in the number of hours of work per employee will lead to increase in hourly productivity so that higher real incomes will be sustainable. If the increase in hourly productivity, plus any increase in total output which might result from an increase in the total number of hours worked, is sufficient to meet the difference between the transfer payments made to the unemployed and their net wages in employment there should be no increase in inflationary pressure from the demand side, although there could be from costs if the difference in net pay and total labour costs of increased employment exceeds the increase in output.

The forecast of this paper is that in some Member countries pressures to reduce "normal" or "expected" hours of work will increase and in some cases will be successful.

Given the weak state of demand and weak expectations and confidence of private business in investment in Member countries, there will be sustained pressures on government to increase employment in the public sector. Clearly political and ideological factors will be important, but even where there is acceptance of the desirability of increasing the output of goods from the private and/or market sector, there will be pressures to use the public sector at least in the shorter term to lead out of the depressed state.

Two major arguments will be used against this. Firstly, the increased burden of taxation frequently associated with such measures will lead to political pressures on government. Secondly, the marginal taxation levels will themselves be increasingly criticised, not only by individual taxpayers but by employers and trade unions, for their adverse effects on incentives. Even in countries in which the trade unions have strong political affiliations with a political party which is committed to a policy of increased government intervention and the provision of more services through the State, there is an increased awareness of the unpopularity, as well as, perhaps, the inefficacy, of high marginal rates of direct taxation. Inflation emphasizes this as, generally, effective tax rates are not adjusted to inflation so that a larger number of employees are pushed into higher marginal tax rates even though there may have been little if any increase in real wage levels.

If, as is assumed, investors are reluctant to undertake significantly larger investment activity in some countries but prefer to consider investment elsewhere, frequently in developing countries, trade unions can be expected to adopt much stronger protectionist views. These will not be confined to imports from Third World countries; there is a danger that protectionism will also cover imports from other OECD countries. Such a process could lead to a worsening of the general level of demand and employment. While it may be possible to produce economic arguments which suggest that employment might be adversely affected if all countries adopted protectionist policies, this will not necessarily lead trade unions to accept them. All economic analyses and arguments rest upon assumptions which may or may not be subsequently validated by events. Trade unions and their members believe that they have in the past suffered too often because of the acceptance of economic analyses and arguments which subsequently turned out to be wrong. Also, most workers and their unions believe that their prime concern is to protect their interests as employees in their current place of employment. Change and uncertainty are considered undesirable.

Inflation

While there is considerable disagreement as to a precise main cause of inflation, and even more disagreement about the specific measures to be adopted to end or reduce it, there is in some sense perhaps more in common between the protagonists of different schools than was formerly the case. Most important, almost all commentators accept that "attitudes" or "expectations" play an important part in the inflationary process. Much work needs to be done on the factors which determine attitudes or expectations, and on how these are translated into pressures which have an effect on pay, and thus on cost and price determination. But even extreme monetarists appear to accept that it is necessary to change expectations in order to break an inflationary cycle, their difference from other schools perhaps relying more on how these can or should be changed. Similarly, it is doubtful if there is an advocate, however extreme, of the desirability of even a direct statutory policy of pay and price controls, who would argue that the level of monetary demand and changes in the money supply were totally irrelevant. It is now a question of balance and of the best ways of changing attitudes and behaviour.

Simple reliance on orthodox demand management policies is nowhere considered sufficient. All governments recognise that they must adopt other supportive measures. These include forms of active manpower policies designed to supplement or speed up the market's response to labour force adaptation to changing circumstances. Thus while economic theory might suggest that in the long run there will be tendencies for labour to adapt to changing circumstances by leaving certain occupations and employments and undertaking the necessary training or re-training to enter others, the time-lags of response are recognised as too great, and the economic consequences which occur during the intervening periods as too severe, to accept.

Moreover, the existence of institutional or social factors in pay determination themselves frequently prevent the market from working in the theoretically assumed manner. Coercive comparisons, the impact of notions of fairness and perceived equity in leading to pay claims based on traditional pay relationships, frequently mean that even if the market forces operate to raise the pay of some skill which is in short supply, the pay of other groups often moves more or less in line or at least to such an extent that the initial relative advantage that has been obtained is subsequently whittled away. This is not to state that pay relationships are fixed and immutable, but that they can prove extremely rigid and difficult to change.

In many countries the appeal to history is accepted as a fair and reasonable argument in pay determination. This is an appeal which is often reinforced by the decisions of arbitrators in issues of interest; it provides them with an apparently acceptable response which does not require them to determine a set or principles by which to seek to establish some new pay relationships.

Further, in all countries, government is a major employer. Frequently it adopts some form of comparability for the determination of the pay of its own direct and indirect employees. This can reinforce the tendencies to the generalisation of pay increases which have been obtained by specific groups, perhaps on grounds of labour market requirements or contribution to increased productivity. The relatively high degree of trade union organisation in the public sector in many countries means that it is often not feasible, even if it is considered desirable, to use the public sector to set the pace by forcing through lower money wage settlements.

In all Member countries trade unions have much increased their use of economic analysis, particularly within the trade union central organisations. This has resulted from two main factors. Firstly, there has been an increasing appreciation of the relevance of macro-economic developments on pay determination in general, and, more particularly, on the response of governments, influenced by macro-economic factors, to individual pay settlements.

Secondly, the growing tendency for trade unions to be consulted by governments about the state of the economy and the type of economic measures which government is considering introducing, or which unions are urging governments to introduce, has, of necessity, required trade unions to form views about macro-economic analysis and policies. Similar developments have taken place amongst employers' organisations.

Consequences of Changes in Governments' Attitudes and Approaches

The most important consequence of the rejection of reliance on demand management policies alone has been the recognition by governments that it is necessary to seek to influence the behaviour of the social partners. This has been combined with pressure by the social partners, and particularly the trade unions, to obtain greater government intervention, either in the labour market, or in the provision of other aspects of economic, social and trade union policies. As trade union aims and objectives have widened so have they sought to obtain more from government. Frequently employers have played a more passive role, responding to or resisting the introduction of additional measures which would further union objectives. However, in some countries changes in the political composition of governments may diminish this somewhat biased approach in the future.

The particular form of government's response to these pressures in its attempts to influence the behaviour of the bargaining parties has been varied. Some constraints have been imposed by the existing bargaining processes and structures, and prevailing political beliefs and attitudes have shaped the government's perceptions of the effective range of options open to it. Thus in some countries the existence of centralised bargaining machinery has led governments to seek to exert influence on the outcome of bargaining by persuasion rather than by direct intervention. In other cases even where no centralised bargaining exists governments have sought to obtain an acceptable consensus regarding the range of settlements which ought to emerge from bargaining, seeking to influence this perhaps by specifying that if settlements were to exceed the desired range government would respond by adopting certain monetary or fiscal policies designed to offset the inflationary settlements. The success of this approach depends upon the way in which the parties themselves react to these threats and whether they believe that is is possible to persuade government to change its views. In other cases governments have intervened directly by income policies which have included direct controls on pay and price increases.

Essentially governments have to choose between seeking to influence the outcome of collective bargaining by packages of economic measures which include those actions normally regarded as orthodox demand management policies; by introducing new measures designed to influence the bargaining, such as changes in taxation, which are not designed primarily to operate as the fiscal cutting edge of demand management policies but rather as attempts to change the bargaining behaviour by providing changes in real income and consumption power through taxation levels rather than through changes in money incomes; or by introducing some form of incomes policies.

The difficulties facing government might be summarised as the change in expectations so that while there is a greater appreciation by the population of the dangers of inflation, there is nonetheless a desire to have steady and continuing increases in real living standards. Trade unions naturally translate these desires into bargaining demands. Improvements obtained by government intervention frequently have one disadvantage from a union viewpoint. They are less easily seen as the result of trade union action, so that the perceived benefits of trade union membership are accordingly less. Trade unions, of necessity, require to be able to demonstrate to members and potential members the advantages of union membership. Thus the tax reduction introduced in the United Kingdom conditional upon agreement that the Social Contract "norm" would be reduced, while perhaps having desirable macro-economic effects and some slight impact on reducing the disincentive effects of taxation, does not have the same attraction to trade unions as a pay increase which would leave their members with a corresponding equivalent rise in real incomes.

Governments may introduce legislation on other issues of interest to trade unions, e.g. employee participation, capital-sharing or trade union recognition and bargaining rights, in an attempt to obtain a trade-off in pay bargaining. Such approaches are more likely to be attempted by Social Democratic or Labour governments. Their use rests on an acceptance that there is a margin of opportunity in pay bargaining within which trade unions can decide which position within that margin or range they will adopt. This depends not only on the acceptance of other than purely economic factors in pay determination, but also upon a view of the options open to trade unions to influence either their members' attitudes and choices, or on the view that unions themselves have some margin of opportunity in relation to their membership, so that they can to some extent withstand membership pressure for higher money wages without suffering unacceptable internal stresses which could challenge either the continuation of the union or the position of the existing leadership.

To the extent that there exists inter-union competition for membership this margin of opportunity will be reduced. Even where there is no direct competition for membership or recognition, there will be forces operating to limit the ability of union leadership to participate in a trade-off of policy objectives with governments. All trade union leadership faces challenges from within. If the policies of the leadership strain the tolerance of membership too far there will be threats, either from electoral challenges or through the form of unofficial strikes by the rank and file. It may well be that the general tendency for employees to want a greater share in decision-taking at their place of employment applies also to their relationship with their trade unions, so that the margin of toleration of leadership policies with which the rank and file disagree might now be somewhat reduced. It is crucial therefore, not only for governments, but also for those responsible for offering advice on policy, to recognise the effective constraints that operate in an economy at a particular time. There is some tendency, understandable perhaps, for governments to try and push beyond the limits of what can be realistically expected even from co-operative trade union leaders.

Moreover, in any situation, the response of trade unions will be much influenced by their views as to the probability that if they accept restraints on their own bargaining they will be let down by the refusal or inability of others to do the same. Even when the realities of the underlying economic situation are accepted, so that unions recognise that some moderation in money wage settlements is necessary, individual unions may feel unable to move unless they are assured that other unions will do likewise.

A combination of potential threats both from without and from within can make it extremely difficult for trade unions to moderate their individual bargaining demands. This is not to suggest that no such moderation is possible or that leadership cannot be exercised in order to moderate increases in money wage increases, perhaps in order to obtain other bargaining goals. Rather, it is to emphasise that there are constraints upon the powers of trade union leadership and that these should be recognised by governments, and that in some circumstances the constraints may be more restrictive than they were previously.

If, as seems probable, trade union expectations in a bargaining situation are firstly backward-looking, and only secondly forward-looking, it is extremely difficult to persuade them to accept settlements which provide for smaller pay increases than the rise in retail prices since the last settlement. The restoration of the past settlement's real living standards is frequently the starting point of negotiation. The forward-looking expectations then reflect views of improvements in real standards. If the reduction in the inflation rate sought is greater than the increase in productivity between settlements, then trade unions will inevitably have immense problems in seeking to co-operate with government, no matter how well-intentioned they might be.

Particular emphasis is placed on the role of trade unions in this situation because it is believed that in present circumstances, with a depressed general level of demand, much of the inflationary pressure in pay determination is coming from that side. Employers are much less concerned by consideration of labour market shortages and so are not, by and large, adopting offensive pay strategies to recruit or retain labour, although in some cases they may be doing so for particular groups already in short supply. In some situations employers may also be prepared to grant relatively larger increases to certain groups which they believe have been adversely affected by solidaristic wage policies, or government incomes policies which have had redistributive provisions.

On the employers' side discussion tends to emphasise measures whereby they can increase their ability to resist trade union demands. Some of the proposals emphasise the importance of the timing of different pay settlements and suggest a need for greater co-ordination of timing so that the consequences of coercive comparisons and use of leap-frogging might be reduced. The difficulties are that unions will not take kindly to putting back their settlement dates in order to obtain greater co-ordination, so it might be necessary to achieve co-ordination by bringing some forward. That could be inflationary. Also it does not follow that there will be sufficient agreement between unions to allow co-ordinated settlements to reach satisfactory solutions. As with centralised bargaining measures the provision of machinery and processes creates the opportunity for certain policies to be introduced, if that is what the parties want, but does not of itself ensure that they will want the same things. Difficulties can be expected therefore not only because of competing objectives of trade unions and of employers' who also have views about fairness in relative pay levels, but also from the existence of different payment systems so that some employees receive pay increases from sources other than the central or co-ordinated settlements. As the Swedish experience shows, the major part of the efforts are directed towards preventing a worsening of the relative pay positions rather than actually changing these.

Efforts to increase employers' solidarity depend primarily upon the prevailing methods and institutions for pay determination and the attitudes and objectives of employers. The Swedish employers' organisation has strong formal provisions for ensuring employer solidarity but in practice these can be used only very occasionally and with great care. Of the two main components of employers' solidarity, actions against union demands made on all employers or more particularly on individual employers, and actions against employers who break the collective policy, it is the latter which creates the greater problems. Indemnity funds can provide some measure of relief in the former case, but even then it is necessary to persuade the individual employers concerned that they should bear the brunt of any trade union action in order to defend the general employer position. In the second case it is necessary to have sufficient sanctions against individual employer members to dissuade them from taking action regarded as harmful to employers generally but which is presumably regarded by the individual firm as in its own interests, at least when compared with the alternative. It is probable that the German employers have been most successful in their solidaristic approach, but this owes more to their attitudes than to any economic factors. The creation of similar attitudes elsewhere has proved either impossible or has not been attempted. However, the current situation is probably the most conducive to such attempts, as employer competition in labour market terms is less than it has been for many years.

It is thought, therefore, that governments' main attempts will continue to be directed towards influencing trade union behaviour by various combinations of exhortation and the offer of trade-offs designed to influence union responses.

Trade Union Responses

While the greater degree of economic understanding and sophistication of analysis amongst trade unions may mean that they are concerned about inflation, unemployment and low rates of economic growth, it does not mean that they necessarily accept the diagnosis of the cause of economic ills or the prescriptions offered by government and employers. Unions have also become more sophisticated in their own prescriptions.

Irrespective of their precise political affiliations or ideology, unions as a whole have shifted somewhat, in that there is increased appreciation of the interrelationship of various aspects of the economy. While unions continue to seek a redistribution of income towards employment incomes, they are more conscious of the role that investment plays in generating employment even though they are also aware of the employment consequences of shifts towards more capital-intensive methods of production. As a result of recognising the importance of retained profits in financing investment the trade unions, or perhaps more specifically the headquarters of a number of continental European trade union movements, have designed proposals for forms of capital-sharing. These have the added attraction to trade unions of seeking to redistribute wealth. Essentially there is an acceptance of the need for enterprises to retain profits but an unwillingness to see the ownership of these increased capital funds accrue to the present shareholders.

In some cases it is claimed that these proposals will ease the inflationary pressures which emanate from a desire to see a redistribution of income and wealth. Whether this would actually be the case were such schemes to be introduced is however unclear. Nevertheless it should be expected that trade union movements in some countries will continue to press for schemes whereby some part of the ownership of capital growth accrues to employees. On a broader perspective this can be seen as adding an economic dimension to the general pressures for greater industrial democracy.

In a situation in which government and other sections of society are seeking to urge trade unions and their members to moderate and modify their behaviour, frequently on the grounds that it is really in their own interests to do so, it must be expected that trade unions will respond cautiously, even with suspicion. Trade unions are well used to outsiders advising them of what is really in their own interests. They are also well used to being criticised as undemocratic if they do not seek to translate into action the desires of their members.

Herein lies one of the basic difficulties for trade unions. They are democratic organisations which must, in order to survive, carry their membership with them. While there is undoubtedly some room for manœuvre and the exercise of leadership (whether this is regarded as responsible or irresponsible leadership frequently depends upon whether or not the commentator agrees with the union on the particular issue) there are nevertheless severe constraints upon this room for manœuvre. Moreover, trade unions believe that they are often asked to exercise moderating influence when other sections of society are not prepared to do so.

While they may be willing to seek to change their members' views regarding the best way of achieving stated objectives (again this is education or indoctrination according to whether or not the commentator agrees with the action) union leaders also recognise that if they seek to go too far and oppose the prevailing views of their membership they are likely to be overturned.

It may be that occasions will arise when trade union leadership may be persuaded that some moderation of their bargaining behaviour would be in the interests of their members as well as the general interest, assuming that all groups displayed similar moderation, but they may nevertheless conclude that it would not be possible to persuade their membership to accept such a policy. In some circumstances it may be more effective for the government to seek to impose such an approach; union leadership is then not required to advocate or defend the constraints.

121

This approach, however, inevitably raises severe difficulties for unions, for they genuinely believe that free collective bargaining in some form or other is a necessary condition for the defence of a free and democratic society. Thus they are naturally alarmed at government intervention to restrict the rights of unions to participate in collective bargaining. It is when government can persuade them that restraints voluntarily accepted are necessary and in their interests, and that their membership will generally recognise the need for such restraints that unions can most easily agree. In this sense voluntarily accepted constraints are no limitation of freedom. Perhaps the major role in fact lies with governments in that they have the prime responsibility for creating that climate of opinion and understanding of the realities of economic life that is conducive to the moderation of inflationary pressures. The election cycle and the temptation for opposition parties to seek advantage, however, makes it extremely difficult for sufficient consensus to be obtained. Moreover there will always be deeply and genuinely held opinions about the "right" or "fair" distribution of income, and in a democratic pluralist society this is to be expected. There is unlikely to be some Golden Society in which there is uniformity of view on relative income levels and in which different groups accept the majority opinion regarding their own relative income position without demur, yet there are some apparently marked differences between countries regarding the extent of disagreements.

Employers' Responses

It is generally true that employers do not like incomes policies much more than do trade unions, also believing that there should not be government intervention in labour markets issues. However, they also tend to believe that the balance of power in the labour market is too much in the unions' favour, even with any changes that may have occurred as a result of rising unemployment. Indeed, in some countries employers believe that rising unemployment has weakened them more than it has the unions, in that as a result of reduced profits and depressed demand in a situation of more intense international competition they are more at the mercy of trade unions and the threat of industrial action than they were in times of full employment. Rising labour costs and measures to provide for greater job security lead them to prefer methods of expanding production which do not require increases in the labour force.

In times of high employment they want to retain their individual freedom to compete for scarce labour. Generally, however, they wish governments to introduce measures to reduce the relative power of unions or to persuade unions to exercise their power more "responsibly".

For the foreseeable future it might be appropriate to conclude that employers will not themselves be generating much inflationary pressures through competitive bidding in a tight labour market generally, although they might do so for certain skills. In addition, employers are likely to prefer a widening of pay differentials.

Possible Developments

There will be increased tripartism in the approach to economic policy making. Governments will seek to influence trade union behaviour by searching for trade-off options to reduce increases in money wages. This will generate considerable difficulties for trade unions, who will be in danger of getting too far ahead of the views and expectations of their own members. Governments will seek a double-barrelled approach, which runs the risk of internal contradiction. While needing the co-operation of trade unions and so entering into consultation or bargaining with them, they will also be tempted to go over the heads of the unions and appeal direct to their membership (and the electorate). The latter step might be necessary if changed attitudes towards money wage increases are to be achieved, but the risk is obvious.

Similarly governments will seek to change the prevailing behaviour patterns in collective bargaining, and particularly the use of comparability. There is at present a conflict between (a) perceptions of fairness which, combined with institutional practices in pay bargaining, lead to the creation of climates of opinion whereby increases received by one group are to a greater or lesser extent passed on to other groups, and (b) the economic forces which may require that relatively larger increases be received by some groups in order that the necessary allocative mechanisms of the labour market can operate. While it is not the only factor, pay is an important one in the allocation of labour. Yet the very existence of collective bargaining makes it far more difficult for labour market forces acting through changes in relative pay levels to operate. If the appropriate responses to changed product and labour market conditions are to be made, and if the structural changes and imbalances are to be obtained and corrected, it is probably necessary that the social value judgments be changed to meet the required economic developments.

This might be seen as striking at the very roots of trade unions as we know them in democratic societies. Whether this is actually so depends upon the general environment in which attempts to change these attitudes take place. If it is possible to create confidence among unions and their members that these are not efforts to destroy the trade union movement, or render it an impotent extension of government, then a positive and constructive response might be forthcoming. This would require increased government efforts to stimulate growth and reduce unemployment, thereby creating higher living standards and increased employment security, even though this might be associated with job change.

In a number of countries trade unions are already recognising that some of their approaches of the past twenty or thirty years are no longer appropriate. In particular, difficulties arise from the fact that most people do not regard an increase or improvement in living standards through the provision of more government services, be these education, health services, roads, etc., as equivalent to a corresponding increase in their private or personal consumption expenditure. It is more difficult therefore for unions to participate in a trade-off with government in that improved educational provision, for example, may not be seen as something sufficiently worthwhile to

123

justify foregoing an extra 1 or 2 per cent increase in money wages, and certainly not some increase in real wages.

The difficulties are compounded by increased union awareness of the disadvantages to their own members, as well as the economy generally, of high marginal rates of direct taxation.

In brief, there is no universally appropriate solution and there is no simple solution for application in any one country. Collective bargaining is about power; both power at the place of work and in an aggregated sense power over the distribution of income and the allocation of resources. Value judgements, beliefs and perceptions of fairness exert strong influence on both sides of the bargaining table. Governments recognise the importance of the outcome of bargaining and will continue to seek to influence it. Basically their success will depend upon their ability to change attitudes and beliefs. The fundamental choice is between an approach that says attitudes and behaviour will change as a result of changed economic circumstances. The simple Phillips Curve can be seen as representing this. The opposite extreme says that attitudes and behaviour may not respond to economic circumstances in any predictable manner. The belief that the Phillips Curve for any one country can change through time reflects this position. Recent events would support the latter view. Increased inflation has accompanied higher unemployment. It is open to debate, and indeed the subject of this conference, as to how far economic forces can change attitudes and behaviour and the extent of change in economic circumstances which is needed to obtain changes in behaviour. Put simply, how much unemployment is thought necessary to obtain acceptable rates of inflation ? It is then a matter of political judgement whether it is possible or feasible to seek to create the required economic circumstances.

The conclusion put forward here is that reliance upon economic circumstances alone will be insufficient. It is also doubtful if our political or our economic systems can tolerate the strains that would necessarily be involved in this approach. Some action to impinge directly on attitudes and behaviour is therefore necessary. At present the scope for this is limited, not least by the extent of the constraints which it is realistic to expect trade unions to bear. In particular countries there will be more opportunity for faster action at some times than at, and in, others. But primarily this should be seen more as a political than an industrial relations problem. Actions to change attitudes cannot be expected to succeed if they are presented as undesirable but necessary short-term measures imposed to meet a particular crisis but to be dropped as soon as the immediate crisis is over. This has been the major defect of British attempts at incomes policies. Our electoral systems make it extremely difficult to provide the necessary longer-term approaches.

It is suggested therefore that while some marginal effects may be obtained in individual countries by modifying the institutions and practices of collective bargaining, these will not in themselves be sufficient to provide the necessary contribution to resolving current problems. By and large the parties to collective bargaining reflect and respond to the views and aspirations of those they represent. The constituency views, while perhaps accepting the objectives of government policies, do not yet accept sufficiently the means whereby those objectives are to be achieved. But it would be placing too great a strain and a burden on the institutions and parties to collective bargaining to expect them to bear the brunt of the responsibility for change.

This is why while collective bargaining, and changes in its processes, can make some contribution to the solution of current problems, such a contribution will not be sufficient to solve them. Even if everyone knows what should be done — and there is much divergence of opinion on this — very few are prepared to do it. Short-term ad hoc ameliorative measures might therefore be the most we can hope for. It is the general package of measures introduced, and the response of trade unions to them, which will primarily determine the perception of the best interests of unions and their members.

The main alternative view is that of the catastrophe. If unemployment, inflation and economic stagnation become sufficiently bad, attitudes will change, trade union power crumble and economies will be in a position to achieve growth, etc. The problem is to know how bad is sufficiently bad; whether governments can politically survive the chain of events which allow things to get so bad; whether attitudes would in fact change amongst all groups or whether those with considerable power, even in a depressed economy, might not still press ahead with their own sectional claims. The same points are relevant to proposals to adopt a very strong tight monetarist position. If some groups resist the measures, comparability and coercive comparisons might spread the high money wage settlements even though unemployment continued to rise.

It is appreciated that this paper does not provide positive proposals which will lead to dramatic improvements over the next five years. This is because none can be found which have the two features of being acceptable and effective. The only comfort is that in practice a pessimist may be a realist surrounded by optimists.

COLLECTIVE BARGAINING AND GOVERNMENT POLICIES IN THE UNITED STATES : FUTURE

John T. Dunlop[1]

The Current Relations

The decentralised system of collective bargaining that has evolved in this country over the past century is inconsistent, and often in open conflict with the aspirations for economic policy by academic economists and macro-economic policy prescriptors. As George W. Taylor stated in 1971, "No simple imposed formula, and no clever gimmick can sublimate the need for an acceptable accommodation of diverse interest".

The guideposts of the Kennedy-Johnson period and the retardation pronouncements of the Carter Administration are illustrative of this conflict. Increasingly, general trade policies and pronouncements by government on international economic relations are likewise widely unacceptable to parties engaged in private collective bargaining.

Fundamentally, decentralised collective bargaining and general incomes policies or macro-economic policies can only be congruent when the parties and the government agree overtly or tacitly upon a no-strike and no-lockout procedure (with some procedure to resolve particular disputes), or the government must have real power to enforce its policy. The ultimate test of an incomes policy — or any macro policy directly affecting wages and prices — is how a strike or lockout against that policy is handled and resolved. Moreover, in a country in which many agreements require the ratification vote of union members to be valid, the rank-and-file are in a position to reject any informal restraints on collective bargaining. In the foreseeable future, and in the absence of a more acute sense of emergency, there is little disposition on the part of the parties of collective bargaining or the members to limit formally the use of the weapons of economic conflict.

In the dispute resolution between the parties, mediators and arbitrators confront special difficulties with a national economic policy in the form of restraints on wage and benefit increases that do not have the force of law. The question has often arisen in the past as to whether mediators have a responsibility to try to enforce the policy or whether their sole mission is to seek a settlement. In general, mediators have eschewed any stabilisation function; they behave that way today, and their loyalties are likely to continue in that form.

The situation in the United States is further characterised at present by the absence of any direct tripartite discussions among organised labour, managements and governments on issues of economic policy. There is no existing mechanism for such continuing discussions. Sporadic discussion between government and some managements or between government and

---

1. Lamont University Professor, Harvard.

the labour federation can never generate the confidence and creativity of an established forum for tripartite discourse. Overseas observers will find it incredible that the nominal reason for the absence of such tripartite discussions is legislation that requires advisory committees to conduct their discussions, with some exceptions, in public, open to the press and media. Imagine trying to hold serious discussions of economic policy among major interest groups on a continuing basis in such an atmosphere. It cannot be done, and the representatives of labour and management will not participate.

There is no appreciation by macro-economists and general economic policy makers of the subtleties and methods of impact of collective bargaining on economic affaires. The same is true in reverse. Macro policy makers have no place for collective bargaining in their intellectual baggage, and it always complicates their relatively simplistic models of fiscal policy and wage and price determination. A single wage equation in an economic model is all they can envisage.

The fact is, of course, that the aggregate of wage and benefit payments or obligations on one hand, and their impact on labour and other costs, productivities and managerial decisions are extraordinarily complex. Issues such as the duration of agreements, methods of wage payments, forms of escalation, structures of collective bargaining, fringe benefit arrangements, rules relating to lay-offs, promotions, transfers and other movements of workers, work rules, manning requirements, training, accident control, etc., each specified to a specific collective agreement, are the essence of the collective bargaining process. The accommodation within groups of workers and within management that is essential to secure concurrence on an agreement — instead of conflict — is outside the macro-economic frame of reference.

There is thus little exchange, and indeed little language or concept for interaction, in the United States, between parties to collective bargaining and economic policy makers preoccupied with the big picture. Never the twain shall meet. Indeed, there is little discourse within government between those interested in collective bargaining and dispute resolution and those concerned with general economic policies.

Spheres of Interaction : Collective Bargaining and Government

If one is to appraise the future of the interaction of government and collective bargaining, it is necessary to specify the spheres of such interaction, since each may follow a somewhat different pattern of development.

1. Substantive regulation

In the United States, as compared with other advanced industrial countries, historically the sphere of substantive government regulation of the terms and conditions of employment was quite narrow and more was left to free collective bargaining, where it existed. In the past decade, particularly, there has been a considerable expansion in the sphere of substantive government determinations such as in health and safety, pension regulation, affirmative action and actions against discrimination in employment by virtue of age, including mandatory retirement at age 65.

These substantive regulations not only narrow to a degree the scope of collective bargaining, but they create numerous issues of interaction between the parties and government agencies. In some instances differences between the parties are exacerbated while in others the parties work together in opposition to positions developed by government agencies and the courts. As the sphere of government activity grows, as the method of legal enactment expands the substantive questions it treats, the more serious are these issues as a threat to problem-solving collective bargaining.

The government regulatory agencies have not learned how to get the parties to work together to formulate practical rules and regulations in the employment field. The regulations are formulated in a legalistic mould rather than developed in the image of rules or provisions under collective bargaining.

The governmental agencies in the United States, in this respect, do not have the device available in many other countries by which the Minister is authorised to extend provisions of a representative collective agreement to all enterprises or workers in an industry or sector.

2. Training and Manpower.

In the area of training, apprenticeship and manpower development, the high promise for the role of collective bargaining in this process a decade ago has not been realised. Indeed, in various areas of apprenticeship and public employment the tensions at times have been acute. Fundamentally, whenever the federal government provides grants and monies for manpower development a detailed set of stringent regulations have accompanied the funding. These intrusions, red tape and bureaucratic irritations have materially made more difficult the co-operative interaction of the public and private sectors and training.

3. Trade

Nowhere is there sharper dispute between general economic policy and collective bargaining than in the approach to trade questions. After almost a century of support for an open economy, the American labour movement has substantially altered its views, seeking more restraints on imports that compete with American manufactured goods. The managements in many sectors have joined forces. Basically, in the present and projected economic climate, these parties are persuaded that the United States has been accommodating to subtle forms of autarchy abroad, non-tariff barriers, with resulting damage to American employment, while at the same time the foreign autarchy subsidises in various ways the costs and exports of its own enterprises. The state trading companies of communist countries and government-operated enterprises elsewhere have compounded the problem. Adjustment assistance is rejected as a significant contribution to the resolution of fundamental trade issues.

4. Public Employment.

As in other countries, public employment raises specialised problems in collective bargaining. In the United States nearly half of the approximately 9.5 million full-time state and local government employees belonged to labour organisations in October 1976. In the Federal government the proportion is higher.

The problems of accommodating the negotiation and administration of collective agreements in the public sector with civil service regulations, the enforcement of equal employment regulations, the budgeting process and the role of legislative bodies in influencing the specific terms and conditions of employment is a most complex matter. While the roles of the strike or lockout, and of compulsory arbitration, have received public attention, these other issues and the task of developing effective public management are the significant longer-term issues if genuine collective negotiations in some form is to operate in the public sector in the United States. The public sector arrangement will be in flux for a long time, with wide variations for some time emerging in various states and localities.

5. Labour-Management Committees

There is a wide variety of labour-management joint consultative committees created by partners to collective bargaining agreements in the United States. Historically, they have arisen in particular industries, plants, or localities to deal with problems of serious concern to the parties such as productivity, bargaining structure, methods of wage payment, competitive conditions, fringe benefits, wage structure, etc. These committees tend to have a limited duration, but they serve vital roles, often relating the problems of a sector to longer-term or wider considerations of public policy. The government has been relatively insignificant in the initiatives or operations of these committees.

6. Incomes Policy

Whatever that maligned term may mean in the United States, in the absence of a genuine emergency, there appears little likelihood of a policy agreement among labour, management and government in the foreseeable future. This statement applies not only to explicit limitations on compensation but also to various fiscal forms of tax-based incomes policies (TIP). Labour and management are opposed to such measures, and it appears unlikely that such policies would be adopted, or be operated successfully, with joint opposition.

If incomes policies simply try to reduce wages or price increases, leaving everything else the same, little if anything can be accomplished except in appearances. But successful voluntary programmes have always sought to induce changes in the more underlying structures and factors affecting wage and price decisions.

Thus on the wage and benefit side the following types of activities can be voluntarily developed: reform in the structure of bargaining so as to reduce rivalries and "leapfrogging"; the elimination of outdated work rules and practices, manning requirement programmes; reforms in methods of wage payment; improving productivity in other ways; recasting of fringe benefit packages and their financing; improved labour supply and training; and specialising agreements which meet the problems of particular branches or plants in an industry.

Such voluntary programmes take time to develop and to produce results in a co-operative and trustful atmosphere. They require personnel with detailed knowledge of sectors and in whom the parties have confidence. Such programmes cannot be imposed by government jawboning or arm-twisting: they can only be developed by persuasion and imaginative and patient leadership.

On the price side, the future course of prices can be affected by early attention to capacity needs, growing out of discussions as to potential bottlenecks which create shortages and price increases; by encouraging government programmes to enhance rather than restrict supply; by stimulation of investment and cost-reducing outlays; by attention to the interface of sectors in manufacturing, transportation and finance, and particularly by attention to governmental activities and regulations which create uncertainty and increase costs unnecessarily.

If incomes policies that explicitly restrain wages and prices are to operate, the central labour organisation is expected to exert significant influence on its constituent local and national unions. The federation level of union government in the United States has little interest, and no constitutional authority, to review negotiating proposals or settlements made by constituent or independent members. Management organisations are even more diffused. In the setting of the United States formal government controls with a tripartite board is a more likely course of development than the sort of structural changes required in the national levels of labour and management organisations to make an incomes policy based on these organisations at all administrable.

PROBLEMS OF RELATING THE OUTCOME OF COLLECTIVE BARGAINING TO THE NEEDS OF NATIONAL ECONOMIC AND EMPLOYMENT POLICIES : SOME VIEWS

Keijo Liinamaa[1]

One of the main purposes of this Conference is to consider the desirability of new forms of collective bargaining as a contribution to non-inflationary medium-term growth. The starting point for the discussion is "that an activity like collective bargaining has such an enormous influence – directly or indirectly – on all parts of the economy that a responsible government intent on securing full employment and price stability must ensure that the outcome of collective bargaining is in accord with its other economic and social objectives" (Blyth in this volume,p. 61). The principles adopted are "that the challenge to governments and collective bargainers is to find ways to get co-ordination of the results of collective bargaining with government aims and at the same time preserve the essential features of free collective bargaining".

In Finland, successive governments and collective bargainers have been co-operating to the best of their ability for over ten years, acting on the starting point and principles quoted above. Organised co-operation began under the difficult conditions following the devaluation of the Finnmark in 1967. The 33 per cent devaluation called for strong and unprecedented measures to prevent inflation. The aim was to preserve the competitive export advantage provided by the devaluation so as to improve employment. To attain these targets a Stabilization Agreement was concluded in March 1968 and in autumn 1969 it was extended to the end of 1970. This agreement is described in Dr. Addison's Report (Addison, 1979).

My own personal experience with Finnish incomes policy is not generalisable. It relates to co-operation between the government, labour-market organisations and other economic interest groups in a small national economy sensitive to external disturbances. The political arena includes two left-wing parties that are a force to be reckoned with when they are both in the government. Traditionally these parties have close ties with the biggest trade union confederation. The powerful political centre is intimately connected with a strong agricultural producers' organisation and partly, too, with industry. In addition, there is a strong right wing that has been in opposition and is closely linked with industry and the employers' organisation.

Several central organisations influence the outcome of collective bargaining and all of them insist on making themselves heard at negotiations. For this reason by no means all income policy agreements made in Finland have been justified by considerations of employment and price stability.

---

1. Secretary-General, Ministry of Labour, Finland.

Some of them have simply been compromises made to keep the peace.

The principle of free collective bargaining is a traditional feature of the Finnish labour market. It is vigorously upheld by the employees' organisations and left-wing parties. But full freedom of bargaining has been limited on two occasions in the past ten years. The Stabilisation Agreement of 1968 included a concession empowering the government to control wages and salaries: a Price and Pay Council was set up on which the labour-market organisations were represented. The pay controls did not have to be applied because the central organisations took care to see that their members kept the agreements. Thus the limitation proved to be only a threat, but even so it served its purpose.

The second occasion was in December 1977, when the government was once again empowered to control pay as well as prices. In this case the government's powers were restricted to the changes that the most powerful bargaining partners consented to make to the current two-year collective agreements. Another limitation was that the government's powers related only to the timing of the pay increases, not their size. In the event, the powers were granted after the majority of the most representative central organisations had agreed to postpone the pay rises to a later time. What the government then decided was to extend the same postponements to the agreements made earlier by the other organisations.

These two examples show that limited deviations from the principle of free bargaining are possible if they are backed by an adequate majority among the collective bargainers.

Naturally the responsibility for national economic policy lies with a country's government and parliament, which enjoy considerable power in matters of economic policy. The extent to which this power is used depends on the majority available for the decisions involved, either in the government or in parliament, or both. And this depends on political power ratios, which vary from country to country. The greater the number of political parties involved in the decision making, however, the more difficult it is to reach the decisions.

But economic power at a national level is exercised by other bodies besides parliament and the government. Apart from the collective bargainers, big industrial and commercial organisations exert influence on economic decision-making both with their own member-companies and as a pressure group acting on the government. Neither should we forget the power of the agricultural producers' organisations, which affects prices of staple foods. Economic power is also exercised by banks and other financial establishments, which not only decide on investments affecting employment but even influence the structure of the investments.

All these examples serve to emphasise that, although collective bargaining is a major factor affecting economic policy, making it responsive to the needs of the economy and employment will not eliminate all the shortcomings. From experience I know how difficult it is to get employees' organisations to limit their discussions to matters on which they themselves can decide — i.e. collective agreements — and to matters the government can decide. They wish to influence the incomes of other groups. This makes consensus difficult, though not impossible.

Full employment and stable economic growth are the approved and rational targets of national economic policy. And there can be no doubt that all decision-makers with any say in the development of the economy are ready to co-operate to achieve these ends; at any rate, publicly. In practice this often means they are ready to co-operate with other decision-makers to secure the best possible result for their own supporters. It seems as if there is always some election ahead, or behind, to leave its mark on negotiations that were intended to achieve an economically sound agreement. My own experience is that only in a very few cases is the national interest paramount.

To co-ordinate the economic policy decisions of the different bodies, agreement must be sought — unless the government has binding powers to say how things should be done. Here I would point out two procedures I regard as essential. First, the state of the country's economy must be analysed as accurately as possible. Secondly, a good relationship based on mutual trust must be created and sustained between the parties to the negotiations.

Experience has shown the need to prepare an analysis of the country's economic state as a background for the negotiations. This analysis must include at least the following:

- A review of the past period — e.g. the period of the last collective agreements. How do results compare with expectations? How have the incomes of different groups developed? Have prices deviated from the targets, etc.?
- Prognoses in broad outline of economic development during the period to be covered by the next agreements — and further ahead if possible — and of means of altering the trends if necessary.
- Recommendations on the main economic policy targets for the coming period and the means of achieving them.

The analysis must be credible to the bargainers. Only a believable analysis will have any effect on the outcome of the negotiations. I have had favourable experience with a procedure by which an analysis of this kind is prepared by a joint study group of the government and economic organisations. Its members are economists. The aim is to provide indisputable data on as many points as possible. Another purpose is to map out areas of disagreements and their reasons. In Finland this technique has eliminated many points of dispute that would otherwise have arisen at the bargaining table. The joint study group has also contributed notably to developing the content and methodology of the analyses.

This raises the question: to what extent do indisputable analyses influence the final terms of the agreements themselves? Agreement policy can never be reduced to mathematics. The outcome is always affected by other factors such as those I mentioned earlier, so the optimum result is seldom achieved however clearly it is indicated by the economic analysis. Obviously a coalition government, such as Finland's, must formulate its targets basing on the economic realities and party-political goals on which it has been able to reach internal agreement. On the other side the economic interest groups start out from the demands of their members and their own organisational targets, which they revise in the light of current feasibility.

The decisive factor is the extent to which the decision-makers are willing to dovetail their own targets with those of others. For all that, I am convinced that joint analyses modify decisions in an economically desirable direction more than would occur otherwise.

Apart from joint economic analyses, the amenability of the decision-makers is affected by confidential and continuous relations between negotiating partners. Such relations cannot be created by fiat. Formal negotiations are easy to arrange, but all they produce is a reiteration of standpoints already proclaimed in public. Results depend on a degree of communication in which responsible leaders in the government and interest groups can sit down together and discuss alternative solutions, their effect on the national economy and their bearing on the targets of all the parties concerned — and can do so regardless of earlier public pronouncements. Such a relationship calls for trust between the negotiating partners. They must be ready to discuss the alternatives, however disagreeable these may be in relation to their own targets. And there must be a clear understanding that such readiness for discussion will not be interpreted by the other side as a relinquishment of their targets. Final stands will be taken only after all the factors affecting the issue are visible.

One condition for such a framework for discussion is that the negotiations are centralised: between the government's representatives and the heads of the central organisations. I can see no rational alternative to this procedure though I know from experience that centralised bargaining raises many problems. For example, it can create difficulties between the government and parliament, because the government is unable to inform parliament adequately of the issues involved that call for a parliamentary decision.

It can also lead to conflict between central organisations and their member organisations or individual members. Centralised agreements are usually rather general in content — apart from detailed provision on pay. This often prevents member organisations from agreeing on specific points relating to their own sector however necessary this may be. Even greater difficulties arise at a company level: local problems sometimes remain unresolved for years on end, and in time they erupt into legal or illegal strikes at a company or local level. Or else they lead to wage drift. Growing differentials due to the wage drift then create discord between different categories of employees.

Can the system of centralised agreements be continued over a period of years without a break? This is a question I have had to ask myself and others. In Finland centralised agreements have produced their best results in slowing down inflation and coping with deep depressions. There is no clear indication that they have done anything to improve employment. Agreements made during booms have been unable to slow down the rise of pay, prices, etc. Matters have got out of hand owing to labour shortages, and the general "overheating". In view of this experience, I am inclined to think that it is not worth insisting on centralised agreements during cyclic rises and booms. But when the cycle turns down, centralised agreements can be used to reduce the residual pressure on pay and prices remaining from the boom.

This leads on to the question of counter-cyclical pay policy – an idea I wholeheartedly approve of: scrape off the top of the boom to fill in the hole of the recession. The idea should be extended to other aspects of the economy. To ensure a smooth growth the public sector – State and local authorities – should refrain from heavy investments during a boom and shift the investments to the following recession. This is not easy in a multi-party system. At times when the State's coffers are full, when the need for reforms and construction projects is evident and greater political support is desired, parties throw their weight behind spending. This leaves no reserves for hard times.

A similar problem arises in company management. The demand for goods and services grows during the boom. Production capacities are fully utilised – often they prove insufficient. So companies try to squeeze the last drop from the boom. In such a situation firms tend to make even non-productive investments, merely to reduce their taxable income. It takes a strong-willed company management to refrain from spending and leave a reserve for the recession.

If the government has not built up a reserve, it will be unable to continue the social reforms begun during the boom when the cycle turns down. Neither will it be able to reduce employees' taxes so as to preserve their purchasing power. If companies have not built up reserves during the good times, they will be unable to give the pay rises required for the counter-cyclical pay policy during the recession. So I regard counter-cyclical pay policy merely as part of counter-cyclical policy as a whole. I do not believe it will succeed unless the same principle is extended to every aspect of the national economy. But steady growth is so important for employment that long-term efforts are worth making to ensure it.

Counter-cyclical pay policy seems to require collective agreements lasting more than one or two years. In a small national economy prone to outside disturbances, like Finland's, long-term collective agreements require some provision for adjustment in the case of need. This can take the form either of indexation or review clauses calling for fresh negotiations. In Finland we have tried out nearly all the alternatives, and our experience is not encouraging. The problem with indexation is that it easily spreads to other sectors of society. Everything has to be indexed to everything else. This creates a self-perpetuating inflationary cycle and any sharp fluctuation of world-market prices triggers off a fresh bout of inflation. The problem with review clauses seems to be the difficulty of agreeing whether the changes in the cost of living are enough to justify fresh negotiations. Further development of the counter-cyclical pay policy will largely depend on improving the procedures for making long-term agreements.

In this contribution I have touched on certain problems that arise in collective bargaining in my own country. Despite the difficulties, the failures and the disappointments, all the interested parties in Finland – the government, labour-market organisations and other economic organisations – have shown themselves to be ready time and time again to sit down and seek a consensus. My own view is that the closer the decision-makers keep in touch, the more credible the economic analyses are; and the better they are used as a basis for the bargaining, the greater the chances are of reaching a consensus.

TRADE-OFFS AND POLITICISATION

Bram Peper[1]

Introduction

From the many reports on the social and economic situation in the OECD countries which have been published recently − including those of the OECD itself − the picture that appears is clearly one of virtual stagnation. Its causes are for the most part well known. Throughout the world, governments are still trying to deal with the consequences of the oil crisis. But even without this crisis it is possible that our countries would have experienced diminishing economic growth, decrease in world trade and a demand crisis, to mention only a few problems.

The ideological link between economic growth and the welfare state had already lost a fair amount of its credibility as a matter of course at the end of the sixties − and for some countries at the beginning of the seventies. Especially the younger generation, which had grown up in economic security, started already in 1966 to criticise the societal order; an order which suffered generally from what could be called a crisis of meaning and purpose. The increasing number of articles and books about the crisis in the welfare state, certainly not written only by progressive radicals, did show a fair amount of concern about the course that western − western for the purpose of this paper including the OECD nations of the Pacific region − societies had taken. However, although socio-economic problems are quite considerable, for most of us economic existence is safely guaranteed; if not by earning wages, then through social security. The remarkable effect that emerges is that a decrease in the rate of economic growth has been experienced as a decline in the standard of living.

The logical answer would appear to be for all groups to moderate their income demands, with the understanding that those who are, economically speaking, relatively strong, should carry a larger share of the burden than the weaker groups. This way to attack the problems is being disregarded: again on the basis of the traditional thinking that only economic growth can solve the problems of demand and unemployment. However, the fact that the governments of various OECD countries have appealed to unions and employers to make a combined attack on demand stagnation, inflation and unemployment, makes it clear that the problem concerned is more societal than economic.

It is very questionable whether the sustained economic growth approach is the right path to take. This panacea from the past, which has been of incalculable significance for the economic and social emancipation of the masses, may well have lost its usefulness for the problems which western nations are facing now. One does not have to be a pessimist by nature to recognise the limitations of pursuing continued economic growth in its

---

1. Professor, Social Economic Policy, Erasmus University, Rotterdam, Netherlands.

relation to, for instance, the problems of poverty in the third world, together with the world-wide problems of energy and scarcity of raw materials.

With due respect and sympathy for the endeavours of the governments of the OECD countries — and of the OECD itself — to curb inflation and unemployment and emerge from stagflation, they have not so far produced more (in the context of the subject of this Conference) than an appeal to unions and employers to pursue wherever possible socially responsible wage and counter-inflationary policies in co-operation with national governments. In some countries this approach has been fairly successful; in others hardly any progress has been made. It is evident — apart from strictly external economic factors (e.g. the oil crisis) — that because of the institutional inertia of industrial relations systems, the problems have been aggravated. By this is meant that since the oil crisis the social partners have continued to act to a great extent on the premises and habits relevant to, and built up over, the days of continuous economic growth. Economic realities have however, forced them, after a few years, to moderate their expectations. How long institutional indolence can go on has been demonstrated by the British example. There, relative economic decline set in years before the oil crisis, yet it was only in 1974 that government, unions and employers arrived at a co-ordinated policy of restraint.

If one feels that the problems with which western countries are confronted are of more than a short-term character, and if one holds the view that it takes economic realities to open the eyes of the social partners and governments, then every single "socially responsible policy" in the sense in which OECD has used this term, is doomed to fail. Because, without a considerable central guidance of their economies our countries will not succeed in righting the structural imbalances which characterise our social systems.

Without underestimating the significance of a price policy (in respect to the employers) and of a wage policy (for the employees), one cannot but conclude that the decidedly modest success of these policies has to be attributed to the limited influence that national governments have or are willing to have on the demand and supply markets of commodities and services. Each of the social partners — be it government, employers, or employees and their organisations — can point to a number of important economic policy spheres which are largely beyond their control. Employers will mention wages, labour can point to investments, and governments to price-setting, wages and technological innovation, just to give a few examples.

Those introductory remarks were not made with the pretension that they import a greater wisdom than what is written in other contributions to this conference, but to warn against conducting illusory policies. A review of the countries that have made an effort to develop a socially responsible wage and anti-inflation policy suggests that either economic reality has forced the social partners — with or without government involvement — into adopting moderate attitudes or an already existing social infrastructure of consultation and co-ordination has led to a better tuning of policies between government and the social partners.

Taking into account the great variety of opinions and differences in the historical backgrounds of the systems of industrial relations in the different countries, it is extremely pretentious to suggest policy recommendations on the basis of past experience. Such recommendations tend to be developed in such general and unspecific terms that for this reason alone they are useless. Nobody will be happy with the commonplaces unless (hopefully) they serve the purpose of making discussion of the matters concerned more meaningful.

This contribution will try − from an economic and sociological point of view − to put forward a number of principles and facts concerning operative social and economic policies. Should these remarks sometimes bear an analytical character, then one can hope that analysis is to be preferred above policy recommendations in which successful efforts in one country are shown as an example to other countries. One does not deny that countries can "learn" from each other, but it must be stressed that the delicacy and the very nature of industrial relations in each country call for great care in "transplanting" institutions and ideas.

The rest of this paper takes the following form. In most OECD countries governments are striving to attack social and economic problems, directly or indirectly taking into consideration the wishes and expectations of employers and unions. By a kind of exchange of measures the government tries to make the partners more sensitive to problems of national economic importance which it is desirable for employers and unions to take into account while they are bargaining. These so-called "trade-offs" are not new phenomena, but appear to have existed in the past under exceptional circumstances (next section). Moreover, it is worth paying attention to the fact that in our type of society, in principle interest groups have both freedom and opportunity to articulate and strive to satisfy their own interests. The relationships have implications for their attitudes towards, and possibilities of, influencing the social and economic policies of the political system (the government). It is possible − very roughly − to develop three models in which the relationship between interest groups and the political system can be represented in outline. In this context it is possible to see the "trade-off" as a form of politicisation, than can be stimulated as well by the government as by the social partners. Further, the question arises whether the "trade-offs" in their different forms can be considered as a continuing or a temporary phenomenon in the near future. Are there factors of lasting character which make it worthwhile to pay attention to this phenomenon, theoretically as well as practically ? And finally, some concluding remarks are made.

Trade-offs : A New Phenomenon?

The intensification of discussion in recent years on the phenomenon of trade-offs − equally in publications as in practical, political activities − could easily lead to the conclusion that we deal here with an entirely new development. Nothing is less true. In the past there were periods in which governments, together with interest groups, were establishing and carrying through common policies.

In the most extreme form we have trade-offs in wartime and similarly calamitous situations. During the economic crisis in the thirties one can find many examples of government intervention and the beginning of co-operation between government and social partners. In the Second World War

141

social and economic developments were completely dominated by governments. In such times of scarcity and national efforts, government directs the societal system – to a great extent with or without the consent of interest groups. In such circumstances the position of the government is – from the viewpoint of legitimacy – normally undisputed. To a less extreme extent, government predominance continued after the war in all OECD countries, for a longer or shorter period. In order to rebuild economy and society many governments appealed to the population, including the social partners, to work together to rebuild the country and to pay less attention to their own sectional interests. During a long period after the war, the population was prepared to exercise considerable restraint on all fronts in respect of making demands. There was a great readiness to submit to a tight economic regime. Through this attitude, among other factors, the foundations were laid for the economic recovery accomplished in the fifties. From that time on, in nearly all the countries, the real free bargaining process was re-established. The government kept a greater distance.

To the above-mentioned, rather extreme situations, many countries owe both more or less institutionalised forms of co-operation or concerted action, and social-economic legislation. These extreme situations show that the social partners in these circumstances were willing and forced to submit to the central guidance of the government. But at the same time it becomes clear that trade-offs which are more than voluntary arrangements are only acceptable in exceptional circumstances. From this we can conclude easily that the more pessimistically we evaluate the present situation, the more likely it will seem that non-voluntary pressures will make for arrangements, necessitating trade-offs. In spite of all the gloomy statements commonly being made there is no impression that the present economic situation is yet considered to be extremely critical. One can therefore conclude that not too much faith should be placed in the effectiveness of the "socially responsible policies".

It might be thought, comparing the present with the past, that there are sufficiently few clear differences to note that it should be relatively easy to derive some comprehensive forecasts from the past experience. Undeniably there are considerable differences over time. For one thing, there is the gigantic and rapid growth of the public (government) sector in the social system (economy). Furthermore one can point to the increasing mutual dependence of the public and private sectors, the improved understanding of the economic process and the more adequate instruments available to influence that process. In spite of this, successful trade-offs, in terms of (inter)national goals, are completely dependent on the willingness of the social partners to engage in them voluntarily. This is the inevitable conclusion one has to draw after reading the national studies made for the OECD. Now we turn to the relationship between interest groups and the political system, and the power of the latter.

Interest Groups and the Power of the Political System

It is understandable that several OECD reports point out that trade-offs can only be realised or succeed if the social partners enter into them willing-

ly. That is both a matter of principle and of pragmatism. The principle is –
to put it simply – that in western societies people and groups are free to
express their opinions; that they are free to associate in interest or pressure
groups. The recognition of this right implies a political philosophy in which
the State, parliament or congress, shares power with other elements in
society.

In all possible sectors of society, private persons and institutions take
part in all kinds of activities. The feasibility of the government influencing
the course of events is rather restricted in many fields of society. Only by
persuasions and consultation and not by force or coercion, can government
keep interest groups on the track which it thinks desirable. Clearly this sharing of power calls for caution when parties or groups call on government to
take stronger measures. Although almost every interest group recognises –
formally and informally – the responsibility of the government for overall
(social-economic) policies, and for their co-ordination and consistency, all
this has to be done in a society where the government often has hardly
enough margin of discretion (power) to pursue firm policies. A wide gap
exists between political theory and political practice. The gap is even further
widened by the fact that interest groups – one by one – call upon the State
to take measures they wish to see adopted. By doing this they strengthen the
fiction of political theory that the government not only has the competence
to take measures but also has the power to put them through.

There are two more circumstances that bring the power of government
into question, no matter how one may think about that power normatively.
First to be mentioned is the fact that when the growth of the public sector
is considered as an indicator of increasing governmental power, it has to be
realised that a great part of the "public" activities are executed by the
private sector. There is an enormous intermingling of private and public
interests, described by Galbraith (1974) as "the bureaucratic symbiosis".

It can be put this way: in practice government and parliament can be
seen as a complex entity of different particular interests, which in one way
or another are related to the interests in the private sector. Against this
background it is difficult to define the substance and boundaries of the
general public interest the government is supposed to serve. Especially in a
societal system with sufficient freedom to encompass a wide variety of
opinions, people tend to disagree – though they may bury their disagreement during crises – as to what the general interest should comprise.

Secondly, one observes that since the war the number of interest groups
has grown strongly. This means that the pressure on the co-ordinating ability
of the political system has increased even more. There is now a strong
impression that the independent power of the government has not grown
in proportion to the display of power outside the sphere of government. If
this impression is correct, high expectations of the guiding power of governments have to be abandoned.

A democracy of interest groups has arisen which makes it extremely
difficult for any government to exercise some forms of control. There is no
other way left for government in its relationships with interest groups
(assuming that they perform essential functions and so have power) than
persuading and consulting. This road is not only preferable from a demo-

cratic viewpoint: the choice of this road — again and again underlined in different OECD publications — is prompted by principle as well as by practical considerations (maybe even more by the latter).

It is possible — very roughly — to distinguish a triad of models to classify the forms of relations between the political system and the (most important) interest groups. As mentioned earlier, every government (no matter how strong or weak) will be confronted by interest groups in conducting its policy. If those interest groups have sufficient power, government will try to enter into an arrangement with them. This enlarges the possibility of government control — mostly indirect, through the channels of authority of those groups — and increases the predictability of its policy.

To the extent to which government (the political system) can enforce the conditions for, and the content of, co-operation in relationships with interest groups, we can distinguish societal systems in which:

a) the primacy of the political system dominates *(political model);*
b) the political system and the interest groups try to accommodate in some more or less institutionalised form *(accommodation model);*
c) the political system tries — in competition with interest groups — to obtain the primacy *(competition model).*

It is evident that from the viewpoint of the interest groups there is hardly any autonomy in the political model, whereas in the competition model autonomy is quite considerable.

The political model

In this model interest groups — if present or permitted to exist at all — take a subordinate position in the political system, both theoretically and in practice. They perform their tasks in co-operation with and subsidiary to what have been formulated as the goals of the political system. Those tasks have been assigned to them: in their performance they are very much dependent on the instructions imposed by the political system. In such a system only a restricted number of interest groups is authorised. The freedom to organise as interest groups and for such groups to present themselves under this title to the government as a partner, is limited or completely absent. A prerequisite for the functioning of the system is the presence of a considerable measure of consensus as to the objectives of society. In this context it does not matter how this consensus comes into existence; nor even whether it really exists. Consensus is at least postulated and the political authority has at its disposal the means of power to demand or to impose unity. Examples of such systems are to be found in the communist world, while the corporatist systems which up to some years ago were to be found in Spain and Portugal can be regarded as a capitalistic form of the political model.

The accommodation model

In this model the position of the political system is much weaker. It is, so to say, together with the large interest organisations (employers, employees,

144

church, science, etc.) one of the factors in the societal power structure. Each interest group has, apart from its societal significance, the right to intervene in the societal conflict. The heart of the system is the endeavour to come to decision-making by way of a complicated system of consultation and bargaining. Because of the dependence of the government on the approval of the interest groups, government is eager to consult those groups in an early stage of (preparation of) decision-making. If possible and feasible those groups are assigned a clearly specified role in this process. The reason for such an approach lies in the expectation that if interest groups are involved in the policy making process in an early stage they can exercise the necessary influence and consequently will give their co-operation in implementing the governmental measures as a result of their combined efforts. One comes across this system in most of the OECD countries with, maybe, particularly clear examples in Germany, the Netherlands, Norway and Sweden.

The competition model

This model can be considered as a special variant of the accommodation model. In this system, which is very much comparable with a market where the different interest groups compete for the best position on the market, the interest groups are involved in a less organised and institutionalised way. They rarely have a role in the preparation of political decision-making. It is characterised − as distinct from the accommodation model − by the existence of relatively few consultative institutions. The interest groups do not accept − at least formally − any responsibility for the contents and outcome of the political decision-making process, which they nevertheless try to influence in all possible ways. They are much more independent of the political system. Naturally, governments do take into account the views of the interest groups. But in the strict political sense governments have to make more efforts to legitimise themselves. Their own field of responsibility is therefore more clearly defined than is the case in the other models (an example is the United States).

It is evident that in the OECD countries the competition and accommodation models are dominant. Within which model a "socially responsible policy" is best realised is not a matter of free choice by the respective governments. But there is reason to suppose that in a policy-making process in which − for whatever reason − graduality is wanted, the accommodation model offers the best opportunities. If, however, very severe measures are required which might have a greater impact on the position and function of interest groups, then it becomes necessary to clarify political and other responsibilities. In that case the competition model presents itself as the best way in which possible trade-offs can develop. It is in this context that the phenomenon of the social contract comes up. It is an interesting fact that in countries with a structure of the accommodation type, signs of erosion can be discerned when there arise strong differences in the judgement on how social-economic problems are to be solved (e.g. the Netherlands, Sweden). Often this is connected with a change in the "colour" of the governement: from social-democratic to conservative, for example.

The models that are marked out here are after all points on a continuum with the criterion: *the degree of consensus on social and economic policy for the medium and long term.*

Trade-Offs as a Form of Politicisation

It is possible, as attempted in this paper, to draw a picture of the power position of the government as being strongly dependent on the position of the social partners. Of course, that does not mean that government behaviour does not have its impact on the social and economic policies followed. There will be an effect not only through the government's incomes and expenditures, which are in large part rigidly defined, but also because whatever measures are taken a certain amount of discontent on the part of some of the interest groups will almost always be experienced. To limit the case to the field of industrial relations: given the fact that employers and employees have basic areas in which they are in opposition to each other (differences in interests), it is hardly possible for any government to satisfy both parties simultaneously. There will always be a feeling of being hurt more (or having benefited less) by the government measures on the part of one party compared with the other.

The increasing interdependence of the behaviour of unions and employers and the government's behaviour — all mass organisations — makes it unavoidable that each experiences the consequences of the others' behaviour. That makes quite a difference from the past, when, broadly speaking, the parties involved were smaller in size, more numerous, more independent of each other and more competitive. In that sense, tendencies in the direction of trade-offs can be considered as a permanent phenomenon.

However, trade-offs can also be looked upon as a process of politicisation of industrial relations. Politicisation can be defined here as the process whereby in the bargaining process between employers and employees about wages and working conditions, the total (social and economic) policy of the government is taken into consideration by these groups.

There are two sources from which this politicisation can be fed. In the first place — of course — by such measures of the government that employers and unions are forced to take them into account. The most obvious examples are measures in the sphere of taxes and prices which directly affect the purchasing power of the employee and the competitive position of the employer. Their effects on the bargaining process are well known. They become problematic and to a large extent questionable in a situation of economic uncertainty and gloomy economic perspectives. Some countries have tried to counter this with (for example) price indexation mechanisms. What makes politicisation so interesting — insofar as it may be introduced by the government — are those government measures which are hard for employers and employees to rate in money. Often those measures are only partly relevant to rank-and-file employers and workers, but call for solidarity with other groups in the national interest. Very much to the point we can read in Addison's (1979) report on Norway that, in a nutshell, the problem of the trade-off is "that it is difficult to ensure that those who are moderat-

146

ing their wage claims are satisfied with the distribution of benefits of government spending".

In this connection we can think of provisions in the fields of education, welfare, social security, health insurance etc. It is understandable that in the first place it has to be the government which – on account of the strong interrelationship between the scope of the public and private sectors – has to convince the parties of the (indirect) significance of this type of provision for the contents of the package of labour conditions. And at the same time it has to be pointed out that negotiations which make no or little allowances for those realities will in time lose a part of their significance in some other respect (inflation, unemployment, wrong investment).

Another, more important source of politicisation can be found in positions taken by employers and employees. This is more important, because it seems logical that the political system in principle has the responsibility of all sectors. This is not a new phenomenon for employers and employees. As, Flanders once very properly observed, "the term 'non-political union' (is) a nonsensical description; there is no such animal" (Flanders, 1970). This holds true both for employers and for labour organisations, although the latter are often more explicit in expressing their vision of society than the former. However, when the social partners broaden their views, more or less explicitly over the entire range of social and economic policy, then industrial relations are really politicised. Dependent on the scope and intensity of their viewpoints, the parties can then hardly avoid a dialogue with the government because of their involvement. Especially in the widening of positions taken – in some countries expressed in underwriting a specific societal vision (in programmes and actions) – lies the characterisation of the phenomenon of politicisation. To the degree in which:

a) the number of societal sectors and problems on which unions and employers express a viewpoint increase;

b) these viewpoints are expressed more officially in long-term (vision) programmes for the long term;

c) the broader societal orientation is taken more into account in the practical working of those organisations;

we can use the term of more politicised industrial relations.

Politicisation of Industrial Relations: A Permanent Phenomenon?

In the previous paragraph the phenomenon of the trade-offs was interpreted as a process of politicisation in which industrial relations became involved. It seems to me that to some extent we have to deal here with an irreversible process. It will become more difficult for the political system to shirk the responsibility – even a derived responsibility – for the outcome of more or less unobstructed negotiations by the social partners. And it is equally impossible for the social partners not to be affected by the consequences of government policy for the bargaining process and its results. This preoccupation with each other's policies can be noticed in almost all countries. It seems that politicisation and trade-offs have become one of the permanent characteristics of industrial relations in OECD countries.

But as far as it concerns future developments, the question of whether politicisation will grow stronger or weaker depends on expectations about the possibilities of a quick recovery of economic growth. If this possibility is regarded as likely to happen — for whatever reason — politicisation and trade-offs will not develop any further in substance and composition from those already known to us. The struggle for division of the economic surplus produced by economic growth will not differ much in character from the fights of the sixties and the seventies. However — and this seems much more likely — should economic growth such as our societies became accustomed to in the past not return, the possibility of zero growth may have to be seriously considered, difficult and gloomy as that prospect may seem. The possible factors leading to what might be called a stabilised economy will not be elaborated here: they are well known. It is nevertheless necessary to realise that under such circumstances drastic societal changes are likely.

There are no indications whatsoever that governments or countries' populations — accustomed as they are to the fruits of growth in nearly all aspects of their lives — have adjusted themselves to a different, more sober way of life. The shock caused by the oil crisis did not — for understandable reasons — last very long and has been superseded by a new orientation towards economic growth, albeit on a somewhat lower level than of old. Already when we consider the effects of this decline, there is not much imagination required to see that zero growth calls for a completely different attitude from governments and the social partners, and their rank-and-file members.

There are hardly any indications that governments or other bodies are ready or are preparing themselves for such a situation and they show little propensity to stimulate scientific research in this direction. Billions of dollars are poured into the arms race or into space projects; little has been spent so far on the development of scenarios for a stabilised economy. And at first sight there is not that much difference between a growth of three or four per cent and zero growth. Nor, as the British example shows, are we talking about a completely imaginary situation.

It is evident that with zero growth several problems will arise. Some of them are: a sharp rise in unemployment, meaning that sharing the amount of available work will become a central problem; a stabilization, and in some cases a certain decrease, in real income; the necessity of a powerful incomes policy, because distribution can no longer be derived from growth but has to come from existing total income.

These are only a few of the immense problems which have to be solved. Because governments, as yet, have neither the power nor the authority to tackle those tasks, the danger exists that the political system will be put under heavy aggregated pressure by interest groups. Although not eager to play the role of a Cassandra, this seems likely to be one of the greatest threats for parliamentary democracy in the future. Governments and democratic organisations which do not want to face up to these problems, and to discuss them publicly, only increase the dangers outlined here.

It is impossible to avoid thinking about, and making a start with, a redistribution policy, combined with striving for greater awareness of the problem. In this respect one cannot value the dogma of a mixed economy other than as a smokescreen that is being used to legitimate what in essence, as far as the problems under review are concerned, is nothing more than *laissez faire* politics. As yet the willingness to take the road described is not strong. This is the more remarkable when one takes into account the fact that several multinational enterprises − by way of scenario painting − are already designing alternative models of economic development.

Concluding Remarks

In Blyth's report (p. 87) an excellent summary is given of the possibilities which governments have at their disposal, or have applied, to arrive at a socially responsible economic policy. There are few further suggestions to add to that. It is for this reason that the present contribution has tried to draw attention to some problems which might arise when, contrary to expectation, the goal of economic growth will not be reached. Especially for the OECD, it can be very fruitful to combine the respectable aim of economic growth with thinking about the implications of a stabilised economy. With due respect to the more "technical" policy propositions in the different OECD publications, whether they may work in practice does not depend so much on their degree of technical sophistication (which is rather high!) but on the willingness of important groups in society, with governments in the first place, to appreciate the gravity of the problems. If the problems in the present paper have been slightly more heavily weighted than usual, it was only to point to the need to be prepared for situations which nobody wishes to happen, but are certainly not entirely illusory. Besides, it is very well realised that this contribution is intended more as a signal than as postulating a final solution. A socially responsible policy would be defined too narrowly if it were only to cover indications and propositions dependent on the willingness of governments and social partners to implement them. This willingness rests solely on the definition and perception of the problem. The conception is that the gravity of the situation is greater than is usually assumed. In this, an important starting point can be found for the design of an alternative, not less socially responsible policy.

149

COMMENT ON PEPER'S PAPER

Tiziano Treu[1]

Basically I agree with the general assumptions of Peper's report. The report appropriately emphasises the difficulties so far experienced by most OECD countries in their efforts to induce collective bargainers to follow socially responsible policies. I also share his view that the gravity of the situation is greater than is usually assumed and that uncontrolled pressures coming from the most important interest groups, or from excluded groups, will present a most serious challenge to the stability and to the very essence of our political systems in the years to come. However, his analysis deserves some further development. It is widely agreed that no solution to these problems can be found by increasing direct state intervention affecting the behaviour of employers and unions through statutory policies. All attempts in this direction have proved unsatisfactory and untenable in the long run, due to the very nature of the pressures which had to be controlled.

On the other hand the situations referred to by Peper, in particular that of post-war reconstruction, where the social partners achieved almost *a priori* consensus on the main objectives of society are not likely to recur, and in many countries such degrees of consensus may not be easy to achieve again. The politicisation of trade unions and of employers' associations is certainly a desirable process which may have a stabilising effect on industrial relations, particularly because the proposition of long-term (i.e. political) objectives is essential to induce moderation in immediate claims. But the signs of growing pragmatism and adaptability shown by many trade unions *vis-à-vis* the present economic difficulties do not necessarily imply that they are willing to abandon their ultimate aims and accept *a priori* a solidary or consensual conception of society. The experience of most OECD countries shows that this consensus can only be won on a case - by - case basis and not simply by way of "persuasion", as euphemistically indicated in Blyth's paper in this volume, or by mere appeals to unions' and employers' sense of responsibility. Voluntary "guidelines", state-oriented mediation in industrial disputes, legal frameworks and institutions for an exchange of views about the condition of the economy also seem to be too weak devices, due to the growing strength of interest groups *vis-à-vis* the State (i.e. the political and economic institutions representing the public powers) and to the deeply rooted or renewed forms of political radicalisation in the labour movement.

More specifically, consensus by the various groups depends on their obtaining, through a process of political negotiation with each other and with the State, precise and frequent material concessions profitable to the hierarchy and/or the components of the groups. This process is a real form

---

1. Professor, University of Pavia, Italy.

of negotiation, even though the word "negotiation" is usually avoided as being inappropriate and incompatible with the essence of parliamentary democracy. For the State in particular, the process of "trade-off" has become more than a question of choice; it has become a compulsory solution. Such a situation can hardly be defined as corporatism if we assume that a basic characteristic of corporatism is that it is founded on cooperative effort by the groups rather than being a competitive process. The need to win consensus from the groups through material concessions keeps the system in an intermediate position between (temporary) cooperation and open conflict, or following Peper's report, between social models *b* and *c*. (See the arguments and evaluation of a number of European experiences by Crouch, 1978, p. 199). The notion of "tripartite bargaining", also often used, can be acceptable only if the qualification derived from the parties involved does not conceal the competitive and conflictual nature of the process. I believe it is analytically misleading and politically ambiguous to obscure this nature, if only because the matter of negotiation involves and impinges on government policies; also it seems hardly enlightening to re-affirm uncritically the idea of government and public institutions as *super partes* entities, not involved in social conflict and representing *a priori* a mythical general interest.

A major implication of these assumptions should be stressed more than appears in Peper's report, i.e. that the stability of both the political and industrial relations systems depends on the quantity and quality of the resources available to the State for trade-off purposes, on their relevance to the members of the groups and on their certainty to acquire them. The experience of various countries shows that most of the measures so far adopted or favoured by the State to win consensus, particularly from the unions, are monetary (indexation of wages, welfare and social security benefits etc.) and are directed mainly at fostering private or social consumption (to a greater extent the former) at the expense of capital accumulation and economic growth. This policy, which is often encouraged or approved of by both unions and employers, is considered as having a most negative influence on economic growth, full employment and inflation. It therefore creates a vicious circle by reducing the real resources to be exchanged in future trade-offs and by restricting the protected area of the work force (regular productive workers) at the expense of the unprotected (young people, peripheral workers, women). Both these consequences have in turn destabilizing effects on the political and social system (Italy being only an extreme case.).

It is hardly conceivable that political trade-offs can function effectively below a certain minimum level of economic growth. Peper's hypothesis that zero growth, or the awareness of its possibility, can induce more political moderation on the part of unions and employers, and therefore favour social peace, does not appear persuasive. However, it can be agreed that the minimum level of growth may be lower in the future than that which has been expected so far and that the social partners have to adapt to it.

The State is faced with the problem of finding a new, more balanced set of measures that will satisfy the two conflicting needs of sustaining production and maintaining expenditure on social services in favour of larger sectors of the population. Such an optimisation between social and economic policies is obviously an immense problem, which cannot be solved solely or primarily by institutional devices and procedures, as some Conference reports seem to believe — particularly if procedural restraints are to be imposed only on collective bargaining. Some political analysis in fact suggests that this is the major contradiction of advanced capitalism and of the Welfare State, a contradiction which could be overcome only through deep changes in the very economic and social structure of the capitalist system, in such a way to alter the basic mechanisms for allocating resources and governing production. Neither can the problem be solved in the same way in different countries by transplanting institutions and ideas, because it involves not only economic factors, which may be tendentially convergent, but also, or mainly, political and ideological systems and mass attitudes which are probably the most important factors distinguishing the various member countries. However, some common trends in policy not mentioned by Peper may well be possible and indeed important for trade-off purposes.

First of all, the State — instead of pursuing non-selective policies of income and wage restraints — should put a greater emphasis on redistribution of wealth and resources, particularly if a period of reduced economic growth is to be expected. Unfairness in income differentials, so far as it is perceived, is one of the major sources of social conflict. The struggle against this unfairness is also one of the most important trade union objectives, but experience teaches us that this objective cannot be achieved by mere wage demands and collective bargaining alone and requires State intervention (public expenditure, etc.). Some OECD Member governments have in fact tried to follow this policy, but with little or only temporary success. It is particularly difficult to meet the need for greater equity for workers generally without overly constraining the market and fostering inflationary pressures — further research is needed on this subject.

In the light of this the State should pay special attention to two lines of action: 1. it should be more responsible and consistent in its role as an employer, and 2. it should give equal emphasis to price and wage policies (so far more attention has been paid to the latter than to the former).

Secondly, the State should put a greater emphasis on problems relating to the quality of life and to the nature of economic growth, to security of employment and of income. Suitable measures for solving these problems can be found both at an institutional level and at the bargaining table between unions and employers. In some countries the parties have shown growing concern for this matter by enlarging the scope of bargaining to deal with problems such as organization of work, investments, labour mobility, and industrial restructuring. But while this scope of collective bargaining should be considered appropriate, contrary to tradition and conventional wisdom, it can hardly be self-sufficient. The experience of countries (like Italy) where the social parties' bargaining in this area has been most clearly a substitute for government inertia or delays confirms that it can be neither effective nor responsive in the absence of consistent and responsible public policies. This is clearly an area where public interventions need not be restrictive nor incompatible with collective bargaining freedom, but may essentially support and guide collective behaviours in various ways: through technical assistance to the bargainers, educational programmes, through active manpower policies and, in general, by providing the social parties with a coherent frame of reference of planned economic and industrial policy.

It should be stressed that these "qualitative" problems are not easily solved and should not be considered, as often happens, as distractions from the "quantitative" problems of growth or as symbolic and temporary concerns to compensate the rank-and-file for the unions' self-restraint in "traditional" economic bargaining. In fact, "qualitative" policies of this kind are necessary to face structural, non-transitory problems of modern society; they call for radical changes not only in social and private attitudes but also in the technical and social division of work, in the distribution of wealth and therefore in the power relations between classes and groups. Peper correctly emphasizes that the problems of sharing the amount of available work, and — maybe even more important — of distributing it differently during the lifetime of the population, will become crucial in any policy of full employment. It is not surprising that attempts to tackle these "qualitative" problems, mainly by pro-labour governments as a response to trade union pressures, have so far met with strong resistance from the employers.

Thirdly, as stated earlier, no trade-off process can avoid facing the problems of power and its distribution among different groups and classes. This explains the growing importance acquired in the last few years throughout the world by the issue of "participation" in its different forms: at the enterprise level by workers' representatives, at the territorial level by groups of citizens represented and organised in different ways, and at the national level by union and employers' representatives. In order to be of significance in trade-off processes, particularly *vis-à-vis* organised labour, participation must be something more than the right to be informed, to be consulted or even to co-determine in private or public tripartite bodies. These are necessary but insufficient initial steps towards achieving greater influence in decision-making, particularly decisions concerning social and economic affairs. Responsibility can only be asked and expected in measure related to the influence given. Today, many solutions and proposals as regards the participation of organised labour do not seem to go far enough. In fact, facing the issue of participation in its broader implications requires changes greater than usually assumed in the fields of production, distribution and consumption. It can even be questioned whether real participation is possible or sufficient in many institutions as they now function in these fields. Significantly enough the proposals advanced, particularly in the Scandinavian countries, and also the debate in some other European trade unions (France, Italy), go as far as to envisage gradual but radical modifications in the proprietal structure of production: e.g., through redistribution of ownership and profit from capital to labour. Modifications of this type might also be useful (and could be devised) to overcome the above-mentioned capitalistic contradiction due to diminishing resources available from economic growth. The shifting from traditional wage demands to such profit redistribution would still be a long-term process, certainly not easy to attain, if only because of the obvious power implications, but it would alter the very terms of the problems of capital accumulation and of decision-making with respect to economic growth. New solutions could be envisaged, although they have been less widely considered, in the field of social consumption, particularly in the organization of social services, in order, among other things, to counterbalance the growing burden of costly and inefficient bureaucracy.

Apart from such broad and clearly controversial perspectives, a proper solution to the issue of participation is somewhat prejudicial to achieving the above-mentioned objectives (redistribution of wealth, full employment, quality of life and of growth, etc.), since these objectives require a fairly large measure of involvement of the social partners in economic and social decisions. Moreover participation in national or centralised bodies is not enough; it must be decentralised to regional and enterprise levels.

Decentralised participation is not only necessary as a matter of principle — no democratic process can be experienced solely at the top — but it is also an essential pragmatic counterbalance to the centralisation which generally goes along with trade-offs and with closer relations between the State and interest groups. Centralisation of trade-offs has in itself a defect, in so far as it reduces the power and benefits of the decentralised constituents of the organisations and of their leaderships, causing tension within the organisations and impairing their capacity to live up to the commitments undertaken centrally. These tensions are particularly dangerous because they tend to combine with other possible dissatisfactions of the rank-and-file connected with political trade-offs (especially because trade-offs offer them future benefits beyond their control in exchange for immediate and certain sacrifices). If the gap between long- and short-term benefits is too great, instead of being an instrument of stabilisation, it becomes a factor of instability. See the comparative and theoretical analysis by Pizzorno (1978), p. 285. The reaction of the rank-and-file to this gap has been negatively experienced by the unions in countries with a social contract in force.

On the other hand, the vexed question of responsibility and control within employers' organisations and unions cannot, it seems, be solved using statutory sanctions or other restrictives measures while relying on trade-offs to persuade the same organisations at a central level to follow an agreed-upon line of conduct. Sanctions or restrictive measures may, on the contrary, be counterproductive. Neither can the acquiescence of the rank-and-file in centrally decided policies be achieved by mere appeals to ideological and political loyalties, except in short periods of extreme crisis, calling for intense collective solidarity.

Once again, consensus from the whole organisation, rank-and-file and apparatus, can only be won at the price of concessions granted from the centre to periphery, including non-monetary benefits, such as effective participation in decision-making on matters relevant to the interest of the constituents. Effective participation at the enterprise level is particularly important for the trade unions, since this level is crucial for obtaining benefits both for the rank-and-file and for their first-level leaders, who are the most severely deprived from a point of view of status and function, as a consequence of centralised processes of trade-off.

The experience of West Germany may be of particular significance in this respect. The long and highly institutionalised use of co-determination at the enterprise and plant level, together with lasting economic prosperity, have contributed to a large extent to stabilising industrial relations from the base upwards and to sustaining, in more general terms, non-conflictual relations between the unions and the State. This is not to suggest that the West German solution can be exported: in fact, it has been criticised by some other European trade union movements that have different histories, political attitudes and a more strongly established bargaining presence at the enterprise level. The choice of the representative organs of participation, for instance, is particularly controversial (and important) also from a point of view of trade-offs; the "dual channel" formula used by West Germany is considered very critically by many other European unions inasmuch as it does not give their local plant representatives enough control or participation.

Other institutional aspects of participation may be relevant to our discussion, particularly in order to avoid negative and counterproductive results. For instance, solutions must be avoided that impose too rigid procedures on the choices of the workers' representatives, which could prejudice their responsiveness to their constituents, or that give these representatives more responsibility than power. Certainly, the institutionalisation of participation, no matter how sophisticated, cannot substitute for actual experience, which in this particular field must be tested in the long run: industrial democracy, like responsible bargaining, must acquire quite a history before it can work and be trusted.

If long-term thinking is essential to trade-off and politicisation, interest groups and their constituents need guarantees that their self-control in the short run is reciprocal and effectively compensated. Lack of such predictability and of mutual trust is a major obstacle to any trade-off; in many cases it has even prevented it from starting, nobody being willing to take the first step. Good experience of bargaining between the social partners themselves, full recognition of unions by employers and by the State (which has only recently been achieved in some countries), an improved legal framework for bargaining and unionisation efforts, are some prerequisites for overcoming this difficulty. The crux of the matter lies, however, for the most part outside industrial relations as such, and depends directly on the structure and working of the political systems itself. It is influenced by the form of government: for instance, it is not surprising that in many countries experiments of socially responsible collective behaviour have been initiated, even by traditionally most diffident trade unions, under a government favourable or acceptable to labour, the most recent case being Italy.

Going further into the question, the practice of, and need for, trade-offs as a necessary means of acquiring consensus, demonstrate the inadequacy of parliamentary democracy and of the existing public institutions to express and mediate all of the collective demands coming from society. If the connection between industrial relations and the political system has become closer and closer, it is bound to work both ways: to the effect not only that the latter is objectively interested to control and somehow "reform" collective bargaining, but, also, vice-versa, that the political system is pressed to "reform" itself and to meet social demands more adequately.

To this question more attention should be devoted, also while dealing with industrial relations. Only one comment is possible here: a socially responsible and balanced trade-off process with the social partners can hardly function and be directed by a State whose institutions are too central-ised, bureacratic and foreclosed to citizens' participation and control. The search for new forms of democratic institutions based on social participation to integrate and not to substitute parliamentary democracy, is also important to this end.

V

PAY AND EMPLOYMENT ECONOMICS

The three papers in this section, by Dodge, Schelde Andersen and Hart and Sloan, together with their respective critiques by Silvestre, Wachter and Shimada, provide a review of the present state of knowledge of the working of those aspects of the labour market which have particular relevance to the relationships between government policy and collective bargaining. Dodge examines the impact of a wide range of government policies on wages and wage determination, concluding that while macro-economic policy continues to play an important part in the process of aggregate wage adjustment, wages respond only slowly to labour market slack. Catch-up for uncompensated past inflation appears to be the most important determinant of aggregate wage behaviour and accounts for the persistence of wage inflation in recent years. Dodge also finds that incomes policies and wage indexation can play an important part in the adjustment process, but that since 1973 their effectiveness has been reduced because they have failed to deal with this catch-up problem. In his comments on Dodge's paper, Silvestre discusses factors which have contributed to the upwards shift of the Phillips curve, drawing attention to the autonomy of wage movements in pace-setting sectors. He also emphasises the complexity of the effect of collective bargaining on wage levels especially when – as in Europe – bargaining takes place at several different levels even in one country.

Schelde Andersen's paper considers three different aspects of recent wage trends. The first part examines the extent to which changes in real wages have diverged from changes in real income in recent years due to changes in the terms of trade. In several countries a substantial gap has emerged between the two measures. The second part of the paper examines the consequences of the growing importance of non-wage labour costs, while the third part tries to assess the extent to which sectoral wage trends have influenced the general rate of inflation. Schelde Andersens's general, although tentative, conclusion that wage changes in the 1970s have become less responsive to business cycle conditions is challenged by Wachter, who argues that the hypothesis that recessions do not reduce the inflation rate is unsubstantiated.

Hart and Sloan's paper is devoted mainly to explaining the opportunities for labour supply adjustment in its various forms: reducing effective weekly or annual working hours, reducing the working lifetime, restricting participation in the workforce and restricting the labour supply. Their conclusion is that in only a small number of areas is a significant impact possible, and the authors emphasise reductions in overtime, shortening the standard working week, earlier retirement and subsidies to short-time working. In his comments Shimada points out that reductions in hours need complementary policy interventions to promote economic growth if employment is to be increased.

161

IMPACT OF SOME GOVERNMENT POLICIES ON WAGE DETERMINATION : AN OVERVIEW

David Dodge[1]

Macro-economic Policy and Aggregate Wage Change[2]

It is now fully twenty years ago that A.W. Phillips (1958) wrote his seminal article presenting empirical evidence to support the proposition that "the rate of change of money wage rates can be explained by the level of unemployment". This paper provided the stimulus for the greatest out-pouring of empirical work on the process of wage determination that has been seen before or since. Simple (many would say simplistic) variants of the trade-off curve were quickly incorporated into accepted economic doctrine. "On the usual time scale of the dissemination of ideas in economics, the Phillips curve and the associated 'Dilemma' problem achieved a prominent place in undergraduate textbooks almost instantly... and the Phillips curve immediately achieved a life of its own in professional discussion... (Leijonhufvud, 1968, p. 738).

Even more surprising, especially to "practitioners" of industrial relations and pay determination, practical men and politicians "who believe themselves to be quite exempt from any intellectual influences" quickly become slaves of the ideas of very much alive economists (Keynes, 1936, p. 383). Buttressed by a mass of empirical studies purporting to have found a national Phillips Curve[3], governments in many OECD countries began with amazing alacrity to base policy decisions on the notion of a trade-off between unemployment and inflation. Especially in North America and the U.K., structuralist arguments about the nature and causes of unemployment were quickly forgotten, and the notion of the trade-off quickly incorporated into the policy-makers' tool kit. If a little more inflation was the only price that had to be paid to reduce unemployment to politically popular levels, then full employment was a bargain and the price would be paid.

But the golden era of the trade-off and fine tuning lasted less than a decade. In the early sixties, the economic literature was replete with articles replicating Phillips' work for countries, provinces, industries, and occupations, as well as searching for new variables to improve the fit of the wage adjustment equation. However, as time periods were extended and variables added, a number of disturbing statistical results began to emerge from estimated wage equations. Coefficients began to wander, temporal instability

---

1. Associate Professor, Johns Hopkins University, School of Advanced International Studies, Washington.
2. I am indebted to Professor David Wilton of the University of Guelph for assistance with most of pages 163 to 167 for which he should be regarded as co-author.
3. It should be noted that most of these early studies used the overlapping annual wage change specification for the dependent variable, and estimated wage equations by ordinary least squares techniques using quarterly data. As Rowley and Wilton (1973) have shown, this leads to a considerable overstatement of statistical significance of the explanatory variables. Much of the strength of the Phillips relation disappears even for these earlier periods when efficient estimation techniques are used.

163

became a major problem, the significance of the unemployment variable began to wane, and the explanatory power of the price change variable increased.

Most of the early researchers had included price change in their wage equation, but their motives for doing so were vague. It was not until the contributions by Phelps (1967) and Friedman (1968) that a more precise theoretical price model was outlined. In their characteristically neo-classical world, "Each morning... workers 'shape-up' for an auction that determines the market clearing money wage and employment level (for the day) (Phelps, 1969, p. 50). Since the future is assumed to be known with certainty and since labour supply is assumed to depend on real wage rates, workers demand and obtain increases in the nominal wage rate commensurate with the rate of inflation expected to prevail over the next day. That is, "compensation" against future inflation is written into contracts *ex ante*, and there is no trade-off available to the policy maker. Unemployment will tend to its "natural" rate.

Because the price variable in the Phelps/Friedman wage equation represents the anticipated rate of inflation, its coefficent should approximate unity. Indeed, as time periods over which Phillips curves were estimated were extended into the early years of the current decade, the coefficient on the price change variable continued to increase and in many recent studies appears to be insignificantly different from unity. Sections on the "trade-off" began to disappear from elementary economics texts, and were replaced by sections on expectations and the natural unemployment rate. In many books, Phillips' notions about the wage adjustment process are now consigned to the same slag heap of discarded ideas on which the sunspot theory and pyramidology are piled. In my view, such consignment is premature, but before discussing my reasons for this view it is important to note the policy-maker's reaction to what might be called to monetarist counter-reformation.

By the late 1960s, it was becoming clear to policy makers in many countries that the price (in terms of inflation) of very low unemployment was rising very rapidly. Wages were increasing more rapidly than they should have done on the basis of estimated wage adjustment functions, and new policy directions were sought. Many countries instituted incomes policies ranging from exhortation to direct controls. The notion of "inflationary expectations" was quickly absorbed from the monetarist literature and these "temporary" interventions were often rationalised as being necessary to reduce inflationary expectations. By the early seventies most OECD countries had tried incomes policies of some form with greater or lesser degree of success as policy makers in an increasing number of countries abandoned hope that macroeconomic policies alone were sufficient to achieve adequate employment and price performance simultaneously. However, prudent macroeconomic policy remains a necessary condition for adequate price and wage performance in the medium run, and so before turning to a discussion of incomes policy I wish to return to the issue of macro-policy and wage adjustment.

The rapid abandonment of the Phillips Curve by economists resulted largely from the deterioration of the coefficients on the excess demand

164

variable in aggregate wage equations. However, these equations were usually built on simplistic notions of the labour market and, as Dow and Dicks-Mireaux (1959) first pointed out, this failure to recognize important institutional features of the labour market can seriously bias the statistical results. First, at least in North America, unions typically sign multi-year contracts with 'lock-in' or deferred increments. Since deferred increments are determined at the time the contract is signed, explanatory variables must be appropriately dated so that when the deferred increment occurs (say two years after the contract was signed) the explanatory variables correctly reflect economic conditions at the time of the contract (two years ago) and not economic conditions at the time when the deferred increment becomes effective. In addition, one must correctly specify a set of weights to reflect the bargaining calendar, as well as front-end loading features of these contracts.

Attempts to incorporate these critical institutional union features into an aggregate time-series wage determination model have, in general, failed to resurrect reliable wage change equations using conventional explanatory variables. For example, Ashenfelter and Pencavel (1975) introduced a *variable* bargaining calendar dimension into a quarterly wage-change model for the United Kingdom, and, utilizing an efficient estimation technique, found that "the results... are not very encouraging with respect to our knowledge of the economic determinants of aggregate wage changes... the conventional economic variables are not of much practical use in accounting for movements in the dependent variables" (p. 168).[4] However, aggregate time series wage models may be inappropriate for analysis of wage decisions since these are made at the micro level. A given settlement is influenced by labour market conditions in the appropriate labour market, by other settlements in that market, and, most importantly, by the nature of the expiring contract. I wish to expand on these points for a moment.

First, the aggregate unemployment rate may be a poor proxy for labour market conditions which affect any given settlement. A given aggregate rate is consistent with a wide dispersion of rates in different labour markets and this dispersion may be very different in two periods during which the aggregate rate is the same. Moreover, because of changed demographic circumstances, changed income levels, and changed labour market structures, the unemployment rate may be a rather unreliable measure of excess demand conditions in labour markets.[5] Thus it is not surprising that crude unemployment variables perform rather poorly in aggregate wage equations.

Second, as anyone familiar with the process of collective bargaining knows well, a wage settlement is made on the basis of conditions at the time of settlement, "expected" conditions over the life of the contract, and on the basis of conditions during the life of the previous contract. If events have turned out to be significantly different from what was expected at the time the last contract was signed, then there is great pressure to tailor the current contract to reflect these unexpected events. For example, if price increases

---

4. Smith and Wilton (1978) have extended the Ashenfelter and Pencavel model to include (i) multi-year variable length contracts, and (ii) deferred increments. Their statistical results for Canada are very similar to those found by Ashenfelter and Pencavel for the United Kingdom.

5. See Ashenfelter (1978a) and Economic Council of Canada (1976).

during the last contract have been much greater than had been expected at the time the previous contract was signed, there will be great pressure for "catch-up" and the wage settlement is likely to be higher than predicted on the basis of current labour market conditions and price expectations. Thus, prices are likely to feed into wages in two ways: first, in terms of expected price increases over the duration of the new contract as per the Phelps/Friedman model; and second, in terms of the catch-up (or catch-down) required to reconcile price expectations at the time the last contract was signed, with actual price increases over the period of that contract. Thus, in economies in which wages are largely determined under multi-year contracts, periods of unexpectedly high (or low) inflation are likely to cause significant amounts of aggregate wage catch-up (or catch-down) which cannot be captured in estimated expectations – augmented Phillips curves.

In this context, four recently published studies have attempted to estimate wage equations from macro data which incorporate variables to measure claims for compensation for past unexpected inflation ("catch-up"), in addition to the *ex ante* demands suggested by Phelps and Friedman.[6] Unfortunately, the treatment of "catch-up" in these papers is not entirely consistent with that of *ex ante* compensation: although their *ex ante* variable does not force all anticipated inflation to be included into the previous contract, their *ex post* variable assumes that all anticipated inflation has been built in, leaving only unanticipated inflation at the bargaining table. A second difficulty with these studies is that the notion of "catch-up" is inherently ambiguous when macro data is utilised because it is not possible to compare anticipated with actual price inflation at the micro level. Because of these difficulties, the addition of a "catch-up" price variable yields only marginal improvement in the explanatory power of their wage equations and does not greatly alter Ashenfelter and Pencavel's conclusion quoted above.

Recent work using Canadian micro data indicated that "conventional price expectations Phillips curve models must be further augmented to include a measure of uncompensated past inflation. In a world of uncertainty, adjustment costs, and wage recontracting, the effects of unexpected inflation are unlikely to be reflected in observable measures of labour market disequilibrium. A measure of uncompensated past inflation may serve as an econometrically powerful indicator of firm specific latent excess demand for labour. Using a large micro data base, the separate effects of price expectations and price catch-up can be disentangled. Both effects are found to be significant determinants of wage changes." (Wilton et al., 1978b p. 27).

It should be noted that the coefficients on the price expectations and catch-up variables indicate that about 3/4 of lagged and expected Consumer Price Index (CPI) increases are reflected in negotiated wage settlements, with over half of the effect being due to catch-up (Wilton, 1978a). Perry's work for the USA indicates that from 4/5 to 9/10 of the combined effect of lagged wage increases, lagged CPI increases and expected CPI increases are

---

6. See Turnovsky and Wachter (1972), Turnovsky (1972), Johnson and Timbrell (1974) and de Mesnil and Bhalla (1975).

reflected in current wage settlements, with most of the impact arising from the lagged wage and CPI variables and only 1/5 to 2/5 arising from the expected price variables (Perry, 1978).

Wilton's work indicates that a statistically robust Phillips curve does still exist in the Canadian case, but that it has "clearly shifted outwards" in the 1970s and that it is depressingly flat so that "none of the long-run inflation-unemployment choices may now be palatable." (Wilton *et al.*, 1978b p.28) On the basis of this estimate, a full two percentage point increase in unemployment held for two to three years would be required to reduce wage increases (in the unionised sector) by 1. 3 percentage points. This is even more pessimistic than estimates based on US aggregate data, which indicate that two to four percentage years of unemployment are required to reduce economy-wide wage increases by one percentage point (Okun 1977, Perry 1978). One final point is worthy of mention: the rate of deceleration of wages in the unionized sector of the US economy is considerably less sensitive to labour market conditions than is suggested by the economy-wide estimates (Perry, 1978 and Mitchell, 1978).[7]

From this review of the evidence of the effect of labour market conditions on the wage adjustment process, several important conclusions can be drawn. The first is that labour market conditions do continue to have an important impact on the rate of increase of money wages, i.e. the Phillips relationship still exists. However, while slack in markets does affect the rate of wage increase, the immediate impact of increased slack is small and sizeable effects on the rate of inflation take a long time, especially in the unionised sector. Moreover, because of changes in demographic composition of the labour force, improvements in social security benefits, increases in average income levels and increased expectation that macro policy will be accommodating, the level of unemployment associated with a given degree of labour market slack has increased, especially in North America. Thus, high rates of unemployment maintained for a considerable period are required to have a significant impact on inflation, if macroeconomic policy is to be used alone.[8]

The second conclusion I draw from the evidence is that restrictive macroeconomic policy has a greater and more rapid impact on wages in the non-union sectors than in heavily unionised sectors. Thus, restrictive policies cause a widening of union/non-union differentials among blue-collar workers and some narrowing of blue-collar/white-collar differentials in North America. These changed relativities may lead to increased pressure for non-union wage increases when labour markets tighten at some future date, although the evidence on this issue is far from clear.[9] At the very least they are likely to lead to increased tensions in labour relations and to increased political pressures for controls on wages and prices in the organised sectors.

The third conclusion I draw from the evidence is that past price increases create great pressure for wage catch-up. The effect of past prices on wages,

7. It should be noted that there is little evidence that the Phillips curve for the 1970s is "flatter" than for the 1960s. In fact, the evidence indicates that (for North America at least) the curve may have a slightly steeper slope in the seventies than in the preceding decade, although it has clearly shifted out from the origin (Wachter 1976, Perry 1978, Wilton 1978a). See also McCracken *et al*, 1977, pp. 104-108.

8. I think McCracken *et al* (1977) were overly optimistic about the speed with which restrictive macro policy could grind out wage inflation (pp. 107-108).

9. For contrasting views on this issue compare Johnson G. (1977) with Dunlop, J. (1977).

which appears to be significantly greater than that of expected prices, creates a strong inertia in wage inflation. This finding has the extremely important, and often overlooked, implication that while wage and price inflation are being wound down, employees must accept the fact that they may have to make do with wage increases which do *not* adequately compensate them for past inflation. The success of the process of winding down wage inflation thus depends not so much on changing employee expectations about future rates of inflation as it does on shaping attitudes about the extent to which employees can expect to be compensated for past inflation. Casual observation suggests to me that the governments which have been most successful in winding down wage inflation since 1974 were those that were successful in selling the concept that employees could not expect to be compensated for increases in the CPI due to oil and commodity price increases, or due to exchange rate depreciation resulting therefrom.[10] This conclusion also has important implications for incomes policies and I shall return to it in the next section of this paper.

Incomes Policies, Indexation and Wage Adjustment

Mandatory Incomes Policies

Because of the high cost (in terms of employment and output) of reducing the rate of wage increase through demand management policy alone, many OECD countries have resorted to the use of temporary wage and price controls or other forms of mandatory incomes policy. Such efforts have usually been derided by economists as useless at best and, more often, as harmful and potentially disastrous.

There can be no doubt that when incomes policies have been misapplied, e.g. when they have been used as a substitute for appropriate demand management policies (UK late 1960s and USA early 1970s), controls have had little long-run effect on slowing wage inflation and have had a harmful effect on the allocation of resources in these economies. However, when mandatory incomes policies are used as a complement to appropriate demand management policies, it seems to me they can have an important role to play in speeding wage adjustment. An appropriate strategy to wind down wage inflation which involves the use of controls may be summarised as follows: Cut the rate of growth of the money supply by two to three per cent each year. This decline would then lead to an increase in rates of interest. Both directly, and via the induced effect on the exchange rate, the higher interest rates would lead to a reduction in aggregate demand. The direct impact of the interest rate increase would operate through a reduction in investment expenditure on plant equipment and through a reduction in investment in residential construction. The higher exchange rate would also act to reduce exports and increase imports, and thus have a downward effect on

---

10. Such an argument is difficult to prove because many of the governments which stressed this concept also adopted restrictive fiscal and monetary policies. Nevertheless, I believe McCracken *et al* (1977), para. 106, overstressed the importance of macro policies in Germany, Japan and the USA. Indeed, the rate of wage increase in heavily unionised sectors in the USA abated extremely slowly after 1973.

prices, since the domestic currency price of most imports and some exports would fall: The decline in demand for domestic output would lead to a reduction in hours worked and in employment. The rise in unemployment would tend to reduce the rate of increase in wages and would continue to do so as long as unemployment remained at or above the natural rate. However, because the responsiveness of wages to unemployment is low, the rate of increase in wages and prices would be forced to adjust downward consistent with reductions in money supply growth and tightened fiscal policy by the imposition of controls. Output and employment would be maintained at reasonable levels as wages and prices were reduced. This reduction would be considerably faster than that which would have been achieved in the absence of controls and, because it would be consistent with demand management policies *ex post*, little or no wage and price rebound would occur when the desired rate of inflation was reached and the controls were removed.

In this strategy, the purpose of incomes policies is not to change expectations directly but rather to force wage decisions to be consistent with monetary and fiscal policy, so that the maximum effect of the more restrictive policy is felt on prices and nominal wages, and the minimum effect is felt on output and employment. As the rate of price increase falls, as the central bank pursues progressively lower target rates of money supply growth, and as workers perceive that their real incomes are not falling even though the rate of nominal wage increase is falling, expectations will adjust. Once this adjustment has been made, then mandatory policies can be removed with minimum likelihood of a new wage explosion.[11]

The Experience with Incomes Policies

The great problem with the execution of this strategy since 1973, however, has been that the successful application of the strategy would have required that money wages rise less rapidly than prices (as measured by the CPI), since a large component of price increases was attributable to the oil price shock of 1973. Under these conditions, an incomes policy based on full compensation for past inflation could not be successful. This created great problems for countries like Belgium, where an extremely high degree of *de facto* wage indexing existed prior to the imposition (or reimposition) of incomes policies. Countries which tried to do so found it politically difficult to implement incomes policies which specifically denied employees the right to maintain real incomes. [12] Countries which did manage to enforce a decline in real incomes (e.g. UK 1976-1977) appear to have achieved a considerable deceleration in underlying rates of price increase, although industrial relations have been somewhat strained as a result.

I would summarise the evidence provided by the last three years' experiences with incomes policies as somewhat mixed, but on balance indicating that these policies, when used in conjunction with prudent demand man-

---

11. Thus far I have talked only in terms of controls. Clearly the same objectives can be pursued with other non-mandatory forms of incomes policies.

12. Time and space does not permit a detailed review of policies pursued. For a summary from 1973 to 1976, see Braun (1978), pp. 15-34.

agement policies, have assisted in moderating rate of wage inflation and/or in maintaining higher levels of output and employment. However, these experiences do appear to have left a residue of problems (e.g. unfavourable current account balances, changed dispersion of wages) which will have to be corrected in the future, and which will continue to create strains on the collective bargaining system.

Indexation

One of the results of the commodity price shocks of 1972-1973 and the subsequent rapid inflation, has been that many governments have adopted, or permitted the parties at the bargaining table to implement, policies of wage indexation. Because keeping up with inflation is seen as fair and equitable, compensation for past cost-of-living increases forms the basis of negotiated and arbitral awards and of incomes policies in most countries. There continue to be strong pressures for inclusion of some form of escalator clauses in centrally bargained agreements.

However, it seems to me that this is exactly the wrong prescription for incomes policy today. Indexation permits little or no downward adjustment in real wages when this is required. The requirement for such downward adjustments from time to time is very great in a world of floating exchange rates and volatile commodity prices. When a country experiences a depreciation in its exchange rate because of current account problems, it is critical that the ensuing increases in the CPI not touch off a general increase in money wages.[13] Similarly, when food or other resource prices increase dramatically, it is critical that these price increases should not feed through to labour costs in the secondary and tertiary sectors. Full wage indexation permits little change in the price of domestic manufactures and services relative to imports and primary products.[14]

Why do past increases in the CPI have such a strong direct impact on wages, even in the absence of full indexation *ex ante*? I believe that the main reason is that the CPI serves as a proxy for a "standard of equity" for wages. It is perceived by employees as only "equitable" that they receive compensatory increases at least equal to past price increases. When their pay increases lag behind the CPI, employees perceive themselves to be unfairly treated by their own employer, particularly in large enterprises. Especially when protected by unions, they may begin to withhold work effort in a variety of ways (absenteeism, longer coffee breaks, increased breakage, etc.). This reduced work effort causes the real unit labour costs to increase. To minimise this increase, the employer finds it profitable to pay the wage perceived as equitable by employees. Thus, in aggregate, resistance of employers to cost of living increases is very low, even when labour markets are slack. Arbitrators usually justify "catch-up" on similar equity grounds.[15]

---

13. In the case of an appreciation, it is equally important that some of the benefits flow through to workers in the form of higher real wages.

14. Such change as does occur requires a sharp reduction in profits in the manufacturing and service sectors.

15. See Annable (1977) for an excellent exposition of these arguments.

Thus the central role that must be played by incomes policy is the creation of a "standard of equity" sufficiently plausible (or enforceable) to unhitch wage adjustments from past CPI increases. Clearly there is no magic formula for such a standard, as the difficulties of the past few years amply illustrate. However, I would venture to suggest that a standard based on a price index for domestic production excluding farm and energy production would be a reasonable starting point. To this index could be added some amount to reflect long-run productivity gain, and, during the period of "disinflation" some number could be subtracted to represent the medium-run expected effect of slowing monetary growth. However, the essence of the "standard of equity" is that employees cannot expect to be compensated for price increases which occur outside of the domestic secondary and tertiary sector of their own economy, but can expect to reap the benefit of outside decreases. In the language of the trade theorist, employees in the secondary and tertiary sector must, in aggregate, shoulder the impact of an adverse movement in the terms-of-trade between their sector and the "rest-of-the-world" (including the primary sector of their own economy) as well as sharing in the benefits of favourable movements in the terms-of-trade.[16]

Although incomes policies have not stressed this intersectoral shift sufficiently, concentrating as they have on the functional distribution of income between wages and profits and on wage relativities within the secondary and tertiary sectors, nevertheless, I conclude that the effects of incomes policies have, on the whole, been beneficial.

Micro-economic Policies and Wages

Because of the wide variety of policies and of differences in institutions, any brief survey of the effects of micro-economic (structural) policies on wages will necessarily be deficient. Moreover, my cursory review of recent literature in this field leaves me with the rather uneasy feeling that there may be significant divergences between the predictions of the effects of policy on wages made on the basis of traditional neo-classical economic theory, and the actual effects observed in labour markets. Thus I approach these issues with great trepidation.

Income Taxation and Wages

The theoretical and empirical literature suggests that direct taxes are likely to affect wages in two ways. First, direct tax changes alter average and marginal wages. Decreases in average wages, due to increased income taxes, cause individuals to reduce their consumption of all commodities, including leisure and, hence increase their supply of labour. This causes downward pressure on wages. On the other hand, increases of the marginal tax rate reduce the price of leisure and, consequently, induce a reduction in the supply of labour, which tends to increase the wage rate.

---

16. For a cogent presentation of a similar argument see Kaldor (1976), pp. 704-708.

The second effect of direct taxation on wages arises due to attempts by trade unions to maintain and increase their real income net of tax. Unions thus attempt to recoup some of the real net income lost due to increases in statutory rates of taxation. Of course, to the extent that taxes are used to finance expenditures which directly increase workers' real incomes, e.g. health schemes, the attempt to recoup increased taxes in higher wages may be mitigated. Moreover, unions may take account of the tax progressivity to demand increased gross wages to compensate them for reductions in real net income due to the interaction of inflation with a progressive tax schedule. The latter effect may cause inflationary pressures to arise, due to the tax progressivity as such rather than due to tax changes.

In countries relying on highly progressive systems of taxation, very rapid increases in wages and salaries under the impetus of sharply rising consumer prices led to unplanned increases in tax liability at given levels of real income. This resulted in a marked rise in the share of gross personal income taken in taxes.[17] Even countries that had already implemented some form of indexation of tax brackets and allowances, such as Canada and Denmark, did not escape this effect, because adjustments for the effect, of inflation were made with a lag of about fifteen months or longer.

The unplanned rise in existing high rates of direct taxation had disturbing repercussions, in intensifying industrial and political conflict, in undermining fiscal control, and making budgetary policy more erratic and less predictable. In some cases the rise resulted in unintendedly large public sector surpluses (as in Canada and the Netherlands in 1973) with a consequent unintentionally severe deflationary impact on the economy, which induced strong political pressures for the adoption of expansionary policies. In other cases, rising revenue encouraged unplanned increases in real public expenditure, which tended to intensify inflationary cost pressures throughout the economy.[18]

The unforeseen rise in direct tax liability itself intensified cost pressures, making it more difficult to bring down the rate of inflation, and in some cases increased the difficulty of maintaining employment and investment in the exposed sectors of the economy.[19] Sharply increasing taxes on unskilled and skilled industrial workers are argued to have contributed to a worsening of the wage bargaining climate. In countries such as Denmark and Norway, unionised workers accustomed to receiving compensation for price increases now found that, with larger price changes, the combined effect of indexation and direct taxes was to reduce their real disposable income. In the Netherlands and the United Kingdom, employees who had recently secured cost of living protection found the benefit largely offset by their increased liability to taxes. In Italy, the newly instituted tax reform and increased taxes on earned income resulted in larger deductions from industrial workers' pay than planned for, and intensified the pressures for further indexation of wages. In many cases larger wage claims were put

17. The system of adjustment had been designed to counter the cumulative effect of creeping inflation, *not* the effect of a sudden inflationary shock. For a description of problems of adjusting taxes see Aaron, H.J. (1975) and OECD Committee on Fiscal Affairs, *The Adjustment of Personal Income Tax Systems for Inflation*, 1976.

18. For a detailed theoretical analysis of the impact of increased public expenditures on output, wages and profits, see Eltis and Bacon (1975).

19. In this paragraph I draw heavily on the judgments of Braun (1978).

forward on the grounds that they were needed to cover the effect of rising tax liability. The phenomenon of "tax push" may well have contributed to the rate of increase in wages and salaries in the Netherlands in 1973-4 and the United Kingdom wage explosion in early 1975.

However, rigorous attempts to quantify the magnitude of the "tax-push" effect have so far been few and generally weak. These studies in the main do not develop the theory in sufficient rigour and detail to pursue meaningful empirical testing. In particular, the tie between theories of labour supply and wage behaviour is generally weak.

There are three studies which attempt to measure the effect of taxes on wage inflation in the U.S. The first two by Gordon (1970 and 1972) and by Eckstein and Brinner (1972) find some degree of forward shifting of the income tax in the form of higher wages. However, the specification of their equations is sufficiently deficient with respect to the tax variables to make their results highly suspect. The third study by Taylor, Turnovsky and Wilson (T.T.W.) (1972) is far more detailed and careful. Unfortunately, the results are extremely ambiguous. The two studies for the United Kingdom by Turner *et al* (1972) and by Johnson and Timbrell (1974) are also somewhat deficient in specification and statistical analysis.

Some of the best empirical studies so far have been performed using Canadian data. The first was carried out by T.T.W. on Canadian manufacturing data, for the Prices and Incomes Commission (1972). While the specification of the wage model in general, and the tax equation in particular, are much more careful than in other work, the results are not entirely satisfactory. The tax variables are generally significant and consistent with some kind of theory but their order of magnitude is entirely unacceptable. Moreover, the extreme sensitivity of other variables in their model, to the inclusion of the tax variables, leads to great difficulties in interpreting the results.

The second was carried out by Kotowitz (1977). In his paper, a competitive model incorporating the effect of taxes on labour supply was developed to yield the tax effects on wages. These were found not to be significant. Then a model to incorporate tax changes into a union bargaining framework was developed. Tests of this model confirm some of the results obtained previously. Some indication that tax changes are shifted forward and stronger indications of the effects of tax levels on wage changes was found.

Kotowitz was unable to determine precisely whether it is the level of taxation (Eltis and Bacon's proposition) or the progressivity of the tax structure (proposition based on casual observation) which contributes most to wage increases. However, his results suggest a very much smaller effect of the tax structure on wage inflation than that suggested by the results using the TTW model. The contribution of tax structure to wage inflation appears to be less than 0.05 % per annum.

The special impact that taxes might have on work effort, wages and labour supply when they constitute part of a negative income tax system has been explored in some depth in the U.S.A. As I read the results, the labour supply response in the U.S. experiments was surprisingly small, suggesting also, surprisingly, that the combined effect of higher incomes plus higher marginal rates for the experimental groups is close to zero. However, the reliability and usefulness of the results are put in some doubt by the difficulties encountered in running such experiments (Pechman and Timpane, 1975).

The general picture which emerges from rigorous testing thus seems to be very tentative. There is clear indication that personal income tax structures and levels do affect wage changes, but at this stage estimates of the impact appear to be much smaller than is suggested by casual observation. Until a considerable amount of additional testing, preferably at a much more detailed industry level, is performed, I would urge caution in imputing much of the increase in wages in recent years to "tax push" causes.

Payroll Taxes

Because payroll taxes are imposed initially partly on earnings of workers and partly on firms, there is some question as to whether the incidence of these taxes will be similar to income taxes. Brittain's work (1971) which indicated that the employer portion of these taxes would be passed back to labour was challenged by Feldstein (1972b) and it appears that there has been no satisfactory resolution of this issue since that time. Subsequent work on wage subsidies (see below) implicitly assumes that these subsidies result in a decrease in labour costs and have the effect of decreasing prices and increasing the quantity of labour demanded, but there is no rigorous examination of this assumption. Similarly, recent European policies involving reduced payroll taxes to encourage employment appear to be based on the assumption that the payroll tax is passed forward to prices and that the demand for labour-intensive goods and services is highly price elastic. On the other hand, recent American work on tax based incomes policies implicitly assumes that, to the extent that these taxes are paid, the burden is borne by profits.

The proper assessment of the static incidence of the payroll tax and its impact on wage rates in equilibrium requires the estimation of a disaggregated simultaneous equation model of supply of, and demand for, labour and capital capable of showing the effects of the tax on relative prices of goods. This is an extremely difficult task, perhaps an impossible one, given the high degree of aggregation of most large-scale econometric models, and to my knowledge has not been carried out. The assessment of the impact incidence of a *change* in the payroll tax is even more difficult as it requires estimates of adjustment functions in addition to supply and demand elasticities. Moreover, the impact on wages and employment will not be invariant to the impact of the payroll tax cuts (increase) on aggregate demand and the method by which the cut is financed or the increased revenues spent.

I thus conclude that at the present time it is not possible to give an assessment of the impact on wages of general changes in the employer's portion of payroll taxes that have taken place in OECD countries during the last decade. Until some very difficult research has been completed on this topic, I am afraid that policy makers will have to continue to rely on highly imperfect estimates, such as those of Brittain (1971) or Dodge (1975),

174

which indicate that 80 % to 100 % of these taxes are ultimately borne by wage earners but give no guidance as to impact of changes in these taxes on money wage rates.

The effect on wages of payroll taxes paid by employees (social security taxes) at first blush might be thought to be the same as the effect of income taxes in a similar structure and magnitude. However, this is definitely not true in countries (such as U.S.A. and Canada) where these taxes are earmarked for special purposes such as health insurance or old age security. For example, there is some evidence that one of the major effects of increases in social security taxes in the U.S.A. has been to reduce personal savings rates. This implies that these taxes are regarded as a form of savings and thus are likely to have had considerably smaller tax push effect on wages than income taxes of a similar magnitude would have had.

This, of course, is just one illustration of a much more general and important point, namely that the impact of taxes on wages depends on the utility to the tax-payer of the goods and services which these taxes purchase.[20] To the extent that social security taxes are regarded as "prices" for a health insurance, unemployment insurance or pensions, then these taxes will only have a tax push effect on wages:

i) to the extent that individuals are forced to "purchase" more of these services than they otherwise would have done; and

ii) to the extent that these taxes are increased to cover increased costs of providing the same level of services due to inflation (in which case the effect is similar to that of an increase in a component of the CPI with the same expenditure weight).

These proportions raise a number of important policy issues, the development of which goes far beyond the scope of this paper. The important implication for wage policy is that earmarked taxes may have a different (and often smaller) impact on wages than general taxes. Policy makers should be aware of these differences and more work should be undertaken to identify their magnitude.

Wage Subsidies

The use of general wage subsidies has also received increasing attention in recent years as a method of generating increased employment during periods of cyclical slack. Temporary selective wage subsidies have been introduced in France, Germany, Japan, Sweden, the U.K. and the U.S. in an attempt to offset the cyclical decline in demand for labour, while Italy has introduced a general subsidy in manufacturing and some services by reducing payroll taxes temporarily. Recently, the federal government in Canada has also introduced an anti-cyclical wage subsidy.

The overall impact of a wage subsidy is the result of three types of effects:

---

20. This is merely an extension of well-known propositions from the field of public finance. For an exposition, see Aaron and McGuire (1970).

i) The factor substitution effect is based on the rise in the use of the subsidised factor relative to other unsubsidised factor inputs which in turn depends on the elasticity of substitution between subsidised labour and other factors and on the elasticity of supply of subsidised labour and other factors. A good estimate of these elasticities is essential to estimating the impact of wage subsidies, but such estimates have proven very difficult to make. Estimates for the U.S. (Kesselman *et al.*, 1977, Hammermesh 1977, Fethke and Williamson (1976), indicate that a reduction of 1 % in the marginal cost of blue-collar labour would lead to employment increases in the order of 0.1 % to 0.3 %, a small reduction in the employment of white-collar labour, a 0.4 % to 0.6 % reduction in demand for capital, assuming output constant.[21] No attempt seems to have been made to estimate the impact of wage rates paid, apparently on the (very tenuous?) assumption that the supply of subsidised labour is perfectly elastic at the going rate. Note that this assumption is totally opposite to the finding of Brittain in his assessment of impact of payroll taxes as discussed above. Because estimates of the employment and wage impact of wage subsidies are highly sensitive both to the elasticity of substitution between subsidised labour and other factors and to the elasticity of supply of subsidised labour, considerably more evidence is required about the magnitude of elasticities at the industry level before an adequate assessment of these programmes can be made.

ii) The scale effect is the rise in employment of the subsidised factor that is brought about by the increase in output produced by the reduced wage cost. This effect depends on the price elasticity of demand for output and the degree of competition in output markets. The larger the fraction of total costs represented by the wage bill for subsidised labour, the greater the degree of competition in output markets, and the more price elastic the demand for output, the greater the employment impact of the subsidy. So far as I can see, little attention has been paid to this effect, and more work is warranted.

iii) In addition to these supply side effects, the overall impact of the subsidy will depend on demand side (multiplier) effects. Here the question arises as to the relative stimulus to employment given when fiscal stimulus is introduced through wage subsidies as opposed to tax cuts, direct employment programs, etc. This problem has been investigated by Fethke and Williamson (1976). Their results indicate that for the United States leakages are smaller for this type of stimulus than for other types of stimulus but it is not clear to me that this would be the case in more open economies.

To sum up, experience with wage subsidies has to date largely been with restricted subsidies, i.e., subsidies related to certain target groups (U.S., France, U.K.) or linked with training schemes (Sweden, Germany). Evalu-

---

21. See the Congressional Budget Office paper (April 1977) for an excellent review of these studies.

ations of the effects of these restricted subsidies seem to show that the employment impact has not been as great as had been hoped, both because the short-run elasticity of demand for labour appears lower than had been thought and because of administrative problems in systems designed to provide limited incremental subsidies.[22] Clearly, programmes designed to save existing jobs have much more serious allocative costs and lower long-run benefits than those designed to encourage new jobs in expanding industries. I could find no evidence bearing on the direct impact of these programmes on wages or wage structures.

Public Sector Pay

One method of influencing rates of changes in economy-wide wages rates that has been both advocated (mainly by private sector employers) and adopted from time to time in many countries, is strict control over public sector pay scales. The efficacy of such a scheme hinges on the propositions either *(i)* that there is a strong and direct spillover of public sector pay awards both to the private sector and to other elements within the public sector, and/or *(ii)* that public sector pay awards play an important role in establishing the general bargaining climate. This conditioning of the bargaining climate is attributed to the effect of public pay awards on expectations about inflation and because they constitute, along with the CPI, part of the amorphous standard of equity to which I referred in the first section of this paper.

While proposition *(ii)* may be valid, and casual observation in some countries suggests a certain degree of validity, it is an inherently untestable hypothesis. Proposition *(i)*, on the other hand, is testable and, although data problems make such testing difficult, the econometric evidence indicates no consistently strong and direct spillovers from the public to private sectors in at least three OECD countries: the U.K., the U.S. or in Canada.[23] While such findings are not surprising from the U.S.A., they are surprising for Canada and the U.K. where it is often alleged that public sector pay awards have touched off rapid increases in private sector pay. The results are not generalizable to other countries. However, they do represent a sufficiently serious challenge to the conventional wisdom that their implications should be considered by policy makers. In particular, they indicate that attempts to moderate private sector wage increases through smaller public sector increases are unlikely to be successful.

Unemployment Insurance

Improvements in social security systems, and unemployment insurance (U.I.) in particular, have undoubtedly had some impact on the rate of wage increase and on the structure of wages during the last decade. Theory would tell us that an increase in the ratio of U.I. benefits to weekly wages would decrease the cost of being unemployed and increase the length of the average

22. For a good overview of the French program and an analysis of general administrative problems, see Kopits (1978). See also Burton's overview (1977).
23. See Copeland (1977), Elliot (1977), Smith (1977) and Wilton *et al.*, (1978a)).

spell of unemployment. This is tantamount to shifting the labour supply curve to the left and hence leads to an increase in the average wage rate. To the extent that U.I. payments are financed by payroll taxes and income taxes borne by wage earners, the supply curve of labour is further shifted to the left and wages further increased. However, to the extent that improved U.I. benefits induce increased labour force participation, the supply curve is shifted to the right. Thus the impact of improved U.I. benefits on the effective supply curve of labour is ambiguous, although in all probability the impact of the first two considerations is far greater than that of the third. The combined impact of U.I. benefits and the taxes to finance these benefits on the demand for labour is also ambiguous.[24] However, to the extent that the employers' share of a payroll tax increase to finance improved U.I. benefits is shifted forward into prices, an increase in U.I. benefits is likely to lead to increased rates of price increase. In sum, theory leads us to predict that the higher the level of U.I. benefits and related taxes, the higher the natural unemployment rate, and hence the greater the rate of wage inflation at any given unemployment rate.

Increases in U.I. benefits are also likely to lead to a change in the structure of wages. In the absence of complete experience rating,[25] improvements in benefits and associated payroll taxes will lead to an increase in the supply of labour to industries in which employment is volatile (for cyclical or seasonal reasons) and to a decrease in supply to industries in which employment is relatively stable.[26] This will put pressure on wage rates in seasonal and cyclical industries to decline *relative* to wage rates in industries offering more stable employment. Of course, unions in industries with cyclical or seasonally volatile employment may be successful in resisting reductions in their relative wages. To the extent that they are successful in doing so, this will add to the overall upward pressure on money wages and further increase the natural unemployment rate.

While little empirical work has been done to my knowledge on the impact of U.I. on wages and wage structures, there has been a veritable avalanche of papers on the impact of U.I. on the unemployment rate.[27] The work of Feldstein (1972a), Marston (1975) and others indicates that changes in U.I. benefit levels in the U.S.A. have added 0.2 to 0.4 percentage points to the natural unemployement rate in the United States. Similar work in the U.K. by Maki, Spindler (1975) and others indicate that a rise in the natural rate of 0.6 to 1.0 percentage points after 1966 could be attributed to changes in the unemployment compensation system in 1965 and 1966 (addition of the earnings related supplement and redundancy pay). Recent

24. To the extent that U.I. benefits and taxes cause the distribution of income to alter in such a way as to decrease (increase) the demand for goods and services with a high domestic labour content, the demand curve for labour will be shifted to the left (right). To the extent that improved U.I. benefits reduce the employer's need to hoard labour, the demand curve will be shifted to the left.

25. By experience rating is meant the linking of the employer share of the U.I. payroll tax to the employer's past layoff experience.

26. The higher the rate of U.I., the higher the total compensation for a week actually worked. For example, if an employee expects to work 40 weeks per year and to receive 10 weeks of U.I. benefits, then his total weekly compensation is equal to his actual weekly wage rate plus one quarter of the weekly U.I. benefit rate.

27. For a survey of the general macroeconomic properties of U.I. systems in major OECD countries, see Mittelstadt (1975).

work in Canada (Green and Cousineau, 1976, and Rea, 1977) indicates that the 1971 amendments to the U.I. system have added about 0.7 percentage points to the natural unemployment rate.

To the extent that improved U.I. benefits can reduce the political pressure on governments to achieve very low rates of unemployment, and to the extent that full employment targets are revised upward, improved U.I. benefits need not add to inflationary pressures. However, to the extent that these targets are not adjusted, then improvements in U.I. benefits can constitute an important source of upward pressure on wages. My own tentative assessment is that targets, at least in the U.K. and Canada, were not revised upward sufficiently during the last ten years to allow for increases in the natural rate attributable to U.I. changes, and hence these changes did contribute to wage inflation.[28] However, this conclusion must remain highly tentative, even for these two countries, pending more careful analysis of the data.

Minimum Wage

The theoretical impact of the minimum wage on unemployment and wages is well known and needs no elaboration here. Increases in the minimum wage will:

i)   lead to increased unemployment among those previously paid less than the new minimum, and

ii) lead initially to a compression of the wage structure and over time to an increase in wages above the minimum as differentials are restored.

The magnitude of these effects will be small or negligible if the increase in the minimum takes place during a period of strong demand for labour and/or if the increase in the minimum is equal to or less than the increase in the average rate of increase in median wages.[29] However, when increases are large relative to the median wage, when increases take place in generally slack labour markets, or when the minimum is set at a "high" fraction of the median wage, then the impact of the minimum may be large. The magnitude of the impact will of course depend on the social and economic institutions of a particular country and on the dispersion of wages prior to the institution of a higher minimum. The greater the fraction of the labour force paid at or near the minimum and the greater the extent to which the minimum serves as a "standard of equity", the greater will be the impact of such a change. Because it does serve as a part of the "standard of equity" in many countries, its impact may be far greater than is suggested by the fraction of the labour force paid minimum rates.

---

28. For an alternative view, see Cubbin and Foley (1977).

29. In a detailed study of the effect of the U.S. minimum wage, Gramlich (1976) concludes that the impact of the U.S. minimum on other wage rates has been very small.

COMMENT ON DODGE'S PAPER

J.-J. Silvestre[1]

Shift of the Phillips Curve and Functioning of the Labour Market

I should like to begin by putting forward some additional ideas on the subject of the upward shift of the Phillips curve to be found in many industrialised countries at the end of the 1960s.[2] It seems to be worthwhile extending and grouping the observations put forward by Professor Dodge, while pointing out how far the emphasis placed on the distinction between the existence of the curve and its shift affects somewhat radically the meaning that can be attributed to the Phillips curve and its recent shifts. It appears to me that the changes that have occurred in the statistical relationship, and in the effectiveness of the traditional policies based on its existence, can be analysed on the basis of three trends:

(1) trends affecting those parts of the labour market in which the workforce is both stable and comparatively well protected, and where the main issue is the generation of wages;

(2) trends affecting the more peripheral areas, mainly defined in terms of the creation of unemployment and mobility of labour; and lastly,

(3) trends affecting the interdependence between these two areas.

Many studies have put forward models of the dynamics of the average money wage based on the pace-setting role of the first labour market sector on the basis of the following assumptions:

i) Wages in these sectors move steadily and independently of fluctuations in general economic activity or the state of the labour market; these wage changes depend mainly on the continuity over time of the contractual relations between employers and wage-earners and the possibilities offered by productivity increases and price rises in those sectors.

ii) The trend of the average wage depends largely on the way these autonomous wage increases are passed on into the other areas of the wage market, in the medium term and also at different stages of cyclical economic changes.

It is admittedly difficult to prove irrefutably the validity of these assumptions from empirical analysis. Many studies have nonetheless shown them to be productive and interesting.[3] It also seems that this approach to wage

---

1. Maître de Recherche au CNRS, Laboratoire d'Économie et de Sociologie de Travail, Aix-en-Provence, France.

2. The work done for France confirms, in the main, the conclusions put forward by the Rapporteur in respect of the United States and Canada. Boyer, (1978), Deruelle (1974).

3. Deruelle (1971); Ertnell, Llewellyn and Tarling (1974); Hall (1975); Silvestre (1971-1973); Turner and Jackson (1970); Wachter (1970).

dynamics brings a better understanding of the relations which can be established, at least in some European countries, between the acceleration in the rise of money wages observed at the end of the 1960s and the changes that have occurred in economic structures, management of the workforce, and the behaviour of workers and trade unions.

First there are the changes which have emerged in the way in which the workforce is managed within firms. Many European countries experienced strong expansion during the 1960s together with large-scale investment and concentration, especially in industry (Jenny and Weber, 1975; Holland, 1978). These rapid and sustained changes facilitated the growth, on a scale well beyond anything previously experienced, of domestic labour markets in which wage movements are more the result of internal pressures within firms (careers, competition between groups) than of external factors. At the same time there were increasingly numerous technical and organisational changes (growth of shift working, industrial restructuring) which all tended to upset the wage structure and thus exert a cumulative upward pressure on the average wage. The consequences of this development were further intensified by a number of trends which became especially important in many countries at the end of the 1960s. Successful claims by wage-earners for increases for particular grades, in order to raise the lowest wages (Reynaud, 1978); pressure to review job classifications in order to create a more homogeneous workforce and reduce the consequences of losses of skills resulting from technical changes (Eyraud, 1975; Sellier, 1971; Mickler, 1978); and strengthening of guarantees of employment by means of collective agreements or legislation (Piore, 1978).

These changes must be stressed in order to understand the strong pressures exerted on the average wage in the most dynamic and concentrated sectors, and the lack of sensitivity of changes in wage increases in the general level of economic activity (Deruelle, 1974; Guillaume, 1976; Silvestre, 1971). Other changes have also affected the wage relativities between the more protected groups of workers and the others.

The behaviour of the workers and their trade unions has aimed, often successfully, at widening the area of interdependence of wages to include categories which were traditionally outside it. This broadening of the field of interdependence has come about as a result either of active trade union policy, as in France or Italy, or through movements not originally under trade union control, as in Germany or the Netherlands (Sellier, 1971; La Porta and D. Valcavi, 1976).

It is important to point out that in many European countries this change in the wage structure has on the whole favoured the lowest paid even at times when economic activity was falling sharply. Thus between 1972 and 1976, the wages of manual workers increased much more rapidly than those of other groups in France and Italy and also, though to a less marked degree, in the Netherlands and Belgium. The same is true if we consider the differences between men's and women's wages, which narrowed during the same period in Germany, the Netherlands and Belgium, and to a lesser degree in France and Italy (J. Bouteiller, 1974). It is also clear that the wage trends observed in the 1970s have on the whole been in the direction of narrowing the differences between high-wage industries (often highly unionised) and the

182

rest (CERC, 1977). These tendencies appear to be somewhat different from those observed in the United States (Perry, 1978).

The trend of the labour market since the end of the 1960s can also usefully be illustrated by analysis of the changes in rates of unemployment among the most vulnerable groups. For Salais (1978), for instance, the rise in unemployment is mainly due to the conjunction of two trends:

i) a rise in the rate of activity and the supply of manpower of the kinds traditionally employed in the most vulnerable and least stable jobs (young people, women, temporary workers);

ii) a change in the policy of firms, for which the growth of this type of workforce is an opportunity, in the face of the growing inflexibility of the domestic markets, to transfer certain jobs so as to make them less stable and more dependent on the location of investments and technical changes; as a result of which a 'perverse' relationship has emerged, on a larger scale than in the past, between job creation and mobility of labour.[4]

These various analyses seem to me to supplement each other and so throw an interesting light in the shift in the Phillips curve and on the policies which these changes involve. They tend, for instance, to draw attention to the autonomy of wage movements — especially in the pace-setting sectors — and the trend of unemployment (Piore, 1974, Chapter 5); the autonomy being more or less marked depending on the structural features of the various labour markets: rigidity in the protected sector; a secondary labour force and its place in production. They also tend to justify the introduction of policies different from those hitherto in favour, which would aim at the same time to keep wages under better control, especially in certain strategic sectors, and limit the generation of unemployment.[5] Finally they emphasize, more than has been done in the past, the role of enterprises and their wage and manpower policies in the functioning of the labour market.

Policies for Incomes and Collective Bargaining

On this question I feel that Professor Dodge tends rather too much to define incomes policy as a complement to demand management policy and to judge its effectiveness by the extent to which wage trend norms are made to approximate to those policies. It may be pointed out, for example, that in many cases the relationship is the opposite, and the success of an incomes policy will depend on the decisions that the government takes on tax or employment matters. The reduction of certain indirect taxes, especially in countries where they are very high, may encourage acceptance by the least favoured groups of limits to rises in money wages.

---

4. These analyses do not rule out other or additional explanations of unemployment based on the strategy of a search for protected jobs adopted by workers who are for the time being 'unstable' (Hall, 1975).

5. This is the significance of the discussions going on in France about the expected effects of a change in the method of financing social expenditure, which at present slows down the growth of employment in labour-intensive industries and encourages high wages in the most capital-intensive industries (Commissariat au Plan, 1977).

Similarly, making income tax less progressive, or even changing the rates, is an important way in which the government can moderate the claims of wage-earners and unions for nominal or real wage increases. Among these ways in which the policies of governments can be adapted to suit their objectives in regard to wages should undoubtedly also be included any action to raise direct family incomes, such as aid to large families, easier access to employment by young workers, or indirect incomes (through collective benefits).

The Dodge report also stresses the fact that a major obstacle encountered by incomes policies is the growing trend towards a systematic catch-up with past price increases — which thus become the norm — in decisions on future wage increases. This tendency is no doubt real, but it is not, I feel, the only one encountered in attempts by governments to slow down rises in money wages to what is considered as "normal". In many European countries the movement of money wages has been marked since the end of the 1960s by a comparatively high rate of growth in purchasing power, fairly independent of changes in the level of economic activity, the rate of inflation and the rise in unemployment. During the period of the greatest fall in industrial activity the purchasing power of the wages of manual workers increased appreciably in all the Common Market countries, and in many cases was at an annual rate of 5 per cent or more. Accurate models tested in the case of France show that, unlike earlier periods, the decade 1967-1977 was marked by a very regular rise in the purchasing power of the wages of manual workers in relation to short-term fluctuations in the rise in prices, unemployment and productivity (Boyer, 1978).

Forces are undoubtedly at work which go beyond the mere incorporation of past price rises in wage claims. Among these forces it is important to mention, at least for some countries in which the growth of powerful and competitive industries is a comparatively recent phenomenon, the raising of the standard of the real wages of industrial workers.[6] This pressure on purchasing power is much weaker, indeed almost negligible, where the wages of non-manual workers are concerned. These market tendencies are not only part of an evolution towards a more equitable wage structure, but are also a necessary condition for the success of industrialisation policies in certain countries and should as such be integrated in wage policies that are even if there is no index-linking; one might go even further and ask, as does then have an appreciable influence on the concept of "standards of equity" the desirability of which is stressed by Dodge as a means of reducing increases in money wages below their present trend.

These observations also make it necessary to reassess the criticisms made of systems whereby wages are linked to price indices. Dodge correctly points out elsewhere that the price index has a very powerful influence on wages even if there is no index-linking; one might go even further and ask, as does Reynaud (1978), whether collective bargaining over these relations between prices and wages does not serve to diminish rather than accentuate that

---

6. The extent to which this is being demanded varies greatly from country to country, so far as Europe is concerned. Some, such as Germany or the Netherlands, have a ratio between non-industrial and industrial wages that is very favourable to industrial workers. Others, like France and Italy, have a ratio that is very favourable to non-industrial workers; while a third group, comprising Belgium, the United Kingdom and Denmark, occupy intermediate positions.

influence. Mention might also be made of the advantages of the "safeguard clause" procedures employed in the public sector in France, which avoid index-linking in the very short term but give guarantees to wage-earners when price rises go beyond the expected effects of a moderate rise in negotiated wages (Piotet, 1978).

In conclusion, some remarks on government policies for regulating wage increases, proposing a few distinctions of use in the discussion.

Dodge discusses mainly the conditions for the introduction and success of stabilising incomes policies whose aim is the short-term adjustment of the rate of increase of wages and prices. The fact that there are possibilities of succeeding in these fields in certain circumstances need not prevent pointing out the advantages of, and the need for, a medium-term income-regulating policy, or a social contract as defined by Professor E.H. Phelps Brown (1974) at the end of an OECD Conference on Wage Determination. Such a concept of government action which, in its more elaborate forms, involves planning in value terms[7], corresponds rather to the approach to the macroeconomic problems of growth and distribution favoured by many European trade unions. I feel that emphasis should be placed on the importance which investment has acquired in the devising of such policies, as regards both their volume (Malinvaud, 1978 and 1971), in order to avoid phases of over-investment, when the rise in real wages is effectively under control, and their nature, which can have a decisive influence on the scale of unemployment and the trend of working conditions of wage-earners (Salais, 1978).

It also seems necessary to distinguish between the problems raised by an incomes policy (short- or medium-term) and those raised by a policy for collective bargaining. In the latter case there is a central issue concerning the effect of collective bargaining on the actual wages paid. The connection between collective bargaining and wages is admittedly sufficiently direct when the negotiations, and the application and management of the bargains, are all carried out at a single level which can only be that of the enterprise. The relationship is undoubtedly much more complex when − as is the case in many European countries − there is a system of industrial relations whereby agreements are concluded at the level of industries, regions or the whole country and are applied and managed at the level of enterprises. This problem of several levels of decision-taking, sometimes associated, as in most Southern European countries, with a multiplicity of unions, seems all the more important since one of the outstanding tendencies of European trade unionism, especially in Italy (La Porta and Valcavi, 1976), France (Reynaud, 1978) and Germany (Sellier, 1972; Weltz, 1978), is to insist more strongly on complementary negotiations by wage-earners and unions at a very decentralised level (the enterprise, the establishment or even the workshop) while maintaining the principle of central negotiation. Working out a policy for collective bargaining must undoubtedly take account of these tendencies. This admittedly involves devising methods for centralised co-ordination and overall norms, but also requires linking processes to enable

---

7. Bernard and Massé 1969; Massé 1964.

account to be taken of the macroeconomic constraints while at the same time keeping the work of bargaining at a level where the workers can feel directly involved. This was, for example, the aim of the procedures tried out with some success in the nationalised sector in France, in which the general direction desired by the government was expressed in terms of total wage-bill, and the decentralised negotiations were concerned with how that wage-bill was to be divided and managed (Piotet, 1978, Toutée, 1964, Rochecorbon, 1968).

RECENT WAGE TRENDS AND MEDIUM-TERM ADJUSTMENT PROBLEMS

Palle Schelde Andersen[1]

The period since the late sixties has seen a coincidence of high rates of unemployment and inflation, leading to widespread beliefs that, compared with the fifties and sixties, the rather stable trade-off between inflation and unemployment has either ceased to exist or undergone a significant deterioration. A number of recent analyses — particularly in the United States — have addressed the question as to why the rate of inflation has remained so stubbornly high despite deteriorating labour market conditions, partly by presenting the problems in an alternative theoretical framework and partly by re-estimating and re-specifying traditional wage relationships. Thus shifts in the composition of the labour force, the influence of lags and price expectations and changes in trade union membership have been more specifically taken into account.[2] Moreover, the general question of whether wage and salary earners bargain in terms of nominal, real, or relative wages has received more attention than in earlier empirical studies. The present paper may be considered an attempt along the same lines, as it addresses three questions, which — though not directly related — concern various aspects of the bargaining process and, at the same time, have important implications for economic policies.

Section 1 discusses whether wage claims are formulated in real or in nominal terms and which set of prices is more important for the final outcome. In a period of stable and largely parallel price movements, employers and employees are likely to have consistent and coincident price expectations, but in the case of large fluctuations in prices external to the wage bargaining process there is a risk of diverging views with regard to the development in real wage costs and real earnings which, in turn, may spark off a strong inflationary process. Against the background of the steep rise in oil and other commodity prices in 1973-74, the response of real and nominal wages is analysed for a number of OECD countries and attempts are made to assess to what extent wage developments have been consistent with a desired adjustment of the foreign balance. A particular aspect of the adjustment process concerns the role of government action. The overall stance of demand management has significantly influenced the development in nominal and real wages, as policies in some countries were accommodating a higher rate of inflation, while in others restrictive measures were appplied to "break" the inflationary spiral. More specifically, the development of

---

1. Head of General Economics Division, Economics and Statistics Department, OECD. In writing this paper the author acknowledges the considerable amount of help and inspiration given by his colleagues J. Chan Lee and A. Mittelstadt.
2. See Perry, (1970); Gordon, (1972), and Wachter, (1976). For studies taking explicit account of the role of trade unions, see Hines, (1969), Ashenfelter, Johnson and Pencavel (1972), and several contributions in Laidler, and Purdy, eds. (1974).

income-tax rates has influenced the trend in real disposable earningss compared with before-tax real wages. Thus, in some countries a steep rise in average and marginal tax rates seems to have induced "tax-push" wage claims while in others, the adoption of tax reductions in a framework of social consensus appears to have dampened nominal wage demands. At the same time, generally higher social security taxes and other employer welfare contributions have, in most countries, raised total labour costs compared with direct wage costs, thereby possibly creating a further divergence of wage claims and wage offers.

Another aspect of this problem — and more generally of recent labour-cost trends — has been the rising share of non-wage labour costs (NWLCs). This can in part be related to higher social welfare contributions imposed on employers, but is also the result of a rapid growth of fringe benefits, partly reflecting a gradual development towards establishing a longer-term relationship between employers and employees. Consequently, the proportion of total labour costs which is directly related to the number of hours worked is today lower than earlier. As further explained in section 2, this implies that fluctuations in unit labour costs have tended to grow more counter-cyclical over time. Section 2 also discusses the origins of this development, including the role of trade unions, and analyses to what extent the share of NWLCs in total labour costs varies across industries and between different countries.

While most empirical studies of the wage formation process have analysed wage developments from a macroeconomic point of view, it has also been recognised that changes in the wage structure may have a particular impact on overall wage development. Through emulations and spillovers, wage gains obtained by unions in certain sectors affect the general pattern. At the same time, the wage claims presented by unions in a particular industry may reflect concerns about real income developments, as well as attempts to maintain a certain relative income position. Section 3 is devoted to an analysis of inter-industry wage trends in selected Member countries, discussing *inter alia* the relative importance of economy-wide and sector-specific developments. In particular, this part considers the cyclical variation of wage dispersions and attempts to assess the extent to which disturbances in the wage structure have influenced the overall inflation rate and possibly contributed to the apparent deterioration of the inflation/unemployment trade-off.

Although seemingly unrelated, the three aspects of recent wage trends dealt with in this paper have similar implications for the general wage formation process and the choice of appropriate anti-inflationary policies. If the determination of wage claims is decomposed into two elements, reflecting the influence of — respectively — current demand conditions (u_t) and wage (and non-wage) targets (w_t^g),[3] the rate of change in total labour costs (w_t) may be approximated by the following equation:

$$\dot{w}_t = a + b\, u_t + c\, \dot{w}_t^g$$

---

3. As further discussed below, the target may reflect attempts to maintain the share of wage incomes or to ensure a "normal" growth of real disposable earnings.

With the share of non-wage labour costs — and partly also of the fixed-cost component (see further below) — rising over time, the constant term (a) will tend to increase while the influence of general demand conditions (u) may diminish and become subject to longer and longer time-lags. Viewed in the framework of a simple two-dimensional Phillips curve, this development implies a shift in both the level and the slope of the short-run relationship between the rates of inflation and unemployment. Thus, with a growing share of more or less fixed employment costs a given rate of unemployment will tend to be associated with a higher rate of inflation and, at the same time, changes in the rate of unemployment will induce a smaller acceleration or deceleration in the rate of price and labour cost increases. With respect to the wt-element, rising concern about the development in real after-tax earnings and relative income positions would, in general, imply that the importance attached to specific wage targets will increase in relation to the influence of current demand conditions; i.e. "c" rises compared with "b" and $\dot{w}_t^g$ itself may increase over time.[4] Assuming that price expectations as well as the influence of shifts in the wage structure can be approximated by a function of past wage changes[5], the process of wage determination as presented in the above equation will more and more appear as an auto-regressive relationship, where current increases in total labour costs are dominated by past wage changes and exogenous components, while the impact of current demand conditions may be small and subject to long lags. Moreover, to the extent that higher taxes are used as an instrument for arresting an inflationary development, the dampening influence of less favourable labour market conditions could, in some countries, be thwarted by "tax-push" effects, reflecting attempts to maintain a certain rate of growth of after-tax earnings.

To what extent recent trends in wages and labour costs justify such conclusions with respect to the scope for demand management policies is considered in the last part of the paper, which also briefly discusses the medium-term outlook for the OECD area and the role of price and wage developments in creating more favourable employment conditions.

1. Real Wages and "External" Price Changes

Prices and the determination of wages

The original Phillips curve — as well as most of the subsequent wage equations estimated for different countries over various time periods — was specified in terms of nominal wage increases. However, since in the

---

4. More specifically, if current wage claims in a certain sector are influenced by past wage changes in other sectors, as well as by price expectations, the responsiveness of wage claims to changes in demand will be smaller or subject to longer lags, compared with a situation where real or relative wage targets are relatively unimportant.

5. This is clearly a simplification. The existence of threshold effects — due to indexation clauses or a certain reaction on the part of wage earners — will produce a discontinuous wage pattern, which is not captured by past wage changes.

long run the demand for labour is determined by real rather than nominal wages and the supply of labour can also be assumed to depend on the development in real wages[6], a substantial part of the literature on wage determination has dealt with the influence of prices; i.e. prices have been introduced as an explanatory variable in addition to one or more expressions for excess demand pressure. A considerable part of this discussion has been concentrated on determining price expectations, while the question of whether the appropriate price term should include output or consumer prices – or possibly both – has received relatively little attention. Thus higher output prices – either by improving firms' ability to pay or by raising the marginal revenue product of labour – would tend to increase the demand for labour and thus raise the rate of nominal wage increase. Similarly, higher consumer prices – either through escalator clauses or real wage targets – might reduce the supply of labour and thus put upward pressure on the rate of wage increase. On the basis of traditional one-equation wage functions, it is not possible to identify separate effects of output and consumer prices and, even for more complete models including both demand and supply functions, separate influences would be difficult to identify, as throughout most of the postwar period the two price indices have followed each other rather closely.[7]

External price changes, wage flexibility and economic policies

However, in conditions of large "external" price changes, the development in consumer and output prices will differ, possibly creating a dichotomy of perception regarding real wages and risking an acceleration of the rate of inflation.[8] Thus, when import prices rise substantially faster than export prices - i.e. the terms of trade deteriorate - the increase in wages (or compensation) deflated by output prices will tend to exceed that of wages deflated by consumer prices. Consequently, there is a potential conflict in the wage bargaining process as employers may not fully realise to what extent real pre-tax wages have been squeezed. Conversely, trade unions may underestimate the true rise in real wage costs and its implications for profits. The reaction of trade unions and employers to this deviation between real wages and real labour costs, together with the stance of demand

6. If both the demand for and supply of labour are determined by real wages, and wage adjustments are flexible and not subject to time-lags, total employment as well as the real wage rate will be determined in the labour market, leaving little room for traditional demand management policies to affect total real output. These assumptions are implicit or explicit in classical models and are also embedded in more recent "accelerationist" formulations of the Phillips curve, which excludes a long-run trade-off between inflation and unemployment.

7. As will be discussed below, this is less likely to hold in a more disaggregated model of wage determination.

8. Broadly speaking, the development in consumer prices (CPI) can be approximated by the following expression :

$$CPI = a\,P_d + (1-a)\,P_x$$

where P_d refers to the average output price of the sector (or the whole economy) for which wage changes are analysed, P_x denotes prices outside this sector, and "a" and "1 – a" are weights. While the following analysis focuses on import and export prices, it would for some countries be more relevant to consider relative prices in the primary and secondary sectors. Thus, a surge in food prices could have an important effect on industrial wages without being reflected in a country's terms of trade. On the other hand, for countries with a large export share of primary products, a commodity price boom would improve the terms of trade, but should not have any direct effect on wage negotiations in the manufacturing sectors.

management, will determine whether this situation leads to an acceleration of inflation over extended periods or to a change in relative factor prices and income shares which facilitates the adjustment to the new external conditions:

(i) in the case of real wage rigidity — either due to strong real wage resistance or indexation clauses protecting the employees against an erosion of real incomes — the initial burden of the terms-of-trade loss will be borne by the employers, who will see real wage costs rising faster than real output per man and, consequently, a declining profit share. At the same time, real wage and salary incomes per employee progress in line with real GNP. However, if policies are accommodating, the acceleration in unit labour costs and import prices, will probably — depending on the initial position of profits and the flexibility of other incomes — lead to sharply higher output prices. In general, the combination of inflexible real wages and accommodating policies will tend to leave factor shares largely unchanged, but "at the expense" of an extended period with high rates of inflation. On the other hand, if policies are non-accommodating, "second-round" price increases will be relatively moderate, while labour market conditions are likely to weaken. Generally, this situation can be expected to entail a marked shift of the income distribution in favour of labour and a relatively short period of high inflation rates;

(ii) in the case of flexible real wages, the adjustment to the slower trend in real national income may be rather fast and the reaction to the inflationary impulse of the terms-of-trade deterioration much smaller. The development in factor shares — which in this case are likely to remain largely unchanged — and relative factor prices can be expected to facilitate a smooth return to the initial balance-of-payments situation.[9] In these conditions, demand management policies are less important for income shares and will mainly influence the length of the period during which inflation will be running at a high rate.

Under the social and institutional arrangements of modern industrial societies, the first case would seem to be the most likely outcome; i.e. the initial effect of a deterioration in the terms of trade and the rise in the overall price level will almost certainly escalate claims for higher wages and other factor incomes in an attempt to recapture the losses of real income. In such circumstances, an accommodating policy stance is unlikely to facilitate the adjustment process, particularly if the high rate of inflation is accompanied by a deterioration in the foreign exchange rate, which may further widen the gap between real wages and the income "norm".

---

9. In this context it is important to note that a return to the initial balance-of-payments position does not normally imply that the loss (in real income induced by changes in the terms of trade) has been eliminated. In fact, if relative foreign prices remain unchanged after the terms-of-trade deterioration, a necessary — but not sufficient — condition for re-establishing the initial foreign balance is that domestic demand fall relative to domestic output, thus creating room for a rise in net real exports. At unchanged spending propensities, this downward adjustment of domestic demand requires that the development in real income will have to "absorb" the terms-of-trade loss.

Policies aimed at choking-off price and wage increases through deflation-ary demand management may be more conducive to a faster adjustment to the changing external conditions, though the "cost" in terms of foregone output will, for most countries, be high. As indicated above, a reduction in domestic demand relative to output is a necessary condition for re-establish-ing the initial foreign balance, but during the period when foreign demand has not risen sufficiently to "fill the gap" between domestic demand and output, employment conditions are bound to deteriorate. Moreover, even though a restrictive demand management policy will reduce the rate of inflation compared with other countries, there is a risk that some of the measures adopted may accentuate the dichotomy of perception regarding real wages. Thus increases in social security taxes will cause total labour costs to rise faster than wage costs and discretionary income-tax increases and/or fiscal drag would lower the rise in real after-tax earnings in relation to the increase in pre-tax earnings or wage costs. Particularly in a situation where sudden external price changes push the rise in real disposable earnings below earlier trends and, at the same time raise average tax rates through fiscal drag, attempts by various groups to maintain their shares in national income may, in some countries, provide an additional source of inflationary pressure and thus complicate the implementation of an appropriate and effective demand management policy.[10/11]

On the other hand, a restrictive policy stance is not necessarily the only alternative, and some countries have relied on incomes policy measures, including modifications of existing wage indexation or escalator clauses. Indeed, it may be argued that in a situation where the real transfer of re-sources corresponding to the terms-of-trade loss can be postponed, the governments are in a position to "match" the change in the foreign balance and "absorb" part of the decline in real incomes by allowing a deterioration in the budget balance and, at the same time, introduce measures to reduce the risk of an acceleration in the rate of inflation. Thus, by lowering income-tax rates and/or increasing subsidies and transfers, the governments may "absorb" part of the externally imposed loss of real income and simul-taneously contain compensatory wage claims. However, while such actions will ease the internal adjustment process, additional measures will be needed to achieve an improvement in the external position, as this policy response will not be conducive to a transfer of resources to the sectors competing with other countries. Indeed, since domestic demand is not reduced relative to output and real national income, there is a high risk that the initial ex-

---

10. Recognition of the risk of tax-push inflation, which essentially implies that wage claims are formulated in terms of real disposable earnings rather than nominal pre-tax wages, is comparatively recent. The validity of this hypothesis depends on both a decline in "tax illusion" and the develop-ment in average and marginal tax rates, making it difficult to measure empirically. Moreover, to the extent that the theory also holds for actual wages, it essentially implies that there are no countervail-ing forces transmitted through employers' roles in the bargaining process.

11. In this context it may also be noted that in conditions of deteriorating terms of trade and hence a lower rate of growth or real income, the scope for pursuing egalitarian wage policies without triggering an acceleration of inflation or a further deterioration in the foreign balance is significantly reduced. If targets for low-income groups are not adjusted to the lower rate of growth of real national income, the implicit adjustment burden for other income groups will be correspondingly larger, which – if not accepted – will push up the inflation rate and/or worsen the balance-of-payments position.

ternal deficit will widen further. Moreover, this policy presupposes a high degree of social consensus regarding the distribution of factor incomes, and in the absence of such an agreement — i.e. in the case of real income rigidity — the accommodating policy stance will — as noted above — tend to exacerbate and perpetuate the inflationary impulse from abroad.

Empirical Analysis of Real Wage Changes

An empirical assessment of the wage response to the terms-of-trade deterioration for the OECD area in 1973-74 and a comparison of the extent to which policies have affected relative factor price changes and the adjustment process in different countries are, for several reasons, difficult:

(i) due to variations in the reliance on imported energy, the immediate — deflationary as well as inflationary — impact of the rise in energy prices differed considerably between Member countries;

(ii) although most Member countries were close to full employment and capacity utilisation in 1973 and inflationary pressures had been building up, there were large differences in the extent to which balance-of-payments and inflation trends were out of line with earlier patterns and, therefore, also in the vulnerability to the external shock. In fact, it may be argued that, for some countries, the adjustment to external price changes was no more than an additional complication in a general attempt to reduce inflation and improve the foreign balance;

(iii) while virtually all Member countries[12] adopted a more restrictive policy stance in 1974-75, differences in the timing of policy measures, as well as in the reliance on respectively fiscal and monetary policy have probably affected the response of prices and wages. In addition, traditional demand management policies have, in a number of countries, been supplemented by specific employment stabilisation measures;

(iv) due to inter-country variations in the short-term trade-off between inflation/unemployment and in the speed with which wages and prices adjust to changes in labour and product market conditions, it is difficult to judge the extent of real wage resistance. Moreover, since the rate of productivity increase tends to fall in a cyclical downturn while the rise in real wages is only partly adjusted to the slower real income growth, the relative trends of *per capita* real output and wages for the 1973-76 period will be influenced by cyclical factors, as well as the adjustment to externally imposed income losses.

Development in Real Wages and Real Income "Norm"

Keeping these caveats in mind, however, it is possible to draw some conclusions with respect to the size of the initial problem posed by the

---

12. Norway, Sweden, Italy, Canada and partly also Austria are the major exceptions.

higher energy prices and the subsequent adjustment process in various Member countries. Thus, by adopting the growth of real national income per employee – i.e. GNP corrected for terms-of-trade changes and divided by total (dependent as well as self-employed) employment – as a "norm" and comparing this to the development in wage costs and earnings deflated by, respectively, output prices and consumer prices, it is possible to get some idea of both the extent to which real wages have adjusted to the "norm"[13] and the potential size of the dichotomy of perception mentioned above.[14] Judging by the results shown in Table 1[15], the United States is the only country where, in 1976, real earnings have actually fallen over the four-year period and more than adjusted to the flat development of the national "norm". Moreover, the rate of productivity increase in the United States has exceeded the advance in total real labour costs, suggesting an improvement in the relative cost and profit position of firms. Developments in Germany also point to a small degree of wage rigidity, as the rise in real wages has been below that of the "norm". Although there was a marked rise in unemployment, the adjustment has taken place in conditions of considerably faster productivity growth than in the United States. In Austria, the Netherlands, Sweden and Finland, real wage earnings by 1976 were largely in line with the "norm", but in all four countries – and particularly in Sweden – real total labour costs have exceeded productivity by some margin. In almost all other countries, real wage earnings by 1976 exceeded

13. Since the national accounts do not allow for productivity increases in the public sector, the "norms" as calculated in this paper will underestimate the "room" for real wage increases. However, private sector output deflators are available for only a few of the countries analysed. On the other hand, considering that during the period 1973-1977 the share of the public sector in total output has generally been rather stable, this bias may in most countries be relatively unimportant.

14. While there is no generally accepted method of measuring terms-of-trade losses and gains, the procedure adopted here defines the real income effect (T_i) for year i – expressed as an absolute amount – as follows :

(a) $T_i = X_{i-1} (P_i^{-1} - P_{x,i}^{-1}) + M_{i-1} (P_{m,i}^{-1} - P_i^{-1})$ where

    X = exports in current prices

    M = imports in current prices

    P_x = export deflator, set equal to 1 in base year

    P_m = import deflator, set equal to 1 in base year

    P_i = $1/2 (P_x + P_m)$

An alternative definition, which gives approximately the same result and is more directly relevant for the problem at hand, would be :

(b) $T_i = GNP_{i-1} (P_{gnp,i}^{-1} - P_{dd,i}^{-1})$ where

    P_{gnp} = GNP deflator

    P_{dd} = domestic demand deflator

While (a) is based on the relative change in foreign prices - measured in relation to the base year - (b) focuses on the corresponding deviation between the domestic output and demand deflators. Due to the large weight of private consumption in domestic demand, a comparison of wages deflated by, respectively, output prices and consumer prices should give a reasonably good indication of the degree to which terms-of-trade changes may create diverging perceptions of real wage developments.

15. The first three columns show various concepts of real income, the next three comparable productivity and cost measures, and the last three indicators of nominal wage increases, cyclical changes and the initial terms-of-trade effect. No adjustments have been made for the impact of cyclical changes, and it may also be noted that, since the employment figures have not been adjusted for changes in the average number of hours worked, the table does not give a correct impression of real wage and productivity developments. However, for a discussion of the adjustment process, this is of minor importance as the employment concepts used are consistent and "cancel out" in the comparisons below.

194

Table 1
Developments in Real Income, Productivity and Costs, 1972-76
(Indices, 1972 = 100, except for column 8)

	"Norm" (a)	Real wages (b)	Real disposable income (c)	GDP per employee (d)	Real total labour costs (e)	Real wage costs (f)	Nominal wages	Terms-of-trade loss (g)	Labour slack (h)
United States.	101.2	98.0	100.3	102.4	100.8	98.0	136.3	− 1.4	96.1
Germany	113.4	112.6	105.2	115.2	117.4	114.3	140.5	− 2.5	93.1
Austria	115.3	115.5	119.7	115.4	115.1	114.0	164.7	0.0	94.4
Netherlands	111.5	112.2	106.0	115.1	118.0	114.3	163.8	− 3.8	93.9
Sweden	103.7	104.8	104.3	104.2	111.5	100.8	163.0	− 3.0	96.5
Switzerland.	106.5	110.2	110.3	104.7	113.4	113.4	132.3	− 2.6	84.0
Finland	111.7	113.3	105.8	110.6	112.8	109.0	199.2	− 0.6	93.4
Norway	105.8	112.0	117.0	110.8	111.5	111.5	182.0	− 3.0	100.5
France	111.0	116.3	108.2	112.8	121.4	118.0	183.8	− 3.5	95.1
Canada	106.5	112.7	112.8	103.5	105.4	103.9	161.9	3.4	97.0
Australia	107.3	121.2	–	106.4	114.1	114.1	196.5	3.3	95.1
Belgium.	111.6	118.2	108.4	114.5	121.8	117.6	187.5	− 1.1	95.5
Italy.	102.4	112.8	106.4	109.4	115.8	113.0	233.4	− 6.4	95.7
United Kingdom	101.7	110.2	103.0	105.5	112.5	109.5	194.3	− 6.4	97.0
Japan	109.1	120.3	118.2	114.8	127.9	126.9	195.5	− 5.1	83.9
Denmark	103.8	117.1	116.0	106.3	114.3	115.0	192.3	− 5.2	92.5

a) GDP in constant prices, corrected for changes in the terms of trade and divided by total employment.
b) Wages per dependent employee as defined in the national accounts, deflated by the private consumption deflator.
c) Disposable household income less transfers, divided by total employment and deflated by the private consumption deflator. For Denmark and Norway the estimates are tentative as disposable income figures are only available for the total private sector.
d) GDP in constant prices, divided by total employment.
e) Total compensation per dependent employee as defined in the national accounts, deflated by the GDP deflator.
f) Wages as defined in (b), deflated by the GDP deflator.
g) Income effect of total change in the terms of trade from 1972 to 1974, in per cent of GDP (for Japan and Norway the terms of trade change relates to the period 1972-75).
h) Actual labour input in per cent of trend, where trend labour input is defined as trend (labour force) × trend (employment rate) × trend (hours worked) × trend (output per man-hour). Trends are defined in terms of simple moving averages and estimates are presented for a moving average of 15 years, except for Australia, where the trend is based on a moving average of 10 years.
Source : OECD, *National Accounts* and Secretariat estimates.

the "norm" by 5 per cent or more and, except for Norway and Canada, this development was accompanied by a considerable deterioration of the cost and profit position of firms, as total labour costs increased markedly faster than productivity. Switzerland is a special case, as real wage earnings have increased moderately faster than the "norm", while the cost position of firms has worsened considerably due to a sharp reduction in economic growth and a rise in real total labour costs of 13 per cent.[16]

According to preliminary data, the above conclusions largely also hold for 1977[17], though in some cases rather large shifts have occurred (Diagram 1). Thus, the "gap" between the "norm" and real wages fell from 8 1/2 to only 2 1/2 per cent in the United Kingdom, while in Norway, Sweden and Australia the "gap" widened by 5-6 percentage points. In most other countries the changes from 1976 to 1977 were only marginal, but the number of countries with real wages below the "norm" rose from 2 to 5, as Finland, the Netherlands and Austria moved "above the line".

Government action

The influence of government action appears in three different forms:

i) comparisons of columns 2 and 3 show to what extent direct taxes may have eased or complicated the adjustment of real earnings to the "norm". In the United States, Austria, Switzerland, and particularly in Norway, lower direct tax rates have enabled wage and salary earners to obtain a higher rise in after-tax earnings than in pre-tax wages, while in Sweden, Denmark, Canada, and partly also in Japan, income taxes have been largely neutral with respect to the adjustment process. On the other hand, in Germany, the Netherlands, Finland, France, the United Kingdom, Belgium and, to some extent, also in Italy, fiscal drag and discretionary policy changes have strongly reduced the rate of growth of after-tax earnings in relation to before-tax wages[18];

ii) a comparison of columns 5 and 6 shows to what extent taxes and other social welfare contributions imposed on employers have affected the relative cost position of firms. In all countries, except for Norway and Denmark, it appears that total labour costs have increased faster than wage costs, with the deterioration in employers' cost and profit positions being particularly severe in Sweden, Germany, the Netherlands, France, Finland and the United Kingdom. In what measure this development has affected the rate of increase in

---

16. This outcome may possibly be related to the effective revaluation of the Swiss franc, which has probably dampened the rate of growth of output prices relative to that of consumer prices. Moreover, the sharp fall in the share of foreign workers in total employment may have tended to raise average wages.

17. Due to data limitations, only a few of the columns shown in Table 1 are available for 1977.

18. As will be discussed below, in a majority of these countries the empirical evidence does not point to any strong "tax-push" effects on inflation.

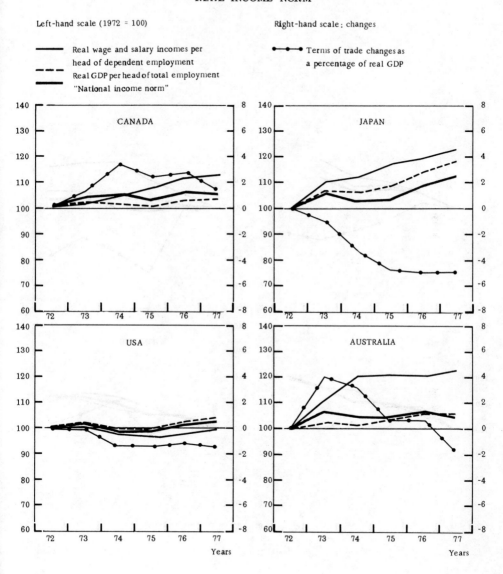

Diagram 1. REAL WAGES, PRODUCTIVITY AND
REAL INCOME NORM

Left-hand scale (1972 = 100)

Real wage and salary incomes per
head of dependent employment
Real GDP per head of total employment
"National income norm"

Right-hand scale : changes

Terms of trade changes as
a percentage of real GDP

197

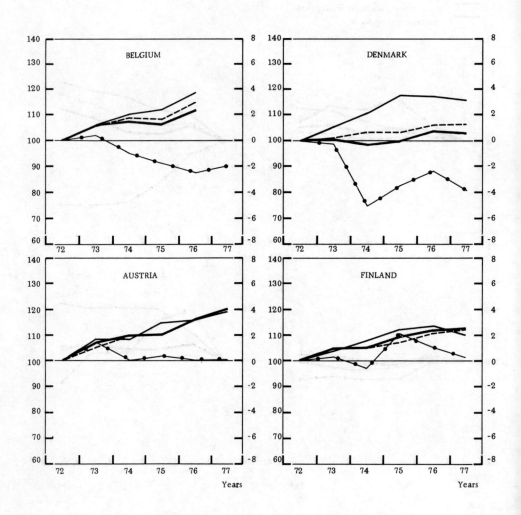

198

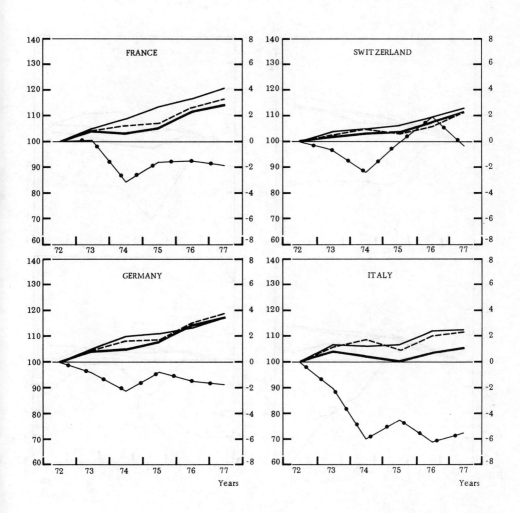

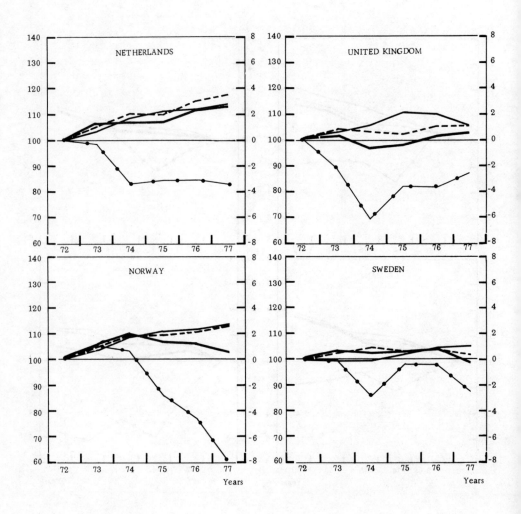

wages is difficult to judge[19], but particularly wide discrepancies between the rise in, respectively, total labour and direct wage costs are likely to have put additional upward pressure on prices;

iii) finally, a comparison of columns 2 and 6 with 1 and 4 may give some indication of a possible influence on the consumption deflator from changes in indirect taxes and subsidies. For a country experiencing a terms-of-trade deterioration, the GDP deflator will normally rise less fast than the consumption deflator, implying that the figure given in column 6 should exceed that of column 2. However, if the difference is considerably smaller than the income effect of the terms-of-trade deterioration — as measured by the difference between columns 1 and 4 — changes in indirect taxes and subsidies are likely to have affected the relative price trends. On this basis, it seems that in Sweden, Norway, Italy and the United Kingdom lower indirect taxes or higher subsidies have allowed the real adjustment to take place at a smaller rise in nominal wages and salaries. In Canada and Finland the output deflator has increased considerably faster than consumer prices, but this may reflect the terms-of-trade gain rather than a change in tax and subsidy rates. In most other countries, subsidies and indirect taxes seem to have been largely neutral with respect to changes in consumer prices.

Tax-push inflation

While the results discussed above do not explicitly measure tax-push inflation, a set of wage equations were earlier estimated to test this hypothesis.[20] On the assumption that the tendency to bargain in terms of real disposable earnings will be particularly pronounced when the increase in real after-tax incomes falls significantly below the rate traditionally expected by wage earners, these estimates included a "catch-up" term together with demand pressure and price variables. The empirical results clearly suggest that in the Scandinavian countries, as well as in Australia, Belgium and in the United Kingdom, there is a significant tendency for nominal wage demands to be raised to "catch-up" a past shortfall of real after-tax wages compared with their "normally expected" increase. No significant effect was found for the United States, Canada, Germany and the Netherlands. These suggests that tax-push effects in some countries may have had a significant impact on the change in relative factor prices.[21] On the other hand, the results obtained for Italy and France, where the deviations from the norm have been quite large, did not point to any significant impact of taxes, and for Japan the coefficient with respect to the "catch-up" variable was also somewhat doubtful.

19. In some countries — for instance in Sweden — it is generally recognised that an increase in employers' social welfare contributions or payroll taxes reduce the "room for wage increases" and such tax changes are, therefore, taken into account in the wage claims presented by the trade unions. Higher employee contributions may, of course, also influence wage claims, but these revenues have been included under direct personal taxes.

20. See "Public Expenditure Trends", Annex B, *OECD* (1978).

21. The existence of automatic or semi-automatic indexation of tax schedules — as in Canada, Denmark and the Netherlands — may have influenced the empirical estimates, but this question has not been pursued in any detail.

Real wage adjustment, nominal wages and initial terms-of-trade changes

Not surprisingly, a "ranking" of countries according to the degree of adjustment of real wage earnings to the national "norms" largely coincides with a "ranking" on the basis of nominal wage increases (Table 1, column 7). The major exceptions are Switzerland, which, as noted earlier, is a special case; Finland, where nominal wages have increased rather fast, possibly reflecting "tax-push" effects as after-tax real earnings are markedly below pre-tax earnings; and Canada, where, despite a relatively slow growth in nominal wages, real earnings have exceeded the "norm" by a considerable margin. Apart from the special factors pertaining to each particular country, it is worth noting that one characteristic feature of the three exceptions is that a terms-of-trade loss either did not occur or was reversed in the course of the four-year period. In general, considerations of the initial terms-of-trade losses provide important information, even though there is not a clear one-to-one correspondence between the potential size of the adjustment burden and the extent to which countries have moved closer to the "norm". Except for Canada, Australia[22] and Belgium, the "largest" "gap" between the "norm" and real wage gains is found among those countries where the initial terms-of-trade deterioration was most severely felt (Denmark, Italy, France, Japan and the United Kingdom until (1976). On the other hand, in those countries where the increase in real wages has been more or less in line with the "norm", the initial terms-of-trade loss was relatively small (1-2 per cent of GDP).

Real wages in a cyclical downturn

An assessment of the impact on real wage adjustments of fluctuations in labour market and general demand conditions is subject to major problems. Country-by-country comparisons of unemployment rates are notoriously difficult — if not impossible — and even comparisons of relative *changes* in rates or levels of unemployment are somewhat uncertain, particularly when the initial levels differ widely between countries. Moreover, to the extent that employment-supporting measures are taken or foreign workers constitute a disproportionately large share of the number of unemployed, the rate of unemployment will tend to understate the degree of slack. Hence, in the present context a more broadly defined measure was applied, and on the basis of the figures presented in Table 1, column 9 it may be tentatively concluded that restrictive policies[23] and a relatively sharp deterioration in labour market conditions probably played an important role in inducing a rapid adjustment of real wages in Germany, the

---

22. Switzerland and Australia may be considered extreme cases with regard to the adjustment of wages to external changes. Thus, in Switzerland the terms-of-trade loss has been reversed in conditions of low nominal wage gains, while in Australia an initial terms-of-trade gain was accompanied by a sharp rise in nominal wages.

23. The change in labour market slack should, of course, not be considered an indicator of the impact of policy changes in a rigorous sense. It merely serves as a measure of deviation from full employment conditions, which policies either have contributed to or failed to prevent.

Netherlands, Switzerland, and partly also in the United States and Austria.[24] At the same time, comparatively favourable employment conditions – partly related to an expansionary policy stance – may explain some of the large discrepancy between real wages and the "norm" in Sweden, Norway, Canada and, to some extent, also in Italy. On the other hand, in Denmark, Belgium, Japan, and partly also in France and Australia, the 1972-1976 developments point to a large measure of real wage rigidity as the gap between real wages and the "norm" remained large or even widened despite a marked weakening in labour market trends.

Apart from the problem of finding internationally consistent indicators, cyclical changes also complicate the analysis of real wage adjustments in other ways.

i) as mentioned earlier, a cyclical downturn is normally accompanied by a shift in the distribution of income in favour of wage and salary earners. In the present context, this implies that the recorded "real wage gap" – i.e. the difference between real wages and the real income "norm", cf. Table 1 – for some countries will indicate a more or less normal cyclical development rather than a structural imbalance;

ii) at the same time, the use of 1972 as the basis of the calculations may introduce another bias, as the countries analysed are unlikely to have been in the same cyclical position during this particular period. Hence, for some countries a recorded "real wage gap" may be no more than a normal correction of an earlier imbalance of factor shares.

A more detailed study of these questions is obviously required before a final verdict on the degree of real wage rigidity can be passed, and work along these lines is currently being done by the Secretariat. Preliminary estimates seem to suggest that an appropriate correction for cyclical factors will not change the "ranking" of the countries with respect to a possible "real wage gap", but the results obtained so far are too tentative to provide any idea as to the size of the problem. A few experiments with alternative base years indicate that in some cases this may have rather a large impact; but again the results are too preliminary to justify a more detailed discussion.

2. Development and Role of Non-wage Labour Costs (NWLCs)

As noted above, the development in social security contributions and other taxes levied on employers may, in a number of countries, have tended to accentuate the dichotomy of perception regarding real wages. While the forward shifting of payroll taxes is difficult to determine empirically, the general rise in the importance of social security contributions and other non-wage labour costs is likely to have influenced recent trends in both inflation

---

24. Both the United States and Austria are difficult to classify in this context. Since the recovery in the United States started earlier and has been more pronounced than in most other countries, the 1976 figure understates the severity of the recession. Thus in 1975, the index of labour market slack was more in line with figures recorded in some other countries, where the deterioration in the terms of trade was met by restrictive policy measures. In Austria, monetary and fiscal policies have been expansionary during most of the 1972-1976 period, and the marked deterioration in employment conditions is probably mainly due to the policy of tying the Austrian Schilling to the German Mark.

and employment. Thus by 1976 employers' contributions to social security schemes, private pension plans and insurance schemes and payroll taxes had in some countries (France, Italy, the Netherlands and Sweden) reached more than 30 per cent of total wage and salary earnings (Table 2). Moreover, the increase in the average share of such labour costs during the 1973-1976 period raised the rate of growth of real compensation by a considerable margin and, since externally imposed taxes are unlikely to affect productivity growth, this development may, in some countries, account for a considerable part of the divergent movements of various real wage measures. Finally, average shares and growth rates of NWLCs have differed considerably between countries, suggesting that the existence of such charges may, in part, explain the diverging adjustment paths.

Origin and nature of NWLCs

The growing importance of NWLCs can be related to changes in the legislation concerning social security and other welfare contributions imposed on the employers, but attempts by trade unions to bargain for non-wage benefits have also played a role. In several countries, structural and institutional changes, such as a relatively slow growth in the civilian labour force compared with that of the inactive population, and unusually rapid increases in health costs and substantial improvements in welfare benefits, have enlarged the financial requirements of self-financed social security schemes. Over and above this trend, the recent recession and the subsequent weak growth in employment have tended to put pressure on the financial resources and probably influenced decisions to increase rates and ceilings, including those applying to unemployment insurance. The role of trade unions in the development of NWLCs is more difficult to determine, but it seems reasonable to assume that greater demand for leisure, the desire to improve health insurance and retirement benefits and − at least in some countries − the high marginal tax rates applying to wages, have led trade unions to put greater emphasis on an enlargement of non-wage benefits.[25]

However, in addition to this more or less externally imposed cost element, the rising share of NWLCs in total compensation seems to reflect a deliberate policy on the part of firms. Thus, certain costs are incurred to increase the productivity of the labour force and/or ensure an employment pattern which is more consistent with expected developments in product demand. Together with the external labour costs discussed above, this development has, for some countries, raised the ratio of NWLCs to average earnings (manufacturing) to more than 70 per cent (Table 2) and has tended to strengthen the fixed component inside labour costs. Due to ceilings and other institutional factors, social welfare contributions are often difficult to vary in the short run, and voluntarily incurred NWLCs are mostly of a long-run nature, reflecting firms' attempts to maximise profits over the medium term.

---

25. Wage guidelines or direct control of wages have probably also tended to raise the share of fringe benefits in countries where such measures have been applied.

Table 2
Non-wage Labour Costs in Manufacturing (a) and the Economy as a Whole (B)

		1965	1970	1974	1975	1976
United States	1	20.3	24.7	30.0	31.3	31.7
	2	20.6	25.1	26.5	–	–
	3	9.5	11.4	14.3	14.9	15.5
Japan	1	13.1	13.2	13.2	14.3	14.3
	2	–	–	–	–	–
	3	4.8	5.4	5.5	6.3	6.8
Canada	1	16.6	19.7	22.8	23.8	25.3
	2	–	19.8	20.4	–	–
	3	4.7	6.0	7.7	8.2	9.1
France	1	62.0	60.3	64.2	66.8	68.0
	2	67.1	65.1	64.1	–	–
	3	31.9	33.0	33.2	34.6	34.4
Germany	1	36.5	42.2	55.6	58.4	60.8
	2	42.3	47.7	54.1	–	–
	3	16.2	18.4	21.5	22.4	23.1
Italy	1	78.1	81.3	–	66.0	66.9
	2	81.8	90.2	88.1	–	–
	3	37.7	40.6	40.5	40.9	39.8
United Kingdom	1	13.3	15.0	19.5	21.4	21.6
	2	15.9	20.5	21.0	–	–
	3	9.8	13.2	11.7	12.7	13.9
Belgium	1	47.9	56.2	68.6	73.0	73.7
	2	48.2	59.3	66.8	–	–
	3	22.2	24.1	24.9	26.4	–
Netherlands	1	43.8	56.7	67.4	67.8	66.7
	2	46.2	63.2	68.6	–	–
	3	17.9	23.8	28.6	29.0	29.3
Sweden	1	22.1	27.7	40.8	45.9	49.8
	2	23.4	28.2	41.6	-	–
	3	11.6	15.8	24.6	27.5	32.0

Note : 1) Manufacturing; preliminary estimates by the U.S. Bureau of Labour Statistics.
2) Manufacturing; estimates by Swedish Employers' Confederation. NWLC also include cost of vocational training, welfare services, etc.
3) Total economy; national accounts data.
a) Ratio of NWLC (including pay for time not worked except for Japan) to hourly earnings for production workers.
b) Employers' contributions to social security schemes, private pensions, insurance schemes, etc. and payroll taxes that are not compensation to employees, but are a labour cost to employers.

205

The proposition that labour costs have both a fixed and a variable component has found rising recognition in the 1960s.[26] According to this theory, fixed employment costs[27] drive a "wedge" between the marginal product of labour and the wage rate, as employers introduce non-wage benefits or raise wages above those prevailing elsewhere. While such wage premia may serve to stabilise the available supply of labour and maintain a queue of applicants to draw upon in the event of an unexpected rise in demand, other elements of the fixed labour-cost component reflect specific training expenditures[28], raising the marginal product of labour, or higher hiring costs, as employers attempt to reduce the risk of damage to sophisticated machinery through a more thorough screening of applicants. Hence part of the rise in NWLCs in recent years can be ascribed to investments in human capital and a longer-term attachment between employees and employers. This suggests that the elasticity of labour demand and employment with respect to changes in the overall level of production is now lower than earlier and recent developments in employment and total output seem to be consistent with this observation. Thus, even though rates of unemployment in most Member countries have reached record high levels for the post-war period, the slowdown in the growth of output per man-hour has been more pronounced than in earlier cycles.[29] This in turn implies that the rise in unit labour costs during the present recession has been unusually fast.

Sectoral distribution of NWLCs

While the lower employment elasticity has dampened the impact on labour market conditions of the sluggish growth of total demand, the

26. See: Becker, Mincer, Stigler, Oi (all 1962); Doeringer and Piore (1971); Becker (1975).

27. It is extremely difficult to draw a sharp distinction between fixed and variable labour costs, as it will depend on the time perspective, institutional arrangements, and more generally on the nature of the cost. Fixed labour costs in this note have been defined as those which change by less than hours worked, but under this definition there can be wide variations in the degree to which costs are insensitive to changes in the number of working hours. Some may vary with changes in standard working time, but not with overtime, while others are completely independent of changes in standard time. In addition, some costs may be invariant to changes in the number of hours worked, but not to the number of employed persons. By contrast, other cost elements, such as outlays of a social nature, do not even change with the number of persons employed. Finally, the existence of ceilings implies that employers' contributions are a variable cost for wages below the ceiling, but a fixed cost for wage earners having incomes above the ceiling, with the share of the fixed cost component depending on the distribution of wage incomes around the ceiling.

28. Specific training raises the marginal product of labour inside the firm, but not elsewhere. Consequently, the "marketability" of a specifically trained worker remains unchanged. By contrast, general training raises the marginal product of labour both inside and outside the firm. Costs for general training are usually borne by the employee or the government, given the risk of people leaving after training is completed. Costs for specific training are likely to be borne by the employer.

29. Due to the marked change in relative prices in 1973-74, the considerable slowdown in the rate of productivity gains during the recession may be the result of structural as well as cyclical factors. Thus, in the United States, where the recovery has been stronger than in most other countries, recent productivity gains have differed only little from those of previous cyclical upturns. This suggests that the apparent rise in labour-hoarding during the recession was due to a once-and-for-all decline in output per man-hour, rather than a slower adjustment of employment to weaker output trends. In this context, it may also be noted that in addition to the possible impact of NWLCs recent employment trends may have been influenced by changing employer attitudes to job security.

accompanying high rate of increase in unit labour costs may have contributed to the persistently high rates of inflation in the face of widespread slack. It is, however, also important to note that the growing importance of NWLCs varies considerably, both between countries and within each country between different groups and sectors. Judging by cross-section analyses (see Annex I), most fixed labour-cost components of a voluntary and internal nature tend to rise faster than wages and salaries; i.e. NWLCs in per cent of wages and salaries are positively related to the level of total labour costs. Hence, this component of NWLCs — and the lower employment elasticity — is mainly found among skilled workers with higher than average incomes. On the other hand, reflecting the existence of ceilings (Diagram 2), social security contributions measured in per cent of total compensation tend to fall with the level of wages and salaries, so that in periods of recession firms may be more inclined to lay off workers of low skill.[30]

Changes in size and nature of NWLCs over time

While the high income elasticity of most internal NWLCs observed in the cross-section analyses is consistent with the rising share of NWLCs in total labour costs over time (Diagram 3), the development in social security taxes and other welfare contributions is more difficult to interpret. Despite a very low income elasticity when measured across sectors[31], the share of welfare contributions in total compensation has tended to rise over time due to higher tax rates and ceilings. In some countries (Sweden, and to some extent also, Canada), higher tax rates have raised the wage share of welfare contributions — as well as the fixed-cost element of NWLCs — supported by a fall of the ceilings in relation to average wages, thereby possibly aggravating the discriminatory employment impact against unskilled workers. In other countries (the United States, Japan, Germany, the United Kingdom, the Netherlands and Norway) however, where the rising share of social welfare contributions has been unusually pronounced due to higher rates and increased ceilings relative to average wages, the fixed-cost component, and hence the risk of a discriminatory employment effect, has probably fallen.

Another implication of the cross-section analyses would seem to be that externally imposed NWLCs tend to narrow labour cost differentials between different industries and possibly by more than is consistent with correspond-

---

30. As can be seen from Diagram 2, the income level where social security contributions become a fixed cost differ widely between countries. In the United States, Canada and Belgium, such contributions become a fixed cost at a relatively low level of income, while in other countries the ceilings are well above average earnings, implying that this component of NWLCs is a variable cost for a major part of the labour force. In assessing the possibility of a discriminatory employment effect, the tax rate as well as the percentage of workers for whom the contributions constitute a variable cost, would have to be considered. On this basis, one may tentatively conclude that the fixed-cost element has been and probably still is relatively important in France, Belgium and the Netherlands.

31. When the share of employers' social security contributions in total labour costs was regressed on the level of labour costs, the estimated coefficient was for most countries negative, implying that the income elasticity of such contributions is less than unity. For further details see Annex I.

Diagram 2. EMPLOYERS' CONTRIBUTIONS TO SOCIAL SECURITY AS A PERCENTAGE OF EARNINGS IN 1976

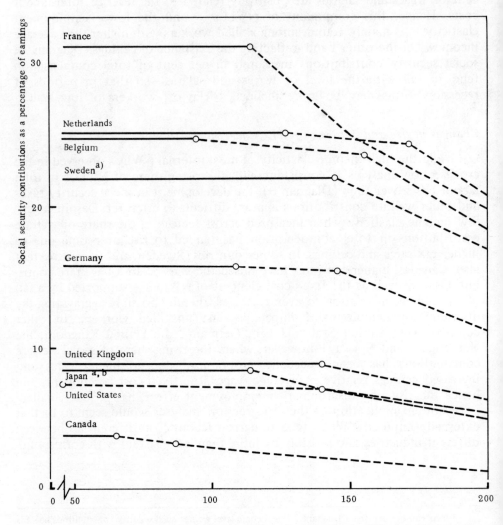

Earnings (annual earnings of average production worker in 1976 equals 100)

NOTE: Circles denote ceilings, i.e. the income level at which various elements of social security contributions become a fixed labour cost.

a) 1975.
b) Total economy.

ing productivity differentials.[32] On the other hand, internal NWLCs have a widening effect on wage cost differentials, but given the nature of these costs this development may well be accompanied by a similar widening of productivity differentials. When aggregating all components of NWLCs and comparing cross-section estimates at different points in time (see Annex I), the results seem to suggest that, along with an increase in the average share of NWLCs, the responsiveness of fixed to total labour costs has weakened at the margin. In other words, even when treating employers' social security contributions as a fixed-cost element, the results still showed that overall fixed labour costs are more important in high than in low labour-cost industries, though over time there has been a tendency for this inter-industry distribution to become somewhat less unequal. Nevertheless the general development in NWLCs has contributed to a widening of inter-industry labour-cost differentials, as will be further discussed below.

3. Differential Wage Changes

The possibility of diverging movements in output and consumer prices — and hence the risk of a potential conflict in wage bargaining — is, of course, the larger the more disaggregated the process of wage determination. Consequently, over and above the impact of changes in NWLCs, which in most countries has been a trend phenomenon rather than a more recent feature, movements in labour-cost differentials may have been strongly influenced by the sharp relative price changes in 1972-73, as the impacts are likely to have differed considerably between sectors. Moreover, to the extent that wage earners — or their unions — not only attempt to protect real earnings, but also to maintain relative income positions, changes in wage differentials may have contributed to the momentum of inflation in recent years.

Macro- and micro-wage relations

In a broader context, the analysis of sectoral wage developments and their possible impact on the general rate of inflation should be structured according to whether the determination of wages is a micro- or macro-economic phenomenon. If, for instance, wages in a particular industry are mainly determined by developments specific to that sector — such as profits, productivity, output prices and sectoral excess demand pressures — the traditional wage equations based on average wages and economy-wide developments cannot be interpreted as behavioural functions. They are merely aggregations of sectoral micro-equations and, therefore, difficult to determine empirically. Moreover if the micro-relationships are non-linear, estimates based on aggregate data will be biased as the general wage rate can

---

32. Thus, the unusually high unemployment rates recorded for teenagers, women and certain minority groups during the present recession may, in a number of countries, partly reflect the differential impact of NWLCs, though the empirical estimates presented in the Annex do not provide sufficient evidence for a more rigorous test of this hypothesis.

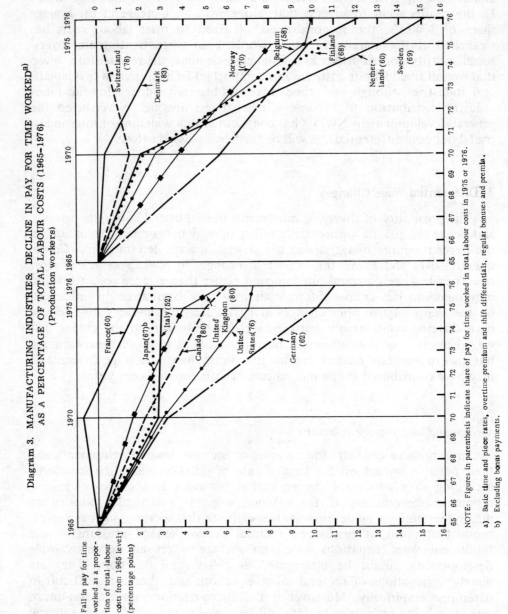

Diagram 3. MANUFACTURING INDUSTRIES: DECLINE IN PAY FOR TIME WORKED[a] AS A PERCENTAGE OF TOTAL LABOUR COSTS (1965-1976)

(Production workers)

NOTE: Figures in parenthesis indicate share of pay for time worked in total labour costs in 1975 or 1976.

a) Basic time and piece rates, overtime premium and shift differentials, regular bonuses and premia.
b) Excluding bonus payments.

be expected to react asymmetrically to variations in the explanatory variables. Finally, the aggregate wage equation will probably be rather unstable, as sectoral changes or movements in other variables not included in the specification of the macro-function will tend to shift it up or down. On the other hand, if wage changes are mainly the result of macroeconomic development — or determined by certain "key" sectors — the traditional Phillips-curve relationship will be subject to only minor aggregation biases, though variations in wage differentials and specific sectoral changes may still exert an influence on the overall rate of inflation.

Theories of sectoral wage developments

Earlier work on the trend and pattern of wage and earnings differentials in industrialised countries has revealed a remarkable stability, as a certain hierarchy of wage differentiation tends to be maintained over long periods.[33] This is particularly so with regard to inter-industry wage dispersions, while differences between various skill groups and between wages for men and women have tended to narrow over time. Most of the earlier empirical work has been concentrated on inter-industry wage relations, where comparable data are more readily available, and has generally attempted to analyse *changes* in sectoral wage rates or wage structures, while existing differences in the *level* of wages between sectors have been more or less taken for granted as reflecting mainly differences in the composition of the labour force and/or in the degree of unionisation and concentration[34]. As regards explanation of wage changes in specific industries or sectors, the analyses have relied upon sector-specific variables — usually some measure of "ability to pay" — as well as on macroeconomic developments and conditions such as changes in consumer prices and the overall rate of unemployment. Finally, with respect to the interrelationship between sectoral wages, earlier work has been based on mainly two alternative specifications:

i)   the key-sector hypothesis[35] according to which pay rates in certain high-wage industries tend to follow a common trend and through spillovers and emulations set a pattern for other industries, while developments in the "non-key" sectors are not assumed to influence key-sector wage trends. In small and open economies, the key sectors are usually found in export industries or in sectors competing with imports, which tend to have the highest output per man-hour and fastest rate of productivity increase.[36]

ii) a distinction between high- and low-wage sectors where spillovers can run both ways and deviations from traditional patterns of the wage

---

33. See, for instance, OECD (1965), *Wages and Labour Mobility;* Turner and Jackson, (1970); and Brown (1977).

34. See Packer and Park (1973), Wachter (1970a), (1970b), (1974a) and (1974b).

35. See Eckstein and Wilson (1962).

36. See Edgren, Faxén and Odhner (1973). According to this hypothesis, wage developments are determined by price and productivity changes in the exposed sectors. Apart from the assumed large impact of international price movements, this theory also implies that the internal rate of inflation will be the higher the larger the difference between rates of productivity increases in, respectively, the exposed and the sheltered sectors.

structure are likely to raise the overall rate of inflation. This hypothesis has mainly been applied to wage movements in the United States,[37] where the high-wage sectors are usually assumed to be highly unionised oligopolistic industries. Since wage developments in those sectors are set according to long-term contracts, the sensitivity to cyclical fluctuations or to unexpected changes in the rate of inflation is normally less pronounced than in the non-unionised low-wage sectors, implying that in a cyclical upturn or in periods of accelerating inflation, wage differentials will tend to narrow.[38] While this distinction between high- and low-wage sectors is also applicable to other countries, differences in sectoral features and in the process of emulation are likely to produce a different response of wage dispersions to cyclical fluctuations. Thus, in countries where contractual increases are determined by centralised bargaining and wage-drift plays an important role in the overall development of earnings, inter-industry wage dispersions can be expected to widen in a cyclical upturn as wage-drift is relatively more important in the high-wage sectors, where the proportion of skilled workers is high.[39] In addition to the cyclical aspects, it is relevant to note that a high degree of centralised bargaining may help to preserve the existing wage structure, but can also provide a vehicle for changing relative wages through discretionary policy actions.

Empirical results[40]

As can be seen from Table 3, the stability of the inter-industry wage structure has been largely maintained during the present recession. Except in France, Italy, Denmark and Iceland, a regression of the 1975 industrial wage structure on that of 1970 yielded R^2s of 0.9 or more. However, within the generally stable wage structures, the development in wage dispersions has differed quite markedly between countries. Thus, there was a clear widening in the United States, Germany , Austria, Belgium and partly also Norway and Switzerland, while in France, Italy, the United Kingdom, Canada, Denmark and the Netherlands the 1970-1975 period has seen a narrowing of wage differentials.

Initially attempts were made to explain changes in wage differentials on the basis of inter-industry variations in output prices and production per man-hour, but regression analyses on cross-section data yielded rather poor results, particularly for more recent years when in some countries industrial wage developments seem to have been quite independent of the simul-

---

37. See Okun (1973) and (1975); Hall (1974); Ross and Wachter (1973); and Flanagan, (1976).
38. See: *A Quarterly Report of the Council on Wage and Price Stability*, (1978) pp. 42-46.
39. In other words, egalitarian wage policies implies a narrowing of *wage-rate* differentials. To maintain *earnings* differentials, skilled workers ask and obtain supplements over and above wage rates, expecially in periods of cyclical upturn.
40. Inter-industry *wage dispersions* are measured by the coefficient of variation, i.e. the standard deviation around the mean in relation to the mean. *Wage differentials* refer to wages in a particular industry relative to the average industrial wage. The term *'wage structure'* is applied more loosely, in some cases referring to the total spread between the highest and the lowest sectoral wages and in other cases to the ranking of industries with respect to wage rates.

taneous price and productivity trends.[41] Estimation of industry-specific Phillips curves on the basis of time series generally showed that the sectoral wage changes have been mainly determined by a common wage trend, while sectoral variables such as profits and value added per employee were of only minor importance. Since, however, the estimated coefficients with respect to the general wage trend spread over a rather broad range, there is evidence of either specific factors or of wide differences in the response of sectoral wages to general economic trends. Hence, the empirical work was concentrated on determining cyclical changes in wage structures, aggregate measures of wage dispersions and the interrelationship between changes in dispersions and the general rate of inflation:

i) on the assumption that the level of wages in each industry depends on some measure of value added per employee and the overall level of demand pressure, the development of wage differentials over time was estimated as a function of relative value added[42] and the inverted rate of unemployment — or an alternative measure of demand pressure. Moreover, to allow for differences in the response to increases in the costs of living and for lags in the adjustment pattern, the rate of change in consumer prices, as well as the lagged relative wage rate, were also included as explanatory variables;

ii) while relative wage functions were estimated for 15-20 industries in five countries, the analyses on the basis of aggregate wage dispersion measures were extended to include 14 countries. Essentially this part of the empirical work rested on the same assumptions as outlined above and coefficients of variation for inter-industry wage earnings,[43] and total labour costs were estimated as functions of a measure of demand pressure and the rate of change in consumer prices. Moreover, to distinguish between cyclical and trend changes in non-wage labour costs, the ratio of total labour costs to wages was also included as a separate variable;

iii) finally, to allow for a possible feedback effect of changes in dispersions on the overall rate of inflation — partly reflecting non-linearities in the microeconomic equations and partly the result of attempts to restore traditional wage patterns — aggregate Phillips curves with and without a measure of wage dispersions were estimated for the same 14 countries. To the extent that fluctuations in wage dispersions can be mainly attributed to current and lagged cyclical changes and rates of inflation, the inclusion of a wage-spread term in the traditional Phillips curve cannot be expected to improve the explanatory power nor provide any new information. However, if incomes policies and other policy measures have an independent effect on wage dispersions, the development in wage differentials may throw additional light on the general inflation process.

41. The cross-section analyses were done on level data as well as on changes over selected time periods. The former yielded extremely poor results for all countries, while specifications on the basis of changes produced acceptable results for some time periods in Japan, Germany, the United Kingdom, Sweden and Denmark, but failed entirely for the United States.

42. i.e. value added per employee for a particular sector divided by average value added per employee. In some cases, though, the absolute value added per employee gave a better fit.

43. Excluding pay for time not worked.

Table 3
Summary Indicators of Industry Wage Structures

	Average annual increase in wages - all manufacturing industries per cent		Coefficient of variation of industry wage levels			Stability (R^2s) of industry wage structures (a)	
	1965-70	1970-75	1965	1970	1975	1970	1975
United States.	5.2	7.6	19.3	17.8	22.0	0.99	0.96
Japan (b)	15.4	20.6	24.3	25.4	26.8	0.96	0.97
Germany	7.7	10.2	12.0	13.5	14.3	0.98	0.93
France	9.7	14.9	15.5	16.1	13.8	0.97	0.77
United Kingdom	8.7	17.3	16.4	17.0	15.0	0.96	0.88
Canada	7.3	10.9	21.1	20.1	18.8	0.98	0.97
Italy.	9.1	19.8	21.8	22.5	16.3	0.93	0.81
Austria.	8.2	13.8	15.2	15.2	17.4	0.95	0.94
Belgium.	8.5	16.7	15.1	16.3	17.2	0.95	0.97
Denmark (c)	10.9	16.1	12.0	11.6	14.4	0.93	0.76
Finland	9.5	18.0	13.8	13.8	13.6	0.96	0.93
Iceland	9.2(d)	33.3	—	14.2	17.0	0.69	0.77
Netherlands	9.7	15.8	11.6	12.9	11.4	0.94	0.97
Norway	9.0	13.8	10.3	10.8	11.6	0.97	0.94
Sweden.	8.7	12.0	10.8	10.0	9.7	0.97	0.89
Switzerland.	7.6	11.5	14.2	10.9	12.8	0.92	0.93

(a) Industry wage structures (in levels) for 1970 and 1975 have been regressed against those of 1965 and 1970 respectively.
(b) Total labour costs.
(c) Including construction.
(d) 1966-70.

Sources: Swedish Employers' Federation and Secretariat estimates.

Inter-industry wage differentials

The hypothesis regarding the development in inter-industry wage differentials (see Annex II) yielded quite satisfactory results as far as explanatory power is concerned. The empirical evidence also supports the assumption that the response of relative wage to cyclical movements and to fluctuations in the overall rate of inflation differs considerably across industries. However, in most cases it is difficult to discern a distinct pattern. Moreover, even though industry-specific variables appear to have had a significant impact on the wage structures, it is difficult to identify a systematic underlying relationship and, for a number of industrial sectors, the sign of the estimated coefficients clearly suggests that the equations are not appropriately specified or that the absolute or relative value-added variables have served as proxies for other factors:

i)   in the United States and Japan an increase in demand pressure seems to benefit the relative position of the low-wage sectors, probably reflecting the existence of long-term contracts and non-competitive product markets in the high-wage sectors and a relatively faster adjustment to changing cyclical conditions in the low-wage industries. In Sweden, on the other hand, where wage-drift plays an important role, the high-wage sectors tend to improve their relative position in a cyclical upturn. In the other countries the impact of cyclical movements on wage differentials is generally quite important, but there does not appear to exist a systematic relationship between the sign of the coefficient with respect to the cyclical indicator and the relative wage positions;

ii) a similar lack of a systematic relationship was found with respect to the impact of consumer prices.[44] Since the influence of price fluctuations on relative wages depends mainly on reaction lags and various institutional factors, the sign of the estimated coefficients is undetermined *a priori*. However, for some of the countries (particularly the United States), the inter-industry variation of the price response is "uncomfortably small", as the condition that the aggregate effect on relative wages should be zero is clearly not satisfied.

iii) the results obtained for sectoral value added also point to errors of specification. Thus, in a number of cases the coefficient of relative wages with respect to absolute or relative value added in the same sector is negative, a result which is difficult to reconcile with current theories of wage determination. For some industries a negative impact of value added coincided with counter-cyclical movements of the relative wage, possibly indicating that the value-added term has acted as a proxy for cyclical changes. In general, the empirical evidence would seem to confirm that sector-specific variables do have some influence on wage differentials, but that these effects do not originate in variations of "ability to pay", a finding which is consistent with the rather meagre results obtained for the cross-section analyses;

---

44. In Germany, though, an acceleration of consumer prices tends to improve the relative position of the high wage sectors, while in Sweden low wage earners seem to obtain a relative improvement.

iv) finally, the estimated impact of lagged wage differentials, which were introduced to allow explicitly for the existence of lags and to capture the stability — or auto-regressive nature — of relative wages, point, for several industries, to a high degree of inertia. While this confirms the earlier observation that aggregate measures of wage dispersions have been quite stable, it may also be important to note that judging by the size of the coefficients with respect to lagged relative wages, the speed of adjustment differs quite considerably between various industries. However, a more detailed elaboration of this point would require a more rigorous specification of the lag structures.[45]

Determination of aggregate wage dispersions

Concerning aggregate dispersion measures, the empirical estimates presented in Table 4 show that the sensitivity of inter-industry variations in wage earnings and total labour costs to cyclical movements and price changes differ widely between countries. In the United States, Japan, Canada, and to some extent also the United Kingdom, wage dispersions appear to change counter-cyclically, while in France, Italy, Denmark, Sweden and partly also in Austria a cyclical upturn seems to be accompanied by a widening of wage and labour cost differentials. With respect to consumer prices, an acceleration of the rate of inflation has a significant widening effect on wage dispersions in Germany, Norway, and partly also in the United States, France, Belgium, Iceland and Austria; while in the United Kingdom, Canada, Italy, Denmark and Sweden indexation schemes and other wage/price adjustments tend to narrow differentials. In most countries the dominating influence of the constant term confirms the earlier observed stability of wage differentials, and in the United States, Germany, Italy, Norway and Sweden, a major part of the fluctuations around the average can be related to cyclical movements and/or changes in the rate of inflation.

In some countries — notably Germany, Canada, Denmark and Austria — there seem to be rather large differences between developments in, respectively, wage and total labour cost dispersions. However, in general it is to be expected that the two dispersion measures should have divergent trend movements, as well as different sensitivities to cyclical changes and price developments:

i) in most countries there has been a rise in the ratio of NWLCs to total labour costs over time (Section 2), implying that over and above the impact of cyclical movements and price changes the inter-industry dispersion of total labour costs has been affected by a trend. In fact, when the ratio of total labour costs to wages was introduced as an additional variable in the CV (TLC) equations, the coefficients were — except for Denmark — always positive, implying that NWLCs have tended to widen dispersions over time;

45. The procedure adopted implicitly assumes that all explanatory variables are subject to the same lag structure with exponentially declining weights. Needless to say, this is a rather crude assumption and the estimates could probably have been much improved by experimenting with alternative lag specifications. However, due to the rather small number of observations, the scope for such experiments was severely constrained.

Table 4
Determination of Inter-Industry Wage and Labour-Cost Dispersions

	Dependent variable	Explanatory variable				R^2	DW
		Constant	1/U	CPI	TLC/W		
United States. . .	CV (W)	0.22**	− 0.11**	0.13		0.63	0.98
	CV (TLC)	0.23**	− 0.11**	0.12		0.62	0.99
Japan (1)	CV (TLC)	0.27**	− 1.66**	0.06		0.45	1.45
Germany (1) . . .	CV (W)	0.12**	0.03	0.24**		0.40	2.30
	CV (TLC)	− 0.06	0.001	0.05**	0.11*	0.95	2.98
France	CV (W)	0.06	0.11	0.24		0.40	2.04
	CV (TLC)	0.06	0.14**	0.47		0.57	2.13
United Kingdom(1)	CV (W)	0.17**	− 1.83	− 0.09**		0.50	1.50
	CV (TLC)	− 0.34	0.26	− 0.02*		0.41	1.65
Canada	CV (W)	0.20**	0.05	− 0.11**		0.49	1.38
	CV (TLC)	0.02	− 0.001	− 0.03**	0.19**	0.95	1.51
Italy.	CV (W)	0.16**	0.20*	− 0.38**		0.81	2.13
	CV (TLC)	− 0.03	0.16	− 0.06**	0.13	0.65	2.70
Belgium.	CV (W)	− 0.06	− 0.02	0.19		0.34	0.79
	CV (TLC)	− 1.54**	− 0.24	− 0.21	1.27**	0.67	1.86
Denmark	CV (W)	0.11**	0.02	− 0.17**		0.45	1.50
	CV (TLC)	0.45	0.003	0.02	− 0.30*	0.22	2.32
Finland	CV (W)	0.14**	− 0.01	0.002		0.08	2.16
Iceland	CV (W)	0.08**	0.01	0.04*		0.31	1.68
	CV(TLC)	− 0.01	−	0.01	0.09**	0.89	1.93
Norway.	CV (W)	0.08**	0.001	0.03**		0.85	1.51
	CV (TLC)	− 0.09	−	− 0.004	0.15**	0.90	1.28
Sweden	CV (W)	0.10**	0.01*	− 0.01		0.47	1.67
	CV (TLC)	0.01	−	− 0.07*	0.14*	0.79	2.17
Austria	CV (W)	− 0.001	0.03	0.11		0.49	1.41
	CV (TLC)	− 4.92*	0.003*	− 0.40**	3.11**	0.90	2.36

Note :   CV (W)   = coefficient of variation, wages
        CV (TLC)   = coefficient of variation, total labour costs
        U   = rate of unemployment
        CPI   = consumer price index, percentage rate of change
        TLC/W   = ratio of total labour costs to wages, per cent
        R^2 = coefficient of determination
        DW   = Durbin-Watson statistic
        **   = statistically significant at 99 per cent level
        *   = statistically significant at 95 per cent level

(1) The ratio of vacancies to number of unemployed has been used as demand pressure indicator.
Sources : Swedish Employers' Confederation and OECD Secretariat.

217

ii) to what extent the cyclical sensitivity of dispersions can be expected to rise or fall when NWLCs are included depends on several factors and *a priori* a general rule is difficult to establish. The empirical estimates also fall within a rather broad range, with the cyclical sensitivity being largely the same for wages and total labour costs in the United States, France, Italy, Denmark and Norway. In Canada, Belgium and Sweden the cyclical sensitivity seems to decline when NWLCs are included, though the coefficients are not very well determined. In the United Kingdom the sign with respect to the cyclical indicator appears to change;

iii) the sensitivity to price changes of, respectively, total labour costs and wage dispersions is also influenced by a number of different factors, but essentially the problem of assessing the relative size of the coefficients can be decomposed in the same way as for the cyclical sensitivity. Judging by the empirical estimates, which statistically are more firmly based than those concerning the cyclical impact, total labour costs are much less sensitive to price fluctuations than wages. This probably reflects that indexation schemes and other automatic adjustments to price changes mainly apply to wages,[46] as well as the fixed-cost nature of most NWLCs. Thus, in Germany, the United Kingdom, Canada, Italy and Denmark the sensitivity of dispersions to price changes clearly falls when NWLCs are included. In the United States, Norway and Sweden the estimated coefficients are largely the same for the two dispersion measures, while in France and Belgium the inter-industry variation of total labour costs may be slightly more sensitive to price changes than that of wages.

Dispersions and the general rate of inflation

Finally, concerning the inter-action between changes in wage dispersions and the rate of nominal wage increases, the results shown in Table 5 would seem to indicate that shifts in relative wages and total labour costs have had a measurable influence on the rate of change in wages and total labour costs. Since no attempts have been made to obtain the "best fit" for the equations based on only demand pressure variables and prices,[47] the estimated impact of dispersions could be seriously affected by specification errors and biases. Moreover, in some cases the inclusion of dispersion measures not only affects the explanatory power of the equations, but also has a marked effect on the coefficients with respect to the other variables, implying that multi-colinearity poses a problem.[48] Nevertheless, the introduction of dispersion

---

46. In fact, since ceilings on social security contributions are usually set in nominal terms, an acceleration of inflation tends to reduce the contributions in real terms and to lower the proportion of NWLCs in total labour costs.

47. For a number of countries (the United States, the United Kingdom, Iceland, Canada and Norway), the coefficient with respect to the inverted rate of unemployment obviously has the wrong sign.

48. Since wage and labour cost dispersions were earlier found to be influenced by price developments and cyclical movements and current prices and cyclical indicators normally have a high degree of auto-correlation, the CV_{-1} terms will, in most cases, not be independent of the other explanatory variables.

measures in a number of countries improves the wage and labour cost relations so considerably that the hypothesis of an interaction between changes in the wage structures and the overall rate of inflation would be difficult to deny.

In Germany, Italy, the United Kingdom, Canada, Denmark, Iceland, Sweden and Austria the addition of dispersion measures raises the R^2s of either the wage or the total labour cost relation. Moreover, in Germany, Canada, Belgium, Denmark, Norway, Sweden and, to some extent also in Austria, specific allowance for changes in the wage and cost structures results in price coefficients which would seem to conform better to *a priori* expectations with respect to the price/wage relationship. On the other hand, measures of the wage structure do not change the estimates very much for the United States, Japan, France and Finland, and in the case of the United Kingdom, Italy and Austria there is obviously such a strong correlation between dispersions and consumer prices that the results would have to be considered of rather doubtful value. With respect to the sign of the estimated impact of changes in the wage structure, a widening of wage dispersions is, in most countries, accompanied by a subsequent acceleration of inflation. However, in Sweden and Denmark — where wage-drift tends to be rather high — and also in Canada, smaller wage differentials seem to induce a subsequently higher rate of inflation. However, a more detailed analysis of just how changes in the wage and labour cost structures affect the rate of inflation would obviously require a more carefully specified model.[49]

4. Conclusions and Medium-term Issues

The conclusions and medium-term policy considerations emerging from the preceding discussion may be summarised as follows:

i) recent years have seen a gradual decline in the relative impact of cyclical movements on wage claims and the outcome of the bargaining process.[50] Instead, wage targets with respect to real and relative income positions have played an increasing role, and for several countries the empirical evidence presented in the previous sections points to the existence of "tax-push" inflation and real wage rigidity. This has been particularly evident since 1973-74, as the rise in real wages has generally exceeded that of real national income and average productivity, in some cases creating structural imbalances and adjustment problems.

---

49. Thus, in a country where the authorities pursue an egalitarian wage policy through the centralised bargaining rounds, but subsequently higher wage-drift tends to eradicate the squeeze on differentials, wage dispersions will be negatively correlated with contractual increases, while the correlation between wage-drift and dispersions is positive, and the sign of an aggregate dispersion measure in an equation determining total wage increases is *a priori* undetermined. For further discussion of this point, see *Norway, Economic* Survey (1975). It may also be noted in this context that Packer and Park (1973) applied a wage dispersion measure, which emphasized deviations from a "normal wage structure", regardless of whether they were positive or negative.

50. To what extent the wage impact of cyclical movements has changed in *absolute* terms is much more difficult to say.

Table 5

Estimated Wage and Labour-Cost Relationships

	Dependent variable	Constant	1/U	CPI	cv_{-1}	R^2	DW
United States	W	0,006**	0.07	0.41**	1.81	0.77	
	W	−0.01	−0.04	0.34**	0.36	0.80	1.71
	TLC	0.06**	−0.05	0.57**		0.74	1.29
	TLC	0.00	−0.02	0.47**	0.24	0.75	1.17
Japan (1).	W	0.08**	0.01	0.76**		0.82	1.08
	TLC	0.03	0.07**	0.83**		0.92	2.40
	TLC	0.43	0.03	0.87**	−1.44	0.93	2.02
Germany (1).	W	−0.01	0.02**	1.34**		0.83	1.53
	W	0.03	0.02**	1.37**	0.09	0.85	1.78
	TLC	−0.01	0.02**	1.35**		0.86	1.59
	TLC	−0.24**	0.02**	0.63**	1.54**	0.96	2.65
France	W	0.04**	0.05**	0.90**		0.96	2.53
	W	0.04**	0.04*	0.90**	0.05	0.97	2.42
	TLC	0.04**	0.05**	0.86**		0.91	2.12
	TLC	0.04**	0.05**	0.85**	0.02	0.92	2.09
Italy	W	−0.24	1.06*	0.57		0.75	2.05
	W	−0.27	1.02	0.64	0.18	0.75	1.95
	TLC	−0.24	1.09*	0.48		0.76	2.12
	TLC	−0.60**	0.16	1.26**	3.08**	0.87	2.80
United Kingdom (1)	W	0.05	−0.001	0.95**		0.80	2.47
	W	−0.41	−0.06	1.18**	2.61	0.85	3.26
	TLC	0.05	0.01	0.93**		0.79	2.41
	TLC	−0.33	0.06	1.05**	2.18*	0.86	3.09
Canada	W	0.11**	−0.36**	0.87**		0.90	1.70
	W	0.40**	−0.30**	0.74**	−1.44*	0.94	2.09
	TLC	0.16**	−0.60**	0.88**		0.88	2.09
	TLC	0.59**	−0.37	0.57**	−2.03**	0.95	2.62
Belgium	W	−0.03	0.15**	1.25**		0.93	1.53
	W	−0.03	0.14**	1.17**	0.08	0.94	1.74
	TLC	−0.03	0.20**	1.08**		0.87	1.70
	TLC	−0.03	0.19**	1.02**	0.06	0.88	1.74
Denmark	W	0.05	0.01	1.08**		0.72	2.09
	W	0.38**	−0.001	0.65*	−2.52	0.84	2.38
	TLC	0.03	0.02	1.22**		0.76	2.18
	TLC	−0.19**	−0.001	0.44	2.06**	0.89	2.21
Finland	W	0.05**	0.06	0.80**		0.87	0.83
	W	−0.21	0.03	0.88**	1.91	0.90	0.63
	TLC	0.05	0.05	0.99**		0.79	0.59
Iceland	W	0.08	−0.04	0.74**		0.50	1.80
	W	−0.03	−0.06	0.65**	1.15	0.58	2.22
	TLC	0.11	−0.05	0.67		0.44	1.64
	TLC	0.03	−0.07	0.56	1.39	0.55	2.09
Norway.	W	0.07**	−0.03	1.09**		0.73	1.47
	W	−0.22	−0.02	0.62	2.89	0.78	1.29
	TLC	0.09**	−0.03**	1.01**		0.80	1.89
	TLC	−0.15	−0.02	0.51	2.26	0.85	1.64
Sweden	W	0.03	0.04	0.83**		0.65	1.75
	W	0.24	0.08	0.58*	−2.20	0.73	1.80
	TLC	0.02	0.03	1.39**		0.74	1.35
	TLC	0.41**	0.10**	0.87**	−3.70	0.89	1.75
Austria	W	0.04*	0.01	1.06**		0.59	2.20
	W	−0.18*	−0.001	0.19	1.94**	0.78	2.49
	TLC	0.05**	0.001	1.20**		0.58	2.29
	TLC	−0.31**	−0.02	−0.19	2.56**	0.83	2.19

Note .
- W = wage rate, percentage rate of change
- TLC = total labour costs, percentage rate of change
- U = rate of unemployment
- CPI = consumer price index, percentage rate of change
- CV_{-1} = lagged coefficient of variation for inter-industry wage and total labour-cost structure
- R^2 = coefficient of determination
- DW = Durbin-Watson statistic
- ** = statistically significant at 99 per cent level
- * = statistically significant at 95 per cent level

(1) The ratio of vacancies to number of unemployed has been used as demand pressure indicator.

Sources : Swedish Employers' Confederation and OECD Secretariat.

220

ii) the tendency towards longer time-lags and less sensitivity to short-term cyclical changes is even more pronounced for total labour costs than for direct wages. In all countries, non-wage labour costs have grown faster than wage earnings. This development has tended to increase fixed costs relative to variable costs and at the same time to drive a "wedge" between changes in real earnings and total labour costs. The growing share of NWLCs is partly the result of legislation concerning employers' social welfare contributions and trade union pressure for non-wage benefits, but also reflects a general tendency towards establishing longer-term relationships between the labour market parties.

iii) while real income rigidities largely result from attempts to protect purchasing power of nominal incomes and income share conflicts, the empirical evidence concerning wage differentials suggests that for some countries sectoral wage developments may have accentuated the problem of inflation. Despite country-by-country differences in the bargaining process, the degree of egalitarian wage policies pursued, and the cyclical sensitivity of various sectors, spillovers and wage emulations have generally contributed to the inflationary momentum. Even though inter-industry wage differentials have been remarkably stable in conditions of large shifts in relative prices and productivity trends and shifts in wage differentials rarely constitute an independent source of inflation, changes in wage dispersions appeared, in some countries, to be an element in explaining the deterioration in the unemployment/inflation trade-off.[51]

As mentioned earlier, the three issues analysed in this paper are not directly related. Nevertheless, most of the empirical evidence — though still preliminary — leads to very much the same conclusion: while in a certain sense a trade-off between inflation and unemployment still exists both in the short and in the long run, an explanation of recent wage trends would have to include a number of factors in addition to a measure of cyclical movements. Some of the additional factors have mainly affected the degree and speed with which wages respond to changes in labour market conditions, while others seem to have exerted a separate influence on wage trends. Consequently, demand management policies and assessments of nominal and real wage developments in both the short and the medium term will have to take account of these developments.

Medium-term prospects

Any assessment of the longer-term prospects, will necessarily have to be based on a number of crucial assumptions, one of which is the likely stance of demand management policies. Given the rising uncertainty regarding the impact of policy measures and constraints on the adoption of a more stimulatory policy stance — particularly fears of reaccelerating inflation and

---

51. i.e. shifts in the inter-industry wage structures were found to raise the rate of inflation at a given level of unemployment.

worsening a precarious balance-of-payments situation — one medium-term growth scenario might be a continuation of present low growth rates.[52] In such conditions the share of private investment would almost certainly fall and, depending on how closely technical progress is related to new investment, potential output growth can be expected to decelerate. Though this may be largely reflected in a lower rate of productivity increase, employment would also be affected and, in turn, provoke some rise in unemployment, even allowing for some decline in participation rates. With respect to wages and prices, it is useful to distinguish between cost and demand pressures. As noted in the preceding sections, real wage claims are only slowly adjusted to weak output trends, and given the present low profit share there is a risk of aggravating the conflict over income shares. On the other hand, it might be argued that lower demand pressures would help to reduce inflation. Certainly commodity prices, which are largely demand-determined in the short run, could be expected to respond to weak OECD demand, though prices in a number of raw material producing sectors are already near, or even below, current costs. Moreover, rising unemployment over an extended period of time is likely to reduce nominal wage increases, even allowing for some increase in structural rigidities, such as lower labour mobility and introduction of protectionist measures. On balance, it is difficult to summarise how the overall inflation rate would be affected in a low growth scenario, and the outcome would no doubt differ considerably from country to country. However, it is reasonably certain that a continuation of present trends would complicate the correction of structural imbalances, which in several ways might affect the bargaining process.

Inflation and real wage prospects in a "high" growth scenario

Alternatively, it might be assumed that demand management policies are shifted in an expansionary direction in order to achieve more favourable employment conditions in the medium term. While stimulatory measures taken in individual countries have a relatively low multiplier effect (as much of the stimulus leaks out into imports) and in a number of cases are subject to constraints, a programme that included a simultaneous expansion of demand in several countries could lead to a significantly higher output growth for the OECD area as a whole. To what extent a concerted action could re-establish full employment conditions in the medium term would, of course, depend on a number of factors, one of which is the inflationary risk. Thus, even in conditions of concerted action, where each country's contribution is graduated according to its balance-of-payments position, as well its rate of inflation, an assessment of the growth prospects would have to take account of the likely development of inflation, both in a transitional period when the economic activity is raised through stimulative policy actions and over the medium term as countries gradually approach

---

52. It might be argued that in view of existing imbalances, a continuation of present low growth rates would lead to an unsustainable situation. Though not at all without interest in the present context, this argument will not be discussed in the following.

the full employment targets.[53] Though some of the problems and issues arising during the transition to a higher level of economic activity are more or less identical to those encountered over the medium term, there are also important differences with respect to the potential inflation risk. Most importantly, reactions to a more expansionary policy will, in several respects, set the stage for what may be achieved in the longer run.[54]

Inflation and concerted action

During the transitional period, when the rate of growth of output will accelerate from present rates to somewhat more than the potential rate, the outlook for inflation will be influenced by two opposing tendencies:

i)   on the one hand, at the present degree of slack — particularly outside the United States — an increment to the rate of growth of GNP might initially be absorbed with only a marginal rise in the demand for labour. In other words, due to a likely sharp rise in the rate of productivity gains, the faster output growth will not be accompanied by any measurable decline in unemployment. Though it is difficult to say for how long the actual rate of productivity increase will exceed present and long-term rates, the existence of wage inertia implies that even some rise in the demand for labour would be unlikely to have any major impact on nominal wage increases.[55]

ii) on the other hand, considering the present low profit shares in most countries, a higher rate of real growth may be accompanied by attempts to raise profit margins, which could more or less offset the dampening effect of above-trend productivity gains. Moreover, an acceleration of commodity prices would seem unavoidable,[56] accentuating inflationary pressures and possibly causing unfavourable terms-of-trade developments in some countries.

The inflationary risk attaching to actions aimed at stimulating the level of economic activity will, of course, depend on the type of measures taken. If wage claims are formulated in terms of real disposable earnings, stimulatory measures in the form of tax cuts might have only a marginal impact on the rate of inflation. Lower indirect taxes and higher subsidies could also reduce the share of a given real wage target which would have to be

---

53. The following is largely based on discussions in the Working Party No. 2, concerning medium-term growth prospects. However, in concentrating the presentation on problems most relevant to the wage bargaining process, a number of important issues have been left out. Since the results emerging from the WP2 discussions are still preliminary, no projections are presented; nor is it discussed to what extent a return to full employment by 1985 will be feasible in all Member countries.

54. It is difficult to draw a clear distinction between the transitional period and the medium term. Generally speaking though, the former refers to a period — lasting a couple of years — during which expansionary policy measures are introduced and the rate of growth of total output will exceed the average rate for the entire 1978-1985 period.

55. This also implies that if the demand for labour should rise faster and earlier than expected, the lagged wage response to changes in employment conditions would provide governments with some time for preparing offsetting measures.

56. Higher prices would also seem desirable from the point of view of creating investment incentives in the raw material producing sectors.

"filled" by nominal wage increases, and a reduction of employers' social charges could improve profits and lessen the pressure on prices.[57]

On balance, it may be assumed that a policy aimed at accelerating the output growth in the OECD area by 2-3 percentage points compared with present rates might, by the end of 1979, raise nominal wage gains by some-what less than 1 percentage point. At present trends, this implies that the rate of wage increases in most countries would be largely the same as that recorded in 1977.[58] However, even assuming a somewhat lower growth of output during the years following the transitional period, it remains un-certain to what extent a gradual approach to full employment may be achieved without raising the inflation rate any further. Moreover, the in-flation problem as well as other medium-term issues have important impli-cations for real wage prospects and the wage bargaining process.

Real wages in the medium term

First of all, a necessary condition for moving closer to earlier low un-employment rates is that the share of GNP devoted to non-residential fixed investment increases considerably compared with present levels. In the absence of a faster growth of capital spending there is a clear risk that capacity constraints may be encountered well before full employment. Though faster output growth would, in most countries, be accompanied by a higher profit share, a sufficiently strong rise in private investment − from the point of view of total demand as well as addition to productive capacity − may require a further change of the income distribution in favour of profits, particularly in those countries where the rise in real wages has significantly exceeded that of both real national income and productivity. A critical condition for achieving a gradual improvement in employment conditions over the medium term without escalating inflation-ary pressures is, therefore, that real wage targets and realised wage gains be consistent with the overall economic objectives. In countries where the potential growth of output per man-hour now seems somewhat lower than earlier[59], this may be particularly difficult to achieve, as it would require a reduction of real wage targets in conditions of more favourable market conditions.

A second condition for realising higher growth rates and lower un-employment in the medium term would seem to be a more equal distri-bution of existing external imbalances. Indeed, for a number of countries, balance-of-payments considerations severely constrain the scope for a more active and expansionary demand management. Whatever policies the deficit countries adopt, medium-term real wage prospects would be less favourable

---

57. The scope for implementing a combined fiscal-income policy approach no doubt varies from country to country, depending *inter alia* on the nature of the bargaining process and the strength of the social consensus.

58. The calculations concerning the increment to GNP growth are based on the assumptions that stimulatory policies will be introduced during the second half of 1978 and that countries in a favourable balance-of-payments position and with a relatively low inflation rate will provide a major share of the overall stimulus.

59. It is, though, relevant to recall that a continuation of present growth trends would probably entail a more pronounced deterioration in potential growth as investment activities in most countries are likely to remain weak.

than in countries with an external surplus and wage bargaining, therefore, likely to be more complicated than in the past:

i) if — for fear of a deterioration in the foreign balance or a depreciation of the exchange rate — demand management policies provide only little stimulus to economic activity, the recovery of labour market conditions will be slow. Hence, the scope for real wage increases may be smaller than in the past, and the probability of a continued weak investment trend creates a risk of decelerating productivity gains;

ii) policies aimed at reducing the external constraint through an adjustment of relative factor prices would have to incorporate either a real exchange-rate depreciation or a reduction in costs relative to other countries. Even though this approach allows a faster rate of output growth, both policy options would require a downward adjustment of real wage aspirations.[60]

In this context it is also relevant to note that a higher level of economic activity for the OECD area as a whole would probably also in the medium term be accompanied by an acceleration of commodity prices. Though it is difficult to estimate the size of the likely price increase, countries depending heavily on imported raw materials might experience a terms-of-trade deterioration, which would put further downward pressure on real incomes, if an unfavourable development in the external balance is to be avoided.

Finally, price and wage trends are themselves subject to a number of uncertainties. Given the high share of labour in total costs, domestic prices may, on average, be assumed to be largely determined as a mark-up on unit labour costs. If — for medium-term projections — it is also assumed that nominal wage increases are mainly influenced by current labour market conditions and wage targets, with the latter being based on what wage earners regard as a "fair" increase in their net after-tax earnings and expectations regarding future price increases, a gradual recovery path may — at least in some countries — be consistent with a slowly decelerating inflation rate. The assumed wage/price system is highly auto-regressive, implying that once a process of deceleration gets started it will continue over an extended period of time. On the other hand, with a high degree of auto-regression external shocks will affect the system for a long period.[61] In fact, given the frequency of external shocks experienced in recent years and the sensitivity of wage and price trends to such events, it may be argued that a medium-term growth projection based on the assumption of a decelerating inflation rate has only a small chance of being achieved.

As mentioned above, non-oil industrial commodity prices are likely to rise and even though projections point to a continuation of excess supply conditions with respect to oil over the next few years, the possibility of a

---

60. With the exception of Japan, countries with a severe external constraint are largely identical to those that have the largest gap between real wages and the real income "norm"; cf. Table 1.

61. Seen in the context of price and wage developments over the last three to four years, the assumed wage/price relations imply that the "underlying" system is basically stable, but that over a short time period it has been exposed to a number of extreme shocks, which all tended to raise the actual rate of inflation.

new increase in oil prices will also have to be considered. The immediate outlook for food prices is relatively favourable, but given the dependence on the weather, this situation can quickly change. Moreover, at present agricultural policies, the risk would seem to be on the "upside" since excess supplies of food products will not be fully reflected in lower prices. Future developments in exchange rates constitute a particular area of uncertainty. Even assuming a narrowing of existing differentials with respect to real growth and inflation rates, exchange-rate adjustments may not proceed sufficiently smoothly to avoid a disturbing influence on domestic wage and price trends. The impact of exchange-rate fluctuations will, of course, differ between appreciating and depreciating countries, but considering the likely asymmetries regarding the sensitivity of domestic prices to changes in import prices, the net effect of developments in exchange markets could well be an additional kick to the overall inflation rate.

Apart from the target of avoiding excess demand pressures, the prospects for medium wage and price trends will, to an important extent, depend on economic policies. With wage targets formulated in terms of real disposable earnings, increases in income-tax rates — whether due to discretionary changes or the effect of fiscal drag — will eventually produce compensating wage claims. Other government actions, such as higher indirect and employers' taxes and regulations regarding the environment, would also increase cost pressures. More generally, however, price and wage developments will be most importantly influenced by the prospects for implementing policies which ensure consistency between real income aspirations and the development in real output. Depending on institutional factors and past experience, a number of countries may want to consider the scope for introducing some type of incomes policy, which might also have certain implications for the wage bargaining process.

Annex I

The Distribution of Fixed Labour Costs by Industrial Sectors

Lack of detailed data on hiring and training costs (and related benefits) by skill, occupation and wage rates has made it hard to directly verify the hypothesis of labour as a quasi-fixed factor. In EEC countries, however, surveys of the structure of labour costs by industrial branches are now established at regular intervals, and these provide an opportunity for gaining at least some insight into the distribution of certain components of non-wage and wage costs for different levels of total labour costs. These components are pay for time not worked; contractual or voluntary payments to insurance schemes (i.e. excluding employers' contributions to social security); benefits in kind and other expenses of a social nature and outlays on vocational training.

For every country, each of these cost components and their sum (expressed as a percentage of hourly labour costs) were regressed on the level of total hourly labour costs (excluding employers' statutory contributions to social security) for both manual and non-manual workers.[62] The results presented in Tables 1 and 2 lend some support to the proposition that the share of (internally created) fixed costs in total labour costs and the level of labour costs are positively related, with the estimated coefficients being somewhat higher for manual than for non-manual workers (except in Italy). An examination of differences between actual and fitted values by industrial sectors revealed a strong concentration of gaps in a few sectors, predominantly mining, extraction and refining of petrol and electricity, gas and water. Thus, the estimated coefficient, as a rule, largely underpredicted the share of fixed in total costs, and this may be related to the unusually high capital/labour ratios which characterise these sectors.[63] When excluding capital intensive sectors, the fit between actual and estimated cost shares for most countries improved.

Examining the various components of fixed labour costs revealed a highly differentiated picture for all countries under review. The regression results indicate a significant positive relationship for private insurance payments and (with the exception of Italy and the Netherlands) for "other expenditure of social nature". By contrast, no general positive relationship was found for benefits in kind (except for France, manual workers; Germany and the United Kingdom, non-manual workers), vocational training (except for the United Kingdom and Denmark, manual workers; and France, non-manual workers) and pay for time not worked (except for Italy). On the contrary, in some instances, the results carry a "wrong" (negative) sign, suggesting that fixed labour costs (as a percentage of total labour costs) lose in importance as the level of labour costs rises.

---

62. The data refer to sub-sectors in industry, ranging from 20 observations for Denmark to 27 in Italy.

63. Introducing the share of gross fixed asset formation in value added as an additional independent variable yielded higher R^2s for France, Italy and Belgium, but the residuals were still rather large.

For the United States, a similar regression analysis was carried out, though for fewer components of fixed labour costs. Both pay for leave time and employers' payments to private pension plans (as a proportion of total labour costs) were found to be positively related to the level of labour costs in 1972. Apparently no significant relationship exists for employers' expenditure on life and health insurance (Table 3). More recent (1975-76) data for Canada show a similar pattern; thus for total costs below C$ 7.50 an hour, the share of pay for time not worked (including sick leave) and payments to private insurance schemes is a positive function of total labour costs.[64]

In contrast to internally created fixed employment costs employers' statutory contributions to social security (as a percentage of total labour costs) can be expected to fall with the level of labour costs.[65] For any given year, the extent to which social security ceilings introduce a fixed-cost element is largely determined by the ratio of ceilings to average wages and salaries; by the distribution of incomes around the average; and by the level of social security taxes themselves. Regressing for each country the share of employers' social security contributions in total labour costs on the absolute level of labour costs, yielded a strong negative relationship for the Netherlands, Belgium, Italy, France (1972) and the United Kingdom (1973) (Table 4). Reflecting the fact that average salaries tend to exceed average wages, the estimated (negative) coefficients were found to be higher for non-manual than for manual workers.

The empirical estimates presented above generally showed that within a given year internally created fixed employment costs in per cent of total labour costs tended to rise with the level of total labour costs. For statutory social security contributions, the opposite pattern was revealed. At the same time there has been a trend rise in the share of non-wage labour costs over the last decade. With detailed data unavailable, it is impossible to show how each of these factors has influenced the distribution of fixed labour costs between industrial sectors over time. However, assuming that the entire difference between total labour costs and pay for time worked represents fixed labour costs, one can, at least, compare for each country the inter-industry distribution of such costs for two different periods. Regressing this difference (expressed as a percentage of total labour costs) on the absolute level of total hourly labour costs produced, as a rule, a positive, but lower coefficient for 1973-75 than for 1965-67 and a higher constant term for the second period (Table 5).

Judging by the Durbin-Watson statistics, the observed inter-industry pattern of fixed and total labour costs is consistent with a linear specification of the relationship between the share of fixed employment costs and

---

64. To the extent that wages paid in the unionised sector are higher than in the non-unionised sector, fixed employment costs are likely to be more important in the former than in the latter sector. Recent data for Canada confirm this hypothesis. Fixed employment costs are significantly higher in union than in non-union sectors, with the difference being most pronounced for pay for time not worked. See: Taylor, (1977).

65. In most countries, ceiling provisions apply and social security contributions are partly a fixed and partly a variable cost. Exceptions may be Finland and Switzerland, where no ceilings are operated.

total labour costs. This suggests that changes in pay differentials have had only a marginal effect on the estimated coefficients.[66] In the case of Canada, France, Belgium and Sweden, the decline in the estimated coefficient seems to be connected with the growing fixed-cost nature of statutory contributions to social security. An additional factor could have been a small fall in the relative importance of payments of private insurance schemes (Canada, France, Belgium). In Germany and possibly Denmark, a more than proportionate rise in pay for leave time could have played a part in lowering the estimated coefficient.[67] As regards the Netherlands, one might have expected a stronger positive relation between fixed and total labour costs, largely owing to the greater importance of employers' payments to private insurance schemes. But a more than proportionate rise in pay for time not worked, together with sharp increases in employers' social security taxes (enlarging the fixed proportion inside these contributions) appears to have swamped this effect.[68]

For the United Kingdom, a higher and significant coefficient was found for 1973-75 (compared with 1965-67), probably reflecting the growing emphasis upon payments to private insurance schemes.[69] For Italy, the results suggest a negative relationship between fixed and total labour costs for 1965-67 and a positive one for 1973-75. The negative function in the early period was probably connected with the exceptionally high level and the structure of employers' social security taxes, which are strongly graduated according to occupation and industry. In addition, the low ceiling set for contributions for family allowances may have played a role. The emergence of a positive relationship in the second period seems to indicate the presence of both the withdrawal of the above ceiling and a more than proportionate rise in pay for leave time.[70]

---

66. However, due to the small number of observations (see Table 5), the Durbin-Watson statistics will provide only an approximate test. Therefore, it cannot be excluded that changes in inter-industry pay differentials have biased the estimated coefficients.

67. For both these countries and also for the Netherlands, a significant but negative relationship was found between pay for leave time (expressed as a percentage of total labour costs) and total labour costs (Tables 1 and 2).

68. Given the negative relationships between social security contributions (as a proportion of total labour costs) and the level of total labour costs, a higher fixed component within social security contributions tends to lower the estimated (positive) coefficient (other things being equal).

69. For the United Kingdom, regression results for 1973-75 suggest an increasingly positive relationship between private insurance payments (as a percentage of labour costs) and the level of total labour costs. Another reason may have been the removal of flat-rate contributions in April 1975, transforming part of employers' social security payments into a variable cost.

70. It will be recalled that in 1972-73 Italy was the only country to show a strong positive relationship between the share of pay for leave time in total labour costs and the absolute level of labour costs.

Table 1
Estimated Relationship between the Share of Fixed Costs and Total Labour Costs (1972) (a)
(Manual workers in industry) (b)

Independent variable: level of total hourly labour costs (c); Dependent variable: share of fixed costs in total hourly labour costs

Dependent variable	Coefficient	t-values	R^2
A. Pay for days not worked :			
France	0.19	0.52	0.01
Germany	− 0.62	− 1.27	0.06
Italy	3.09	4.65	0.46
United Kingdom	0.21	0.60	0.02
Belgium	− 0.26	− 1.43	0.08
Netherlands	− 0.87	− 4.23	0.50
Denmark	− 0.38	− 5.12	0.59
B. Private insurance payments			
France	2.03	5.08	0.52
Germany	3.88	3.53	0.34
Italy	2.19	6.71	0.64
United Kingdom	4.98	3.98	0.45
Belgium	1.91	4.85	0.52
Netherlands	8.27	5.78	0.65
Denmark	0.83	2.56	0.27
C. Benefits in kind			
France	2.87	2.52	0.21
Germany	0.93	1.55	0.10
Italy	0.06	0.87	0.03
United Kingdom	0.14	1.84	0.15
Belgium	0.19	1.29	0.07
Netherlands	0.35	1.57	0.12
Denmark	0.14	2.17	0.20

Dependent variable	Coefficient	t-values	R^2
D. Other expenditure of social nature			
France	2.62	6.51	0.64
Germany	0.91	2.68	0.23
Italy	0.50	1.12	0.48
United Kingdom	1.13	2.28	0.21
Belgium	1.55	10.63	0.84
Netherlands	− 0.33	− 1.04	0.06
Denmark	1.27	3.00	0.33
E. Vocational training			
France	0.72	1.95	0.14
Germany	0.13	0.42	0.01
Italy	− 0.74	− 3.92	0.38
United Kingdom	1.58	3.24	0.36
Belgium	0.01	0.96	0.00
Netherlands	0.07	0.30	0.00
Denmark	1.10	2.11	0.20
F. A to E. together			
France	8.42	7.61	0.71
Germany	5.21	4.35	0.44
Italy	5.15	4.94	0.49
United Kingdom	8.06	3.79	0.43
Belgium	3.40	6.66	0.67
Netherlands	7.50	6.31	0.69
Denmark	2.96	5.11	0.59

(a) For the United Kingdom and Denmark the results to 1973.
(b) For the Netherlands the results relate to both manual and non-manual workers.
(c) Excluding statutory contributions to social security payable by employers.

Table 2

Estimated Relationship between the Share of Fixed Costs and Total Labour Costs (1972) (a)
(Non-manual workers in industry)

Independent variable: level of total hourly labour costs (b);   Dependent variable: fixed costs as a percentage of total hourly labour costs

Dependent variable	Coefficient	t-values	R^2
A. Pay for days not worked			
France	0.10	0.39	0.01
Germany	− 0.70	− 2.24	0.17
Italy	4.72	6.73	0.64
United Kingdom	0.31	1.15	0.06
Belgium	0.20	0.68	0.02
B. Private insurance payments			
France	1.08	3.17	0.29
Germany	3.30	3.49	0.34
Italy	0.95	6.22	0.61
United Kingdom	4.56	5.49	0.61
Belgium	2.40	7.71	0.73
C. Benefits in kind			
France	1.20	1.70	0.11
Germany	0.67	3.30	0.31
Italy	0.06	0.65	0.01
United Kingdom	0.38	3.51	0.39
Belgium	0.17	1.89	0.14

Dependent variable	Coefficient	t-values	R^2
D. Other expenditure of social nature			
France	1.27	4.47	0.45
Germany	0.78	5.44	0.55
Italy	0.15	0.80	0.02
United Kingdom	1.87	4.53	0.52
Belgium	0.66	4.31	0.46
E. Vocational training			
France	0.63	5.42	0.55
Germany	− 0.33	3.10	0.29
Italy	− 0.08	− 1.63	0.10
United Kingdom	0.39	1.78	0.14
Belgium	0.01	0.24	0.00
F. A to E. together			
France	4.28	5.94	0.59
Germany	3.71	4.17	0.42
Italy	5.80	7.72	0.70
United Kingdom	7.51	5.64	0.62
Belgium	2.57	6.55	0.66

(a) For the United Kingdom the results refer to 1973.
(b) Excluding statutory contributions to social security payable by employers.

Table 3

**Estimated Relationship between the Share of Fixed Costs
and Total Labour Costs, U.S. (1972) (a)**

Dependent variable : share of fixed in total labour costs

Independent variable : level of total labour costs

(Private non-farm economy)

	Estimated coefficient (b)	R^2
A. Paid leave (excluding sick leave)............	0.69 (3.39)	0.53
B. Employers' expenditure on private retirement programmes........................	0.47 (2.09)	0.30
C. Employers' expenditure for life insurance and health benefit programmes	−0.12 (−0.57)	0.03

(a) 12 observations
(b) Figures in parenthesis indicate t-values.

Source : U.S. Bureau of Labor Statistics, *Bulletin 1878, "Employee Compensation in the Private Non-farm Economy 1972"*, pp. 28-29.

Table 4

Estimated Relationships between Social Security Payments and Total Labour Costs

Dependent variable : share of mandatory payments to social security in total hourly labour costs

Independent variable : total hourly labour costs

	Estimated coefficient		t-statistics		R^2	
	Manual	Non-manual	Manual	Non-Manual	Manual	Non-manual
France	− 0.86	− 1.48	− 1.89	− 10.10	0.15	0.82
Germany	0.15	− 0.12	0.26	− 0.54	0.03	0.01
Italy	− 0.81	− 1.06	− 3.22	− 9.22	0.32	0.77
United Kingdom	− 1.22	− 0.90	− 7.79	− 8.96	0.76	0.81
Belgium	− 1.72	− 1.75	− 7.25	− 18.31	0.71	0.93
Netherlands	− 3.12		− 8.00		0.80	
Denmark	− 0.19	—	− 0.97	—	0.05	—

Table 5

Estimated Relationship between the Share of Fixed Costs and Total Labour Costs
(Industrial workers)

Dependent variable : total labour costs minus pay for time worked (a) as a percentage of total labour costs
Independent variable : total labour costs.

	Number of industrial sectors	Constant term		Estimated coefficient		t-values		R^2		Durbin-Watson statistics	
		1965-67	1973-75	1965-67	1973-75	1965-67	1973-75	1965-67	1973-75	1965-67	1973-75
United States	15	14.27	20.27	0.013	0.006	2.91	2.77	0.40	0.37	1.62	1.61
Canada	14	5.70	6.13	0.033	0.019	4.31	3.78	0.61	0.54	1.88	2.19
France	15	30.10	24.15	0.072	0.043	3.11	7.40	0.43	0.81	2.10	1.85
Germany	15	13.82	18.55	0.099	0.028	4.28	6.32	0.58	0.75	2.61	2.33
Italy	15	50.45	43.37	− 0.039	0.010	− 3.99	2.63	0.55	0.35	1.80	1.52
United Kingdom	15	13.60	11.42	0.010	0.020	0.34	2.15	0.01	0.26	1.49	1.80
Austria	15	26.20	33.60	0.140	0.029	3.32	4.42	0.58	0.71	1.31	1.87
Belgium	15	27.02	36.00	0.042	0.005	4.17	1.21	0.57	0.10	1.33	2.31
Denmark	12	3.05	5.58	0.063	0.021	2.94	6.75	0.46	0.82	1.34	1.57
Finland	14	12.06	15.90	0.068	0.038	2.96	4.56	0.42	0.63	2.27	2.75
Netherlands	15	17.70	16.86	0.120	0.044	8.74	4.20	0.85	0.58	1.67	1.73
Norway	13	18.43	23.79	0.021	0.011	1.27	2.90	0.13	0.43	0.93	1.67
Sweden	15	12.30	25.83	0.037	0.006	1.90	3.18	0.22	0.44	2.15	1.94

(a) Pay for time worked includes basic time and piece rates, overtime premium and shift differentials, regular bonuses and premia.

Source : Swedish Employers' Federation, "*Wages and Total Labour Costs for Workers 1965-1975*", 1977.

Annex II

Inter-Industry Wage Relations

The following tables present the results obtained for the United States, Germany, Japan, the United Kingdom and Sweden, applying the theory explained in Section 3 of the main text. For all countries the dependent variable is relative hourly earnings for sector i (W_i / W_a) and the following notation has been used:

Pr_i = value added per employee in sector i.

Pr_a = average value added per employee for all sectors.

W_i = hourly earnings in sector i.

W_a = average hourly earnings for all sectors.

$\dfrac{W_i}{W_{a-1}}$ = relative hourly earnings lagged one year.

$\dfrac{W_i}{W_a}$ ave. = relative hourly earnings, average for observation period.

        * = statistically significant at a 95 per cent degree of confidence.

       ** = statistically significant at a 99 per cent degree of confidence.

Table 1
United States: Industrial Wage Differentials, 1966-76
Relative Wage Equations

Industry	Explanatory variables						R^2	$\dfrac{W_i}{W_a}$ ave.
	Constant	Pr_i	Pr_i/Pr_a	Unemployment rate (a)	Consumer prices	$(W_i/W_a)_{-1}$		
Apparel and leather goods	0.55**		-0.28*	0.17**		0.39*	0.95	0.69
Textile mill products	0.34**		0.03	0.08***	-0.08	0.47***	0.92	0.71
Lumber and furniture	0.36			-0.06		0.61	0.75	0.86
Food and tobacco	1.00**		-0.13**	-0.09**	0.15	0.09	0.91	0.93
Rubber and miscellaneous manufactures	0.21	-0.57**		0.06	-0.25	0.75**	0.92	0.94
Electrical equipment and supplies	1.05***			-0.09			0.90	0.95
Instruments and related products	0.23*		0.17**	-0.10***	-0.16	0.56***	0.98	0.97
Stone, clay, glass and concrete	0.92**		-0.17	-0.16*	0.01	0.29	0.73	1.00
Fabricated metal products	0.84***		0.18**	0.04	0.02		0.72	1.04
Paper and printing	1.19**	-0.57**		-0.14**	0.42		0.85	1.08
Chemicals and allied products	1.46**			-0.11**			0.67	1.09
Machinery except electrical	0.97***		0.12**	0.03	-0.25	0.08	0.79	1.11
Primary metals	0.98***	1.15**			-0.25		0.88	1.21
Transportation equipment	1.13***	0.76**		0.07	-0.24		0.63	1.22
Petroleum and coal products	0.90			-0.28**	-0.37	0.36	0.69	1.27

(a) Reciprocal of the male unemployment rate.

236

Table 2

Japan: Industrial Wage Differentials, 1966-1975
Relative Wage Equations

Industry	Explanatory variables						R^2	$\frac{W_i}{W_a}$ ave.
	Constant	Pr_i	Pr_i/Pr_a	Vacancies/ Unemployed (a)	Consumer prices	(W_i/W_a)-1		
Apparel and leather goods	0.23**	0.57**		0.18	− 0,14	0.51*	0.83	0.63
Textile mill products	0.32**	0.09		0.42**		0.44**	0.89	0.70
Lumber and furniture	0.53**		0.39**	− 0.31	0.18**		0.94	0.77
Food and tobacco	0.77**		0.08		− 0.14		0.65	0.85
Instruments and related products	0.82**		0.16	0.11	− 0.16		0.58	0.87
Stone, clay, glass and concrete	1.10**	− 0.35**		− 0.47**	0.22*		0.87	1.01
Fabricated metal products	0.98**	0.27**		6.16	− 0.13		0.77	1.03
Paper and printing	0.71**		0.56	− 0.30*	− 0.18	0.10	0.89	1.04
Electrical equipment and supplies	0.90**		0.13**	− 0.19			0.74	1.05
Transportation equipment	1.03**	0.37**		− 0.21**	− 0.27**		0.83	1.05
Machinery except electrical	0.99**		0.12**	0.07			0.76	1.21
Petroleum and coal products	1.53**		− 0.49**	− 0.22**	0.37	0.26	0.89	1.25
Chemicals and allied products	1.55**			− 0.16	0.27	− 0.21	0.96	1.30
Primary metals	1.30**		0.15	− 0.63**			0.65	1.46

(a) The ratio of job offers to applicants (excluding new graduates) all industries.

237

Table 3

Germany: Industrial Wage Differentials, 1966-1975

Relative Wage Equations

Industry	Constant	Pr_i	Pr_i/Pr_a	Vacancies/Unemployed	Consumer prices	$(W_i/W_a)_{-1}$	R^2	$\dfrac{W_i \text{ ave.}}{W_a}$
				Explanatory variables				
Apparel and leather goods	0.58**		0.40**		-0.01		0.80	0.77
Textile mill products	1.22**		0.08	-0.17	-0.10	-0.49	0.34	0.84
Food and tobacco	1.42**		0.06	-0.66**		-0.67*	0.78	0.90
Instruments and related products	1.15**		0.16	-0.22	-0.33*	-0.46	0.58	0.93
Lumber and furniture	0.80**		0.17**	-0.37**	-0.01		0.60	0.96
Fabricated metal products	1.02**	-0.41**		-0.11			0.96	0.97
Stone, clay, glass and concrete	0.36			0.92**	0.55*	0.65*	0.72	0.99
Rubber and miscellaneous manufactures.	0.26		0.06**	0.40**	0.02**	0.66**	0.83	1.03
Paper and printing	1.08**	-0.24**		-0.09			0.81	1.03
Machinery except electrical	0.87*			0.13	0.39	0.17	0.42	1.07
Chemical and allied products	1.77**			-0.19	0.21*	-0.63	0.58	1.07
Primary metals	0.60**		0.08*	0.27	-0.41**	0.39**	0.93	1.10
Petroleum and coal products	1.34**		-0.57**	-0.70			0.57	1.12
Transportation equipment	1.52**		0.03	-0.12		-0.37	0.14	1.15

Table 4
United Kingdom: Industrial Wage Differentials, 1968-1976
Relative Wage Equations

Industry	Explanatory variables						R²	$\frac{W_i \text{ ave.}}{W_a}$
	Constant	Pr_i	Pr_i/Pr_a	Vacancies/Unemployed	Consumer prices	$(W_i/W_a)_{-1}$		
Apparel and leather goods	0.11	0.21		0.33**	− 0.21**	0.82**	0.95	0.75
Textile mill products	1.29**	0.12**		0.06		− 0.55	0.89	0.85
Lumber and furniture	0.95**	0.30**		0.52**			0.91	0.96
Food and tobacco	0.24		0.18	− 0.34	− 0.15	0.57	0.60	0.96
Stone, clay, glass and concrete	0.95**		0.06	0.20			0.35	1.01
Fabricated metal products	0.60*		0.09		0.14**	0.33	0.94	1.02
Chemicals and allied products	0.71*	− 0.14		− 0.40	0.23	0.36	0.67	1.09
Paper and printing	0.63		0.10	0.18	− 0.25	0.34	0.82	1.09
Primary metals	1.19**				0.26		0.45	1.14
Machinery except electrical (a)	1.21**			− 0.30**	0.05**		0.93	1.18
Petroleum and coal products	0.74					0.50	0.45	1.19
Transportation equipment	1.25**		0.45**		− 0.37		0.61	1.20
Instruments and related products (a)	0.90**			0.93	− 0.14	0.03	0.85	1.42
Electrical equipment and supplies (a)	1.52**	0.34**		− 0.51**	− 0.15**	0.64	0.98	1.56

(a) Data available only for 1970-1976.

Table 5
Sweden: Industrial Wage Differentials, 1963-1976
Relative Wage Equations

Industry	Explanatory variables					R^2	$\frac{W_i}{W_a}$ ave.
	Constant	Pr_i/Pr_a	Unemployment rate (a)	Consumer Prices	$(W_i/W_a)-1$		
Textiles	0.71**	− 0.14**		0.14*		0.88	0.80
Wood.	0.44**	− 0.03*	− 0.63*	0.44**		0.60	0.87
Sheltered food production. . . .	0.57*	0.44	− 0.10	0.12	0.25	0.50	0.88
Other manufacturing	0.41	− 0.02*	0.03		0.42	0.73	0.88
Import competing food products . .	0.29**	− 0.06**	− 0.13		0.74**	0.93	0.93
Non-metallic minerals	1.00**		− 0.16			0.44	0.96
Electricity and gas	0.66		− 0.81	− 0.36	0.74**	0.78	0.96
Rubber products	0.58*		− 0.31*		0.32	0.24	0.97
Beverages and tobacco	0.52*		− 0.92*	0.18	0.33	0.51	0.98
Paper.	0.08	0.02*			0.98**	0.95	1.00
Industrial chemicals	0.80**		0.40**		0.20	0.46	1.03
Fabricated metals.	1.38**	− 0.13		− 0.28*		0.46	1.03
Electrical machinery	1.63**	− 0.06	0.20	− 0.53**		0.76	1.05
Base metals		− 0.03*	− 0.33	0.37*	0.56**	0.94	1.07
Printing	0.90**	− 0.07	0.25	− 0.22	0.41*	0.40	1.07
Shipbuilding.	1.11**	− 0.10**	0.36*			0.71	1.12
Mining and quarrying		− 0.01	0.17	0.60**	0.53**	0.91	1.13
Construction	1.15**	0.07	0.86**	− 0.49**		0.96	1.13
Petroleum refining	1.10**	0.01	0.46		0.38	0.05	1.14

(a) Reciprocal of the total unemployment rate.

COMMENT ON SCHELDE ANDERSEN'S PAPER

Michael L. Wachter[1]

Schelde Andersen argues that wage changes have become less responsive to business cycle conditions, at least during the 1970s, and that this is due to three factors: "tax-push" inflation, related to workers' interests in maintaining after tax real wage growth; the growing importance of fringe or overhead labour costs; and the increase in structural imbalances in the relative wage structure.

The author presents evidence on all of the OECD countries and this ambitious undertaking leads to somewhat mixed results. The scope of the paper encourages the presentation of broadly based and detailed evidence. The findings, however, do not appear to yield systematic inter-country comparisons. In some cases the countries can be ranked in terms of their support for the author's overall conclusions but there are few explanations for why some countries "fit" better than others. Perhaps a focus on fewer issues would have yielded better cross-country results.

On the overall issue of whether inflation has become less responsive to aggregate demand, the paper is somewhat ambiguous. On page 189 the author suggests that the slope of the Phillips curve has been reduced, implying less of a short-run trade-off between inflation and unemployment. In addition, he argues that inflation has become more of an auto-regressive process, with wage increases feeding on past and promoting future wage and price increases. But his model and evidence can be interpreted differently with the implication that inflation has, in fact, not become less responsive to business cycles. In part, the alternative case is based on the fact that the fluctuations in wages during the 1970s were caused by factors other than traditional cyclical effects. Assuming a zero covariance, the variance in the inflation rate ($\sigma^2_{\dot{w}}$) is the sum of cyclical (σ^2_c) and non-cyclical variances (σ^2_{nc}). It happens that during the 1970s the σ^2_{nc} term was unusually large so that $\sigma^2_{\dot{w}}$ was dominated by those effects. The cyclical responsiveness was simply swamped by these exogenous factors. This, however, does not imply a, *ceteris paribus*, reduced responsiveness (or elasticity) of wage inflation to cyclical fluctuations.

That Schelde Andersen concentrates on the 1970s is important in reaching policy conclusions. It is the case that the OECD economies suffered a slowdown in growth during the middle 1970s which coincided with an

1. Professor, Department of Economics, University of Pennsylvania, Philadelphia, Pennsylvania.

increase in the inflation rate. This, however, need not suggest that inflation and unemployment (or growth) are no longer related. Cyclical effects on inflation may well be as important as ever - even though the exogenous shocks of the 1970s had the major effect on swings in the inflation rate over the past few years. Indeed the author's evidence supports the notion that those countries which augmented the exogenous food-fuel shocks of the 1970s with monetary and fiscal stimulus did have the relatively highest inflation rates.

Schelde Andersen's most provocative point is that tax increases, contrary to prevailing wisdom, may be inflationary on balance because wages are determined in a bargaining context that stresses the after-tax real wage. The paper's evidence to support this assertion, however, is not strong enough to convince the sceptical reader. The technical problems raised by the evidence include the fact that the definition of the after-tax wage variable seems somewhat arbitrary, its statistical significance varies considerably among equations, and the pattern of the quantitative size of the coefficient or its significance across countries cannot be explained. Moreover, the real wage rigidity effect is based largely on the reaction of economies to one event; namely, the OPEC oil increase. Given these technical problems, it is possible that, where the variable is significant, it may be measuring other effects that were occurring during the oil crisis and it may not be relevant to the more general "tax-push" question. As a result, there is little hard statistical evidence in this paper to contradict the traditional view that, on balance, tax increases (decreases) are restrictive (stimulative) in their impact on nominal GNP growth rates.

The notion that there exists a "norm" or target after-tax real wage growth rate is difficult to test, in part because of the problems in clearly specifying the hypotheses for aggregate data. If such a norm exists at all, it presumably exists for individual workers. But workers are at different stages of their life cycle and should therefore have different norms. Real wage gains should be higher for younger than for older workers. Wage settlements can take account of this since they distinguish between across-the-board wage gains and movements across job categories. The latter changes account for the larger wage increases of younger workers. Aggregate wage data, however, cannot allow for these life-cycle complexities.

Indeed, the large demographic changes affecting many OECD countries — the decreasing average age of the work force and the increasing percentage of female workers—introduces a systematic bias into the aggregate wage data. Specifically, the aggregate (or even industry) rate of wage increase is biased downward by this compositional shift. For example, in the United States, whereas the "representative" worker of ten years ago was a 45-year-old male machinist in manufacturing, the "representative" worker today is a 35-year-old worker (40 per cent female) in the service sector. Of the real wage slowdown that appears in the aggregate data, that component which is accounted for by demographic changes is certainly not a violation of after-tax real wage norms for individuals.

The increasing number of female workers and the decreasing size of families introduces another set of problems. Are norms set for individual hourly wages, family income, or family income per capita? The present writer's view is that family income "counts" a great deal in both setting and achieving norms. As a result, the slowdown in real wage growth is in part responsible for the increase in two-worker families. But a two-worker family, with fewer children, may be able to satisfy its real wage norm even at the slower recent growth rate of real wages.

A separate issue is whether all age groups are suffering a real wage slow-down. Data for the United States, for example, indicates that most of the real wage slowdown is for younger workers. If the older workers are a key factor in union politics, their preferential position may dictate against a strong bargaining stance in favour of real wage norms.

To summarise, attempts to capture real wage norms with aggregate data are bound to have severe difficulties. Part of the violation of the norm in the 1970s is a statistical artifact due to the compositional shift in the labour force. Perhaps more important, individuals adjust their norms in reaction to labour market realities--the growth in two-wage earner families and the decline in fertility in many OECD countries are just manifestations of this process. But, if the real wage norm can be "satisfied" in many different ways, how important will it be in causing cyclical rigidity of money wages?

Having indicated all of these reservations with the Schelde Andersen hypothesis on the importance of after-tax real wage gains, I still believe that it may be relevant. The problem is to formulate the hypothesis in a fashion which avoids the questions raised above. This is very difficult to accomplish with aggregate data alone.

The second factor, the rising share of non-wage labour costs, does have a greater potential for introducing an inflationary bias into the economy that is independent of aggregate demand factors. A problem, however, is to distinguish between government mandated changes in compensation and those agreed upon by the private sector. In terms of economic theory, the former should be more of a problem than the latter. Non-statutory fringes are as much a part of unit labour costs to the firm as are wages. Presumably during recessions firms will be more reluctant to add to their fringe package and the cost of services already provided might be expected to be increasing with the general inflation rate. It seems to be the case, however, that over the recent decade, the tendency of fringes to increase as a percentage of total costs has been a secular rather than a cyclical development. New programmes are initiated at prespecified dates which adds an acyclical element to the wage inflation data. In addition, a major benefit provision, health care, has been a source of above-average and acyclical cost increases. This seems to be due to institutional factors specific to that benefit. In particular, the growth of insurance or government programmes that reduce the relative marginal cost to the consumer, has permitted demand to increase without regard for the self-policing market mechanism of rising supply costs.

Due to the array of institutional and governmental barriers that seem to prevent fringe benefit growth from adjusting to cyclical factors, the compensation variable should be treated differently from the direct wage component. Since they affect unit labour costs and the supply price of labour, both need to be studied. They are sufficiently different in their underlying motivation, however, as to necessitate separate treatment. Granting the acyclical nature of fringe increases, it is useful to address the changing cyclical responsiveness of direct wage payments independent of overhead or fringe costs.

The final topic in the paper, the role of the inter-industry wage structure in the wage equation, is of substantial interest on its own account. The present writer differs from Schelde Andersen on the relationship between the coefficient of variation of inter-industry wages (i.e., wage disparity, denoted CV) and the rate of wage inflation. Specifically, he argues that the former is an explanatory variable in the wage equation. But CV itself is a function of the same variables that appear in the wage equation. If CV is a function of the unemployment rate, the inclusion of CV in the wage equation is likely to lower both the significance and quantitative size of the coefficient on the unemployment variable. This, however, does not imply a reduced cyclical responsiveness since the total cyclical effect now includes the coefficient on CV as well as on unemployment. The author acknowledges this point, but maintains his interpretation of this result.

The paper is rewarding to read. However, the main point of the paper on the declining responsiveness of wage inflation is not well supported by the evidence. The hypothesis itself is somewhat ambiguously stated and this hinders a well specified set of empirical tests. In addition, the arguments for the three major causes of this phenomenon-after-tax, real wage norms, overhead costs, and the inter-industry wage structure - are not well established as independent causes. Only the case for the increasing importance of overhead or fringe costs as part of the overall compensation package has strong supporting arguments.

The notion that excessive aggregate demand stimulus causes accelerating inflation is only too well supported by the data. The case for decelerating inflation and recessions is less well established. The one steep recession of the last decade did result in a slowdown in the inflation rate. But both the sharp upswing in inflation in the early 1970s and the subsequent moderate decline in inflation were influenced by exogenous factors such as wage and price controls, OPEC oil increases, and agricultural problems.

The potential deflationary impact of recession is often confused with the political distaste for such policies. For example, it can be argued that a pre-announced recession of the depth and direction of 1974-75, with the slow recovery of 1975-76, without the exogenous inflationary forces of OPEC oil increases and government increases in transfer payments, would have caused a significant downward adjustment of the inflation rate. The decision not to adopt such a policy is based on the perceived costs of unemployment measured against the perceived costs of inflation. It is useful, however, not to confuse a preference for low unemployment policies with the unsubstantiated hypothesis that recessions do not reduce the inflation rate.

In an economic environment where inflation cannot be reduced because of its unemployment cost, and unemployment is difficult to reduce because of the fear of accelerating inflation, new policies are needed. I suggest that such policies should be based on improving the productivity and potential output growth of the economy by increasing incentives for investment in human and physical capital. That is, governments should switch from policies that would directly stimulate consumption to those which directly stimulate investment. Such policies may require somewhat slower growth in the short run, but they offer the potential for faster, non-inflationary growth in the future.

WORKING HOURS AND THE DISTRIBUTION OF WORK

R.A. Hart[1] and P.J. Sloane [2]

Introduction

For the first time since the inter-war period persistently high unemployment rates have in recent years re-emerged in many OECD countries. Fears have been expressed that such unemployment is not of a demand-deficient variety which may be remedied by traditional monetary/fiscal stimulants, but reflects long-term structural forces which require new approaches. Two broad policies, implemented by various governments, appear worthy of note here. First, various forms of temporary employment subsidy have been introduced which either discourage employers from making workers redundant (i.e. are job-preserving) or encourage employers to take on more new recruits than otherwise would be the case (i.e. are job-creating).

The second main approach is to examine possibilities for expanding the number of workers in employment by restricting the effective utilisation of the existing workforce (i.e. work-sharing), notably reflected in the unions' pursuit of a 35-hour week. The focus of attention may, indeed, be shifting away from problems of income distribution towards the achievement of a more equitable distribution of work. It is on the latter approach that we concentrate here, though in general the importance of examining components of manpower policy in terms of their interaction with each other cannot be overemphasised.

We may identify four general areas where policies to restrict total working hours may be applied, thereby, hopefully, producing work-sharing possibilities: *(a)* reducing effective working hours per worker per unit of time *(b)* reducing the average working lifetime of the workforce *(c)* restricting the size of the potential workforce *(d)* restructuring the labour supply. Certain policy measures fall into two or more of the above categories. One example, which straddles *(a)* and *(b)* above, involves work-sharing in its more immediate, literal meaning, that is where two (or more) workers share the same job; this may be attractive in particular to married women. Alternatively, an older, skilled worker may be given the opportunity to share his job with a young, new recruit. The older person would then enjoy a phased, or partial, retirement while the youngster could combine classroom education with valuable on-the-job training.

While it is the intention of this paper to consider the feasibility and implications of most of the above measures for collective bargaining agreements, the bulk of the discussion will purposely be devoted to category *(a)*. The view is taken that it is success in reducing working hours per existing

---

1. Senior Lecturer, Department of Economics, University of Strathclyde, Scotland.
2. Professor of Economics and Management, Paisley College, Scotland.

employee which would have the greatest potential quantitative importance in reducing unemployment.

Reducing Hours of Work to Increase Employment - Some Policy Implications

There would appear to be three general policy strategies towards increasing employment by reducing working hours. The first involves agreement among firms, government and trade unions to achieve direct reductions in working hours. The second involves trying to achieve the same objectives by indirect means; that is, by legislation designed to alter the relative price structure of the labour services components. The third involves general macroeconomic management.

In this section each of these possibilities will be discussed in turn and an attempt made to evaluate their relative strengths and weaknesses.

Direct reductions in working hours

It is the practice in several OECD countries (e.g. Belgium, France, Germany, Japan, Netherlands, Spain), to set legal limits on the length of the working week. Commonly, this takes the form of defining a 'standard' or "normal" workweek by collective agreement and then imposing upper limits on overtime working. However, such upper limits are often generously high and, moreover, exclude many key occupations.

There is little doubt that successful attempts to control overtime working in order to create employment could be quantitatively quite significant given the coexistence of high levels of both overtime working and unemployment in several countries. For example, in October, 1977 total registered unemployment in Britain comprised about 6 % of the adult labour force (roughly 1.5 million workers) while the number of overtime hours in manufacturing industry alone was equivalent to 400,000 persons working a "standard", 40-hour week. However, since this latter figure excludes manufacturing firms employing fewer than 25 persons and the whole of the service sector, it is clear that overtime hours amount to a significant proportion of the unemployment rate. Indeed, in approximately half of the industries which comprise the manufacturing sector of British industry, if total overtime hours worked were converted to 40-hour week jobs then the employment thus created would exceed the registered unemployment figures.

However, attempts to reduce overtime hours directly involve a number of fundamental problems. It is clear that there are economic cost considerations which make some use of overtime highly desirable. A crude reduction of overtime hours, in the absence of other measures, may well prove to lead to adverse long-run employment effects. For example, the work by Ehrenberg (1971) would seem to indicate that an important use of overtime is to offset increases in non-wage costs. Now, if such costs are rising relative to wage costs, and we present evidence below which strongly indicates that they are, then a reduction of overtime working will increase the total labour costs to the firm. Thus, while an employer's immediate reaction in the face of effective overtime constraints may be to increase employment, in the longer term he may well be induced to substitute more labour-saving machinery for less employment (i.e. *both* workers and hours) in order to counteract his rising wage bill. A similar cost effect will also occur on the supply side if, as is likely, trade unions demand compensation (through higher standard rates and/or more fringe benefits) for the reduction in average overtime earnings.

Even in the absence of such long-term cost effects, it is not certain that the short-run consequences of reducing overtime hours will be generally beneficial. There is evidence that a substantial lag exists between employers wishing to increase their effective labour force by a given magnitude and such an increase taking place. For instance, time must first be devoted to searching for, hiring and training new labour. If overtime hours were cut abruptly, therefore, serious production bottlenecks might result with accompanying adverse price effects and delivery delays. If, on the other hand, a reduction in overtime hours is phased in gradually, then time may be given for employers to substitute capital for labour, thereby circumventing even the short-run employment increases.

An alternative approach in this area would be to attempt to reduce the length of the standard working week. At the time of writing this strategy is currently being pursued in several key industries in Belgium. For example, a breakthrough has recently been achieved by the Belgian trade unions which have negotiated reductions to below 40 hours in several sections of industry and individual firms, without loss of pay. Several key American agreements have reduced standard hours to as low as a 35-hour workweek (see Zalusky, 1978).

Of course, there has been a long-run gradual reduction in standard hours in all countries with the current average typically around the 40-hour week level. It would seem reasonable to argue that collective bargaining agreements have been successful in the perspective of long-time horizons since it has been possible to achieve compensatory offsets in the form of improvements in technology and work methods. Significant short-term reductions in standard hours, on the other hand, may prove to be even more counterproductive than comparable reductions in overtime working. Not only do such reductions involve all the intrinsic difficulties mentioned in the case of overtime hours but they would also provide an added "job-creation" cost. A fall in standard hours *(ceteris paribus)* will tend to lead firms to substitute more overtime working for new employment. If, to meet such a contingency, reductions are proposed in both standard and overtime working, then the tendency for firms to substitute capital for labour will be even more pronounced.

Recently, the Department of Employment (1978) in Great Britain has attempted to estimate the effects on employment, labour costs and public expenditure of a general reduction in standard hours from 40 to 35 or to 38 hours. The estimates, shown in Table 1, are achieved after imposing varying assumptions concerning changes in overtime, output per man-hour, output and employment. These findings support our contention that reductions in standard hours will significantly increase employers' labour costs. While, for example, reduction of 5 hours in the standard workweek could reduce unemployment from between 100,000 and 500,000, total labour costs could rise from between 6 % and 8 %. The Department of Employment conclude that "the inflationary effects of the increase in labour costs resulting from a fall in hours would weaken our competitive position and damage employment prospects beyond the short term".

Table 1

Effects of reducing normal weekly hours without corresponding loss of pay - Great Britain

Example	Reduction to 35 hours			Reduction to 38 hours		
	Registered unem- ployment (000s)	Labour costs per cent	Govern[1] ment expendi- ture million	Registered unem- ployment (000s)	Labour costs per cent	Govern- ment expendi- ture million
Large employment effect (a)	− 480	+ 7.0	− £ 650	− 200	+ 2.5	− £ 250
Intermediate employment/ low productivity (b).	− 350	+ 8.5	− £ 950	− 150	+ 3.0	− £ 350
Intermediate employment/ high productivity (c)	− 250	+ 6.1	− £ 700	− 100	+ 2.2	− £ 250
Small employment effect (d)	− 100	+ 6.4	− £ 800	− 40	+ 2.2	− £ 300

1. Government expenditure is measured at 1977 prices and benefit levels.
2. A proportion of the potential output lost by a reduction in hours would be made up through:
    a) 48 % increased employment, 40 % higher output per man-hour, 12 % more overtime.
    b) 35 % increased employment, 20 % higher output per man-hour, 35 % more overtime, 10 % lower output.
    c) 25 % increased employment, 40 % higher output per man-hour, 25 % more overtime, 10 % lower output.
    d) 10 % increased employment, 40 % higher output per man-hour, 40 % more overtime, 10 % lower output.

Source : *Department of Employment Gazette,* April, 1978.

We have mentioned one aspect of the cost-reaction of limiting working hours which is particularly relevant to collective bargaining agreements, namely employee compensation. Such compensation may either be assimilated into the firm's existing cost structure or 'externalised' in the form of government compensation. In this latter respect, governments in certain European countries (Austria, Belgium, France, Great Britain, Italy, Luxembourg, the Netherlands, Norway, and West Germany) have introduced schemes which provide partial compensation to employees who lose wages due to reduced hours. For example, the West German Government, through its Employment Promotion Act, 1969, has tried to encourage manpower reductions by reimbursing 68 per cent of wages lost due to shortened working weeks. Initially such payments were continued for up to 6 months but as the recent depression has deepened the period has extended to between one and two years. Recently a limited number of experiments along these lines have been conducted in Canada (see Crowley [1978], and Sadlier-Brown [1978]).

It has been argued that such 'partial unemployment schemes' have been successful in both increasing the amount of short-time working and reducing unemployment. For example, Levitan and Belous (1977) quote figures for Germany where over the year ended May 1975, unemployment more than doubled (450,000 workers to 1 million) while the number of short-time workers increased more than fourfold (225,000 workers to 925,000). They also cite the fact that German government statisticians have estimated that, without short-time compensation, the 1975 unemployment average would have been 175,000 workers higher. They show similar trends following unemployment compensation schemes in France and the Netherlands. (See also Clark [1977], where evidence and argument from a number of studies is quoted).

However, without a much deeper analysis, reliance on such evidence can be dangerously misleading. It is by no means certain that partial unemployment schemes either create new employment (by work sharing) or even prevent layoffs. Most of the schemes have been operating principally during periods of economic depression. Now, it is well established in a number of studies (for a useful summary see Fair (1969) that output falls more than proportionately to employment during depressions as firms hoard labour in order, for example, to safeguard their human capital investments. If governments decide to subsidise shorter working hours during depressions this may simply mean that hoarding payments are effectively transferred from the firm to the government without any significant employment creation or unemployment prevention taking place. If, without the government schemes, firms were to hoard anyway, then the above-quoted figures would overestimate the effect of the subsidies.

Irrespective of whether reduced working hours are financed by the firm or the government, a fundamental problem remains with all initiatives which are designed to constrain working hours directly. If such constraint occurs without regard to the relative cost structure of labour (for example, between wage and non-wage costs or between total wage and capital costs) then any work creation which does result may be only temporary as firms substitute out of the relatively costly factor.

It is to such underlying cost considerations that we turn our attention in the following sub-section.

Reductions in working hours and changes in labour costs

The ratio of non-wage to wage costs (nw/w) is an important determinant of labour service employment: a rise in nw/w induces employers to substitute more overtime workers for fewer employees. This proposition is strongly supported in a detailed study by Ehrenberg (1971), using U.S. data for 1966 and concluding, "in the vast majority of both manufacturing and non-manufacturing industries the observed annual overtime hours per man are significantly positively related to the ratio of weekly fixed labour costs per man to the overtime premium wage". (Laudadio and Percy [1978] found a similar relationship between these two variables for Canadian manufacturing in 1968). It may be assumed that this phenomenon has recently led to adverse effects on new employment in the U.S. since, according to Clark (1977), fringe benefits, an important component of nw, now average 35 percent of total labour costs and have been increased twice as fast as wages.

It should be emphasised that a rise in the ratio, nw/w is not limited to North America. Table 2 shows the trend in the proportion of non-wage costs to total wage costs for six major European countries. By 1972 this proportion was well over 30 percent in all cases except the U.K. (and in the case of Italy well over 40 percent) and all of them (where full information is available) experienced appreciable rises over the period 1966 to 1972.

It would be surprising if during the last few years such a trend had not continued despite the high proportion of non-wage costs achieved by 1972. See, for instance, Incomes Data Services International Reports *(passim)*. During the recent depressed economic climate, the growing use of statutory or voluntary incomes policies would tend to limit the growth of the wage part of the index while government and union pressures would tend to accelerate the growth of the non-wage part. Such pressures manifest themselves in a number of ways. First, governments, faced with the problem of growing unemployment, are inclined to introduce policies designed either to alleviate the hardships of the newly unemployed or to make employers more reluctant to create new redundancies. Such policies, however, can produce higher non-wage costs to the employer, such as higher redundancy payments contributions, and thus, while jobs may be preserved for a time, the worsening nw/w ratio may gradually lead to the substitution of longer hours for fewer workers. One such series of measures in Britain is contained in the Employment Protection Act, 1975, which has been attacked on the employer's side as reducing employment, principally because of the higher non-wage payments imposed on the employer, and this issue is currently being investigated by the Government. Secondly, unions, faced with incomes policy constraints on their direct wage bargaining, tend to switch their emphasis to bargaining for better fringe benefits, thus exacerbating the non-wage increases.

There is little doubt that policies designed to reduce the ratio, nw/w, may well make a significant contribution to new job creation. Further, in certain respects, such policies provide the most fruitful avenue for successful collective bargaining agreements to reduce working hours. There are two basic strategies which may be adopted singly or in combination to reduce nw/w. The first involves directly affecting earnings through incomes policy while the second involves reducing the employer's non-wage payments.

Government policies concerning limits on the growth of incomes embrace a wide area of macroeconomic decision-making with, of course, many ramifications which lie outside the immediate subject matter here. One limited area of incomes policy, however, has particular relevance to the present discussion. Certain countries legislate the rate at which hours worked in excess of standard hours should be paid. An obvious policy strategy, therefore, would be to legislate for higher premium rates, thereby increasing the relative price of overtime hours compared to additional employment.

Table 2
Trend in the proportion of non-wage to total wage costs[1]
in six European countries
All Industries[2]

	Manual Workers (% hourly labour costs)					
	Germany	France	Italy	Netherlands	Belgium	UK
1966	26.77	36.65	37.92	32.50	32.01	n.a.
1969	27.36	35.70	40.11	35.02	33.62	n.a.
1972	32.25	39.27	47.56	n.a.	39.23	17.35[3]
	Non-Manual Workers (% monthly labour costs)					
	Germany	France	Italy	Netherlands	Belgium	UK
1966	25.82	32.70	33.74	29.01	27.61	n.a.
1969	27.23	31.30	36.19	32.45	28.65	n.a.
1972	32.24	37.61	43.58	n.a.	37.96	23.55[3]

1. Proportion of non-wage costs calculated as total wage costs minus items 1 (direct pay), 2 (other bonuses and gratuities) and 3 (benefits in kind) as listed in the Eurostat tables.
2. Extractive, manufacturing and construction industries employing in excess of 50 persons.
3. Includes net subsidies.
Source : 1966 : *Coûts de la main d'œuvre 1966;* Eurostat 4-1969; Tables 0/1-4/3, p. 81 and Tables E 1-4/3, p. 156.
1969 : *Coûts de la main-d'œuvre dans l'industrie, 1969;* Eurostat, *Statistiques Sociales* 3-1971 - pp. 389 and 507.
1972 : *Coûts de la main-d'œuvre dans l'industrie 1972;* Eurostat., *Statistiques Sociales* 6-1975, Table II pp. 302/303.

Employers should be encouraged, therefore, to substitute extra jobs for less utilisation of existing jobs.

Two legislative measures were introduced in the U.S. in the 1930s which impose such constraints on premium payments. Under the Fair Labor Standards Act employers are required to pay premium rates of time-and-a-half for hours worked in excess of a standard 40-hour week. The Walsh-Healy Public Contract Act imposed such overtime premiums on work in excess of eight hours in one day. Ehrenberg, (1971), in his study attempted to quantify the employment implications of increasing the above premium payments from 150 to 200 per cent given *ceteris paribus* assumptions. He found that the employment increases so induced were generally stable across the 16 two-digit manufacturing industries in his 1966 sample, ranging between 1 and 3 per cent. The overall absolute increase in employment in these industries was found to be 218,000 jobs from an existing base of 3,616,000. Analogous results were obtained for the non-manufacturing sector. (Similar estimates for Canadian manufacturing industry (Laudadio and Percy, 1978) suggest that an identical increase in the overtime rate would increase employment by 23,711 on a base of 1,639,400 workers).

In order to obtain his employment estimates, Ehrenberg made the critical assumption that the fall in total overtime hours due to the rise in premium payments (which, incidentally, was estimated to be a 'substantial proportion' of the existing overtime hours worked) would be totally accommodated by a rise in man hours comprising new employees each working 2,000 hours per year. A consideration of various offsetting effects, however, led Ehrenberg to be extremely cautions over his induced employment estimates. Such effects include, on the demand side, capital for labour substitution given the relative price increase of the latter factor and, on the supply side, an hour's substitution effect as workers increase their demand for overtime due to the higher premium payments. In the latter case one possibility worthy of further consideration is to introduce a special tax on employers who carry out overtime work beyond an agreed margin. Another problem not mentioned by Ehrenberg is that standard rate increases may subsequently erode the overtime-standard pay gap thereby making new employment less attractive. For example, unions in industries where overtime working is not prevalent may bargain for higher standard rates in order to restore the differential with the high overtime sectors (see Hart, [1973] for a discussion and empirical tests on such compensation criteria).

However, the possible advantages of increasing overtime premiums should not be underestimated. Certainly, such an approach compares favourably with imposing severe direct restrictions on the amount of overtime which may be worked. On the demand side, there is the advantage of permanently changing the underlying labour cost structure (in the absence of compensation effects) in favour of new employment while, at the same time, there is no curtailment of the use of high levels of overtime working in the event of unforeseen economic circumstances. On the supply side, it is hard to believe that collective bargainers would encounter as many difficulties over the introduction of increased premium rates compared with direct action to limit overtime working. Indeed, it might be expected that the income effect of an increase in premium rates should overwhelm the substitution effect. In a climate where both government and trade unions desire to reduce unemployment, it is probable that existing workers may be willing, or persuaded, to use the higher premium rates as a means of substituting more leisure time for shorter working hours.

An alternative, or parallel, strategy towards reducing the ratio $\frac{nw}{w}$ to the employer is to reduce the burden of non-wage costs themselves. As mentioned earlier, the large growth in non-wage costs experienced in several countries in recent years has been due to the fact that bargaining over earnings has been constrained.

However, in one important area of non-wage payments, fringe benefits, employers and trade unions have had other incentives to concentrate more bargaining power. This arises because taxation systems often fail to cover certain fringe benefit items and, where such systems are progressive, marginal rates of tax are often higher than equivalent fringe benefit costs, such as life and health insurance premiums. One approach towards making non-wage payments less attractive, therefore, is to extend the personal income tax base to cover more fringe benefits and to increase the tax payment on existing taxable items. Such a taxation policy has been receiving growing attention in

Britain (see Incomes Data Services [1976]) as exemplified by the 1976 Finance Bill.

As a somewhat simpler, and probably more effective, device, the burden of non-wage payments on the employer may be reduced by government decisions to subsidise a higher proportion of such costs. This would have the advantage of offsetting any harmful effect on the creation of human capital which might be implicit in alternative approaches. Examples here may include the reduction of payroll taxes (especially where earnings ceilings are incorporated), subsidising more of collectively agreed redundancy costs and extending the availability of government financed job training schemes. In this instance, bargaining among government employers and trade unions would concern reducing such costs to the firm while increasing personal and indirect taxation to cover them. While perhaps of limited appeal, an added advantage of this approach is that the employment creation through the reductions in non-wage payments may be reinforced by increases in direct taxes acting to discourage employees from working longer hours. Of course we must not ignore the wider implications of increases in taxation on other policy goals.

There is a fundamental advantage of a greater proportion of non-wage costs financed by the government. In the short run there would be a net fall in total labour costs to the firm while the long-run growth rates of the total wage bill would probably be less than if subsidies were not applied. This would tend to circumvent the problem, inherent in all the other strategies outlined so far, of labour costs rising relative to capital costs with accompanying adverse substitution effects from an employment viewpoint.

However, there is a trade-off involved in attempts to reduce the ratio $\frac{nw}{w}$ through non-wage cost reductions. The expectation of employment creation has to be weighed against the expectation of greater employment instability. As mentioned earlier it is well established in many empirical studies that output fluctuates more than proportionately to labour as employers hold a buffer stock of labour during recession periods. One of the major reasons for such labour hoarding is the fact that the employer wishes to recoup, or not incur, certain non-wage costs. For example, if a firm employs a relatively skilled labour force it may have to invest heavily in the human capital of its employees through specific training schemes. In order to maximise the average time period over which such investments are recouped it is sensible to try to minimise labour turnover rates. One way of achieving this is to offer the sort of fringe benefit, such as an attractive company pension scheme based on longevity of service, which encourages the employee to stay with the firm. Here, one type of non-wage cost, training, encourages the employer to extend the working period of employees in his firm, while another type, pensions, encourages a similar extension by the employees (for an interesting discussion of this area, see Mabry [1973] pp. 95-106). A somewhat different stimulus on employers to retain workers is provided by another type of non-wage cost, redundancy payments. It is possible that the operating losses of hoarding labour during falls in product demand may be less than the costs incurred through making workers redundant. This is particularly true in the situation where there is a temporary, cyclical fall in demand and thus, where firing labour may be shortly followed by the need to rehire labour.

Thus, we would anticipate that the greater the reduction in non-wage costs, the greater the propensity for the firm to vary its employment numbers more directly with variations in its sales, thereby creating less employment stability. For this and other reasons it is essential that all sides of industry should endeavour constantly to achieve smooth, predictable changes in demand conditions. We now turn briefly to this aspect of policy.

Macroeconomic Management

In the absence of a reasonably stable economic climate all possible collective bargaining agreements concerning reductions in working hours may be regarded as merely ephemeral measures in their impact on employment. Of paramount concern in this respect are attempts to minimise unforeseen variations in firms' sales expectations. In its macro-context, such stability would appear to be the current aim of the strategically important economies of Japan, the United States and West Germany, whose governments seem to favour a gradual expansion from the world recession rather than adopting more strongly inflationary, and therefore more volatile, strategies.

In the context of the present discussion, the establishment of smooth, predictable changes in output will achieve two valuable objectives. First, it will help to reduce the extent to which employers will need to use longer hours in order to meet unexpected, short-lived increases in sales. This in turn will reduce the levels of 'guaranteed' or 'permanent' overtime, whereby employers are willing to allow previously high rates of overtime to continue when demand falls off in order to retain manpower and/or prevent industrial unrest (see National Board for Prices and Incomes, 1970, for British evidence of such overtime working). Secondly, it will help to offset the potential increases in employment variation resulting from policies designed to reduce non-wage costs to employers.

Alternative Methods of Work-Sharing

There are a number of approaches to work sharing in addition to the reduction of overtime, the shortening of the standard work-week and the encouragement of short-time working as an alternative to lay-offs. In the case of hours reductions there are several forms this could take: fewer hours per day, days per week, weeks per year, or years per working lifetime. More specifically, questions are raised concerning part-time work (i.e. sharing a given job amongst a number of workers), double-jobbing (or moonlighting), holiday entitlement, educational leave (or sabbaticals), age of entry into the labour force and exit from it, and the question of shiftwork. In recent years attention has been increasingly focused on the need for greater flexibility in working hours arrangements, notably including the development of flexible working hours systems in a large number of countries (see OECD [1976b]) and I.L.O., 1978). This rests upon the assumption that workers' tastes with respect to patterns of work are heterogeneous and a greater range of choice in this area is more likely to maximise employee welfare than rigidly fixed working arrangements (see Sloane, 1977). As Moses (1962) has suggested we may broadly distinguish between two groups – income preferrers and leisure preferrers. The former group would prefer to work longer hours than are currently offered by the employer (that is desired hours exceed the length of the standard working week) and their needs can only be met by the provision of overtime working or a second job, whilst the latter group would prefer to work shorter hours than the current standard and where they cannot obtain part-time employment are likely to absent themselves from work. Collective bargaining arrangements which impose a common rule on all employees regardless of individual needs are therefore unlikely to maximise individual welfare even if a common rule is necessary to maximise the welfare of a group as a whole. Such analysis suggests that as far as possible work-sharing through collective bargaining is to be preferred to that obtained by legal limitation, and that collective bargaining itself should allow some freedom of choice for the individual worker, whilst recognising that certain actions (such as recourse to overtime under conditions of high unemployment) may impose social costs upon other workers. There is a conflict in particular between the interests of those who are in work and the interests of those who are unemployed but seeking work. However, gains could be obtained, without corresponding disadvantages, if it were possible to devise work-sharing arrangements which were limited to leisure preferrers as opposed to income preferrers, since the former group would actually benefit from such arrangements whilst the latter would be excluded from policies which worked to their detriment. To the extent that this is not achieved under work-sharing arrangements there is always the danger of workers substituting one form of work for another. Thus, would those forced to retire early, refused overtime or provided with a shorter work-week simply take a second job, in addition to their existing one? A means of overcoming this problem would be to offer financial compensation to such workers which is conditional upon their not taking up further work. There does, however, remain the problem of policing such a policy. A movement towards greater flexibility in working life is likely, by widening the range of choice for potential employees (particularly married women), to increase the supply of labour (in itself beneficial in times of overfull employment), thereby raising the number of workers among whom the work is to be shared. There is a trade-off, therefore, between greater flexibility and work-sharing, which is exacerbated where the latter is rigidly imposed. It is now necessary to examine briefly the implications of particular patterns of work for policies of work-sharing.

Part-time work

In the last decade there has been a sharp increase in part-time employment in many industrialised countries, mainly but not exclusively involving married women, such that in some cases as many as 5 % of the total male labour force and in excess of 20 % of the total female labour force are part-time (defined as work of a substantially shorter duration than current normal

257

or statutory hours). The question is could this process be intensified by converting presently full-time jobs into part-time ones? The scope for doing this may in practice be limited not only by the fact that relatively few men undertake part-time tasks, but also by the fact that many part-time jobs may be complementary to full-time ones. Thus two major factors causing an increase in part-time work are shortages in particular skills, usually where training and experience are built up over a fairly long time period, in occupations such as nursing and teaching, and the nature and duration of the work which may be concentrated into a particular time period such as cleaning, canteen work and public transport. Further, fears have sometimes been expressed by trade unions that the extension of part-time work may pose the threat of displacement to full-time employees (i.e. part and full-time work are competitive). This could occur where the fixed costs of employment (as discussed above) were lower in the case of part-time employees. Whiting (1978) suggests that in the United Kingdom these are substantially lower where hours worked are less than 14 per week and particularly where initial costs of employment resulting from the need for training are low. There would appear to be scope for the further development of job-sharing where two women perform a job by alternating mornings and afternoons, days, or weeks and possibly for part-time work for those approaching retirement age, but these are unlikely themselves to make a major impact in the unemployment problem.

Multiple job-holding

Multiple job-holding would seem potentially to be a major threat to attempts to reduce employment by hours reductions since shorter hours may considerably enhance the possibilities for the worker to undertake a second job. Much depends, however, on the extent to which primary and secondary jobs are complementary or competitive and on the capacity for growth in the secondary job market. Because of problems of tax evasion it is difficult to obtain accurate estimates of the extent of double-jobbing but at least 5 % of the workforce in both the U.S.A. and U.K. appear to have more than one job. In a number of countries trade unions have expressed concern over double-jobbing as with overtime work. Thus in Belgium a law was passed following trade union pressure designed to make 'travail noir' including some moonlighting illegal, and similar concern has been expressed in France, Germany, the Netherlands and Sweden. However, there is reason to suppose that the elimination of double-jobbing would have a negligible effect on reducing the level of unemployment. For the United States, research suggests there is little correlation between unemployment and double-jobbing rates. This may be a result of the fact that most second jobs are of a few hours' duration or intermittent (e.g. seasonal work), are dependent upon or complementary to a primary task (e.g. examination marking by teachers) or involve an unacceptable level of risk (see Shishko and Rostker, 1976). Further, as Alden (1977) points out, over 30 % of second jobs in Britain and the U.S. are held in a self-employed capacity with skills and resources outside the scope of the majority of the unemployment, and there is a spatial and industrial mismatch in many cases. Despite the above it is possible that reduced hours of work, flexible working hours arrangements, compressed work-weeks, a growing service sector and part-time employment will increase the extent of double-jobbing in the economy, perhaps in new areas.

Increased Holiday Entitlement vs Reduced Hours

At first sight it would appear to be a matter of indifference from the job creation point of view whether an hours reduction takes the form of fewer hours per day, days per week (i.e. the compressed work-week) or weeks per year. However, in certain types of work, performance may be affected by fatigue effects so that there will be an optimal distribution of work in terms of output. When daily hours are reasonably short it is possible that a greater recuperative effect is to be obtained from additional holidays rather than a further reduction in daily hours. However, to the extent that productivity increases as a consequence of reduced hours the demand for additional labour to meet a particular output level is reduced, whilst to the extent that there are no productivity gains the increased cost to the employer will reduce his demand for labour. Given current levels of working hours it does not seem likely that there is much further potential for productivity improvement as a consequence of a reduction in daily, weekly or annual hours. Owen (1976) reports that:

"Most investigators agree that in a range from 0 to 40-48 hours a week an additional hour of work contributes to output an amount not less than that contributed by the average of hours up to this point: that as hours rise from 40-48 to some level between 60-120, output rises with hours, but at a decreasing rate, i.e. each successive hour makes a smaller contribution to output: and finally that an entrepreneur foolish enough to schedule hours per week at a level above the 60-120 range would find that total output was declining as hours rose".

Suggestions, therefore, that the costs of further reduced hours could be substantially paid for by productivity improvements seem to be rather wide of the mark and it would appear also that the job-creating effect of additional holiday entitlement is minimal. Further, any job creating effect of reduced hours is dependent upon employees accepting the trade-off between increases in wage income and hours reductions. More jobs will be created only if the rate of wage advance is slowed down as a consequence of greater pressure for hours reductions under collective bargaining.

Length of Working Life

Delayed Entry into the Labour Force

The tendency for an increasing proportion of young people to remain in full-time education beyond the minimum school-leaving age and the raising of the school-leaving age itself have already contributed to some shortening of the length of working life. In general the legal school-leaving age varies between the ages of 14 to 17. The effect of raising the school-leaving age on unemployment is, however, limited by the fact that already substantial numbers extend their education beyond the legal minimum. Further, there may be resistance to further schooling on the part of potential employees themselves. However, in many countries, including the United Kingdom, France, Sweden and Belgium work experience programmes have been introduced to reduce the unemployment level of the vulnerable young post-school-leaver group. The effect of such schemes is essentially to blur the rigid division between education and work and emphasise the need to consider employment policies in conjunction with educational policies rather than in isolation.

Recurrent Education

An alternative approach to extending holiday entitlement is to grant extended leave (sabbaticals) to workers with long service in a particular firm or establishment. In some countries, such as the United Kingdom, such arrangements are limited to a small number of white collar occupations, particularly education, but in some other countries more extensive arrangements are being introduced. Thus in France workers who have left the educational system between the ages of 16 and 20 and who wish to return to education after three years of working life before the age of 25 or 26 are paid for up to one academic year of full-time education, with the possibility of an extension for one year. Facilities for such educational leave are available in other countries, including Belgium, Germany and Sweden; it would be unwise, however, to anticipate major possibilities for additional replacement employment in such cases since many workers may be reluctant to take advantage of such facilities, even if inclined towards them, on the grounds that it may hinder their advance up the promotional ladder. This will not apply, of course, where promotion is dependent upon the acquisition of a particular qualification which it is desired to obtain.

Early Retirement

A number of countries have introduced early retirement schemes for older workers in order to release jobs for the registered unemployed. Belgium was the first country to introduce such a scheme, in April 1976, initially open to workers three years or less from the statutory retirement age and from September 1976 to these five years or less from the statutory retirement age. The scheme applies throughout the country, but requires that any worker volunteering for the scheme is replaced by his employer with an unemployed person under 30. The older worker receives a sum mid-way between his former net wage and unemployment benefit until pensionable age. By the end of August 1977 (after 17 months) 15,000 older workers had made use of the scheme, a much higher proportion of the total unemployed rate than in the British scheme introduced in January 1977. It would seem that to be successful such schemes require to be open to a wide range of workers and to offer an allowance reasonably close to the older worker's initial wage. However, problems arise in cases where experience is important since it is not possible for a new young employee simply to replace the older departing worker, but a number of changes of personnel must occur. Manpower planning is also made more difficult. In other countries early retirement has not been limited directly to job replacement. Thus in France full retirement pension at 60 became available to unemployed manual workers whose work was particularly heavy or involved unsocial hours in 1976 provided such workers had made sufficient insurance contributions. In 1977 such arrangements were extended to all workers with compensation fixed at 70 % of gross (and 80 % of net) earnings until the age of 65 when normal pension arrangements apply. It was estimated that a quarter of those eligible (or 100,000) would opt for early retirement. Such schemes have generally been welcomed by the trade unions, although the approval is presumably dependent on the provision of adequate income support. However, the effect of any voluntary early retirement scheme on unemployment is largely governed by two factors — 'take-up' or the proportion of the relevant age group taking advantage of the scheme and 'replacement' or the proportion of vacated jobs filled from the unemployment register. The former will be influenced by the coverage of the scheme, the level of benefits offered and attitudes towards earlier retirement, whilst the latter will be influenced by the state of the economy for when demand is depressed employers may take the opportunity to reduce their workforce and raise labour productivity. Bearing in mind these factors the British Department of Employment (1978), estimates that the effect of reducing the statutory retirement age for men from 65 to 60 would be to reduce registered unemployment by nearly 200,000 in the first year of operation, building up to nearly 600,000 after firms and employees had fully adjusted to the change at a net financial cost (taking into account offsetting gains of extra tax from and lower expenditure on benefits to those who were previously unemployed) in excess of $ 1,000 million. The report goes on to suggest that whilst selective retirement schemes would not reduce unemployment to the same extent as a general scheme they are to be preferred as they could be more cost-effective on account of higher replacement rates.

Furthermore, schemes allowing workers near to retirement age to work part-time would produce only roughly half as many jobs for the unemployed as a full-time scheme for the same level of expenditure. Clearly the work-sharing potential of early retirement is substantially greater than the other possibilities outlined above in this section, but the cost implications of equivalent pension rights are daunting.

Limiting the Supply of Labour

A number of countries including Austria, France, Germany, the Netherlands and Switzerland have limited their overt unemployment by tightening up on the use of immigrant labour. Thus in France permission for the entry of foreign workers into the country was restricted in July 1974, other than in the case of EEC nationals. As a consequence the number of foreign workers entering the country to work on a permanent basis fell from 153,419 in 1973 to 64,462 in 1974 and 25,591 in the following year. In Switzerland restrictions on the employment of foreign workers including limitations on the issue of annual work permits were introduced in the early 1970s and later extended. Over a three-year period August 1973 to

August 1976 the number of foreigners in gainful employment fell by one quarter (or 228,000) equivalent to 6 % of the labour force. Similarly in Austria in 1974 the authorities became more reluctant to renew expiring work permits or issue new ones and the foreign labour force fell from a peak of 250,000 in the final quarter of 1973 to approximately 180,000 in the final quarter of 1975. The use of such a policy to alleviate unemployment is, of course, only open to countries with substantial numbers of foreign workers and such "exported' unemployment may be regarded as undesirable in the wider context. Similar reservations occur in relation to possible limitations on the entry of secondary workers into the labour force. A prominent feature of labour supply in most OECD countries has been a substantial rise in the number of married women entering the labour force. Any barriers imposed here would of course conflict with equal opportunities legislation.

Shiftwork

Finally, it is necessary to consider shiftwork in analysing the possibilities of work-sharing, particularly in view of its rapid growth in the industrialised economies (see Sloane, 1978). In its survey of work-sharing the EEC Standing Employment Committee seemed to imply that a *reduction* in shiftwork would create additional job opportunities (EEC, 1978). This is, in fact, erroneous. In the long run the firm faces the choice for any given level of output of building a large plant and utilising it with one shift or building a smaller plant and working it more intensively with multiple shifts. Clearly in the latter case more workers will be employed. Generalising this case to the whole economy leads to the suggestion of a favourable effect of multiple shifts on employment, since with surplus labour scarce capital can be shared among a greater number of workers. However, there is likely to be a depressing effect on the capital goods sector, since demand for its products will be diminished through the fall in the capital/labour ratio. On realistic assumptions this temporary negative effect on employment is not likely to predominate. The net effect on employment will be a function not only of the size of the capital goods sector, but also the importance of economies of scale, the size of the shiftwork wage premium and that of the capital/ output ratio. In the short-run situation, with size of plant given the addition of an extra shift must increase employment and the removal of a shift reduce its level.

A reduction in the length of the work-week will itself stimulate the introduction of shiftwork, on account of the consequent decline in capital utilisation and similarly an increase in shiftwork may encourage a reduction in average hours worked in order to compensate employees for work at inconvenient hours. Such relationships make it difficult to assess the relative merits of reduced hours (with constant hourly earnings) and shiftwork as employment-creating devices, but they are clearly complementary.

Conclusions

In the course of this paper we have tried to cover most of the areas in which policies have been implemented or proposed for the redistribution of working patterns in order to reduce unemployment. Whilst not wishing to undervalue any specific policy we nevertheless feel that only in a few areas is a significant impact possible. Thus, emphasis has been placed on the potential of reductions in overtime, a shortening of the standard work-week, earlier retirement and subsidies to short-time working. Taking British estimates as an example of the possible effect of each of these measures the attainment of a reduction in the order of half a million in the number of registered unemployed workers is claimed to be roughly equivalent to eliminating the major part of overtime working or reducing the length of the standard work-week from 40 to 35 hours or the bringing forward of the retirement age for men from 65 to 60. Again, whilst reductions of this magnitude are not feasible through subsidies to short-time working, nevertheless a substantial contribution is suggested. However, it must be emphasised that these rough estimates are very much dependent upon the assumptions made, particularly for instance in relation to the effects on labour costs. At least part and possibly most of the advantage may be eroded in the longer term.

Accordingly, this paper has tended to favour policies which are designed to minimise possible adverse labour cost repercussions. The emphasis has been placed upon the adoption of policies involving government subsidy of employers' non-wage costs in order to reduce the ratio of non-wage to wage costs, while at the same time spreading the burden of such costs more widely over the community. In the same vein, an attractive aspect of early retirement is that the government and not the employer bears the direct cost of implementation. If, as is likely, employees are not agreeable to bearing the full costs most other work-sharing policies have the built-in disadvantage of raising the price of labour to the employer and therefore act as a deterrent to employment creation.

Given the particular needs of different sectors of the economy and the possibility of adverse effects deriving from the introduction of work-sharing arrangements legal regulation would seem to be too crude an instrument to achieve the desired effects. For this reason it seems preferable to proceed on the basis of collective bargaining initiatives by employers and trade unions, who are more able to accommodate the particular needs of their own sector. Further, legal regulations are more likely than collective bargaining to impinge severely on the freedom of choice of the individual worker between income and leisure.

It is encouraging to observe the groundswell of interest in work-sharing that has occurred in various OECD countries if this is taken as a sign of determination to deal firmly with the problem of unemployment. However, such measures represent no more than a palliative and do not constitute a substitute for policies designed to tackle the fundamental causes of high unemployment in industrialised market economies.

COMMENT ON PAPER BY HART AND SLOANE

Haruo Shimada[1]

Implications of Recent Trends: a Micro View[2]

There are three conspicuous trends in working time and arrangements of working patterns. Firstly, working time has been reduced steadily and substantially over a long period of time (Leicester, 1979). Secondly, working time tends to fluctuate with business cycles.[3] Thirdly, arrangements of flexible an new patterns of working time have grown increasingly prevalent recently among industrial countries.[4]

The main policy implication associated with the reductions in hours of work currently being advocated vocally by unions and also by the governments of various Member countries is to distribute employment opportunities to a greater number of people. In other words, shorter working time and work-sharing are regarded as two sides of the same coin for the purposes of increasing the number of employed persons and reducing unemployment.

The key question before us, however, is whether or not a reduction in working time will *really* increase employment. In order to answer this question, we need to examine immediate microeconomic outcomes as well as macroeconomic consequences. Let us take first the microeconomic effects of a reduction in hours of work.

Our assessments of employment effects will depend heavily upon the assumptions made in our conceptual models. Consider in turn, under alternative assumptions, three models of different complexities.

Model 1: This is a very simple model with two sets of simplifying assumptions. One is that the production function has only one kind of input, which is labour, and changes in productivity are not allowed for. The other is that hours of work are treated in a simple abstract form and not in terms of specific forms such as standard work-week, overtime, etc.

a) If demand for the amount of work is fixed regardless of the wage rate of a worker, a reduction of hours of work per worker will certainly increase the number of workers employed. This is the simplest interpretation of what is implied by assertions often made by unions and governments about

---

1. Associate Professor of Economics, Keio University, Tokyo.
2. As well as the Hart and Sloane paper in the present volume, useful reviews may be found in OECD (1973),and Levitan and Belous (1977).
3. ILO, *Yearbook of Labour Statistics,* various issues. See also for a concise presentation of the data, OECD, 1973, pp. 17-44.
4. OECD (1973), OECD (1970), OECD (1976) and OECD (1973).

reducing hours of work in an attempt to increase employment; one should note, however, that this is in fact the case in which the demand for labour is assumed to be "inelastic" with respect to wage rate. This is obviously a very special case of a variety of alternative cases.

b) A more realistic and general formulation is to allow for alternative degrees of elasticity of demand for labour with respect to wage rate. In other words, we allow for the possibility that demand for labour decreases as wage rate increases, although to a different extent depending upon the value of demand elasticity.

If in this case workers are unwilling to accept reductions in earnings in return for reductions in hours, then the number of employees would have to decline since this means in effect an increase in hourly wage rate. There are, however, cases in which a reduction in hours will not necessarily decrease employment or could even increase it in spite of the elastic demand. These are cases in which: *(i)* workers accept lower earnings with reductions in hours, *(ii)* the state subsidises the adjustment so that workers are neither discharged nor their earnings reduced despite reductions in hours, and *(iii)* the aggregate demand of the economy is controlled appropriately so as to prevent employment reductions. In summary, the employment effect of reductions in hours in this case is likely to be negative unless some other co-ordinating policies are also taken into account. However, since this model is unrealistically simple, let us consider a more realistic model.

Model 2: To make our model of employment demand more realistic, let us relax the first set of assumptions attached to Model 1 and allow for changes in productivity. Since changes in productivity depend importantly on capital input, we need to take into account explicity the effect of capital input in order to isolate the net effect of reductions in hours. The net effect of reductions in hours of reductions in hours on productivity may vary from positive to negative values depending upon the influence of various factors, such as production technology, workers' preferences, fatigue, and motivation, etc. The actual value of the net effect can be known only through empirical analysis and cannot be presumed *a priori*.[5] Let us, therefore, consider the alternative cases of an increase and decrease in productivity in turn.

a) In the case in which productivity increases, demand for labour for the same wage rate will increase, since the demand schedule shifts outward. But since the same amount of work can now be performed with a smaller labour input, the number of employees will be reduced unless the total amount of

---

5. By analysing the data for the manufacturing sector during the 1960s, Tsujimura has found that the net effect of overtime on labour productivity and the standard work week on labour productivity are negative and positive, respectively, after controlling for influences of capital input and capacity utilisation. A typical result of analysis may be expressed by the regression model

$$X/Lh = a \left(\frac{K}{L}\right) 0.96 \frac{}{h} - 0.37 \left(\frac{h}{H}\right) 7.54_H - 1.71 \quad (R = 0.998)$$

where X is output, Lh is man-hour labour input, K/L is capital labour ratio, h is overtime, h/H is the ratio of actual hours worked to standard work week which is a proxy for the level of capacity utilisation, and H is standard work week. The exponential value attached to each of the independent variables implies percentage changes in labour productivity in response to one percent increase in the value of respective independent variable. Tsujimura, K., "Working Hours and Productivity (in Japanese)". Mimeo, Japan Ministry of Labour, 1970. A similar result has been obtained by analysing more recent data using a multisectoral model of the Japanese economy which allows for interdependent relationships of the economy.

work demanded is expanded to offset this negative employment effect. It is usually the case, however, that increases in productivity tend to go hand in hand with economic growth and as a result employment increases. It is nevertheless important to recognise that an increase in productivity alone, without supplementary policies which increase the aggregate demand, will not increase employment.

b) In the case in which productivity decreases, demand for labour will decrease if other things are held constant. But if the amount of work demanded is fixed, the number of employed workers would increase to fulfil the fixed demand. However, it is usually the case that the aggregate demand too diminishes with productivity. In other words, under circumstances of declining productivity some policy interventions to stimulate economic growth are called for in order to maintain or increase the level of employment.

Model 3: To make our conceptual model still more realistic, we drop the second assumption. This means that we will now take into account explicitly specific forms of working time arrangements such as overtime, standard work week, paid holidays, vacations, time off for training and education, etc. The focus of our interest in dealing with these specific forms of arrangements is in their differential effects upon employment. In other words, the same amount of reduction in working time may give different employment effects depending upon the specific types of reduction of working time. Hart and Sloane's comprehensive analysis clarifies systematically these differential employment effects.

Overtime Hours, Standard Work Day and Standard Work Week

According to Hart and Sloane's analysis, a direct reduction of overtime will have hardly any, or even a negative, employment effect, contrary to commonly held expectation. This is because the direct restriction of overtime gives rise to bottlenecks in production in the short run and encourages substitution of capital for labour in the long run.[6]

Overtime hours fluctuate sensitively with business cycles. It is also known that employment changes only sluggishly with time lags. These phenomena reflect the common practice of employers in using overtime as a short-run adjustment factor. Two hypotheses seem useful in explaining this behaviour: one is the "internal labour market" hypothesis and the other is the "specific human capital" hypothesis.[7] As the degree of internalisation or the specificity of human capital increases, the employers are more inclined to "hoard" their core labour force. If employers in modern industries are constrained by these conditions, a direct reduction of overtime will not increase employment of regular employees although employers may want to increase temporary or part-time employment which does not involve high non-wage labour costs.

---

6. Hart and Sloane, op. cit.
7. Doeringer and Piore (1971), Oi (1962) and Becker, G. (1964).

Similarly, a direct reduction in standard work day or standard work-week is not likely to produce a positive employment effect since this means an increase in unit labour cost of the core labour force. As a means to mitigate these negative effects, Hart and Sloane recommend policies to reduce the relative cost ratio of non-wage costs. Although such policies are certainly useful in making employers less reluctant to recruit new workers, the policy of reducing non-wage costs may have an undesirable effect through weakening the process of human capital development of already employed workers.

Paid Holidays, Extended Vacations and Time Off for Training and Education

Increases in holidays and vacations seem to have appreciable effects in increasing productivity of workers by means of refreshing and motivating them and, moreover, giving opportunities for retraining themselves.[8] Whether the effects of increased productivity outweigh the increased labour cost occasioned by these policies, however, is an empirical question. It should also be borne in mind that an expansion of aggregate demand is necessary if the increased productivity, and also the reduced work year per person are to lead to an increase in employment.

Finally, a comment on actual means to implement shorter working time. Two principal instruments mobilisable for this purpose are collective bargaining and legislation. The preceding discussion suggests that a reduction of working time of certain types could have a positive employment effect if accompanied by policies to increase the aggregate demand of the economy. Much of the achievement in shortening working time has been attained by collective bargaining in many countries. However, the collective bargaining approach has one drawback; it regulates only the sector covered by the agreement. In other words, this approach has a potential effect of altering competitive positions of employers. Since a reduction of working time tends to increase labour costs, employers affected by the agreement may well dislike it as weakening their competitive positions. The legislative approach, in contrast, is advantageous in this respect since it has a uniform impact and therefore does not affect relative competitive positions. However, since the legislative regulation determines the minimum "standard" rather than the maximum "target" its use is naturally limited. Collective bargaining and legislative approaches, therefore, should best be used in combination to produce a desired effect in the labour market.

Implications for Economic Policies — A Macro View

Our examination of microeconomic outcomes in the previous section suggests that reductions in hours alone will not increase employment unless complementary policy interventions are made which will promote economic growth.

---

8. In contrast, since the standard work-week in many industrialised countries today is already short enough little incremental productivity may be expected in return for an additional reduction in standard work-week. See Reader (1959) and Owen (1976), as quoted by Hart and Sloane, op. cit.

Reductions in hours in effect will increase wage rates unless workers agree to accept reduced earnings. Workers usually will not accept lower earnings unless it is guaranteed that their lost earnings will be supplemented by some other means, such as subsidies. Therefore, in the absence of government policy actions either to provide reduced hour subsidies or to stimulate aggregate demand of the economy, the wage rate will have to rise. And if employment were to be preserved in the face of the rising wage rate, then inflationary pressure would be intensified in the economy.

The single most important remedy to ease these difficulties is to promote investment. Vigorous capital formation is most helpful in the sense that it increases productivity and consequently moderates inflationary pressure on the one hand and that it helps to increase the aggregate demand and thereby increase employment on the other. Needless to say, other components of GNP should be controlled appropriately in addition to capital formation. As Hart and Sloane aptly stress in their report, what is important is to control the aggregate demand so as to make people confident in the future growth and well prepared for predictable future changes.[9]

However, current economic conditions for most Member countries are not such as to assure stable and adequate growth. The prospect for growth is poor especially because of the adverse conditions for investment such as a pessimistic prospect for future demand, increased social costs associated with investments, and intensified constraints concerning natural resources, etc. Under these circumstances, relatively defensive economic policies of preventing unemployment rather than increasing employment should perhaps receive more attention.

In many European Member countries and Japan, various schemes of reduced hour or employment subsidies have been developed during the last several years for the purpose of preventing unemployment from increasing.[10] Although specific provisions of the systems are different their functions are essentially common. That is to maintain on the payroll a certain portion of relatively unused or under-utilised labour who would otherwise be laid off. This may be regarded as a subsidised scheme of work-sharing. On the other hand, the conventional alternatives, which have been substantially built up in OECD Member countries in recent years, are unemployment insurance and other social security policies for minimum income maintenance. These latter policies aim at protecting the livelihood of unemployed workers outside the firm, whereas the former policy attempts to protect workers' livelihoods while keeping them within the firm. A few comments on these alternative policies are in order.

Although both policies are quite costly, which one is more inefficient (and thus inflationary) than the other is hard to tell, *a priori*. The former system is inefficient in that it makes the allocation of workforce rigid and inflexible. The latter is inefficient in that it envisages a completely idle labour force within the economy. The former is advantageous in that it prevents human capital embodied in employees from being destroyed

9. Hart and Sloane, op. cit.

10. See the review of Levitan and Belous, op. cit., pp. 60-73. The Japanese "Employment Adjustment Subsidy" which subsidises partially wages paid to idle workers on the payroll plays an essentially similar role. For a brief explanation of this system, see Shimada (1977).

during the period of unemployment. The latter is advantageous in that it helps to maintain the flexible allocative function of the labour market.

These systems, accompanied by their own merits and demerits, may not necessarily be alternative choices and instead can be combined to produce more desirable outcomes. In West Germany and Japan, for instance, both of these systems have been developed well and yet inflationary pressure appears to have been decreased. In the United States, in contrast, the former system has been largely ignored as a policy instrument and yet inflationary pressure remains quite strong. One of the keys to understanding this seemingly contradictory phenomenon lies in the nature of union-management relationships and the system of conflict resolution between workers and management.

In other words, in order to understand the employment-income-inflation nexus more properly we need to introduce another important variable, namely labour-management relations. It may be hypothesised that in countries where workers' participation in management is practised substantially, whether formally or informally, resources can be allocated efficiently along the lines of macroeconomic policies without much friction, whereas in countries in which conflict resolution is entirely left to collective bargaining, the efficient allocative function of the economy may sometimes be sacrificed. Although much has to be analysed on this topic before one can reach a reasonable understanding of the nexus, it would nevertheless not be unreasonable to stress at this stage that labour-management relations and the nature of collective bargaining influence importantly the efficacy of government policies and the performance of the economy.

Implications for Social Policies

Let us discuss in this section some of the remaining policy implications relating to freedom, security and equity in society.

There are increasingly pronounced trends towards flexible work arrangements such as flexible working time, shift work, part-time work, job sharing, extended vacations, time off for recurrent education and training, early retirement, etc. These arrangements increase the scope for free choice of workers in selecting their preferred work patterns apart from reducing total hours of work per worker. The adoption of flexible work arrangements should be encouraged, insofar as they increase welfare of workers in the sense of increasing freedom in determining their occupational careers. It must be added, however, that recent developments of these systems are not entirely commendable in this sense since some arrangements have been developed largely for the purpose of preserving jobs rather than of fulfilling the increasing desire of workers for greater freedom.

One of the major policy objectives of reducing hours and encouraging work-sharing, as repeatedly underlined, is to reduce unemployment, or, in other words, to maintain the job security of workers. As is well-known, unemployment incidence tends to be concentrated in some segments of the labour force, notably youth, in the recent experience of Member countries. But the hardship associated with unemployment seems much greater for relatively older persons, as partially reflected by their longer duration of unemployment. From the viewpoint of protecting the security of occupational life, it would seem necessary to re-examine which segments of unemployed population really suffer the greatest hardship. Even among the recently increasing young and/or female unemployed persons, for example, some search for jobs in order to make up for lost earnings of household heads while others join the labour market seeking for higher incomes for themselves.[11] It would not be unjustifiable to suggest, especially in view of the current severe labour market conditions, that policy efforts for redistributing job opportunities through reduced hours and increased worksharing should be used selectively for those who need such help more seriously than others.

Related to this is the differential aspect of working conditions and hours. Hours of work are not uniform across different sectors of an economy and different segments of labour force. In sectors characterised by high productivity, large firms, and a high degree of unionisation, workers enjoy relatively shorter hours and better working conditions. In peripheral sectors (secondary labour markets), in contrast, workers work longer hours under poorer working conditions.[12] From the viewpoint of social equity, it is difficult to affirm or accept such differentials. However, these differentials are often closely related to the conditions of survival of respective industries. If this is the case, the hasty and rigid imposition of uniform conditions can sometimes be harmful for weaker sectors.[13] In view of this, statutory regulation of hours and working conditions should be confined to the uniform minimum standard since it is neither easy nor desirable to make legislative regulations highly selective. On the other hand, collective bargaining is quite forceful and effective in the sense that collective agreements are well fitted to meet specific conditions and desires of workers and employers in different sectors.

Finally, let me emphasise that reduction in working time is by itself a valuable and meaningful objective to be pursued in society especially since it will humanise working conditions and increase freedom in occupational life. However, since the general and substantial reduction of working time in society necessarily involves changes in the life-styles and value systems of people, it will take a long time, though the direction of change itself is irreversible.

---

11. It is well known that the labour force participation of married women varies negatively with the income of husbands but positively with their own expected market wage rates. The former trend produces the so-called "additional worker effect". However, more serious problems may be associated with the phenomenon known by the name of the "discouraged worker effect".

12. Averitt (1968). In the case of Japan, for example, while average hours worked per worker during a week in September 1977 were 41 hours, average hours worked in small (with 30 to 99 employees), medium (100 to 999 employees) and large (more than 1,000 employees) firms respectively were 45, 42 and 39 hours.

13. The same topic can be applied analogously to the case of international competition. Although it is desirable to make competitive conditions uniform throughout the competitors, it might cause an even more detrimental effect if the survival conditions of weaker competitors are threatened.

Concluding Remarks

The main purpose of this comment has been to examine the implications of a reduction of working time and the distribution of work opportunities for employment, economic and social policies. Attention has also been paid to means to implement shorter working time; namely collective bargaining and legislation. To summarise briefly the major points implied by the discussion:

1) A reduction in working time alone is not likely to produce a positive employment effect.

2) A reduction in working time could increase employment if accompanied by appropriate supplementary policies which increase the aggregate demand of the economy.

3) Labour-management relations influence importantly the efficacy of government policies and the performance of the economy.

4) While a collective bargaining approach is useful in improving the working conditions of unionised sectors; it needs to be supplemented by legislative action to be really effective in the labour market.

5) Although it takes time to realise, reduction in working time is by itself a valuable and meaningful social goal in the long run.

VI

COLLECTIVE BARGAINING ATTITUDES AND TRENDS

The papers in this section cover a variety of views about the functioning, achievements and problems of collective bargaining as seen by the participants and observers of industrial relations. Oswald surveys the broad field of bargaining activity in several countries, drawing attention to the fact that what in some countries are the subjects of bargaining are in others the subjects of legislation, and analysing the effect of recent economic events – particularly inflation and high unemployment – on bargaining. The papers of McBride and Rasmussen explore in detail one of the most important subjects of recent bargaining and legislative activity: job security. The link between the concern with job security and high unemployment is stressed by Crispo, who sees a clear danger in what he regards as defeatist, supply and adjustment measures.

The role of collective bargaining in the inflationary process is discussed in several of the papers. Oswald sees unions responding to inflationary pressures. Crispo would attach more importance to their political than their economic activities as sources of inflation, although he makes a plea for revitalising and reforming the market system including collective bargaining. Roberts is clearly of the opinion that collective bargaining has aggravated inflationary pressures, and unlike Crispo sees a need for restraints on completely free bargaining.

Verschueren's paper explores changes in recent years in bargaining levels, the content of bargaining and the development of public sector bargaining. In his comments, Scharpf draws attention to Verschueren's argument that recent trends show evidence of moves to both greater decentralisation and greater centralisation. He suggests that the only safe generalisation is that there is a trend to greater diversification. Scharpf explores some of the consequences of this for policy and his conclusions may be compared with those of Peper and Treu above.

DEVELOPMENTS IN COLLECTIVE BARGAINING AND THEIR IMPACT ON NATIONAL ECONOMIC AND EMPLOYMENT POLICIES

Rudolph A. Oswald[1]

Over the past decade national economic policies have had a profound impact on collective bargaining. Trade unions' collective bargaining efforts in developed countries have had to adapt to a deep world-wide recession and the highest unemployment levels of the post-war era. At the same time, the economies of the developed countries and collective bargaining as well have been afflicted by the highest inflation rates of the post-war era.

These persistent and chronic economic problems of the 1970s -- unemployment and inflation -- have disrupted the orderly development of collective bargaining which had occurred during the previous decade. The 1960s was a decade in which collective bargaining played an increasing role in raising workers' living standards and contributing to reasonably stable upward trends in economic growth.

Then the recessions of the 1970s led to the deportation of immigrant workers in Europe, massive lay-offs in the United States and Canada and challenges to Japan's lifetime employment policies. Inflation rose to unprecedented heights, spurred by sudden spurts in food prices and by the four-fold increase in oil prices. International monetary policies -- national and international -- added to the crisis. Collective bargaining was called upon to respond to broad economic issues that were beyond its abilities to redress. Nevertheless, unions attempted to negotiate employment protection and inflation protection provisions and used their political powers to influence governments to create jobs and protect purchasing power. They sought overall governmental action to spur their respective economies and provide for greater economic growth, and to alleviate inflation. No trade union centre ignored governmental policies designed to attain full employment and most argued, correctly, that full employment was a necessary corollary to stable prices.

The governmental policies urged by the various union federations were remarkably similar -- overall economic stimulus complemented by specific targeted job stimulus. Unions supported monetary and fiscal policies that would spur overall economic growth. Unions suggested specific job stimulus in a number of countries, public works programmes, and housing programmes -- sectors suffering greatly as a result of the recession.

During the recession many unions emphasized again a number of programmes and measures that required substantial pre-notification for mass layoffs and provided for specific targeted employment policies and programmes to meet the particular problems of severe unemployment in specific

---

1. Director of the AFL-CIO Department of Research, Washington, D.C.

industries and geographic areas. It was believed that general economic expansion would spur new investment and bring about more efficient operations. Unions believed that an economy operating at full employment would be operating at the optimal cost per unit of output. Thus trade unions tied anti-inflation programmes to full employment policies.

Collective Bargaining and Unemployment

Collective bargaining has tried to address the problems of unemployment and inflation. While it is not able to solve unemployment, it has mitigated its effects. These collective bargaining efforts included reductions in working time, increases in job security arrangements, and specific industry approaches. In many countries these approaches have been interspersed with legislative changes.

Working time has been reduced through early retirement programmes, shorter hours of work and increased vacations and holidays. In the United States a major way work time is being reduced is by early retirement. Age 65 is no longer the normal retirement age in America, and most workers are retiring much earlier. If retirement income is adequate, workers can look forward to retirement and carefully planned social security benefits, negotiated pensions and savings for the day they can leave work. Today 32 per cent of the U.S. labour force in the age group 62-64 is retired and drawing social security benefits compared with only 8.6 per cent who were in this category 16 years ago.

Many collective bargaining arrangements allow for even earlier retirement, as a number of major contracts permit retirement at full pension after 30 years' service, regardless of the worker's age. Many of these contracts provide a supplement through the private pension plan to increase retirement income until the worker becomes eligible for social security, so that the worker's retirement income will be level before and after receipt of social security payment at age 62. In a 1976 study of auto retirement practices, it was found that about a quarter of those retiring that year were under the age of 55. Liberalised early retirement provisions, of course, provide additional job opportunities for younger workers.

U.S. contracts frequently have special early retirement provisions for workers faced with job losses. For example, under the agreements of the United Steelworkers with the basic steel companies, workers confronted by a plant shutdown, extended layoff, or disability can retire after 20 years of service provided they have attained age 45. In addition to the normal private pension benefit, the worker receives a $300 per month supplement until he is eligible for social security. This benefit is particularly significant in times of plant shutdowns.

In many countries similar early retirement programmes were undertaken either through collective bargaining, or special legislative acts. What may traditionally be a collective bargaining solution in one country may be a legislative approach in another country.

In France in recent years both legislation and collective bargaining have been concerned with early retirement. Japanese unions have negotiated to raise the retirement age; in Belgium, Germany, Italy and the United Kingdom legislation has attempted to deal with the problems of early retirement.

Another popular method of reducing working time is through increased public holidays and vacations (annual holidays). Most OECD countries, except for the United States, legislate minimum requirements. These are frequently augmented by more liberal collective bargaining provisions. The liberalisation of these provisions over the years has reduced the annual hours worked by regular employees. In the United States, union contracts generally provide for 2 weeks of vacation for new employees, with workers with longer service becoming eligible for 3, 4, 5 or 6 weeks of vacation. The number of public holidays continues to rise from the traditional 6 holidays to 17 paid holidays in some contracts. The increase in both holidays and vacations has substantially reduced working hours during the last decades in the U.S. Similar trends have taken place in other countries as collective bargaining agreements have extended the basic legislative holiday and vacation requirements.

In contrast to the general trend of liberalizing holidays and vacations, note must be made of Italy's reduction in the number of public holidays. It was believed that Italy's much higher than normal number of public holidays placed the cost impact of the holidays upon manufactured products, and disadvantaged them in international trade.

Reductions in working time have also taken the form of contracts or legislation which reduce the hours worked per week. While the 40-hour work-week is the basic standard, many workers are now working under contracts that call for fewer hours per week at no loss in pay. In the United States approximately 14 per cent of all full time workers are on work-weeks of less than 40 hours.

In Belgium the unions last year had called for the gradual introduction of a 36-hour week by 1980. The employers' organisations were unreservedly opposed, but a number of agreements have been negotiated providing for the reduction of the working week in certain industrial sectors -- in electricity to 38 3/4 hours starting July 1977 and to 38 hours starting July 1978; in gas to 38 hours starting January 1978 and to 37 3/4 hours starting October 1978; and in the ports, to 36 1/4 hours starting July 1978. In Ireland and in Germany the unions have been calling for a 35-hour work-week. German and French unions continued to negotiate reductions in hours for those still working more than 40 hours per week.

Job Security

Job security concerns of unions were expressed not only in public policy recommendations of unions, but also in collective bargaining. All the trade union centres have pressed their governments during the last few years to undertake broad fiscal and monetary policies as well as specific structural programmes to mitigate unemployment. In collective bargaining, unions sought lay-off protections, advance notice of layoffs, and supplemental income for workers laid off. In the United States, the longshoremen's union extended its pay guarantees to a full year in its New York agreement. Thus

279

workers under that agreement are guaranteed a full year of work, or, if work is not available, full pay for those hours.

A number of United States collective bargaining agreements provide for private supplements to the public unemployment insurance programmes. These so-called Supplemental Unemployment Benefits (SUB), first negotiated in the mid-1950s, have been improved substantially since their initial introduction into collective bargaining in the mid-1950s. Today, senior employees under the steel agreements are guaranteed two years of production. Benefits under the public and private plans replace 90 per cent of lost purchasing power. Short work-week benefits are also provided. If a worker is reassigned to a lower paying job because of a plant shut-down or disability, the fund provides for two years of wage protection.

In Germany, in 1978, the metal workers negotiated protections against demotions for economic reasons as well as new income security clauses and extended information rights for works councils. Under this new agreement no manual worker can be downgraded by more than two wage levels, and a non-manual worker's demotion can only be to the next lowest salary level. Demotions will only be possible where there are no opportunities for transfer to equivalent work or retraining.

Collective Bargaining and Inflation

Although the entire post-war period is often pictured as an inflation-prone era, the inflation rates of the 1950s and 1960s look insignificant in the light of the experiences of the 1970s. Among the OECD countries the 1950 inflation rates varied from compound annual rates of about 1 per cent a year in Belgium, Canada, Germany and the United States to about 4 per cent a year in France and New Zealand. During the 1960s these rates rose to a range of 2 per cent a year in Germany and the United States, to 5 per cent a year in Denmark and Japan. Such rates of inflation appear modest in comparison to the 10 per cent or higher rates that raged in most of the OECD countries during the 1970s. Even in the "best" countries in terms of price increases the general inflation rate exceeded 5 per cent a year.

All of the countries tried to meet their special inflation problems with classic fiscal and monetary restraints. These actions led to a general recession in most of the developed countries, as the rate of growth diminished, and sometimes turned negative. In many cases, inflation persisted even though the economies of particular countries were plagued with the worst recessions experienced since the Great Depression of the 1930s. Unemployment obviously could not "cure" an inflation that was related to specific events and not "demand-pull" factors.

Many countries also experimented with various types of wage and price controls. However these programmes did not seem to be particularly effective in curtailing inflation and in some cases merely postponed or aggravated those pressures. Several different voluntary programmes of wage and price restraint were also tried and many of these were also found wanting. Experiments continue among the various countries as each struggles to lessen its respective inflationary pressures. Unions and managements have frequently entered into "national understandings" or "social contracts" to deal with the problems of inflation. Some unions and managements were subjected to controls against the wishes of both business and labour.

In some countries unions have tried to adjust to inflation through the collective bargaining system by indexing wages to changes in consumer prices, through frequent renegotiation of wage levels, or through special reopenings of contracts to assure adequate protection from extraordinary price rises.

In the United States, 60 per cent of the workers under large contracts — those covering 1,000 or more workers — are now covered by cost-of-living escalator clauses. The prevalence of such clauses has increased nearly three-fold during the past decade. However, few if any of these clauses provide full protection for changes in the cost of living. Even the better contracts generally only recover two-thirds of lost purchasing power. Moreover, these adjustment mechanisms are after the fact and generally disregard the tax impact on the higher earnings, and thus further understate the real adjustment necessary to maintain purchasing power. The typical industrial contract in the U.S. provides the same cents-per-hour increase for all the workers, with the most usual clause calling for a quarterly wage adjustment of 1 cent per hour for each 0.3 point increase in the Consumer Price Index.

In the Netherlands the unions in their national negotiations have been firmly committed to the maintenance and full application of indexation. The adjustments in the Netherlands are generally made on a biannual basis. In Sweden there is no formal policy of indexation, but the most recent national agreement allows for early cancellation of the contract if prices rise by more than 7 1/4 per cent in 1978 or more than 5 per cent in 1979. In many of the other countries annual wage bargaining has become the usual pattern, with negotiations concerned with the maintenance of real purchasing power, as well as attempting to improve the real conditions of the workers. The negotiations in Japan during the annual "spring offensive" generally have been able to improve real wages. However, the 1978 gains seem to fall short of previous rates of improvement. In many other countries the regular annual negotiations have not been efficient guarantors of maintaining real purchasing power in the light of the inflation of the 1970s.

Government imposition of wage controls interferes with the collective bargaining process. However, such programmes have not exemplified either outstanding success in controlling inflation or in achieving greater rates of real income growth. On the contrary, in the United States the rate of inflation was more than twice as great after the control period than before it. Similarly the British experience showed a higher rate of inflation after six years of control than that experience prior to control, and a faster rate than that in most other European countries not under a strict wage control mechanism. In Canada the inflation rate tended to be reduced during the first year of the programmes, only to begin to rise again during the second year. Also the price rises in Canada were more rapid than in neighbouring United States during the same period, when the United States had abandoned its earlier experiments with controls. My interpretation of these control programmes is that they did not curb inflation but actually may have aggravated existing inflationary conditions. Nearly all of these programmes ended up as primarily wage control measures rather than price control measures.

Wages in nearly all developed countries are a major factor in the costs of production, but they have not shown a simplistic correlation to changes in consumer prices. Government judgments as to appropriate wage increments have not shown signs of being any better than the decisions the parties might have arrived at without governmental interference. In national economic policies such as those undertaken by these various countries one cannot establish what would have happened without such interference. There is no simple test of what would have happened *ceteris paribus* if no wage control programmes had been undertaken in these countries. No proof exists that wage control programmes have had significant success in controlling inflation. The rate of inflation during the past decade has been the most modest in Germany, which has not imposed a wage control programme.

General data for manufacturing industry indicate that real hourly compensation of workers during the past decade failed to rise with the general trend in productivity. This was particularly true in some of the countries with control programmes such as the United States and Canada. In these countries then, the workers failed to maintain their previous share of real gains in productivity. As the following table demonstrates manufacturing output per man-hour in the United States increased nearly 10 per cent faster than the rate of real compensation during the past decade. These gains then redounded to other income recipients in the economy.

The biggest real gains in compensation took place in Italy, Japan, Germany, and the Netherlands. However, only the latter country had some type of formal "social contract". Biggest real compensation gains above productivity took place in Italy and Germany.

Governmental attempts to control inflation through controlling wage changes of organised workers did not address the core problems of the type of inflation that characterises the 1970s. The problems were frequently external to particular national economies, and were caused more by the oil crisis, the world-wide food crisis, and the shocks in international monetary affairs.

Unemployment became so pervasive in the 1970s that the palliatives of collective bargaining adjustments had little impact on the overall levels of unemployment. Certainly the job security arrangements of particular collective bargaining agreements preserved the job opportunities of some currently employed workers, and some of the actions to reduce hours of work through early retirement, shorter hours of work and longer vacations and holidays contributed to an increase in employment opportunities. But all these collective bargaining measures could not overcome the general unemployment problems.

Unemployment doubled in many of the OECD countries between 1965 and 1975. And while some improvement was made by 1977 in some countries, others suffered a worsening of unemployment.

These conditions reflected the general economic downturns that occurred in most of these nations in 1975. While 1976 was a general recovery year, some economies stuttered again in 1977 and took a turn for the worse. This lack of economic growth aggravated employment problems, particularly for new entrants to the labour market.

Manufacturing output continued to increase in all of the developed countries during the past decade, but at a much slower rate of growth. Clearly, the substantial reductions in the rate of growth in manufacturing were a major factor in the general malaise of the developed countries during the 1970s. The lower rate of growth coincided with substantial increases in the labour force, particularly in the United States and Canada. Thus, the slower rate of growth compounded the job needs of a rapidly growing labour force. Germany was an exception as the labour force actually declined with the departure of the "guest workers".

Corporations complained about the need for new investment, and sought tax concessions to spur such investment. However, in spite of tax breaks for corporations in many of the developed countries, no great strides were made in expanding investment. Corporations frequently faced overcapacity problems in specific industries such as textiles and steel which suffered from a world-wide glut and lack of sufficient demand.

In the United States, a large part of investment by American firms was abroad and not in the United States. According to the U.S. Department of Commerce, U.S. direct private investment abroad totalled some $140 billion in 1976, almost double the 1970 total. And, even during the two recessions during that period, U.S. direct investment abroad continued to rise. Over these years U.S. firms have been investing abroad amounts equivalent to some 20-25 per cent of their domestic spending on plant, machinery and equipment.

Now, when the U.S. is trying to solve its problems of slow growth, lagging productivity, inadequate public investment and severe unemployment, U.S. firms are planning to increase – by 12 per cent – their investment in overseas subsidiaries while at the same time calling for huge tax breaks and restraints on public investments to promote lagging domestic private capital investment and productivity.

These examples of national and international developments merely underline the central experience of the 1970s -- inflation and unemployment have been twin devils in the world. National and international government policies have tried to cure them, but have not succeeded. Collective bargaining has been able to make some improvements, but the experience of industrial countries has shown the need for government policies to augment collective bargaining policies in meeting problems of inflation and unemployment. Governments should not try to use collective bargaining as a scapegoat in trying to address these issues.

The American labour movement has called upon the government to undertake a number of specific policy programmes to alleviate this nation's economic problems. The AFL-CIO believes that a full employment programme is an essential ingredient for curing not only unemployment but also inflation. The AFL-CIO is urging a wide-ranging series of measures to deal with the need for overall economic growth and for measures targeted to deal with special problems of those who tend to be left behind even if the economy was advancing rapidly. The AFL-CIO is calling for enactment of a tax programme that provides a substantial income tax cut for low- and

Comparison of Productivity Gains with Real Compensation Gains in Manufacturing, Ten Countries 1967 to 1977 – Indexes : 1967 = 100

	United States	Canada	Japan	Denmark	France	Germany	Italy	Netherlands	Sweden	United Kingdom
Index of Output per Hour in Manufacturing 1977	126.9	143.3	206.6	185.1	171.6	169.6	162.3	198.9*	156.6	126.6
Real Hourly Compensation in Manufacturing 1977	116.8	139.8	198.8	156.0	170.6	186.9	215.1	184.4*	167.7	133.7

* Netherlands data refer to 1976

Source : U.S. Department of Labor, Bureau of Labor Statistics.

Unemployment Rates in Selected Industrial Countries 1965 - 1975 - 1977
(percentages)

Year	United States	Canada	Australia	Japan	France	Germany	Italy	Sweden	United Kingdom
1965	4.5	3.9	1.3	1.2	1.4	0.7	3.6	1.2	1.4
1975	8.5	6.9	4.4	1.9	4.1	4.7	3.3	1.6	4.1
1977	7.0	8.1	5.2	2.0	5.2	4.5	7.2	1.8	6.2

Source : U.S. Department of Labor, Bureau of Labor Statistics.

middle-income Americans as a means to prevent consumer purchasing power losses that are primarily the result of higher costs of energy, food, housing and medical care. The income tax programme contains a number of reform measures which would end some of the tax privileges available to U.S.-based multinational enterprises and wealthy investors and speculators.

Another series of labour proposals deals with the serious problems of older cities. These proposals include establishment of a National Development Bank to make grants and guaranteed loans to cities and to enterprises which locate, remain, or expand in urban areas with high unemployment. Expanded federal aid for housing construction and rehabilitation is also part of the programme.

The AFL-CIO is also calling for enactment of a series of direct job creation measures which include expansion of public works programmes, particularly in older city neighbourhoods where poverty and unemployment is severe, an expansion of the federally subsidized service employment programme, an expansion of job-training for youths, and more funds for public transportation facilities. These programmes would create a million jobs directly and another million indirectly, as the purchasing power spreads through the economy.

The AFL-CIO also calls for a reversal in the high interest policies of the Federal Reserve Board, the nation's central bank. By pushing up interest rates now, the Board is signalling a return to the recession-producing policies of monetary restraint that characterised the Federal Reserve Board under the previous Administration and led to two back-to-back recessions.

At the same time, the AFL-CIO is urging a programme to help resolve the serious and growing problems American workers face as a result of dislocations due to international trade and investment in today's world. The AFL-CIO believes that the U.S. should share its markets and keep them as open as possible, but that such trade should be fair to American workers.

Growth of the Labour Force in Eight Countries
1967-1977
(Numbers in Thousands)

	United States	Canada	Japan	France	Germany	Italy	Sweden	United Kingdom
1967	77,347	7,748	49,830	20,118	26,409	19,525	3,774	24,540
1977	97,401	10,616	54,520	21,971	25,984	21,608	4,174	25,402
Percentage Growth	25.9 %	37.0 %	9.4 %	9.2 %	− 1.7 %	10.7 %	10.6 %	3.5 %

Source : U.S. Department of Labor, Bureau of Labor Statistics.

A major legislative goal of the AFL-CIO is enactment of pending legislation called the Full Employment and Balanced Growth Act. This legislation would firmly commit the U.S. to specific targets of reducing unemployment. Under the terms of this legislation the President and the Central Bank would have to submit to Congress programmes and policies to achieve these targets

285

within five years and maintain genuine full employment. The Bill provides for a comprehensive planning process aimed at specific goals and timetables for reaching full employment and outlines a wide variety of programmes, including "last-resort public jobs", which can be used to meet the full employment goals and timetables. And, perhaps most significantly, it affirms the right of all Americans who are able, willing, and seeking work to "... full opportunity for useful paid employment at fair rates of compensation".

To meet specific inflationary pressure points, the AFL-CIO calls for the establishment of reserve stockpiles of agricultural commodities and other raw materials that may potentially be in short supply. The labour federation has urged an overall energy programme to alleviate the inflationary pressures from this sector upon the whole economy. The labour movement has also long been urging that medical care delivery be changed to a national health insurance programme.

In order to enhance the collective bargaining rights of workers, the AFL-CIO is supporting basic reforms in the nation's labour law. These reforms would assure prompt elections to determine workers' desires for forming unions, and appropriate protections for workers wishing to seek collective bargaining.

Unions recognize the fact that many major national economic problems that affect the well-being of workers (1) cannot be solved at the bargaining table and (2) can undermine any progress achieved through collective bargaining. But unions will continue to seek to improve the lot of workers through collective bargaining. And they will urge governmental policies that will further that goal.

No free nation can remain free without free collective bargaining. Government wage and price controls are not an acceptable alternative to free collective bargaining. However, government policies to spur economic growth, assure full employment and maintain price stability are essential prerequisites for a stable economic environment in which free collective bargaining can be nourished and expanded.

COMMENT ON OSWALD'S PAPER

B.C. Roberts[1]

In Oswald's opinion the dramatic change of the 1970s which "disrupted the orderly development of collective bargaining which had occurred during the previous decade" was largely brought about by the rise in food prices occasioned by poor harvests, the four-fold increase in oil prices and the actions of national governments and international monetary agencies to prevent inflation. There can be little doubt that these factors were of considerable importance, but it may be questioned whether there would not have been both a significant increase in the level of inflation and unemployment had the oil price shock not occurred. Pay and prices had already risen significantly in most industrial countries before 1973 and it was the view of many economists that these increases were not unrelated to the rising strength of the trade unions. Oswald does not examine the possible influence of collective bargaining in causing the problems of inflation and unemployment, either as a factor raising labour costs or as an influence on government economic and social policies.

Oswald is clearly correct in arguing that national incomes policies have an influence on pay structures. In Europe they have led to a narrowing of pay differentials: a narrowing which has been made more severe by the additional effects of high levels of inflation and taxation policies. This development has in itself been a stimulant to further inflation since it has encouraged the unionisation of white-collar, technical and professional employees who have sought to restore their relative pay levels by militant bargaining. The interaction between unionised occupational groups is a central feature of the dynamics of collective bargaining which has confronted pay policies with many problems, which have often not been satisfactorily solved.

As Oswald observes, it is difficult to measure the effect of pay and prices policies as a counter-inflationary measure, but it is difficult to accept his reasoning that they have made inflation worse and at the same time led to a fall in real wages by preventing the collective bargaining process from pushing wages up to higher levels. Had money wages risen to higher levels in Europe it is virtually certain that prices would have risen by a similar proportion and unemployment would almost certainly have been made worse. Oswald provides a table which indicates that real hourly compensation

---

1. Professor, London School of Economics.

went up less than the index of output per hour in the U.S.A., Canada, Japan, Denmark and the Netherlands; but in Germany, Italy, Sweden and the U.K. real compensation rose more than the index of output. These figures, in so far as they establish anything, demonstrate that a redistribution of income either towards a narrowing or widening of income differences is possible under an incomes and prices policy.

There has been a decline in profits in all the advanced industrial countries but changes in the share of the national income have varied between countries; however, there has been no general tendency towards a shift from wages and salaries to rent, interest and dividends, or from personal consumption to capital formation. Indeed the tendency has been in the other direction.

As OECD studies show, profits have been falling generally in most advanced industrial countries since the beginning of the 1970s and the rate of productivity has also declined. In Britain the fall in profits and productivity has been a dramatic one and with this drop there has been a serious decline in private investment. Reluctance to invest had been an important contributing factor to the rise in unemployment which has occurred in all the advanced industrial countries. There have been some tax concessions designed to encourage investment, but private corporations faced by insufficient home demand and uncertainties in export markets brought about by fluctuations in currency values, anti-inflationary policies, the O.P.E.C. dollar problem, and a tendency to move towards more restrictive trade policies, have not been persuaded that the time is ripe to launch into new ventures.

There has been a tendency for government expenditure to increase in most countries and employment in the government sector has grown, offsetting, sometimes to an important extent, declines in employment in the private sector. Limits to government expenditure are set by political ideology and tax capacity. In the OECD countries it is clear that confronted by inflation and a revolt against tax levels there has been a curtailment of fiscal growth and borrowing has been limited by the need to impose a degree of monetary discipline - reinforced by IMF rules and OECD guidance.

Oswald indicates that unions in the U.S.A. have favoured expansionary fiscal and monetary policies in spite of current levels of inflation. This view would be shared by trade unions in many other countries. Unions generally would also support Oswald's demand that there should be greater public expenditure on specific job creation policies. One of the major problems, however, in persuading governments that they should pursue more expansionary monetary and public expenditure policies is that they will lead via the collective bargaining systems to rapid increases in wages that will far outstrip productivity and employment gains, thus leading to a further upsurge of domestic inflation and balance of payments crises.

Trade unions in other countries would also share Oswald's apprehension at the rise in imports from other countries and the flow of capital overseas. It is doubtful, however, whether they would be in favour of the U.S. government restricting the flow of capital overseas or closing the American market to imports. Union interests are inevitably divided on the issue of protection. Those who have members in industries threatened by imports wish to see them curtailed, those who benefit from exports take a different view. The net effect of a general policy of trade restriction would have profound economic, political and welfare implications and ought not to be determined by sectional interests alone.

As Oswald accepts, these problems cannot be resolved through the collective bargaining process. They require the action of governments, but collective bargaining can reinforce government action or make it ineffective. Unfortunately, the demand for pay increases in excess of output, opposition to adjustments in pay structures, resistance to labour mobility, refusal to accept changes in work methods have led to conflicts with government policies. One of the difficulties that has to be faced is that unions are often divided and unable to act effectively in concert; there is also the fact that in many countries the unions organise only a minority of workers - although it is often a crucial section of the labour force. The tendency for bargaining power to move from the level of the industry to the shop floor and the enterprise has weakened the ability of union leaders to enter into binding commitments at a national level. Given these facts, governments have no choice but to act independently if national union leaders, through fear of losing their authority, give in to rank-and-file pressures.

Whilst recognising that there are inevitable conflicts of interest it is clear from the experience of the last thirty years that failure to achieve a level of co-ordination between the process of collective bargaining and the policies of governments is a factor of major importance in overcoming the current obstacles to regaining prosperity, lower levels of unemployment, more stable prices and currency values. It is also clear that so far systems of wage and price controls based upon rigid formulae and bureaucratic administrative procedures have at best succeeded for only a limited period and may even have made the fundamental problems more difficult. The evidence, however, also indicates that policies of restraint and mutual accommodation can be effective, but recognition of this degree of success is lacking in Oswald's paper.

Nevertheless, there is reason to hope that employers, unions and governments are becoming increasingly aware that the demand for a return to "free collective bargaining" is a misleading slogan. While it is likely that collective bargaining will continue to be the most important means of determining levels of pay and other conditions of employment, it is inevitable that governments will be directly concerned in its outcome, both as the largest employers and because they have final responsibility to the public as a whole for the economic and social progress of society. If it proves not possible to reconcile the process of collective bargaining with the achievement of the wider goals that, as Oswald recognises, must be the responsibility of governments, it is likely in the long run that the collective bargaining process will have to be changed. The task before employers, unions and governments is to so adjust their relations by developing appropriate institutional and procedural changes that will enable them to achieve their common goals, reducing inflation, lowering unemployment, increasing economic growth and advancing social welfare.

DEVELOPMENTS IN COLLECTIVE BARGAINING AND THEIR IMPACT ON ECONOMIC AND EMPLOYMENT POLICIES

Albert Verschueren[1]

Bargaining Levels

General comments

The essence of this paper's remarks on bargaining levels concerns the extent to which the recession has affected negotiating structures.

Let it be said at the outset that the view according to which economic prosperity encourages enterprise bargaining whereas a recession favours more centralised bargaining is no longer corroborated by the facts.

The trend towards diversification of bargaining levels, noted in particular in certain ILO studies, and which dates back to before the crisis, has not been weakened by the recession but seems on the contrary to have accelerated.

In countries with highly centralised bargaining, where national agreements had become increasingly detailed, leaving little room for manoeuvre at lower bargaining levels, more and more cases have been seen of "loss of control" following additional bargaining intended to be more exhaustive (Scandinavian countries, Netherlands). In countries where the enterprise was traditionally the level preferred, a trend towards consolidation is to be seen in some industries (Japan, United States, etc.). And lastly, in countries where industry bargaining was predominant, movements towards both decentralisation and centralisation are to be seen (Belgium, France, Italy).

The economic situation, generally characterised by high rates of inflation and by under-employment with a wide range of consequences, seems to be a major explanatory factor. It is of course appreciated that other complex factors have also played a part in these changes. Among such factors are the degree of cohesion of employers' organisations and trade unions, strategic considerations linked to fluctuations in the balance of power, the nature of the issues negotiated and the desire or otherwise of workers to participate in management. There have been clear interactions between these various factors.

Diversification of bargaining levels has focussed attention with growing urgency on the problem of co-ordination between them. Employers' organisations, often reticent in relation to this policy of diversification of "bargaining counters"; which, in the absence of a clear division of responsibilities at each bargaining level, may lead to additional or improved benefits being accorded and higher costs incurred, have sometimes been led to lay down prior conditions *vis-à-vis* the trade unions and to strengthen procedures

---

1. Director-General, Federation of Belgian Enterprises, Brussels.

guaranteeing their own internal cohesion. In some cases, certain bargaining levels have been called into question and a trend has appeared towards reduction in the number of "counters". The superposing of bargaining levels has alarmed some governments, concerned that this development will undermine their anti-inflationary policies. In Italy relations between bargaining levels were thus the subject of study by a parliamentary commission which concluded its work on 27th July, 1977.

Explanatory Factors

Moves towards decentralisation

The economic recession has frequently affected industries in a very uneven way. Alongside industries said to be sheltered, usually operating in the home market alone, are to be seen highly vulnerable industries whose competitivity on foreign markets has been gravely impaired (textiles, clothing, footwear, shipbuilding, iron and steel, etc.). Even within individual industries, the situation of firms frequently varies greatly depending on the type of products, labour and capital intensivity, management etc. As a result it became increasingly difficult to find a common denominator for everyone either at national level or even within certain industries. Framework agreements providing for lowel-level negotiations were not sufficient to prevent breakaway movements.

In those industries and individual firms which the unions consider to be most buoyant, the latter are inclined to see national agreements, even where these are supposed to have resolved problems exhaustively, as setting out minimum terms to be supplemented where appropriate. It also seems that, more generally, in this period of recession, a tendency is appearing on the part of the bargaining parties to look for *ad hoc* solutions better adapted to the circumstances of economic units of the smallest possible size. This is also related to the nature of issues negotiated. The narrow margin for wage increases, the priority given to questions of safeguarding employment and the change which this has brought about in the content of negotiations has led to a search for tailor-made solutions. The limits to what is negotiable may be more easily altered at enterprise level than at a higher level. The move towards decentralisation also seems linked to a more pronounced desire for participation in decision-making at enterprise level.

Professor Reynaud's study on France (1978) reveals the trend towards increasing power at shop floor level. In Italy, the emergence of a new climate in factories and new forms of representation within the enterprise have intensified enterprise bargaining. The growth of a kind of shop-steward organisation in the Belgian metalworking industry is also an example of this. In addition to increased shop floor awareness, this trend is in some cases strengthened by changes in status introduced by legislation. Sweden provides a good example. The Act of 1976 on the joint regulation of working life and that on the status of shop-stewards at the workplace have significantly strengthened the powers of workers at their place of work. It cannot be denied that increased power on the shop floor increases the risk of conflict. Enterprise bargaining does not lend itself so readily "to the reassuring procedures of a game where the rules are respected and a contract faithfully applied". In particular it appears that the decentralisation of bargaining has been one of the reasons for the fresh outburst of strikes which has affected certain countries over the last year, and which followed on notably calm periods (in the Netherlands after the breakdown of national negotiations in 1977, in Belgium from the beginning of 1978 and in Germany in metal-working and printing at the beginning of 1978).

Moves towards centralisation

Although in countries where bargaining is centred on the enterprise, some tendencies towards greater co-ordination have been noted in the past (Japan: trade union strategy for the spring offensive; United States: electrical engineering, copper, etc.) this does not appear to be significant or far-reaching, except in Ireland where national agreements have been concluded for future wage increases.

Somewhat prior to this the movement towards centralisation seemed to be more typical of countries where bargaining had traditionally taken place at industry level. Note the celebrated interconfederal agreement in Italy of 26th January, 1977 designed to hold down labour costs, and the various agreements concluded in France over the last few years (security of employment, supplementary waiting allowance, improvement of working conditions, adult education, monthly payment of wages). In the case of Belgium, it will be noted that the most recent national agreements on social planning, particularly that of 7th February, 1975, have become increasingly wide ranging (working hours, annual leave, minimum income, pension in advance, etc.). In other countries (Germany, Austria), although no resort is made to formal procedures, machinery has been introduced for concerted action at the highest level. The difficulties temporarily confronting concerted action in Germany should, however, be noted.

The problem of co-ordination between different levels

Diversification of bargaining levels has obviously accentuated the problem of co-ordination between the different levels. One legal device to make bargaining more orderly entails the use of industrial stability clauses which provide that agreements concluded at a certain level terminate the bargaining process and may not subsequently be called into question. We can only note that such clauses are frequently ignored in practice.

We have also noted the fragmentation which occurs in individual industries in countries where bargaining is centralised. At the time of writing, national negotiations in Norway are deadlocked since the employers' organisation has insisted on the prior agreement of the unions to the limitation of wage variations for the duration of the agreement. In Sweden the difficulty encountered in concluding the last two national agreements must be viewed in the same perspective.

In other countries, national negotiations have foundered on the impossibility of co-ordinating bargaining. Thus in Finland: "when the central organisations had agreed upon the guidelines to be adopted, they were often ignored by the branches in their own negotiations. Furthermore, privileges that exceeded the guidelines set by the central organisation, were often forced through by strikes... After many years of centralised negotiations, a return to the previous more decentralised system can now clearly be noticed. In the spring of 1977 no comprehensive agreements were concluded but the collective agreements were made after negotiations at branch level" (ILO, 1977, p. 11-12).

In the Netherlands, the 1977 national negotiations reached deadlock on the question of linking wages to the cost of living. The failure of these negotiations led to an unusual series of strikes. The protocol of the Hague, which was a result of government action, should have enabled the deadlock to be broken and new negotiations to be started at industry level. It was rapidly seen that national negotiations for an agreement for 1978 would not be successful and that it was preferable to start negotiations at industry level from the beginning. The virtual absence of the Government due to the continuing government crisis was also an important factor in the deadlock at national level.

It seems undeniable that national bargaining in the present economic circumstances runs into an increasingly clear desire for decentralisation, corresponding on the part of employers to a wish to reduce the number of negotiating tables so as not to dissipate or overstretch the slim margin available to them due to the recession and, on the part of the workers, to the wish not to sacrifice possibilities of satisfying their demands within smaller units to the problems of an industry or the national economy as a whole.

Belgium is a good example of this trend. All attempts to reach a new general agreement for industrial workers after the last one expired in 1975 resulted in failure. At industry level, a move to restrict bargaining levels has become apparent, confining bargaining either to individual firms (metalworking, iron and steel, glass, chemicals, etc.) or to particular industries (textiles, clothing, food). However, in cases where bargaining has been more widely decentralised, the employers' organisation has made efforts to set up strengthened machinery for internal co-ordination (Netherlands, Italy, etc).

Lastly, it will be found that the failure of national negotiations in some countries or the fact that these negotiations are becoming more difficult, has led to greater intervention by the public authorities, anxious or tempted to fill the gap left by employers and unions.

Content of Bargaining

General comments

The urgent need to control inflation and the profound concern felt in the face of rising unemployment, the structural aspects of which are becoming increasingly apparent, have led to the emergence of new approaches to bargaining and to new forms of agreements.

First let us explain the employers' standpoint. Employers' organisations are unceasingly having to stress that increasing production costs have significantly reduced firms' profit margins. These have in numerous cases moved into losses as a result of inflation. The poor outlook for profits discourages the propensity to invest. The price spiral seriously compromises competitiveness and obliges many firms to export at a loss to avoid losing their share of the market. Renewed profitability and competitiveness have thus become the principal policy objectives of employers' organisations. Without claiming that increased wages are the only reason for this deterioration, it cannot be denied that they play an important part in it. For this reason there is a marked desire to reduce and moderate labour costs. In countries with elaborate arrangements for the automatic adjustment of wages to price changes this system has become a subject of controversy. Employers' organisations have stressed its inflationary effect and advocated the search for other techniques. On the other hand, trade unions have energetically defended the social progress represented by guaranteed purchasing power. It should be noted that the controversy has been fierce in the Netherlands (a central issue of the 1977 conflict), in Italy and Denmark (where it was the subject of compensation measures by the Government) and in Belgium (where indexing was abandoned on a temporary basis for wages over F. 40,000).

The desire of employers' organisations — and also of many governments — to contain overall wage increases, from any source, within tolerable limits has favoured the emergence of demands of a more qualitative nature. For unions and employers are still anxious to retain the possibility of concluding agreements, essential for the sound working of any system of industrial relations.

As stated in an Italian report "trade unions then had to give priority to the more political aspects of their demands, i.e. questions concerning more general issues such as investment, safeguarding employment and the organisation of work, at the expense of aspects directly related to wages" (Triola, p. 17).

New Trends

The greater stress placed on problems of security of employment and income and on questions of work organisation should be noted. In the Federal Republic of Germany, there has since 1973 been an extension of agreements in favour of older workers, giving them some guarantee of continued income in the event of transfer to less well paid jobs. Various arrangements have also been introduced for workers affected by rationalisation schemes or by technical changes. In the Netherlands, the demand for the conclusion of "arbeidsplaatsenovereenkomsten" (agreement on work places) is at the centre of current discussions. The recent agreement in the metalworking industry introduces the principle of concerted action on employment problems within the enterprise (prevention of lay-offs, procedure for filling vacancies, limitation of overtime, employment possibilities for vulnerable categories of job applicant, sharing of available jobs, etc.). In Italy, one of the basic features of 1975-1976 was the inclusion in workers' demands and in subsequent agreements, of the right to obtain information about, and exercise supervision over, investment and its consequences for employment. A good example is the Fiat agreement, which contains clauses whereby the company undertakes to invest in southern Italy. In Belgium, the question of sharing out available work, notably by reducing hours worked per week and taking on additional labour, has been the subject of considerable argument. Agreements reached in this respect in the services sector, the energy sector and in certain electrical engineering firms, have demonstrated in practice that, although shorter working hours are a factor in social progress, they are not a suitable way of sharing out available employment.

Unions and Employers and the Public Authorities

General remarks

The Background Paper prepared by the ILO for its Symposium on Collective Bargaining in Industrialised Countries, referred to above, notes that over the last few years, government interventions to influence wage levels as part of their efforts to control inflation and under income policy "have become increasingly frequent and increasingly detailed in a great many (industrialised market economies). This action, and its possible effect on the autonomy of the bargaining parties, is probably the most significant recent development in collective bargaining in these countries and, at the same time, poses the most delicate problem currently facing such bargaining". (ILO, 1977b, p.28). Intervention has taken various forms, from mere general recommendations to legally binding measures.

There are various causes for this increased intervention. The relations between a situation of inflation and underemployment on the one hand and collective bargaining on the other may be examined from two angles: the effect of the former on the latter, which is more important for our consideration of the level and content of bargaining, but also, conversely, the effect of collective bargaining on inflation and unemployment. Some governments have thus accused collective bargaining of being in its turn a cause of inflation and hence of unemployment. As part of their plans for economic recovery, they have therefore been tempted to intervene in the collective bargaining process. The difficulty of reaching national agreements has led some governments to get round the deadlock, notably by fiscal or parafiscal measures, while the absence of national agreements has, moreover, led several governments to fill the gap left by unions and employers.

Relations between the public authorities and unions and employers

A strengthening of tripartite action is to be seen in many countries, sometimes at the expense of long-standing bilateral contacts. This development is a logical consequence of the common desire to bring collective bargaining into line with the requirements of policies to control inflation and promote employment, in which the public authorities, as representatives of the public interest, play a predominant part.

Although this development seems to be based on a broad consensus, this is not by any means so as regards measures of compulsion unilaterally introduced by governments. In such cases, government action has provoked discussion, sometimes violent, on the delicate issue of the sharing of responsibilities between public authorities and unions and employers.

296

In Italy, the Decree-Law of 7th February, 1977 provided for machinery to impose penalties on firms which paid wages higher than those specified in national agreements. Trade union opposition to this was so strong that an Act of 7th April, 1977 annulled the measure. Furthermore, the above-mentioned report of an Italian parliamentary commission, which maintained that issues such as holidays, wages structure, etc., could be determined either by legislation or by industrial agreement, received scant applause.

As emphasized at an ILO Tripartite Advisory Meeting in Geneva on collective bargaining in 1976: "Without the support of employers' and workers' organisations any incomes policy [is] destined to fail " and consequently "every possible effort should be made to base the whole of anti-inflationary policy on the agreement of all parties concerned" (ILO, 1977b, p.29). In our opinion, observance of this principle explains the considerable success of policies for tripartite action, while demonstrating the generally short life of direct intervention measures.

Indeed, it seems that such measures are only justified when collective bargaining breaks down or for urgent reasons of an exceptional nature. The perpetuation of this type of intervention would lead to the continued existence of collective bargaining systems being questioned, resulting in a permanent conflict situation. This view is a major reason for inducing unions and employers to draw up a socially and economically responsible wages policy.

COMMENT ON VERSCHUEREN'S PAPER

Fritz W. Scharpf[1]

General Notes and Comments

Verschueren has offered convincing evidence against all hypotheses suggesting that there might be a universal trend toward more centralisation or more decentralisation of collective bargaining, or even that economic prosperity might, in general, favour enterprise bargaining while recession might encourage more centralisation. Apparently, the only universal movement is toward greater diversification, with countries starting from a highly centralised bargaining pattern developing some facilities for lower-level agreements while central discussions (usually with government participation) have assumed greater significance in countries where decentralised bargaining was the prevailing pattern.

The resulting convergence of overall bargaining patterns among different countries may be partly due to increasing opportunities for cross-national imitation resulting from more intensive communication and exchange among OECD countries. But, as Verschueren suggests, there may also be functional imperatives at work: To the extent that inflation control has become a central political concern and that incomes policy is being regarded as a major instrument to be used in the fight against inflation, governments are more or less forced to provide opportunities for central wage discussions even in countries where decentralised collective bargaining has traditionally prevailed. And to the extent that issues of job security and work organisation increase in importance, even countries where wage bargaining is highly centralised must provide opportunities for "tailor-made" solutions at the industry or enterprise levels. I would expect, therefore, that a precise tabulation of bargaining levels and of the substantive issues settled at each level would provide very powerful evidence for the increasing convergence of bargaining patterns among OECD countries.

Nevertheless, the degree of convergence will be less than perfect as long as one disregards (as Verschueren tends to do) the functional equivalence between collective bargaining on the one hand and government regulation, services and institutions on the other hand. If, for instance, unemployment insurance is subject to collective bargaining, this in itself will increase the importance of central bargaining levels. If, on the other hand, the protection of individual rights at the workplace is the concern of an elaborate body of labour law whose application is entrusted to a fully developed system of

---

1. Director, International Institute of Management, Berlin.

(public) labour courts, the importance of shop-floor bargaining between employers and unions will be much reduced in comparison to systems in which the "legalisation" of labour relations is less pronounced. These differences in the institutional framework must be kept in mind when "functionalist" hypotheses regarding the relative weight of central and local levels of collective bargaining are to be evaluated.

With regard to the substantive content of collective bargaining agreements, Verschueren offers the interesting hypothesis that (successful) efforts by employers and by governments to contain wage increases may be responsible for the emergence of union demands "of a more qualitative nature", such as "security of employment" and "questions of work organisation". This hypothesis assumes that, on the one hand, wage increases could be "voluntaristically" controlled by employers or governments and that, on the other hand, agreements regarding the security of employment and work organisation might be alternatives which could satisfy qualitative union demands without adding to the cost burden of industries. It seems to me that both assumptions ought to be examined very carefully before the "wage displacement" hypotheses of the widening scope of bargaining contents should be accepted.

An alternative explanation might be based upon a distinction between qualitative demands pursued by unions (or voluntarily conceded by management) under conditions of full employment, and demands pushed by unions under conditions of high unemployment. In the first case, it might be that management's concern with labour scarcity and high labour turnover was the main force behind attempts at "job enrichment" and the "humanisation of working life" as exemplified by the Volvo innovations and similar efforts in other countries. In the second case, demands for job protection and for labour intensive work organisation seem to have been prompted mainly by union concern over the effects of rapid rationalisation in the face of high general unemployment — as exemplified by strikes in the German printing and metalworking industries in 1978. Generalising hypotheses that do not distinguish between these two cases are unlikely to provide valid explanations of apparent shifts in bargaining content.

On the subject of government intervention in collective bargaining, a most interesting general point emerges from the description of new trends in Verschueren's report: governments seem to have been concerned primarily with wage bargaining, and their attempts to influence the outcome of bargaining processes seem to have been acceptable only when they have taken the form of advice, consultation or "exchange of views", while all attempts to determine wages directly or to impose "legally binding" controls upon wage bargaining have met with massive protests and resistance, and have usually been abandoned after relatively brief trial periods. It seems that governments, in their concern about controlling inflation, have universally attempted to pursue some form of incomes policy through influencing wage increases, but that the "voluntary" cooperation of unions and employers is essential to the success of such efforts while seemingly stronger measures are likely to fail. It may be that democratic governments which are, at the same time, politically responsible to a majority of wage earners among the electorate, and "technocratically" responsible for macroeconomic policy and inflation control, are intrinsically incapable of pursuing an effective policy of wage restraint through direct controls. Wage settlements, after all, are the most visible manifestation of class conflict in capitalist societies, and any attempt by democratic governments to intervene directly in this conflict is likely to be politically self-defeating. As a consequence, governments seem capable of influencing wage settlements only to the degree that they can do so through indirect means which leave the immediate responsibility for the outcome with the representatives of capital and labour at the bargaining table or at the strike front. Thus, the mechanisms of persuasion, consultation, or "concerted action" which provide for government influence without formally destroying the "autonomy" of collective bargaining seem to be essential to the success of government incomes policies under the conditions of capitalistic democracies. If they appear to be less than successful under present conditions, it is still unlikely that an increase of direct governmental controls and regulations would provide effective solutions. This does not mean, of course, that any other solution will be more effective under present conditions.

Inflation, Unemployment, and Collective Bargaining

The primary focus of Verschueren's report, as well as of public discussion and government efforts, is on wage bargaining. Other issues, such as work organisation and the protection of employment appear as secondary concerns of minor importance whose potential effectiveness, at least in the case of strategies aimed at sharing out available work, is viewed with scepticism. This is probably the dominant view among governments and employers' associations, but it is doubtful whether it will be able to prevail if present levels of unemployment in OECD countries should continue much longer.

The central importance attributed to wage bargaining is based upon the belief that wage costs are the crucial factor determining rates of inflation and, at the same time, real growth and employment. Wage increases are simultaneously seen as the causes of cost-push inflation which decreases international competitiveness and of a profit squeeze which discourages domestic investment. Thus, not only inflation but also unemployment are mainly attributed to "immoderate" union demands on the wage front. There are two reasons, however, which make it doubtful whether the "wage theory of unemployment" can be maintained.

First, there seem to be several factors, apart from wage increases, that tend to reduce the potential for sustained growth of industrial output and employment in OECD countries:

— overall demand for industrial products seems to be approaching relative saturation among the "rich" countries of the world while massive transfers of purchasing power to the poor countries are nowhere in sight;
— at the same time, the industrialisation of third world countries (much aided by the world-wide activities of multinational enterprises) reduces the market shares of high-wage countries in the markets for standardised industrial products;

— finally, the rapid development of micro-electronic control technology will provide vast opportunities for labour-saving automation and rationalisation.

Thus, productivity gains are likely to exceed output increases in highly industrialised countries, and the resultant losses in employment are unlikely to be compensated by corresponding increases in the commercial service sector (where automation is also taking its toll) or in the public service sector (which is threatened by taxpayers' revolts).

For the OECD countries as a whole, none of these factors are likely to be significantly affected by a policy of voluntary or enforced wage restraints. Drastic wage limitations might further reduce overall demand but they could surely not reduce wage costs to the level of third world countries or to the level where firms would find it profitable to ignore the possibilities of replacing human labour through reliable and completely submissive automatic equipment. For the OECD countries as a whole, therefore, wage restraint (whether voluntary or imposed) does not seem to be a promising strategy for increasing economic growth or maintaining present levels of employment (much less for returning to conditions of full employment).

But if these conclusions were universally accepted for the group of OECD countries as a whole, they might not necessarily impress any single country. Each country might still hope to increase its share of the export markets for industrial products if it could only improve its competitive advantage through lower production costs and, hence, through lower wage increases. In a shrinking world market for the goods produced by highly industrialised countries, this may be an instance of "beggar-thy-neighbour" thinking which seems to have dominated international economics for some time. Under present conditions, however, not only the morality but also the wisdom of this philosophy has become questionable.

Under the regime of fixed exchange rates, a country could hope temporarily to improve its competitive advantage in international markets through wage restraints that would limit cost increases. Eventually, of course, it would have to pay for this advantage through "imported inflation" caused by export surpluses and international currency speculation. Under the regime of floating exchange rates, however, these conditions have changed. If one country is more successful than others in containing its wage increases, it may also succeed in reducing its rate of inflation compared to other industrialised countries. Any competitive advantage in export markets, however, which might result from this will be quickly nullified by corresponding revaluations of its own currency. Within the present international monetary system, individual countries have lost the option of generating export-led growth through a successful policy of wage restraint.

If this is so, national incomes policies intended to constrain wage bargaining may still be successful in reducing the rate of inflation, but they seem to have become powerless if used to achieve increased rates of economic growth and increased employment. Conser\-vely, if unemployment has become the dominant problem, national incomes policy and wage restraints, voluntary or imposed, are unlikely to provide an effective solution even for individual countries. At least in this regard, beggar-thy-neighbour policies are frustrated by the regime of floating exchange rates.

If full employment cannot be restored through wage restraint, it is obvious that unions concerned with rising levels of unemployment must attempt to enlarge the scope of collective bargaining so as to include measures which might help to protect existing employment and, perhaps, to create new employment. That such efforts have come relatively late and have not yet achieved much momentum is, perhaps, best explained by the fact that in most countries unemployment has not yet reached union members to a considerable degree. By and large, the unemployed are still primarily found among women, among the young, the old, the unskilled and the non-unionised members of the workforce. Accordingly, and with the notable exception of Sweden, unions have concentrated more on increasing benefits for those who are employed than on increasing employment opportunities for those who are unemployed. Priorities will change, however, as increasing numbers of skilled and unionised workers are threatened by technological unemployment caused by the electronics revolution.

I would disagree, therefore, with Verschueren's judgement that union interest in issues such as the security of employment or question of work organisation should be regarded primarily as symbolic concerns compensating for higher constraints on wage bargaining. On the contrary, these are likely to be the dominant issues of the future. The unprecedented intensity of this year's conflicts in the German printing and metalworking industries and the degree of job protection achieved there are more likely to set the pattern for the future than to remain ephemeral aberrations.

Contrary to Verschueren's expectations, I think it is also likely that the reduction of working time will play a major role in any portfolio of strategies aimed at maintaining employment in highly industrialised countries. It is unlikely, however, that the protection of employment can be achieved without much more intensive government participation in collective bargaining processes. Thus in several important respects the future of collective bargaining will differ from the immediate past.

JOB SECURITY THROUGH COLLECTIVE BARGAINING IN THE STEEL INDUSTRY OF THE UNITED STATES

Lloyd McBride[1]

The United Steelworkers of America and the American labour movement rely primarily upon the collective bargaining process to provide job security and all the other benefits that we seek in order to provide economic justice for workers. What we obtain at the bargaining table, of course, must be protected and supplemented by legislation at all levels of government.

Job security has been a trade union concern from the very beginning. It is certainly not new. I will first discuss some of the different approaches by different unions in this country in this area of job security and then say in more detail what the United Steelworkers of America have done about job security. The major thrusts in the most recent negotiations reaffirmed historical U.S. collective bargaining objectives – the improvement of wages, fringe benefits, pensions and conditions of work for American working people, including the emphasis on job and income security. Job and income security proposals were a central focus of several important contract negotiations last year. They were the major theme, not only in our union's negotiations, in steel and container, but in the negotiations by the Communications Workers and the International Brotherhood of Electrical Workers in the telephone industry, Longshoremen at Atlantic and Gulf ports, and our union and the Aluminum Workers in the aluminum industry. These agreements covered about 1.2 million workers, or a fourth of the total workers covered under major contracts that expired during 1977.

Union negotiators sought job and income security for their membership through a wide variety of proposals suited to the special characteristics of the particular industry and the most pressing problems faced by that group of workers. Some contracts added clauses that supplemented and strengthened existing contract provisions designed to guarantee adequate incomes during working lives and after retirement. Job security clauses designed to increase workers' leisure time and maintain or expand employment opportunities also featured in negotiations during recent months.

Touching briefly on some of the security features of recently negotiated contracts, to cite some specifics, job guarantees were negotiated by members of the Typographical union at commercial printing firms in New York. The 10-year contract – an unusually long contract – covering 4,400 workers, allows major changes in work rules designed to increase productivity in return for complete job security for printers at full pay.

A many-faceted job and income security package was also a feature of contracts negotiated by the Communications Workers, the Telecommunications Union and the International Brotherhood of Electrical Workers

1. President, United Steelworkers of America, Pittsburgh.

with the operating and manufacturing companies of the American Telephone and Telegraph Company. The president of the Communications Workers, Glenn Watts, had said that the paramount issue for his union and the other two unions was the preservation of jobs because of increasing automation in the industry and the resulting cutbacks in employment. The settlement package that finally emerged included a supplemental income protection plan for workers who face lay-off or involuntary assignment and who are eligible for retirement; a reassignment pay protection plan providing loss-of-income protection for workers transferred to lower paid jobs as a result of lay-offs; a clause permitting employees to decline overtime in excess of 10 hours a week; and increasing the number of holidays or so-called "excused workdays" -- three days with pay and two without pay by 1980.

Longshoremen in New York City, also confronted with job losses because of technological changes, first negotiated an income security plan in 1966. Similar plans were adopted by Longshoremen at other Atlantic and Gulf ports. And as I mentioned briefly at the outset of these remarks, agreements negotiated last year strengthened this job and income security plan. The plan, briefly, sets a floor under the annual number of hours for which regular Longshoremen receive pay, regardless of the hours they work.

Job security was also emphasised by teachers in a New York school district last year where they won provisions precluding lay-offs or reductions in the workforce. In Yonkers, New York, a teachers' contract specified that all teachers covered by the prior contract must be guaranteed employment during the life of the new contract.

Early retirement provisions and shorter work hours are two other approaches used by unions to increase jobs and job security. America's trade union members are spending less and less time on the job because of paid holidays, longer vacations and a variety of other days off. But a major way that work time is being reduced is by earlier retirement. The age of 65 is no longer the normal retirement age in the United States. Consider this startling fact: 32 per cent of the labour force in the age group 62-64 is now retired and drawing social security benefits. Sixteen years ago this figure was only 8.6 per cent.

Many unions started to negotiate special early retirement plans in the 1960s and early 1970s, and the growth in these plans has been most dramatic. The U.S. Department of Labor did an analysis of the changes in major retirement plans between 1970 and 1974 and found that nearly 20 per cent of the plans included special early retirement provisions, and these were almost all negotiated plans. It was in the 1960s, for example, that both the United Auto Workers and the Steelworkers negotiated what are called "30-and-out" retirement provisions. They allowed workers with 30 years of service to retire with full benefits regardless of age. Special early retirement programmes have also been negotiated by the Rubber Workers and the Fire Fighters, and the Seafarers last year won a pension plan that amounts to a 20-year retirement plan after reaching 55 years of age. Early retirement plans are especially interesting because they relate retirement, supplemental unemployment benefits and other programmes with the whole concept of worker income and job security.

Turning to how the work-week has been decreasing as unions pursue this approach to create more jobs and enhance job security, in the 1860s, the average work-week in the United States was estimated at 68 hours a week – the six-day, 12-hour day was common practice. If that were common today, the result would be economic disaster. If today, we in the United States worked 70 to 75 hours a week without vacations, holidays and early retirement, the unemployment rate would be near half the work force ! We would have a working elite with high incomes and the other half would be on unemployment compensation and welfare. The shorter work-week, then, has historically created jobs and job security along with retirement plans, holidays and vacations.

In 1938, the Fair Labor Standards Act provided for the payment of time-and-a-half for work over the 40-hour work-week. This was done as a means of providing more job opportunities. It is true that hours of work have not declined as rapidly since then as they did before, but they have been decreasing. Higher overtime rates, voluntary overtime clauses, and negotiated shorter work-weeks are beginning to have an effect. The U.S. Labor Department's Bureau of Labor Statistics notes a steady decline from 41.1 hours per week in 1948 to 38.2 in 1976 for industrial and salaried workers. The Bureau has also done studies that show the trend to the shorter scheduled work-week. In 1964-65, the average scheduled work-week for office workers was 38.9 hours, while for plant workers it was 40.4 hours. In 1973-75, the average scheduled hours decreased to 38.7 and 40.1 respectively. In fact, scheduled work-weeks of less than 40 hours are increasing in negotiated settlements slowly but steadily and by 1975 11.1 per cent of major collective bargaining agreements had scheduled hours of less than 40 per week, up from 9.6 per cent in 1972.

The printing trades, including the International Typographical Union and the Newspaper Guild, generally have achieved the 35-hour week. The International Brotherhood of Electrical Workers has 25 agreements that call for 35 hours or less. The Service Employees' agreement covering 12,000 workers in Metropolitan New York nursing homes provides a 35-hour week. In Los Angeles, 8,000 workers under the Maintenance Contractors Agreement have a 37-hour week. The 35-hour work-week is a way of life in the New York garment industry and has been for many years. The Clothing and Textile Workers and the International Ladies Garment Workers have negotiated for the 35-hour week for many years.

In the AFL-CIO we have urged a shorter work-week in order to put the unemployed back to work. In part the shorter work-week is a demand for more leisure time. Its major purpose, however, is the effort to protect and increase jobs. I might interject here that our union favours a shorter work-week – a four-day, 32-hour week. There have been suggestions for a four-day, 10-hour day, or the usual 40-hour week to be worked in four days. But labour worked too long and too hard to establish the eight-hour day, to agree now to turn the clock back by lengthening the work day. And so we strongly oppose and condemn any attempt to lengthen the working day beyond the 8-hour day as a regularly scheduled work day.

In addition to all these examples of efforts to promote job security, there is also the increasing use by labour of co-ordinated bargaining where a number of unions represent workers in a conglomerate or in an industry.

307

A common tactic of multi-union employers and industries has been to play off one union against another and thus prevent any kind of a solid, collective bargaining front. The frequent result of such conquer-and-divide strategy, of course, is inferior contracts with little job security and inadequate wages and benefits. Individual unions, many of them small, and bargaining separately are no match for a conglomerate or an industry. But by coordinating their efforts, they are more nearly able to match the power of a conglomerate or industry.

For example, in one of the major industries in our union's jurisdiction, the copper industry, there are 26 unions, including the Steelworkers, which is the largest union of the 26. When we negotiate with the major copper companies the 26 unions coordinate their bargaining. We bargain together and we settle together. Since we have done this -- and we had to undergo numerous strikes in the industry -- the job security and other benefits of the workers of the copper firms have improved dramatically. Before the 26 unions agreed to the coordinated bargaining approach, the copper industry was very successful in playing one union against another. In addition, there were attempts by some of the unions to raid other unions. This inter-union industrial warfare, and the industry's conquer-and-divide tactics, cost the workers dearly. But now, fortunately, those days are gone.

Turning to show more specifically what the United Steelworkers have done in regard to job security, since the union was organised in 1937, the job and income security of our members have been our first priority. One of the resolutions introduced at our first convention in 1937 called for a guaranteed annual wage. In 1944 the guaranteed annual wage was made part of our collective bargaining proposals to the basic steel industry.

Even before our union was organised, those who later became our leaders recognised that the problem of job and income security must be dealt with through legislation as well as collective bargaining. They helped persuade Congress to pass the Social Security Act that established public pensions for retired workers and unemployment insurance for laid-off workers. Later, in 1946, our union was active in the campaign that won Congressional approval of the Employment Act of 1946 that established full employment as national policy.

Our early union pioneers realised that the road to job and income security would be a long one and so they set out to make progress on a step-by-step basis. Our first contract with U.S. Steel in 1937 made history because the company had fought unionisation since 1901 with every weapon it could command. Significant in the first contract, in addition to union recognition, were provisions for a grievance procedure, and a seniority system in cases of promotion or increase and decrease of the workforce. Thus, in this first contract, the union prevailed upon the company to accept basic rights of the worker for job security. In succeeding negotiations during our formative years, the emphasis was on wages, vacations, premium pay for overtime, and shift differentials. However, during these negotiations we also began to extend and clarify the principle of seniority for promotions, demotions, lay-offs and recalls. In 1949 a priority bargaining goal was a company-paid pension plan which the steel industry had previously refused to discuss, claiming it was not a bargainable issue under the law. We took the case to the U.S. Supreme Court and won our point that under the law companies were required to negotiate on paid pensions. After a five-week strike we won our first pension plan providing for $100 a month at age 65 with 25 years of service and including social security payments. In every contract since then we have negotiated improvements in pensions. By August 1979 a worker who retires under our present steel agreement with 30 years of service will receive a minimum pension of $427 a month, *excluding* social security. He will receive social security on top of his regular pension. If a worker should die while an active employee, and have 10 years' service, his or her surviving spouse receives one-half of the worker's earned pension.

In the negotiations of 1949 and 1950 we also won the beginning of a social insurance system. We now have a fully company-paid system of insurance that includes life insurance benefits for the active or the retired steelworker's family when he dies. It pays the full cost of hospitalisation and virtually the full cost of medical care, including dental and vision care.

We had not forgotten our original demand for a guaranteed annual wage. In 1955 in the can industry, and in 1956 after a six-week strike in the steel industry, we made a major breakthrough on this problem when we won agreements that provided supplemental unemployment benefits by the companies in addition to unemployment compensation paid by the States. In steel, the total of the two payments will normally equal 26 hours pay each week, or about 80 per cent of the average worker's after-tax take-home pay. The programme not only provides income security for laid-off workers, it creates a financial incentive for companies to plan production to avoid lay-offs.

Later, a "short work-week" provision was added under which a worker who works less than 32 hours in a week is paid for 32 hours. In 1962 we began to add additional building blocks into our structure of job and income security. In 1962 we negotiated 13-week vacations every fifth year for the senior half of steel company employees. This was an effort to create jobs in an industry with declining employment. Later we won extended vacations every five years of three additional weeks for the junior half of the workforce. Both the extended vacation programme and the "30-and-out" pension for workers with 30 years of service regardless of age, increased job opportunities in the mills and also meant added job security. In 1968 we negotiated an Earnings Protection Plan under which workers who are transferred to lower paid jobs are guaranteed 85 per cent of their average hourly earnings on their previous job.

When steel imports started to play havoc with the steel industry and the jobs of our members, our union and the 10 major companies agreed to a new bargaining format aimed at meeting the import threat. Other steel-producing nations started to make inroads on the American market during our 116-day strike in 1959. In following negotiations the import flow increased and became a flood. Because of stockpiling during negotiations, our members had to undergo long lay-offs after peaceful settlements were reached in the years following 1959, and the industry had to absorb costly shutdowns in production facilities. The new bargaining format -- called the Experimental Negotiating Agreement – ENA -- was agreed to after prolonged discussions between our union and the companies; but it was finally agreed to use it in the 1974 negotiations.

Briefly, the ENA prohibited industry-wide strikes or lockouts, thus guaranteeing continued production and eliminating the need for stockpiling; it called for a minimum 3 per cent wage increase each year of the three-year agreement; it allowed the parties to negotiate freely on virtually all other issues; and called for the voluntary arbitration of any unresolved national bargaining issues. It did allow local unions to strike over local issues, or largely non-economic matters, that affect workers in an individual plant.

Our 1974 contract, negotiated under the new bargaining format, was the best in our history, and not one issue had to be submitted to the arbitration panel. It worked so well that both sides agreed to use the ENA in the 1977 negotiations when, again, a full settlement was reached without resort to arbitration, and again it was agreed to use the format in our negotiations in 1980. We think that through the ENA we have eliminated a major source of job insecurity.

In the 1977 negotiations with the major steel companies, we were successful in making a historic breakthrough in adding to the job and income security of our basic steel members. On approaching negotiations we were confronted with a worldwide slackening of demand for steel and a continued high level of imports -- in fact imports set an all-time record in 1977. Out of these negotiations came what we called the Employment and Income Security Programme. This applies to those employees who have 20 years of service or more, who make up approximately 40 per cent of the workforce of the 10 companies. The centrepiece of the Programme is called the Rule of 65 pension. Under this provision, a 20-year employee out of work because of a plant shutdown, extended layoff or extended disability, and whose age plus service equals 65, must be provided either with suitable long-term employment or his regular pension plus a monthly supplement of $300. Under this plan, a worker with 20 years of service, whose plant is closed, is entitled to $557.50 a month if the company cannot provide him with another suitable, long-term job. With 25 years of service, he is entitled to $627.50 a month; 30 years of service, $697.50 a month; and 35 years of service, $772.50 a month. Another feature of the Programme is that supplemental unemployment benefits are guaranteed for up to two years, regardless of the solvency of the company's SUB fund. And full coverage under the insurance programme is continued for such laid-off employees for up to two years. The Earnings Protection Plan for 20-year workers who are demoted but not laid off is increased to 90 per cent of previous hourly earnings. Finally, we established a joint union-industry task force to study ways to expand this programme in the 1980 negotiations.

In conclusion, it should be said that in bargaining for greater job security our union has left the companies free to install whatever technology or processes they wish to. Our union's leaders have been convinced that technological progress is necessary for workers to enjoy a steadily rising standard of living, and our members have accepted that philosophy. Our concern has been to share in such technological progress.

We can do a great deal as a union to accomplish our objectives but we cannot do it all. We need the assistance and cooperation of our government in pursuing an economic policy that promotes the kind of economic climate that results in jobs for all those able and willing to work. That is why the Steelworkers and the labour movement in general have been urging Congress to pass the pending full employment legislation known as the Humphrey-Hawkins Bill. The Bill is designed to implement the full employment promise of the 1946 Employment Act, 32 long years ago.

Not only must the government act in respect to a national economic policy; it must exert itself on the international level, particularly -- from our union's standpoint -- in the area of steel imports and the general question of fair trade. Our union believes in international trade while insisting that it be fair trade. That is why we have been demanding that our government enforce the fair trade provisions of our 1974 Trade Act. That is why we have called for sectoral negotiations on steel under the General Agreement on Trade and Tariffs. We believe that through multilateral negotiations on steel, the needs of the workers of the steel producing nations can best be met and that in an uncertain world we can at least give them the certainty of a job. What we want to do is to build job security in a free world, under conditions of fair trade.

JOB SECURITY : A EUROPEAN COMMENT

Poul N. Rasmussen[1]

Job security — an important element in a coherent policy for employment security

The intention of this note is to present some main tendencies in collective bargaining and government policies on job security as they have developed since the beginning of the 1960s in Europe. What is the picture, in broad terms, at the moment? What are the main social and economic implications of current trends? The main part of this paper deals with the term *job security* in the sense of security of wage earners' jobs with their *existing* employers.

The Background

Greater job security — a contribution to the improvement of the quality of working life

There are three major lines in the development in Western Europe within the last 15-20 years:

1) Since the beginning of the 1960s and until the start of the present recession western industrialised countries experienced periods of substantial economic growth and relatively high levels of employment. Most wage earners got a substantial increase in real wages, material consumption and leisure in that period. Parallel to that development, considerations and strategies for the improvement of working and living conditions in the broadest sense — that is the qualitative aspects of economic growth and development — got increasing importance. The need for security and progress in qualitative aspects of wealth got still more weight in social policies and especially in trade union activities. These initiatives concentrated not only on the traditional means for improving work safety and health. In addition, they focused on the humanisation of the whole working life, including organisation of work, working environment, possibilities of educational and social progress. Wage earners, their representatives and trade unions, obtained important new roles and responsibilities for participation in decision-making on the shop-floor and at company level. A greater job security was seen as a natural and integrated part of trade union efforts to improve the qualitative aspects of working life.

---

1. L.O., (Danish Confederation of Trade Unions).

2) Under the present international employment crisis job security has been brought further into focus. Claims for greater job security are thereby also seen as one means — among several — of limiting unemployment.
3) In addition, considerable technological changes have characterised the development, and not only during the years of strong economic growth. In many countries we find several examples showing that technological changes have even accelerated in the course of the last few years. This has further stressed the serious and far-reaching structural aspects of the present unemployment situation: The term "technological unemployment" has become more and more common in most countries in Western Europe. Claims for further preventive job security arrangements are seen as one of the means to counterbalance the adverse effects of uncontrolled technological changes in working life.

In short: job security is not a totally new term or trade union claim which has been brought to the fore under the present employment crisis. Greater job security through collective bargaining and legislation has for several years been an integrated part of the development of the qualitative aspects of working life.

The recession and technological changes have strengthened claims for greater job security. What are of importance are the implications of job security in relation to the growing recognition that the recession is no longer a short-term, mainly conjunctural, phenomenon but is of a long-term nature and does include serious economic/structural problems.

Collective bargaining and consultation

Collective bargaining in all countries in Western Europe has for many years included important claims for greater job security. Collective agreements typically include minimum periods of notice in case of individual dismissals, often related to length of service. Furthermore, severance pay and other means to contribute to maintaining income during unemployment are often collectively bargained in some countries. Protection against arbitrary dismissals when firms close are either subject to collective bargaining, an integrated part of the system of labour law on which the collective agreements are based, or subject to direct legislation. Progress has been made also through collective bargaining in many countries with regard to consultations with workers' representatives in case of and prior to dismissals — progress which again has been a natural and important element in industrial relations agreements.

Some of the major elements in collective bargaining for greater job security have been supplemented — partly or totally — by direct legislation. By collective agreements and legislation in each country in Western Europe important results have been achieved in the four major aspects of greater job security: 1) extended periods of notice, 2) severance pay as a contribution to maintaining income in case of unemployment, 3) protection against arbitrary dismissals or closure of firms, and 4) consultation with workers' representatives prior to dismissals when firms close.

314

Under the present recession the efforts and claims of trade unions have obviously been strengthened to avoid redundancy and keep employees in jobs. As a supplement to the progress in job security already mentioned the measures agreed upon between unions and employers have included: suspension of recruitment; reduction or elimination of overtime; work-sharing; and employer-financed payments to supplement State unemployment benefits. Some of the provisions agreed upon represent common minima for industry as a whole, others are adapted to the economic and structural problems of specific sectors.

Government policies and job security

For years the governments of most countries have sought – to a greater or lesser extent – to increase the protection of jobs or income by providing legislative rights and obligations which give some sort of security for employees in temporary or permanent lay-offs. In some countries – most far-reaching in the Federal Republic of Germany and the Netherlands – consultations with workers' representatives prior to dismissals have also been pursued through legislation. As a consequence of the recession, governments in many countries have taken initiatives to protect employment in individual enterprises by, for example, jobs subsidies and financial assistance to industry.

New initiatives within the European Communities

Additionally, the gradually more intensified collaboration on labour market questions within the European Communities has resulted in several initiatives in the course of the last few years. Of special interest is the Council of Ministers' directive of notification in the event of mass dismissals. This directive has now been transformed into national legislation in all EEC member countries.

Consequences and evaluations of some important measures of job security

Advance notification

As the trade union movement sees it there are three obvious advantages of advance notification by the employer in case of "economic" dismissals:

1) It is in the interest of the individual wage earner and gives him better opportunities to plan and try to find alternative employment.

2) The employer will be more oriented to think and plan ahead with a longer time horizon than usual as far as his manpower policy is concerned. Experience shows that the public sector has indicated greater willingness to plan ahead.

3) Advance notification makes it possible for the relevant public authorities to plan social, educational and other "follow-ups" in case of

unavoidable dismissals, while it enables the time interval between changing jobs to be reduced to a minimum.

In other words it is in the fundamental interest of society as a whole that employers should be obliged to notify a public authority of expected future redundancies and to provide relevant information about the redundant employees.

Consultation with workers' representatives

Prior consultation by employers with workers' representatives about expected redundancies can bring considerable advantages to employers, trade unions and the community. The first reason for this is that such consultation will assist further investigation of the possibilities of helping the employees of the firm. Secondly, management must give proper consideration to how to deal with redundancy. As part of its manpower planning workers' representatives should be kept informed about the economic environment, etc., facing the company. Thirdly, prior consultations enable workers' representatives and trade unions to suggest alternative ways to tackle the company's economic problems so that the workers' jobs may be protected and the company may re-establish its competitiveness.

Collective bargaining measures to avoid redundancy

In many countries agreements on measures to avoid redundancy have probably resulted in saving a number of workers from becoming unemployed. The most effective measures, as trade unions see them, have been suspension of recruitment, reduction or elimination of overtime, and lay-offs without loss of earnings. Although the introduction of short-time working has assumed massive proportions in some countries, it is the opinion of the European trade union movement that short-time working or part-time working cannot be any long-term solution or acceptable measure to protect employment.

Employment subsidies

In the present recession various forms of financial support — especially wage subsidies — to promote employment in the private and public sectors have been used. In most countries this instrument is more or less designed to bridge short-term employment deficiencies. Many arguments can be formulated against employment subsidies as such: for example, they have adverse effects on competition, their net effect on employment is doubtful, collectively bargained wage structures are damaged, there is great risk of abuse. Trade unions are not very happy about this instrument as a general measure to combat unemployment. On the other hand, experience and evaluations from countries where employment subsidies have been used most extensively underline that this instrument has had positive effects on the efforts to limit unemployment, although these positive effects depend on:

a) the arrangement having a selective character, either in relation to specific groups (young unemployed who have been out of employment for a longer period) or particular industries with difficulties,

b) abuses by employers being combated effectively (particular abuses being the creating of redundancies on one hand and hiring of workers with public wage subsidies on the other hand, and the abolition of jobs which have been promoted by public subsidies after these subsidies are finished), and

c) the promoting of qualified jobs in order to avoid occupational, financial and social downgrading for those employed in subsidised jobs.

The employment effect of selective employment premiums is probably more secure than more general subsidies to private investments.

Conclusions

The evaluation of trade unions in most European countries is that the measures taken to protect jobs have been effective. That is, the various measures introduced both by governments and through collective bargaining have been relatively successful in keeping people in employment who would otherwise have been unemployed.

Job security and optimal economic development

According to traditional economic wisdom it is doubtful whether the strengthening of job security is in accordance with the optimal working of our economic system in Western industrialised countries. The main arguments are that job security can be a barrier to the optimal allocation of resources in the total economy. Thereby economic growth is dampened, employment opportunities are limited, and it becomes more complicated to re-establish long-term solutions to the present recession. The traditional economic wisdom advises wage earners to accept the old "recipe" from the years of full employment in the 1960s, i.e. emphasis should be placed on offering relatively continuing employment but not necessarily specific employment security in particular enterprises. In theory the most effective use of resources will occur when labour is completely mobile.

In practice such mobility is of course an unrealistic notion, not only because of social considerations but also for pure economic reasons. The validity of the argument about the optimal allocation of resources includes unrealistic ideas about, for instance, the existence of competition and the allocation of capital resources. Consequently, although trade unions have no illusions about the effects of a frozen or inflexible job security policy, they regard a realistically formulated and stipulated job security policy as an important contribution to a more "socially" oriented economic development.

317

Job security and "segmentation" on the labour market

It has been argued that job security contributes to an unfortunate segmentation on the labour market: "Security of employment for some is in effect achieved at the expense of increased insecurity for others, especially the groups with most difficult employment problems, as young people, elderly workers, etc." It is difficult to see why missing employment opportunities for one group should be used as an argument to worsen conditions for other wage earners.

As trade unions see it, the case is rather for strengthening the selective approaches to creating employment and educational opportunities for the groups which are most severely hit under the recession, and, in fact, that is what is going on in many countries.

Job security and technological unemployment

There are strong indications that the constant increases in investment in new, advanced technology in the industrialised countries are responsible for, and will continue to an even greater degree to be responsible for, employment problems in the form of growing "technological unemployment". This spreads far beyond the limits of known restructuring problems, i.e. the traditional "bottleneck problems" on the labour market and the specific form of "structural unemployment" found in the industrialised countries' development areas.

There is good reason to believe that normal cost calculations covering labour and capital are not the decisive factor in companies' consideration of possible means of rationalisation and choice of technology. Industry's explanation of this can frequently be summed up as "invest or die". Unless a company can constantly invest in the very latest techniques designed to create the most "up-to-date product", it runs the risk of "limping along" behind its competitors. When it comes to investing in new technology, it would no longer seem to be a question of "if" for companies, but simply of "when".

This separate source of pressure towards the use of the very latest techniques also means that market prices become extremely uncertain, or at all events no longer determined by theoretical supply and demand. This creates a separate series of problems in the struggle against inflation and in the context of rational utilisation of a nation's resources.

The time gap between the technical and the economic obsolescence of the production apparatus is becoming longer. The rate at which industry is replacing old plant is, in other words, increasing all the time. This causes considerable waste of resources and creates, as already mentioned, a completely separate series of employment problems.

It is still too early to be able to present a complete strategy designed to solve these problems. The trade union movement is not against technical progress. But, on the other hand, it is not possible to sit and watch while large numbers of people lose their jobs, a development which is also accompanied by certain environmental effects. Discussions in the trade

318

union movement on a new strategy have throughout contained two main elements:

1) An obvious requirement must be for employers to be made liable to hold talks in advance with workers' representatives on the consequences which a given investment in a new technique will have for employment, training and so on.

2) Secondly, one must try to obtain more direct evaluations of technological development for the national economy and draft a separate technology policy for the community as a whole on the basis of these evaluations. The goals of technology policy will have to be coordinated with the primary goals for the country's development. Here efforts should include a wide range of preventive measures in the fields of social welfare, training and active labour market policy, while extensive selective measures will need to be introduced in the field of industrial policy.

From short-term actions to long-term strategies

Many of the means realised to counteract the recession are short-term in nature. In the light of the prolongation of the recession and the fact that most of the fundamental structural problems have not yet been attacked, many of the measures introduced to limit unemployment must be reexamined. Trade unions do not doubt that flexibility must be an important permanent part of a more coherent employment security policy. Future job security policies should not be formulated and evaluated insolated from the broader manpower policy. Job security can only be done full justice if it is evaluated as part of a greater effort to secure employment.

COLLECTIVE BARGAINING AND JOB SECURITY:

A Commentary

John Crispo[1]

Both in North America and Western Europe unions and workers are demanding more job security. Even the basic quest for cost-of-living protection has given way in some instances to this now more pressing priority. This shift in emphasis is to be explained by the prolonged nature of the current recession and the extensive lay-offs growing out of it.

It is worth stressing that such a shift in emphasis is not a new phenomenon. It re-occurs whenever the livelihood of large numbers of employees is or appears to be threatened. One need only recall a previous OECD conference in Washington in 1964 when the automation scare was at its peak. Then as now everything from guaranteed annual wages to shorter hours was being proposed to alleviate the perceived crisis. Nonetheless the major emphasis at that time was still on a number of approaches which collectively became known as active labour market policies.

These highly constructive and positive programmes featured the following set of measures: ample advance notice of any changes likely to have a disruptive effect on workers; complete disclosure of information concerning any such changes and their effects; full consultation by employers with unions and government employment agencies; and an integrated set of private and public adjustment mechanisms including relocation, retraining and upgrading. While Sweden moved more effectively in most of these areas than other countries virtually every OECD country followed suit with varying degrees of effectiveness.

What most differentiates the present situation from that of the sixties is the persistently higher levels of unemployment which the OECD countries have been experiencing. This has led to a shift in union and worker thinking away from active labour market policies stressing reallocation between positions and firms. Much more emphasis is now being placed on the preservation of individual jobs within specific enterprises.

Understandable as the pressures for such protective measures are, they are bound to have many regrettable side effects. Take the various demands that are being made to secure and stabilise the jobs of those now employed in particular jobs by specific firms. Economically they are turning labour into more and more of a fixed cost, thereby further rigidifying total costs. This contributes to inflexibility, reduces competitiveness, and, perhaps worst of all, discourages engagement of new employees. In the longer run, moreover, it is bound to slow down improvements in productivity and increases in standards of living.

---

1. Professor of Industrial Relations and Public Policy, University of Toronto.

Socially, the confinement of job security and stability measures to those enterprises able to afford them tends to create two types of workers within the labour market. On the one hand, there are those privileged enough to be in or able to break into the more protected sanctuaries. On the other hand, there are those left outside these preserves who must bear much of the brunt for ups and downs in the economy. This balkanization or segmentation of the labour market is probably most pronounced in Japan, where only the large firms provide something close to lifetime employment security.

A manifestation of an even more defeatist-type approach to the current job security challenge is to be found in the growing demand for reduced hours of work in one form or another. It would be difficult to quarrel with these demands if they represented a clear-cut case of a desire for more leisure as opposed to more income. They would then be a logical step in the long-term trend to share some of society's growing productivity in this manner. Nor could one quarrel if such demands were for temporary work-sharing arrangements designed to avoid lay-offs for a relatively short period of time. The problem arises when the rationale for such demands is based on the forlorn hope that they will somehow create more permanent employment. Although some new jobs may be created and more unemployment thereby reduced it will be at the expense of more general underemployment as more and more workers are asked to work less than they have been and for the most part would like to. Without some heroic and unreal assumptions about pay and related matters the real incomes and standards of living of most of those affected would also decline.

The task of reducing unemployment is, of course, made the more complex by the inflationary potential which plagues most OECD countries. This forces one back to the central subject matter of this conference which is intended to address itself to the issue of better integrating collective bargaining with government policy formulation. Space and time will permit only a few random thoughts concerning the tangle of issues involved in this equation.

First of all one should question the amount of attention which is focused on collective bargaining as a source of inflation. In most OECD countries domestic fiscal and monetary policies and foreign oil and food price shocks have been more important causes of inflation than anything transpiring in the collective bargaining arena. Without these other sources of inflation collective bargaining would not have much of an independent inflationary impact, since it appears to be less an originator than a transmitter of in-flationary forces.

As an aside it is worth pointing out that if one wants to criticise organ-ised labour for contributing to inflation one would be better advised to focus on its political than on its collective bargaining activities. By pressing govern-ments for more deficit spending and looser money the labour movement probably contributes far more to inflation than it does through its nego-tiations with employers.

A second focal point for general criticism is the unduly strong emphasis which is being placed on consensual decision-making in the hope of more responsive or socially responsible collective bargaining. Even assuming one could make a great deal of progress in this direction - a valiant assumption in many countries - it would have precious little effect in the absence of sensible and steady fiscal and monetary policies. Perhaps of equal importance is the need for more appropriate competition, institutional and structural policies; priorities all too briefly dealt with in this forum and in others like it.

A third concern relates more directly to the possibility of effective union participation in the kinds of consensual activities which are being recommended at this Conference. When engaging in these kinds of activities unions are subject to their own kind of internal trade-off the significance of which should not be understimated. On the one hand, unions are to be offered a greater role in the formulation of national decisions provided they are prepared to modify their collective bargaining claims accordingly. On the other hand, any such moderation or restraint can fly in the face of the fact that unions are supposed to be democratic institutions responsive to the aspirations of their members. Suffice it to say that the trade-off involved can and has been strained to the breaking point, thereby driving workers to rebel in one way or another against what they perceive to be overly statesmanlike behaviour on the part of their leaders.

Finally there is surely room to protest against the lack of emphasis placed on reform and revitalization of what is left of the free enterprise or market system, including the collective bargaining process itself. One does not have to be a disciple of Adam Smith or Milton Friedman to appreciate that the interacting play of supply and demand can still provide an effective disciplinary force in many situations. It is all too easy to dismiss the role of market forces simply because they have been rendered less operational in some cases. Worse still, one can contribute to the diminution of their role by interfering unnecessarily in the market place. Those who do not believe in the role of market forces can almost become self-fulfilling prophets by adding to the measures which undermine them. The net result can be one distortion after another, all leading to a less and less effective market system.

As stressed earlier, much more emphasis should be placed on competitive, institutional and structural measures designed to improve the effectiveness of the market. Indeed, if one wants to think in terms of more responsive collective bargaining - and, for that matter, fee and price setting and other forms of cost and price determination - one would be better advised to promote more responsiveness to market forces than to government policies.

In the meantime one could suggest that unions, employers and governments avoid permanent commitments to some of the demands which the present high levels of unemployment are producing. Job security and stability schemes, "employment-creating" reductions in hours of work, and other such demands should be resisted except as short-term temporary palliatives. Otherwise they could do far more harm than good even to the point of helping to undermine what is left of the enterprise or market system.

Collective bargaining is unlikely to survive in the absence of something akin to an enterprise or market system. Both could go down to defeat - as well as democracy and pluralism - if too much reliance is placed on government to solve society's problems.

BIBLIOGRAPHY

AARON, H.J. (1975). − Inflation and the Income Tax − Washington, Brookings.

AARON, H.J. and M. McGUIRE (1970). − Public Goods and Income Distribution − Econometrica.

ADDISON, J.T. (1979). − Wage Policies and Collective Bargaining Developments in Finland, Ireland and Norway − OECD, Paris.

ALDEN J. (1977). − The extent and Nature of Double-Jobholding in Great Britain, Industrial Relations Journal, Vol. 8, No. 3, autumn.

ANNABLE J.E. (1977). − A Theory of Downward Rigid Wages and Cyclical Unemployment − Economic Inquiry, XV/3.

ASHENFELTER, Orley (1978). − Unemployment as a Constraint on Labour Market Behaviour, Working Paper No. 107, Industrial Relations Section, Princeton University.

ASHENFELTER, O.C., JOHNSON G.E. and PENCAVEL, J.H. (1972). − Trade Unions and the Rate of Change of Money Wages in United States Manufacturing Industry − Review of Economic Studies.

ASHENFELTER, O.C. and PENCAVEL, J.H. (1975). − Wage Changes and Frequency of Wage Settlements. − Economica, May.

AVERITT, R.T. (1968). − The Dual Economy: the Dynamics of American Industry Structure, − New York, Norton.

BECKER, Gary S. (1962). − Investment in Human Capital: A Theoretical Analysis, Journal of Political Economy, Vol. LXX supplement, October.

BECKER Gary S. (1964). − Human Capital − New York, Columbia University Press.

BECKER Gary S. (1975). − Human Capital, New York, Columbia University Press, 2nd Edition.

BOUTEILLER J. (1974). − Wage Structure in France: The Problem of Wage Hierarchy. − International Journal of Social Economics, N° 1.

BOYER R. (1978). Approche de l'inflation, l'exemple français. − Ronéo, CEREMAP.

BRAUN, A.R. (1978). − Incomes Policies in Industrial Countries since 1973 − I.M.F., mimeo, Washington, January.

BRITTAIN, John A. (1971). − The Incidence of Social Security Payroll Taxes. − American Economic Review, 3.

BROWN E.H.Phelps (1974). − in: Wage Determination, − Paris, OECD.

BROWN E.H.Phelps (1977). − The Inequality of Pay, − Oxford University Press.

BURTON J. (1977). − Employment Subsidies. The Cases for and Against, National Westminster Bank, − Quarterly Review, February.

CERC, CENTRE D'ÉTUDE DES REVENUS ET DES COUTS (1977). − Dispersion et Disparités de salaires à l'étranger. États-Unis; Grande-Bretagne; République Fédérale d'Allemagne. Comparaison avec la France. − Documents nòs 29-30.

CLARK, R. (1977). − Adjusting Hours to Increase Jobs, − National Commission for Manpower Policy, Special Report No. 15, September.

CLEGG, H.A. (1976). − Trade Unionism Under Collective Bargaining, − Oxford.

COMMISSARIAT GÉNÉRAL DU PLAN France (1977). − Assiette des charges sociales et industries de main-d'œuvre, − Ronéo, June.

CONGRESSIONAL BUDGET OFFICE (1977). − Employment Subsidies and Employment Tax Credits, − U.S. Congress, 4.

COPELAND, Laurence (1977). − Wage-Inflation, Productivity and Wage-Leadership, The Manchester School of Economics and Social Studies, 9.

CROUCH, C. and PIZZORNO, A. eds. (1978). − The Resurgence of Class Conflict in Western Europe since 1968. − Vol. 2. London, Macmillan.

CROWLEY, R.W. (1978). − Work-sharing and Lay-offs. − Paper presented at the Annual Meeting of the Canadian Industrial Relations Research Institute, London, Ontario, May 29-30.

de MESNIL, G. and S.S. BHALLA (1975). − Direct Measurement of Popular Price Expectations. − American Economic Review, March.

DEPARTMENT OF EMPLOYMENT (1978). – Measures to Alleviate Unemployment in the Medium Term; Early Retirement, – Department of Employment Gazette, March.

DEPARTMENT OF EMPLOYMENT (1978). – Measures to Alleviate Unemployment in the Medium Term; Work-Sharing, Department of Employment Gazette, April.

DERUELLE, D. (1971). – Diffusion des hausses de salaires dans l'industrie chimique. Annales de l'INSEE, n° 7, May-Aug.

DERUELLE, D. (1974). – Détermination à court terme des hausses de salaires : études sectorielles et régionales. Annales de l'INSEE, May-December, nos 16 et 17.

DICKS-MIREAUX, L.A. and J.C.R. DOW (1959). – The Determinants of Wage Inflation: United Kingdom, 1946-56. – Journal of the Royal Statistical Society, A.

DODGE, D.A. (1975). – Impact of Tax Transfer and Expenditure Policies on the Distribution of Personal Incomes in Canada. – Income and Wealth.

DOERINGER, Peter B. and PIORE, Michael, J. (1971). – Internal Labor Markets and Manpower Analysis, Lexington (Mass).

DUNLOP, J. (1977). – A Reply, Industrial and Labor Relations Review.

ECKSTEIN, O. and WILSON, T.A. (1962). – The Determination of Money Wages in American Industry, Quarterly Journal of Economics.

ECONOMIC COUNCIL OF CANADA (1976), People and Jobs, A Study of the Canadian Labour Market, Ottawa.

EDGREN, G., FAXEN, K.O. and ODHNER, C.E. (1973). – Wage Formation and the Economy, London, Allen and Unwin.

E.E.C. (1978). – Working Paper on Work Sharing. – Meeting of the Standing Committee on Employment, Brussels, March.

EHRENBERG, R.G. (1971). – Fringe Benefits and Overtime Behaviour. – Massachusetts, Heath.

ELLIOT, R.F. (1977). – Public Sector Wage Movements: 1950-1973. – Scottish Journal of Political Economy, June.

ELTIS, W.A. and R.W. BACON (1975). – The Implications for Inflation. Employment and Growth of a Fall in the Share of Output that is Marketed. – Oxford Bull. Econ. Stat., November.

ERTNELL J., LLEWELLYN J., TARLING R. (1974). – Money wage inflation in industrial countries – Review of Economic Studies, February.

EYRAUD F. (1975). – La fin des classifications Parodi. Ronéo, – Centre d'Études des Relations Sociales. Faculté des Sciences Économiques, Aix-en-Provence.

FAIR, R.C. (1969). – The Short-Run Demand for Workers and Hours. – North-Holland.

FELDSTEIN, Martin S. (1967). – Specification of the Labour Input in the Aggregate Production Function. – Review of Economic Studies, 34, October.

FELDSTEIN, Martin S. (1972a). – Lowering the Permanent Rate of Unemployment, – October 1972 (mimeo - subsequently published by the Joint Economic Committee, U.S. Congress).

FELDSTEIN, Martin S. (1972b). – The Incidence of the Social Security Payroll Tax: Comment. – American Economic Review, 9.

FELLNER, W. et al. (1961). – The Problem of Rising Prices. – Paris, OECD.

FETHKE, G. and H. WILLIAMSON (1976). – Employment Tax Credits as a Fiscal Tool. – J.E.C., Washington.

FLANAGAN, R.J. (1976). – Wage Interdependence in Unionised Labor Markets. – Brookings Papers on Economic Activity.

FLANDERS, A. (1970). – Management and Unions. – Faber and Faber, London.

FRIEDMAN, M. (1968). – The Role of Monetary Policy. – American Economic Review, March.

GALBRAITH, J.K. (1974). – Economics and the Public Purpose. – London.

GERMANY, ECONOMIC SURVEYS (1977). – Paris, OECD.

GORDON, R.J. (1970). – The Recent Acceleration of Inflation. – Brookings Papers on Economic Activity.

GORDON, R.J. (1972). – Wage-Price Controls and the Shifting Phillips Curve. – Brookings Papers on Economic Activity.

GRAMLICH, E.M. (1976). – Impact of Minimum Wages on Other Wages, Employment, and Family Incomes. – Brookings Papers on Economic Activity, 2.

GREEN, C. and J. COUSINEAU (1976).— Unemployment in Canada - The Impact of Unemployment Insurance.— Economic Council of Canada, Ottawa.

GUILLAUME, H. (1976).— French medium-term forecasting model.— European Meeting of the Econometric Society. Helsinki.

HALL, R.E. (1974).— The Process of Inflation in the Labor Market.— Brookings Papers on Economic Activity.

HALL, R.E. (1975).— The rigidity of wages and the persistence of unemployment.— Brookings Papers on Economic Activity No 2.

HART, R.A. (1973).— The Role of Overtime Working in the Recent Wage Inflation Process.— Bulletin of Economic Research, 25 May, 73-87.

HART, R.A. and SHAROT, T. (1978). — The Short-Run Demand for Workers and Hours: A Recursive Model. — Review of Economic Studies.

HINES, A.G. (1969).— Wage Inflation in the United Kingdom, 1948-62.—A disaggregated Study, Economic Journal.

HOLLAND, S. (1978).— The Influence of Dominant Enterprises on Employment and its Sectoral Development, in Employment Policies, Incomes and Growth in the Medium Term.— Paris, OECD.

ILO (1977a). — Collective Bargaining in Finland: Recent Trends and Problems, paper to ILO Symposium on Collective Bargaining in Industrialised Countries (mimeo).

ILO (1977b).— Background Paper prepared by the International Labour Office for Symposium on Collective Bargaining in Industrialised Countries (mimeo).

ILO (1978).— Management of Working Time in Industrialised Countries.— Geneva.

ILO (yearly).— Yearbook of Labour Statistics.— Geneva.

INCOMES DATA SERVICES (1976). Fringe Benefits.— Study 127, August. London.

INFLATION (1970).— The Present Problem.— Paris, OECD.

JOHNSON, George E. (1977). — The Determination of Wages in the Union and Non-Union Sectors. — British Journal of Industrial Relations, Vol. 15, N° 2.

JOHNSON, J. and TIMBRELL (1974).— Empirical Tests of Bargaining Theory, in Laider and Purdy.— Inflation and Labour Markets.

JENNY, F. and WEBER, A.P. (1975).— Concentration, syndicalisation et rémunération salariale dans l'industrie française.— Revue Économique, July.

KALDOR, N. (1976).— Inflation and Recession in the World Economy.— The Economic Journal, December.

KESSELMAN, J. et al. (1977).— Tax Credits for Employment.— American Economic Review.

KEYNES, J.M. (1936).— The General Theory of Employment, Interest and Money.— London, Macmillan.

KEYNES (n.d.).— How to Pay for the War.— In Collected Writings of John Maynard Keynes, Vol. IX.

KOPITS, George (1978).— Wage Subsidies and Employment: An Analysis of the French Experience. I.M.F. mimeo. 2/9.

KOTOWITZ, Y. (1977).— The Effect of Direct Taxes on Wages.— Anti-Inflation Board, Ottawa, mimeo.

LAIDLER, D. and PURDY, D., eds. (1974). — Inflation and Labourmarkets. — Manchester University Press.

LA PORTA, A., et VALCAVI, D. (1976). — I Piu recenti sviluppi della contrattazione aziendale in Italia. — Economico et Lavoro (Padova), January.

LAUDADIO, L. and PERCY, M. (1978). — Some Evidence of the Impact of Non-Wage Labour Cost on Overtime Work and Environment. — Vol. 28, No 2.

LEICESTER, C. (1979). — Unemployment and the Working Year in Britain, 1961 to 1976, in Structural Determinants of Employment and Unemployment. — Vol. II, Paris, OECD.

LEIJONHUFVUD, A. (1968).— Comments: Is There a Meaningful Trade-Off Between Inflation and Unemployment.— Journal of Political Economy, July.

LEVITAN, S.A. and BELOUS, R.S. (1977a).— Work-Sharing Initiatives at Home and Abroad.— Monthly Labour Review, Vol. 100, No. 9, September.

LEVITAN, S.A. and BELOUS, R.S. (1977b). — Shorter Hours, Shorter Weeks: Spreading the Work to Reduce Unemployment. — The Johns Hopkins University Press, Baltimore.

MABRY, B. (1973). – The Economics of Fringe Benefits. – Industrial Relations, 12, February.

MALINVAUD, E. (1971). – Peut-on mesurer l'évolution du coût d'usage du capital productif. – Economie et Statistique, No 22., April.

MALINVAUD, E. (1978). – Nouveaux développements de la théorie macro-économique du chômage. – Revue Économique, January.

MASSE, P. (1964). – Rapport sur la Politique des Revenus. – Documentation Française. Recueil et Monographie No 47.

MASSE, P. et BERNARD, P. (1969). – Les dividendes du Progrès. – Éditions du Seuil.

McCRACKEN, P. et al. (1977). – Towards Full Employment and Price Stability. – OECD, Paris.

MICKLER, D. (1978). – Quelles sont les conséquences de l'évolution technico-économique pour les procès de travail qualifié et pour la situation d'ouvriers qualifiés de l'industrie. – SOFI Göttingen. Ronéo. (Translation J. Duplex).

MINCER., Jacob (1962). – On the Job Training: Costs, Returns and Some Implications. Journal of Political Economy, Vol. LXX supplement, October.

MITCHELL, D., (1978). – Disaggregating Wage Equations: A Note. – mimeo: Brookings, May.

MITTELSTADT, Axel, (1975). – Unemployment Benefits and Related Payments in Seven Major Countries. – OECD Economic Outlook, Occasional Studies, July.

MOSES, L.N. (1962). – Income, Leisure and Wage Pressure. – Economic Journal, Vol. 72, June.

NATIONAL BOARD FOR PRICES AND INCOMES (1970). Hours of Work, Overtime and Shift-Working, Report No 161.

NORWAY, ECONOMIC SURVEY (1975). – Paris, OECD.

OECD (1965). – Wages and Labour Mobility. – Paris.

OECD (1973). – New Patterns for Working Time. – Paris.

OECD (1973). – Flexibility in Working Life. – Paris.

OECD (1975). – Socially Responsible Wage Policies and Inflation. – A Review of Four Countries' Experience, Paris.

OECD Committee on Fiscal Affairs (1976a). – The Adjustment of Personal Income Tax System for Inflation. – Paris.

OECD (1976b). – Lifelong Allocation of Time. – Paris.

OECD (1977). – The Development of Industrial Relations Systems: Some Implications of Japanese Experience. – Paris.

OECD (1978). – Public Expenditure Trends, Studies in Resource Allocation. – Paris, June.

OECD (forthcoming). – Collective Bargaining and Government Policies in Ten OECD Countries. – Paris.

OI, Walter, Y. (1962). – Labour as a Quasi-fixed Factor. – Journal of Political Economy, December.

OKUN, A. (1973). – Upward Mobility in a High-Pressure Economy, Brookings Papers on Economic Activity.

OKUN, A. (1975). – Inflation. Its Mechanics and Welfare Costs. – Brookings Papers on Economic Activity.

OKUN, A. (1977). – Efficient Disinflationary Policies. – Paper presented at American Economics Association meetings, December.

OWEN, J.D (1976). – The Price of Leisure. – Rotterdam University Press, Holland.

PACKER, A.H. and PARK, S.H. (1973). – Distortions in Relative Wages and Shifts in the Phillips Curve. – Review of Economics and Statistics.

PECHMAN, J. and TIMPANE (1975). – Work Incentives and Income Guarantees. – Brookings.

PERRY, G.L. (1970). – Changing Labor Market Conditions and Inflation. – Brookings Papers on Economic Activity.

PERRY, G.L. (1978). – Slowing the Wage Price Spiral. The Macro-Economic View. – Mimeo. Brookings.

PHELPS, E.S. (1967). – Phillips Curves, Expectations of Inflation and Optimal Unemployment Over Time. – Economica, August.

PHELPS, E.S. (1969). – The New Microeconomics in Inflation and Employment Theory. American Economic Review, Papers and Proceedings, May.

PHILLIPS, A.W. (1958). – The Relation Between Unemployment and the Rate of Change of Money Wage Rates in the United Kingdom, 1861-1957. – Economica, November.

PIORE, M. (1974). – Labor Market Stratification and Wage Determination. – Mimeo.

PIORE, M. (1978). – Dualism in the labor market: a response to uncertainty and flux. The case of France. – Revue Économique, January.

PIOTET, F. (1978). – Sept ans de politique contractuelle. – Ronéo.

PIZZORNO, A. (1978). – See Crouch and Pizzorno, eds.

Quarterly Report of the Council of Wage and Price Stability (1978). – No. 13, April, G.P.O. Washington.

REA, Samuel (1977). – Unemployment Insurance and Labour Supply: A Simulation of the 1971 Unemployment Insurance Act. – Canadian Journal of Economics, 5.

REDER, M.W. (1959). – The Cost of a Shorter Work Week. – Annual Proceedings of Industrial Relations Research Association.

REYNAUD, J.D. (1978). – Évolution et tendance de la négociation collective. – France. Ronéo.

ROBINSON, D. (1974). – Solidaristic Wage Policy in Sweden. – Paris, OECD.

ROCHECORBON (1968). – Feu la Procédure Toutée ?. – Droit Social, November.

ROSS, S.A. and WACHTER, M. (1973). – Wage Determination, Inflation, and the Industrial Structure. – American Economic Review.

ROWLEY, J.C.R. and D.A. WILTON (1973). – Quarterly Models of Wage Determination: Some New Efficient Estimates. – American Economic Review, June.

SADLIER-BROWN, P. (1978). – Work-Sharing in Canada: Problems and Possibilities. – HRI Observation Series No. 18, June, C.D. Howe Research Institute, Montreal.

SALAIS, R. (1978). – Les besoins d'emploi: contenu et problèmes posés par leur satisfaction. – Revue Économique, January.

SELLIER, F. (1971). – Les transformations de la négociation collective et de l'organisation syndicale en Italie. – Sociologie du Travail, No. 2.

SELLIER, F. (1972). – La fonction de négociation dans la codécision simple en Allemagne. – Droit social, November.

SHIMADA, H. (1977). – The Japanese Labour Market After the Oil Crisis. – Keio Economic Studies, Vol. 17, No. 1.

SHISHKO, R. and ROSTKER, B. (1976. – The Economics of Multiple Job Holding. – American Economic Review, Vol. 66, No. 3, June.

SILVESTRE, J.J. (1971). – La dynamique des salaires nominaux en France. – Revue Économique, May.

SILVESTRE, J.J. (1973). – Les salaires ouvriers dans l'industrie française. – Bordas, Collection Études.

SLOANE, P.J. (1977). – The Economics of Hours and Hourly Working Patterns. – Participation Paper No. 3, Symposium on Arrangement of Working Time and Social Problems Connected with Shiftwork in Industrialised Countries, I.L.O., Geneva.

SLOANE, P.J. (1978). – Economic Aspects of Shiftwork and Nightwork in Industrialised Market Economies. – International Labour Review, Vol. 117, No. 2, March-April.

SMITH, Philip, M. and WILTON D.A., (1978). – Wage Changes - The Frequency of Wage Settlements, the Variability of Contract Length, and 'Locked-in' Wage Adjustments. – Economica.

SMITH, S. (1977). – Equal Pay in the Public Sector: Fact or Fantasy. – I.R. Section, Princeton.

STIGLER, George, J. (1962). – Information in the Labour market. – Journal of Political Economy, Vol. LXX, supplement, October.

SUPPANZ, H. and ROBINSON, D. (1972). – Prices and Incomes Policy: The Austrian Experience. – Paris, OECD.

SWEDEN, ECONOMIC SURVEY (1978). – Paris, OECD.

TAYLOR, R. (1977). – The Composition of Total Compensation based on Reports Submitted to the Anti-Inflation Board. – Anti-Inflation Board (internal draft), October.

TAYLOR, TURNOVSKY and WILSON (1972). – The Inflationary Process in Canadian Manufacturing. – P.I.C., Ottawa.

TOUTEE, M. (1964). – Rapport sur l'amélioration des procédures de discussion des salaires dans le secteur public. – La Documentation Française. Notes et Études documentaires. March.

TRIOLA, A. (1977). – La négociation collective en Italie: Tendances et problèmes récents. – Paper for ILO Symposium on Collective Bargaining in Industrialised Countries, (mimeo).

TSUJIMURA, K. (1970). – Working Hours and Productivity (in Japanese). – Ministry of Labour, Tokyo (mimeo).

TURNER, H.A. and JACKSON, D.A.S., (1970a). – On the Stability of Wage Differences and Productivity-based Wage Policies: An International Analysis. – in British Journal of Industrial Relations.

TURNER, H.A. and JACKSON, D.A.S. (1970b). – On the Determination of the General Wage Level. A World Analysis. – The Economic Journal. December.

TURNOVSKY, S.J. (1972). – The Expectations Hypothesis and the Aggregate Wage Equation: Some Empirical Evidence for Canada. – Economica, February.

TURNOVSKY, S.J. and M.L. WACHTER (1972). – A Test of the 'Expectations Hypothesis' Using Directly Observed Wage and Price Expectations. – The Review of Economics and Statistics, February.

ULMAN, L. (1976). – Unionism, Inflation, and Consensus, in J.S. Cramer, A. Heertje, P.E. Venekamp (eds), Relevance and Precision: From Quantitative Analysis to Economic Policy, Essays in Honour of Pieter de Wolff, Amsterdam, Sawson/North Holland.

WACHTER, M. (1970a). – Cyclical Variations in the Interindustry Wage Structure. – American Economic Review. March.

WACHTER, M. (1970b). – Relative Wage Equations for U.S. Manufacturing Industries 1947-67. – Review of Economics and Statistics.

WACHTER, M. (1974a). – Phase II, Cost-Push Inflation and Relative Wages. – American Economic Review.

WACHTER, M. (1974b). – The Wage Process: An Analysis of the Early 1970's. – Brookings Papers on Economic Activity.

WACHTER, M. (1976). – The Changing Cyclical Responsiveness of Wage Inflation. – Brookings Papers on Economic Activity.

WELTZ, F. (1978). – Procès de changements organisationnels et relations professionnelles en R.F.A. – Ronéo. (Translation: Jean Duplex).

WHITING, E. (1978). – The Economics of Modes of Employment. – Personnel Review, Vol. 7, No. 1, winter.

WILTON, D.A., CHRISTOFIDES, L., SWIDINSKY, R., AULD, D. (1978a). – Determinants of Negotiated Wage Settlements in Canada: A Microeconomic Analysis. – A.I.B., Ottawa.

WILTON, D.A., CHRISTOFIDES, L., SWIDINSKY, R. (1978b). – A Micro-Econometric Analysis of the Canadian Wage Determination Process. – Mimeo.

ZALUSKY, J. (1978). – Shorter Hours - The Steady Gain. – AFL-CIO American Federationist, January.

LIST OF PARTICIPANTS

[Rapporteurs are indicated by (R), Discussants by (D) and Observers by (O)]

AUSTRALIA

Mr. M.B. Keogh, Deputy Secretary, Department of Employment and Industrial Relations, 239 Bourke Street, Melbourne 13000.
Mr. E.L. Waterman, Australian Embassy, 1601 Massachusetts Avenue, Washington D.C. 20036.

AUSTRIA

Mrs. Helga Konrad (O), Austrian Embassy, Washington D.C.
Dr. Thomas Lachs (D), Director, Konsumgenossenschaft-Wien, Gerhard Fritsch-Gasse 71, 1170 Vienna.

BELGIUM

M. A. Schellekens, Economic Counsellor, Belgian Embassy, Washington D.C.
M. Albert Verschueren (R), Director-General, Federation of Belgian Business, Brussels.

CANADA

Prof. Frank R. Anton, Department of Economics, University of Calgary, 2920 24th Ave. N.W., Calgary, Alberta T2N 1N4.
Prof. Frances Bairstow, Director, Industrial Relations Centre, McGill University, 1001 Sherbrooke Street West, Montreal, Quebec, H3 A 1G5.
M. Yvan Blain, Assistant Deputy Minister Staff Relations, Department of Labour and Manpower, 255 boulevard Crémazie, Montréal.
Prof. John Crispo (D), University of Toronto.
Mr. Ross V. Dixon, Canadian Manufacturers Association, 1 Yonge Street, Toronto, Ontario.
Prof. David Dodge (R), Johns Hopkins University and Department of Finance, Canada.
Mr. Craig Dotson, Executive Director, Development Board, Department of Labour, Regina, Saskatchewan, S4P 2Y5.
Mr. J. Ken Eaton, A/Director, International Information Services, Labour Canada, Ottawa, Ontario, K1A OJ2.
Mr. Jim Goodison, Labour Counsellor, Canadian Embassy, Washington D.C.
Prof. John Kervin, c/o Centre for Industrial Relations, University of Toronto, 123 St. George Street, Toronto, Ontario, M5S 1A1.
Mr. Rod McLeod, Chief, Programme Planning and Development, Employment Relations Br., Labour Canada, Ottawa, Ont. K1A OJ2.
Mr. Guy de Merlis, Director, Mediation & Conciliation, Labour Canada, Ottawa, Ontario, K1A OJ2.
Mr. Victor Pathe, Executive Director, Industrial Relations Division, Ontario Dept. of Labour, 400 University Ave., Toronto, Ont., M7A 1T7.
Mr. Ken Phythian, Professional Institute of the Public Service, 786 Bronson Avenue, Ottawa, Ont.
Mr. Wayne Simpson, Economic Analysis Directorate, Labour Canada, Ottawa, Ontario, K1A OJ2.
Mr. J. Slater, Economic Council of Canada.
Mr. Gerald Swartz, Director, Research Branch, Ontario Dept. of Labour, 400 University Ave, Toronto, Ont. M7A 1T7.

Mr. Bob Wing, Centre for the Study of Inflation and Productivity, Economic Council of Canada, 333 River Rd., P.O. Box 527, Vanier, Ontario, K1P 5V6.

DENMARK

Mr. C.J. Clemmensen, Director, Danish Employers' Confederation, 113 Vester Voldgade, 1503 Copenhagen V.

Mr. Einar Edelberg, Head of Division, Ministry of Labour, Laxegade 19, Copenhagen.

Mr. Henrik Hassenkam, Consultant, Ministry of Labour, Laxegade 19, Copenhagen.

Mr. Holger Jensen, Chief Economist, Danish Federation of Trade Unions, Landsorganisationen i Danmark, Rosenørns allé 14, 1970 Copenhagen.

Mr. Poul Rasmussen (D), Consultant, Danish Federation of Trade Unions, Landsorganisationen i Danmark, Rosenørns allé 14, 1970 Copenhagen.

Mr. P. Schade-Poulsen, Director, Danish Employers' Confederation, 113 Vester Voldgade, 1503 Copenhagen V.

Mrs. Kirsten Thorball, Head of Section, Ministry of Labour, Laxegade 19, Copenhagen.

FINLAND

Mr. Timo Kauppinen, Secretary-General, Committee for Labour Relations, Ministry of Social Affairs and Health, Snellmaninkatu 4-6, SF-00170 Helsinki 17.

Mr. Stig-Erik Leiponen, Director, Confederation of Commerce Employers, Etelaranta, 10 SF-00130 Helsinki 13.

Mr. Keijo Liinamaa (R), Secretary-General, Ministry of Labour, Annankatu 25, Helsinki 10.

Mr. Antero Tuominen, Secretary for Economic Policy, Confederation of Finnish Labour Unions, Siltasaarenkatu 3-5 A, SF-00530 Helsinki 53.

FRANCE

M. E. Boursier, Union des Industries Métallurgiques et Minières, 56 avenue de Wagram, 75017 Paris (Co-Chairman).

M. Bernard Brunhes, Chef du Service des Affaires Sociales au Commissariat Général du Plan, 18 rue de Martignac, 75007 Paris.

M. D. Lacaze, Ministère du Travail, 1 Place Fontenoy, 75007 Paris.

M. J.J. Silvestre (D), Centre National de la Recherche Scientifique, Chemin du Coton-Rouge, 13100 Aix-en-Provence.

GERMANY

Mr. Hermann Boedler, Federal Ministry for Labour and Social Affairs, Postfach - D - 5300 Bonn.

Mr. Gisbert F. Faust, Federal Ministry for Economics, Bundesministerium für Wirtschaft, Postfach D-5300 Bonn.

Prof. Fritz Scharpf (D), Director, International Institute of Management, Platz der Luftbrücke 1-3, 1000 Berlin 42.

GREECE

Mr. R. Christodoulis, Directeur Général Adjoint au Ministère du Travail, Ministère du Travail, Pireos Street 40, Athens.

Mr. R. Fakiolas, Directeur Général Adjoint au Centre de Planification et de Recherches Économiques (KEPE), Ippokratous 22, Athens.

IRELAND

Mr. Nicholas Fitzgerald, Principal, Department of Labour, Mespil Road, Dublin 4.
Mr. Felix M. Larkin, Administrative Officer, Department of Economic Planning and Development, Upper Merrion Street, Dublin 2.
Mr. Luke Leonard, Deputy Secretary, Department of Economic Planning and Development, Upper Merrion Street, Dublin 2.
Mr. Daniel J. McAuley, Director General, Federated Union of Employers, 8 Fitzwilliam Place, Dublin 2.
Mr. Tadhg O'Carroll, Secretary, Department of Labour, Mespil Road, Dublin 4.
Mr. Harold O'Sullivan, Vice-President, Irish Congress of Trade Unions, 19, Raglan Road, Dublin 4.
Mr. William P. Smith, Deputy Secretary, Department of the Public Service, Kildare House, 36 Kildare Street, Dublin 2.

ITALY

M. Paolo Annibaldi, Directeur central des relations avec les syndicats, Confindustria.
Prof. Franco Archibugi, University of Calabria, Director of Research Department, C.I.S.L.
Prof. Enzo Avanzi, Conseiller juridique intersyndical, I.R.I.
M. Domenico Buttinelli, Secrétaire confédéral, U.I.L.
Dr. B. de Cesaris, Vice-President, ASAP, Petroleum and Chemical Company, Management Association.
M. Pietro Merli Brandini, Secrétaire confédéral, C.I.S.L.
Mr. G. Migliuolo, General Director for Immigration and Social Affairs, Ministry of Foreign Affairs, Rome.
M. Gianni Salvarani, Dirigeant du bureau d'études, U.I.L.
M. Ugo Tavernini, Directeur Général, Ministère du Travail, Via Flavia 6, 00100 Rome.
M. Bruno Trentin, Secrétaire confédéral, C.G.I.L.
Prof. Tiziano Treu (D), University of Pavia, Via Conca del Naviglio 22, Milan.
M. Antonio Triola, Directeur Adjoint de Division, Direction Générale des Relations du Travail, Ministère du Travail, Via Flavia 6, 00100 Rome.

JAPAN

Mr. Kazuo Hiromi, First Secretary, Japanese Embassy in Washington.
Mr. Takeo Naruse, Acting Director, International Division, Japan Federation of Employers' Associations (Nikkeiren), 4-6 Marunouchi 1-Chome, Chiyoda-Ku, Tokyo.
Mr. Kozo Okabe, Director, Labour Legislation Division, Labour Policy Bureau, Ministry of Labour, c/o International Labour Affairs Division, Ministry of Labour, 1-3-1 Otemachi, Chiyoda-Ku, Tokyo.
Prof. Haruo Shimada (D), 1561-78 Takada-cho, Kohoku-ku, Yokohama 223.
Prof. Taishiro Shirai, Hosei University, Tokyo, No. 508, Daini New Nogeyama Mansion, 4 Oimatsu-Cho, Nishi-Ku, Yokohama City, Kanagawa Prefecture.
Mr. Masao Uenishi, Assistant General-Secretary, Japanese Confederation of Labour (DOMEI), Yuai Kaikan Building, 20-12 Shiba 2-Chome, Minato-Ku, Tokyo.

LUXEMBOURG

M. Romain Schintgen, Conseiller de Gouvernement, Ministère du Travail et de la Sécurité Sociale, Luxembourg.

NETHERLANDS

Mr. L. A. Ph. van der Leij, Ministry of Social Affairs, Zeestraat 73, The Hague.
Prof. Bram Peper (R), Erasmus University, Rotterdam.
Mr. W. Q. J. Willemsen, Ministry of Economic Affairs, Bezuiden-Routseweg 63, The Hague.

NEW ZEALAND

Mr. G. L. Jackson, Secretary of Labour, Department of Labour, Wellington.
Mr. R. E. Taylor, Director, Research and Information Division, New Zealand Employers' Federation, Wellington.

NORWAY

Mr. Øistein Guldbrandsen, Under Secretary of State, Ministry of Consumer Affairs and Government Administration, P.O. Box 8004 Dep., Oslo 1.
Mr. Ingolv Haereid, Director General, Ministry of Consumer Affairs and Government Administration, P.O. Box 8004 Dep., Oslo 1.
Mr. Jan Halvorsen, Head of Division, Ministry of Finance, P.O. Box 8008 Dep., Oslo 1.

PORTUGAL

Mme Odete Esteves de Carvalho, Bureau d'Études et de Planification, Ministère du Travail, Av. Defensores de Chaves 95-4, Lisbon 1.
M. Jose A. Leitao, Direction Générale des Relations Collectives du Travail, Ministère du Travail, Praça de Londres, Lisbon 1.
M. João Pereira de Moura, Directeur du Bureau d'Études et de Planification, Ministère du Travail, Av. Defensores de Chaves 95-4, Lisbon 1.

SPAIN

M. Arturo Cayuela Miro, Attaché à l'Ambassade d'Espagne, Washington D.C.
M. José Miguel Prados Terriente, Directeur Général du Travail, Ministère du Travail, Avenida del Generalisimo, Madrid.

SWEDEN

M. Lennart Nilsson, Director, Ministry of Economy, Fack, 103 10 Stockholm 2.
Mr. Björn Pettersson, Labour Attaché, Swedish Embassy, Suite 1200, Watergate 600, 600 New Hampshire Avenue N.W., Washington, D.C. 20037.
Mr. Carl Tham, Under-Secretary of State, Ministry of Labour, Fack, 103 10 Stockholm 2.

SWITZERLAND

Mr. Silvio E. Arioli, Counsellor (Economic Affairs), Embassy of Switzerland, 2900, Cathedral Avenue, N.W., Washington, D.C. 20008.

UNITED KINGDOM

Mr. Robert Hart (R), Department of Economics, Strathclyde University, 173 Cathedral Street, Glasgow G4 ORQ.

Mr. M.G. Jeremiah, Assistant Secretary, Counter Inflation Policy Division, H.M. Treasury, 18 Parliament Street, London S.W1.
Prof. B.C. Roberts (D), London School of Economics, London, W.C. 2.
Mr. Derek Robinson (R), Magdalen College, Oxford.
Prof. P.J. Sloane (R), Paisley College of Technology, High Street, Paisley.
Mr. M. Wake, Under Secretary, Incomes and Industrial Relations Division, Department of Employment, 8 St' James Square, London S.W. 1.

UNITED STATES

Mr. Edward Ayoub, Research Director, United Steelworkers of America.
Mr. S. Lester Block, Senior Vice President, R.H. Macey Co., New York, New York.
Mr. Francis X. Burkhardt, Assistant Secretary of Labor Management Relations, Department of Labor (co-chairman).
Mr. Harold P. Coxson, Director of Labor Law, Chamber of Commerce of the United States.
Dr. John Dunlop (R), Harvard University.
Mr. David J. Fitzmaurice, President, International Union of Electrical Radio and Machine Workers (co-chairman).
Mr. Ronald Van Helden, Executive Assistant to Assistant Secretary Burkhardt, U.S. Department of Labor, Washington, D.C.
Mr. Sidney McKenna (D), Vice President, Ford Motor Co, Detroit, Michigan.
The Hon. R.E. Marshall, Secretary of Labor, Department of Labor, (co-chairman).
Mr. Kenneth Moffat, Federal Mediation and Conciliation Service.
Mr. Paul O'Day, U.S. Department of Commerce, Washington, D.C.
Dr. Rudoph Oswald (R), Research Director, AFL-CIO, Washington, D.C.
Mr. Arnold Packer, Assistant Secretary for Policy, Evaluation and Research, Department of Labor.
Mr. Peter J. Pestillo, Vice President, B.F. Goodrich Co. Akron, Ohio.
Mr. Richard Prosten, Research Director, Industrial Union Department, AFL-CIO, Washington, D.C.
Mr. Jerome Rosow, President, Work in America Institute and Chairman, U.S. Business and Industry Advisory Committee to the OECD.
Mr. Howard D. Samuel, Deputy Under Secretary for International Affairs, Department of Labor.
Mr. Charles L. Schultze, Chairman of the Council of Economic Advisers to the President.
Mr. Charles H. Smith Jr., Chairman, SIFCO Industries, Cleveland, Ohio.
Mr. Brian Turner, Bureau of International Labor Affairs, U.S. Department of Labor, Washington, D.C.
Prof. Lloyd Ulman (R), University of California, Berkeley.
Mr. Richard D. Vine, Deputy Assistant Secretary of State, European Affairs, State Department.
Prof. Michael Wachter (D), University of Pennsylvania.
Mr. Don Wasserman, American Federation of State, County and Municipal Employers.

INTERNATIONAL ORGANISATIONS
Observers

COMMISSION FOR EUROPEAN COMMUNITIES

Mr. Robert Bistolfi, Directorate General of Economic and Financial Affairs.
Mr. K.H. Schilz, Directorate General for Employment and Social Affairs.

INTERNATIONAL LABOUR OFFICE

Mr. E. Cordova, Labour Law and Labour Relations Branch.
Mr. J. Schregle, Industrial Relations and Labour Administration Department.

INTERNATIONAL INSTITUTE FOR LABOUR STUDIES

Mr. Alan Gladstone, International Institute for Labour Studies, Geneva, Switzerland.

INTERNATIONAL MONETARY FUND

Mrs. Anne Braun, Research Department.

ORGANISATION FOR ECONOMIC COOPERATION AND DEVELOPMENT

Mr. Charles G. Wootton, Deputy Secretary-General.
Mr. J.R. Gass, Director, Directorate for Social Affairs, Manpower and Education.
Mr. W.R. Dymond, Deputy Director, Directorate for Social Affairs, Manpower and Education.
Mr. Palle Schelde Andersen, Head of General Economics Division, Economics and Statistics Department.
Mr. Conrad Blyth, Consultant, Directorate for Social Affairs, Manpower and Education.
Mr. R.O. Clarke, Principal Administrator, Directorate for Social Affairs, Manpower and Education.
Mr. P. Gaskell, Information Service.
Mrs. U. Ranhall Jeanneney, Information Service.

JOINT CONFERENCE SECRETARIAT

Mr. Donald P. Avery, Special Assistant to the Associate Deputy Under Secretary OECD, and the staff of the Bureau of International Labor Affairs.
Mr. Y. Hoflack, Directorate for Social Affairs, Manpower and Education.
Mr. E. Ekers, Washington Office.
Mr. H. de Vroom, Washington Office.
Mrs. D. O'Sullivan, Washington Office.
Mrs. K. Edenhein, Washington Office.

OBSERVERS

Mrs. Ahern, Eileen, Human Resources Consultant, New York City.
Mr. Aho, Mike, Foreign Economic Research Staff, ILAB, Department of Labor.
Mr. Allstrom, Peter, Food and Beverage Trades Department, AFL-CIO.
Mr. Anderson, Mark, International Department, AFL-CIO.
Mr. Ayoub, Ed, Director of Research, United Steelworkers of America.
Mr. Balogh, Jules, Labor Management Services Administration, Department of Labor.
Mr. Bambrick, James, Labor Economist, Standard Oil Company of Ohio.
Dean Banks, Robert, Michigan State University.
Mrs. Barnes, Ann - CBS, New York City (Labor Analysis).
Mrs. Baume, Edith, Minority Counsel, House Education and Labor Committee.
Mrs. Becnel, Barbara, Industrial Relations Research Association.
Mr. Bernhardt, Charles, National Federation of Federal Employees.
Mr. Bier, Joseph, Industrial Relations Research Association.
Mr. Bistolfi, Robert.
Mr. Black, Stanley, Special Assistant to Under Secretary Cooper, Department of State.
Mr. Brill, Lawrence, Department of Commerce.
Mr. Brodeur, Harold, Director, Industrial Relations, American Trucking Association.
Mrs. Broff, Nancy.
Mr. Brumfield, Jesse, W., Assistant European Labor Adviser, Department of Labor.
Mr. Brunz, Kevin, U.S. Senate Staff.
Mrs. Burgoon, Beatrice, Labor Management Services Administration, Department of Labor

Mr. Cantfil, Gus, Labor Management Services Administration, Department of Labor.
Mrs. Capdeville, Patricia, Bureau of Labor Statistics, Department of Labor.
Mr. Chaffins, Gary, Labor Management Services Administration, Department of Labor.
Prof. Chernick, Jack, Rutgers University.
Mr. Ciccone, Charles, Congressional Research Staff, Library of Congress.
Mr. Clowes, Dean, United Steelworkers of America.
Mr. Cohany, Harry, Bureau of Labor Statistics, Department of Labor.
Mr. Cole, Isaac, Office of Administration and Management, Department of Labor.
Mr. Conn, Harry, Press Associates, Inc., Washington, D.C.
Mrs Cooper, Janet, National Federation of Federal Employees.
Mr. Davey, Harold, Bureau of International Labor Affairs, Department of Labor.
Mr. Dawson, Irving, Labor Management Services Administration, Department of Labor.
Mr. Dunford, David, Bureau of Economic and Business Affairs, Department of State.
Mr. Equitz, Howard, Director, Corporate Employment Relations, Allis Chalmers Corporation.
Mr. Fidandis, Nicholas, Federal Mediation and Conciliation Service.
Mr. Finan, Vincent, Labor Management Services Administration, Department of Labor.
Mr. Floyd, Eric, Treasury Department.
Mr. Foose, R.T., Department of Commerce.
Mr. Foster, John, Labor Management Services Administration, Department of Labor.
Mr. Friedman, Marvin, Washington, D.C.
Mr. Gilson, Thomas, University of Hawaii.
Mr. Good, Dale, Special Assistant to the Secretary of State for International Labor Affairs
Mr. Goodwyn, Jack, Labor Management Services Administration, Department of Labor.
Mr. Goott, Daniel, European Labor Adviser, Department of State.
Mr. Greenberg, Leon, Leo Kramer Associates, Washington, D.C.
Mr. Gronkiewicz, Harry, Office of Administration and Management, Department of Labor
Mr. Goldberg, Joseph, Special Assistant to the Commissioner, Bureau of Labor Statistics, Department of Labor.
Mr Halperin, Michael, Office of the Secretary, Department of Commerce.
Mr. Henle, Peter, Deputy Assistant Secretary, Policy Evaluation and Research, Department of Labor.
Mr. Hewitt, William, Director, Office of Policy, Evaluation and Research, Employment and Training Administration.
Mr. Holmes, Gerald, P., European Labor Adviser, Department of Labor.
Mr. Irving, John S., National Labor Relations Board.
Mr. Jenkins, Howard, National Labor Relations Board.
Mr. Johnson, Richard, Department of Commerce.
Prof. Jones, Dallas, Graduate School of Business Administration, University of Michigan.
Mr. Kane, Arthur, International Brotherhood of Teamsters.
Prof. Karsh, Bernard, Department of Sociology, University of Illinois.
Prof. Kassalow, Everett, Congressional Research, Library of Congress.
Mr. Kelley, John, Research Director, Communications Workers of America.
Mrs. Kemble, Eugenia, American Federation of Teachers.
Mr. Kirsch, Henry, Department of Labor.
Mr. Kline, Sheldon, Labor Management Services Administration, Department of Labor.
Mr. Koczak, Stephen, Special Projects Officer, American Federation of Government Employees.
Mr. Kramer, Leo, Leo Kramer Associates.
Mr. Laase, Paul, OECD Affairs, Department of State.
Mr. Lambert, Walter, International Association of Fire Fighters.
Mr. Lawbaugh, William, International Association of Bridge and Structural Iron Workers.
Mrs. Leotta, Joan D., Department of Labor.
Mrs. Lewis, Beverly, Labor Management Services Administration, Department of Labor.
Mr. Lindrew, Jerry, U.S. Senate Labor Subcommittee.
Mr. Linsenmayer, Tadd, Bureau of International Labor Affairs, Department of Labor.
Mr. Lonergan, Edward, Bureau of International Labor Affairs, Department of Labor.
Mr. Loope, Nicholas, Research Director, United Brotherhood of Carpenters and Joiners of America.

Mr. Lowenthal, Al., American Federation of Teachers.
Mr. Lunden, Leon, Labor Management Services Administration, Department of Labor.
Mr. McKenzie, Jack, Labor Studies Center, University of the District of Columbia.
Dr. McLennan, Kenneth, Committee for Economic Development.
Mr. McElroy, Robert, Employment Standards Administration, Department of Labor.
Mr. Marchant, Douglas, Labor Management Services Administration, Department of Labor
Mr. Martin, Benjamin, Carnegie Endowment.
Mr. Master, W. Frank, National Education Association.
Mrs. Miller, Betty, Office of Administration and Management, Department of Labor.
Mr. Moffett, Kenneth, Federal Mediation and Conciliation Service.
Mr. Monier, J. Scott, Bureau of Economic Research, Department of State.
Mr. Mowry, Patrick, Department of Labor.
Mr. Narasimham, Gorti, Office of the Chief Economist, Department of Commerce.
Mr. Nichols, Donald, Deputy Assistant Secretary, Policy, Evaluation and Research Department of Labor.
Mrs. Payne, Sally, International Brotherhood of Teamsters.
Mr. Price, John, Labor Management Services Administration, Department of Labor.
Mr. Raff, Martin, Labour Attache, British Embassy.
Mr. Reed, Ted, International Union of Operating Engineers.
Mrs. Reiner, Helen, National Labor Relations Board.
Mrs. Reynolds, Joy, Labor Management Services Administration, Department of Labor.
Mr. Riccobono, Phil., Labor Management Services Administration, Department of Labor.
Mr. Ross, Fred, Washington Forum.
Prof. Rowan, Richard L., Industrial Research Unit, University of Pennsylvania.
Mr. Salsburg, Sidney, Manager, Research and Planning Systems, Chrysler Corporation, Detroit.
Mr. Segal, Ben, Employment Standards Administration, Department of Labor.
Prof. Seltzer, George, Department of Industrial Relations, University of Minnesota.
Mr. Senior, Kent, Building Trades Department, AFL-CIO.
Mr. Sheehan, Francis, Accounting Department, ALCOA.
Mr. Sheets, James, Laborers International Union of North America.
Mr. Sherman, O.M., Goodyear Tire and Rubber Company.
Mr. Smith, Albert, Assistant Comptroler, Bethlehem Steel Company.
Mr. Soffer, Benson, Labor Economist, Department of Commerce.
Mrs. Stein, Josephine, Department of Labor.
Mr. Stewart, Charles D., Washington D.C.
Mr. Sullivan, Scott, American Federation of Government Employees.
Mr. Sullivan, Sean, Council on Wage and Price Stability.
Mr. Swan, Thomas, Manager, Employment Compensation, General Electric Company.
Mr. Talbot, Joseph, Policy Evaluation and Research, Department of Labor.
Mr. Taylor, Merlin, the International Union of Brick and Allied Craftsmen.
Mr. Tella, Alfred, Bureau of the Census, Department of Commerce.
Mr. Truesdale, John, National Labor Relations Board.
Mr. Turner, Brian, Bureau of International Labor Affairs, Department of Labor.
Mr. Wagner, K. Peter, Economist, Department of Commerce.
Mr. Wallerstein, Lou, Labor Management Services Administration, Department of Labor.
Mrs. Walstedt, Jane, Women's Bureau, Department of Labor.
Mr. Wallick, Frank, United Auto Workers.
Mr. Weinberg, Donald, Prince George's County Personnel Officer.
Prof. Weinstein, Paul, University of Maryland.
Mr. Weinberg, Edgar, Industrial Relations Research Association.
Mr. Werner, John, Office of Administration and Management, Department of Labor.
Prof. Weisz, Morris, Industrial Relations Institute, University of Wisconsin.
Mr. Wilson, Henry, International Brotherhood of Painters.
Mr. Wooddruff, Thomas, Labor Management Services Administration, Department of Labor.
Mrs. Young, Carmen, National Federation of Government Employees.

OECD SALES AGENTS
DÉPOSITAIRES DES PUBLICATIONS DE L'OCDE

ARGENTINA — ARGENTINE
Carlos Hirsch S.R.L., Florida 165, 4° Piso (Galería Guemes)
1333 BUENOS-AIRES. Tel. 33-1787-2391 Y 30-7122

AUSTRALIA — AUSTRALIE
Australia & New Zealand Book Company Pty Ltd.,
23 Cross Street, (P.O.B. 459)
BROOKVALE NSW 2100   Tel. 938-2244

AUSTRIA — AUTRICHE
Gerold and Co., Graben 31, WIEN 1. Tel. 52.22.35

BELGIUM — BELGIQUE
LCLS
44 rue Otlet. B 1070 BRUXELLES . Tel. 02-521 28 13

BRAZIL — BRÉSIL
Mestre Jou S.A., Rua Guaipà 518,
Caixa Postal 24090, 05089 SAO PAULO 10. Tel. 261-1920
Rua Senador Dantas 19 s/205-6, RIO DE JANEIRO GB.
Tel. 232-07. 32

CANADA
Renouf Publishing Company Limited,
2182 St. Catherine Street West,
MONTREAL, Quebec H3H 1M7 Tel. (514) 937-3519

DENMARK — DANEMARK
Munksgaards Boghandel,
Nørregade 6, 1165 KØBENHAVN K. Tel. (01) 12 85 70

FINLAND — FINLANDE
Akateeminen Kirjakauppa
Keskuskatu 1, 00100 HELSINKI 10. Tel. 625.901

FRANCE
Bureau des Publications de l'OCDE,
2 rue André-Pascal, 75775 PARIS CEDEX 16. Tel. (1) 524.81.67
Principal correspondant :
13602 AIX-EN-PROVENCE : Librairie de l'Université.
Tel. 26.18.08

GERMANY — ALLEMAGNE
Alexander Horn,
D - 6200 WIESBADEN, Spiegelgasse 9
Tel. (6121) 37-42-12

GREECE — GRÈCE
Librairie Kauffmann, 28 rue du Stade,
ATHÈNES 132. Tel. 322.21.60

HONG-KONG
Government Information Services,
Sales and Publications Office, Beaconsfield House, 1st floor,
Queen's Road, Central.   Tel. 5-233191

ICELAND — ISLANDE
Snaebjörn Jönsson and Co., h.f.,
Hafnarstraeti 4 and 9, P.O.B. 1131, REYKJAVIK.
Tel. 13133/14281/11936

INDIA — INDE
Oxford Book and Stationery Co.:
NEW DELHI, Scindia House. Tel. 45896
CALCUTTA, 17 Park Street. Tel. 240832

ITALY — ITALIE
Libreria Commissionaria Sansoni:
Via Lamarmora 45, 50121 FIRENZE. Tel. 579751
Via Bartolini 29, 20155 MILANO. Tel. 365083
Sub-depositari:
Editrice e Libreria Herder,
Piazza Montecitorio 120, 00 186 ROMA. Tel. 674628
Libreria Hoepli, Via Hoepli 5, 20121 MILANO. Tel. 865446
Libreria Lattes, Via Garibaldi 3, 10122 TORINO. Tel. 519274
La diffusione delle edizioni OCSE è inoltre assicurata dalle migliori
librerie nelle città più importanti.

JAPAN — JAPON
OECD Publications and Information Center
Akasaka Park Building, 2-3-4 Akasaka, Minato-ku,
TOKYO 107. Tel. 586-2016

KOREA · CORÉE
Pan Korea Book Corporation,
P.O.Box n° 101 Kwangwhamun, SÉOUL. Tel. 72-7369

LEBANON — LIBAN
Documenta Scientifica/Redico,
Edison Building, Bliss Street, P.O.Box 5641, BEIRUT.
Tel. 354429—344425

MALAYSIA — MALAISIE
University of Malaya Co-operative Bookshop Ltd.
P.O. Box 1127, Jalan Pantai Baru
Kuala Lumpur, Malaysia. Tel. 51425, 54058, 54361

THE NETHERLANDS — PAYS-BAS
Staatsuitgeverij
Chr. Plantijnstraat
'S-GRAVENHAGE. Tel. 070-814511
Voor bestellingen: Tel. 070-624551

NEW ZEALAND — NOUVELLE-ZÉLANDE
The Publications Manager,
Government Printing Office,
WELLINGTON: Mulgrave Street (Private Bag),
World Trade Centre, Cubacade, Cuba Street,
Rutherford House, Lambton Quay, Tel. 737-320
AUCKLAND: Rutland Street (P.O.Box 5344), Tel. 32.919
CHRISTCHURCH: 130 Oxford Tce (Private Bag), Tel. 50.331
HAMILTON: Barton Street (P.O.Box 857), Tel. 80.103
DUNEDIN: T & G Building, Princes Street (P.O.Box 1104),
Tel. 78.294

NORWAY — NORVÈGE
J.G. Tanum A/S
P.O. Box 1177 Sentrum
Karl Johansgate 43
OSLO 1   Tel (02) 80 12 60

PAKISTAN
Mirza Book Agency, 65 Shahrah Quaid-E-Azam, LAHORE 3.
Tel. 66839

PORTUGAL
Livraria Portugal, Rua do Carmo 70-74,
1117 LISBOA CODEX.
Tel. 360582/3

SPAIN — ESPAGNE
Mundi-Prensa Libros, S.A.
Castelló 37, Apartado 1223, MADRID-1. Tel. 275.46.55
Libreria Bastinos, Pelayo, 52, BARCELONA 1. Tel. 222.06.00

SWEDEN — SUÈDE
AB CE Fritzes Kungl Hovbokhandel,
Box 16 356, S 103 27 STH, Regeringsgatan 12,
DS STOCKHOLM. Tel. 08/23 89 00

SWITZERLAND — SUISSE
Librairie Payot, 6 rue Grenus, 1211 GENÈVE 11. Tel. 022-31.89.50

TAIWAN — FORMOSE
National Book Company,
84-5 Sing Sung Rd., Sec. 3, TAIPEI 107. Tel. 321.0698

THAILAND — THAILANDE
Suksit Siam Co., Ltd.
1715 Rama IV Rd.
Samyan, Bangkok 5
Tel. 2511630

UNITED KINGDOM — ROYAUME-UNI
H.M. Stationery Office, P.O.B. 569,
LONDON SEI 9 NH. Tel. 01-928-6977, Ext. 410 or
49 High Holborn, LONDON WC1V 6 HB (personal callers)
Branches at: EDINBURGH, BIRMINGHAM, BRISTOL,
MANCHESTER, CARDIFF, BELFAST.

UNITED STATES OF AMERICA
OECD Publications and Information Center, Suite 1207,
1750 Pennsylvania Ave., N.W. WASHINGTON, D.C.20006.
Tel. (202)724-1857

VENEZUELA
Libreria del Este, Avda. F. Miranda 52, Edificio Galipàn,
CARACAS 106. Tel. 32 23 01/33 26 04/33 24 73

YUGOSLAVIA — YOUGOSLAVIE
Jugoslovenska Knjiga, Terazije 27, P.O.B. 36, BEOGRAD.
Tel. 621-992

Les commandes provenant de pays où l'OCDE n'a pas encore désigné de dépositaire peuvent être adressées à :
OCDE, Bureau des Publications, 2 rue André-Pascal, 75775 PARIS CEDEX 16.
Orders and inquiries from countries where sales agents have not yet been appointed may be sent to:
OECD, Publications Office, 2 rue André-Pascal, 75775 PARIS CEDEX 16.

OECD PUBLICATIONS, 2 rue André-Pascal, 75775 PARIS CEDEX 16 - No. 41 081 1979
PRINTED IN FRANCE
(S - 81 79 07 1) ISBN 92-64-12006-8